ArtScroll Series®

Rabbi Nosson Scherman / Rabbi Meir Zlotowitz
General Editors

Pathways
of the

Published by
Mesorah Publications, ltd

Prophets

A Treasury of Torah Thought and Law —
Looking at Ourselves Through the Lens of the Prophets

RABBI YISROEL REISMAN

FIRST EDITION
First Impression … March 2009

Published and Distributed by
MESORAH PUBLICATIONS, LTD.
4401 Second Avenue / Brooklyn, N.Y 11232

Distributed in Europe by
LEHMANNS
Unit E, Viking Business Park
Rolling Mill Road
Jarow, Tyne & Wear, NE32 3DP
England

Distributed in Australia and New Zealand
by **GOLDS WORLDS OF JUDAICA**
3-13 William Street
Balaclava, Melbourne 3183
Victoria, Australia

Distributed in Israel by
SIFRIATI / A. GITLER — BOOKS
6 Hayarkon Street
Bnei Brak 51127

Distributed in South Africa by
KOLLEL BOOKSHOP
Ivy Common
105 William Road
Norwood 2192, Johannesburg, South Africa

ARTSCROLL SERIES®
PATHWAYS OF THE PROPHETS
© Copyright 2009, by MESORAH PUBLICATIONS, Ltd.
4401 Second Avenue / Brooklyn, N.Y. 11232 / (718) 921-9000 / www.artscroll.com

ALL RIGHTS RESERVED
The text, prefatory and associated textual contents and introductions
— including the typographic layout, cover artwork and ornamental graphics —
have been designed, edited and revised as to content, form and style.

No part of this book may be reproduced
IN ANY FORM, PHOTOCOPYING, OR COMPUTER RETRIEVAL SYSTEMS
— even for personal use without written permission from
the copyright holder, Mesorah Publications Ltd.
except by a reviewer who wishes to quote brief passages
in connection with a review written for inclusion in magazines or newspapers.

THE RIGHTS OF THE COPYRIGHT HOLDER WILL BE STRICTLY ENFORCED.

ISBN 10: 1-4226-0893-X / ISBN 13: 978-1-4226-0893-7

Typography by CompuScribe at ArtScroll Studios, Ltd.
Bound by Sefercraft, Quality Bookbinders, Ltd., Brooklyn N.Y. 11232
Printed in Canada

This volume is dedicated to the memory of our husband, father, grandfather, and great-grandfather

Ernest Mermelstein ז״ל
נפתלי שמחה בן אברהם ז״ל
נפ׳ ד׳ שבט תשס״ט

He was a holocaust survivor who, together with his dear wife, built a new life in America, a life filled with Torah and *ahavas Hashem*.

In a slave labor camp, he worked in the kitchen. Unable to watch his brethren starve, he sneaked out food, risking his own life to save fellow Jews. Surely, this *zechus* earned him longevity and much nachas from his children, grandchildren, and great-grandchildren.

All who knew "Zeidy" loved him and treasured his friendship and guidance. It seemed as if everyone, from the teenaged neighbor to former employees and aides, came to pay respects at his funeral.

Daddy never asked for anything; he only wanted to do things to help others. He never looked for כבוד, but people gave it to him because he earned it. As Daddy watches over us in the עולם האמת, may we continue to follow in the path he paved and strive to emulate his wonderful traits.

Mrs. Ruth Mermelstein
Evelyn and Shalom Orkaby and family
David and Nina Mermelstein and family
Zvi and Tova Mermelstein and family

לעילוי נשמות
אבי מורי שמואל משה בן מאיר ז״ל
Sam Fuchs ז״ל
נפטר י״ג טבת תשס״ה

ואמי מורתי חנה בת מאיר יצחק ז״ל
Helen Fuchs ז״ל
נפטרה א׳ דר״ח אדר ב׳ תשמ״ה

Holocaust survivors who rebuilt their lives through tremendous *emunah* and *bitachon* in ה׳. It is our great זכות to dedicate this book by our Rav, Rabbi Reisman, to their memory.

May they be מליצי יושר for their family and all of כלל ישראל.

By their children
Meir and Shandee Fuchs

and their children
**Raphael and Leora Fuchs
Daniel Meir and Chana Heyman
Aviva, Shira, Rachel, Daniel and Esti Fuchs**

and their grandchildren
**Shmuel Moshe and Yehuda Zev Fuchs
Michael and Shmuel Moshe Heyman**

לעילוי נשמות
עזריאל בן רב אריה הכהן ז״ל
Dr. Edward E. Hoenig ז״ל
נפטר ח׳ כסלו תש״מ

פעסיל הדסה בת רב יעקב הכהן ז״ל
Paula Hoenig ז״ל
נפטרה י״ג אדר ב׳ תשס״ח

Dr. Edward E. Hoenig was a נקי כפים ובר לבב, a skilled and dedicated physician — whether in labor camps, D.P. camps or America — who healed and helped many.

Paula Hoenig was an אוהבת חיים whose courage, perseverance, spirit, חסד, and beauty enabled their survival of the Shoah — and rebirth.

May their נשמות be elevated.

Children: **Michael and Alisa Hoenig**
Grandchildren: **Drs. David and Holly Hoenig, Rebekah and Adam Ingber**
Great-grandchildren: **Eva Rose, Bella Pearl, Israel Lev**

Children: **Dr. Leonard and Ellen Hoenig**
Grandchildren: **Suri and Eric Kinzbrunner, Shayna and Jeremy Bekritsky,
Zisa and Yossi Farkas, Ezriel Hoenig**
Great-grandchildren: **Avrum Yitzchak, Eliyahu Eliezer**

Table of Contents

Acknowledgments 11
Introduction: Turning Saturday Night Into *Motza'ei Shabbos* 17

SECTION I
Otzar HaMachshavah — A Treasury of Jewish Thought

Prava Galus	25
Moods: Getting a Hold of Yourself	41
Central Jerusalem	55
My Favorite *Segulos*	65
Plan B	79
Lessons for In-Laws	92
Great Expectations	104
Emulating Hashem	122
Judging Others	137
Judging Yourself	148
Sha'ar HaSimchah	153
Shalom Bayis for Husbands	171
Shortcuts to Gan Eden	187
Matches Made in Heaven	198
From the Yeshivah to the Workplace	205
The Longest *Berachah*	214
Israel at War	226

SECTION II
Otzar HaHalachah — A Treasury of Jewish Law

The Great Siddur Controversy	237
Prayers for *Yiras Shamayim*	255
Rav Zalman Henna & the *Tenuah Kallah* Controversy	263
Astronomy for Beginners	272
By the Dawn's Early Light	286
The Moon and the *Molad*	300
Rules of *Dikduk*	312
Rules for *M'leil* and *M'lra*	326
Dikduk for Aramaic Words	336
Ben Asher and Ben Naftali	340
The Mystery of the Missing Years	363
Prayer Problems	370
Educating Children: Two *Dinim*	378
My Favorite Synonyms	387

SECTION III
Imponderables

Imponderables	405
Why Do Two *Yuds* Refer to God's Name?	406
Kosher Giraffe Meat	407
Why Are There Two Days of Rosh Chodesh?	408
The Missing Chicken Leg	409
Which Woman's Name Appears Most Often in Navi?	410
Caleiv Is Missing!	411
How Did the Dispute Between *Rashi* and *Rabbeinu Tam* Regarding Tefillin Begin?	413
Would *Rabbeinu Tam* Use Our *Rabbeinu Tam* Tefillin?	415
A Clean-Shaven Shimshon?	416
Kosher Succos Decorations?	417
Why Do We Refer to the Splitting of the Sea as *Krias Yam Suf* — The Ripping of the Sea?	417
What Is the Hebrew Word for Sunrise: Neitz or Haneitz?	419
How Do You Forget Something Purposely?	420

Why Is *Zichrono L'vrachah* Used To Refer to Someone Who Is No Longer Alive?	421
Why Do We Refer to a *Choleh* by Using His Mother's Name?	422
Moshe Rabbeinu's Missing Year	423
How Many Verses Are There in *Parashas Tzav*?	424
How Many Verses in *Parashas Pikudei*?	425
Should Megillos Be Read Before *Krias Hatorah*?	426
3,550 Missing Jews!	427
Where Was Bavel?	429
When Rashi Is Not Rashi	430

SHABBOS IMPONDERABLES

Waving at the Candles	431
Why Say Half a Verse Before Kiddush?	432
Chassidim Making an Early Shabbos?	433
Using Chickens to Determine Nightfall	435
Why Do Women Come to Shul for Mussaf?	436
Sleeping Late on Shabbos	436

SIDDUR IMPONDERABLES

Where Is the *Neshamah*?	437
Shimoneh Esrei: Why Does Only One *Berachah* Begin With the Letter *Vuv*?	439
Forgiveness for a Previous Life?	440
Bircas Kohanim: Three Mysteries	441
A Prayer for Tomorrow	442
The Last Words of *Shemoneh Esrei*	443
The *Migdal–Migdol* Mystery Revisited	444
Why Does the *Chazzan* Face the *Aron* When Saying "*Gadlu*"?	445
Why Do We Refer to a "Second and Third" Kiddush in Our *Zemiros* of Shabbos?	446

CHASUNAH IMPONDERABLES

Why Do the Mothers Break the Plate?	448
How Do You Say "Son-In-Law" in Hebrew?	449
Why Doesn't the Kesubah Contain the Family Names of the *Chasan* and *Kallah*?	450
Why Does the *Kallah's* Family Pay for the Wedding?	450
Why Is the *Kesubah* Signed by People Who Haven't Read It?	451
Why Do We Say "Mazel Tov" at a Wedding?	452
Why Don't We Make a *She'hechiyanu* at a Wedding?	453
Bashert or Not *Bashert*?	454

INDICES

Parashah Index	459
Index	460

Acknowledgments

*E*very author begins his work by acknowledging those who made it possible. The question of whether anyone actually reads these lines seems irrelevant; acknowledgments are seen as the author's solemn obligation to be a *makir tov* to those who've helped him.

If this is correct, my job is particularly daunting. This book has two sets of people who deserve acknowledgment: those who've brought the book to reality and those who've been instrumental in the success of the *Motza'ei Shabbos Navi Shiur*, upon which the book is based.

A question bothers me. There were many *Rishonim* and *Acharonim*, Torah giants, who published *seforim* in eras when publishing was far more difficult. These *seforim* do not begin with acknowledgments or references to their wives who (presumably) encouraged them.[1] This is not only true of earlier *seforim*, such as those written by the *Rambam*, *Ramban*, and *Rabbeinu Yonah*, but also of more recent *seforim*.

The *Igros Moshe* begins with a long *hakdamah*. Not a name is mentioned in the entire piece! Rav Elozor Shach wrote seven different *hakdomos* to different editions of his *Avi HaEzree*, without mentioning his wife — or editor. The Chofetz Chaim wrote Introductions to *Mishnah Berurah*, *Shmiras HaLashon*, and *Sefer Chofetz Chaim*, with nary a thank-you to anyone. Didn't the Chofetz Chaim have a publisher, a proofreader, or an editor? In fact, his son wrote part of *Mishnah Berurah*, but is not mentioned in the Introduction.

Apparently, the *hakoras hatov* was always understood, perhaps obvious. It may be that the sense of partnership of husband and

---

1. An interesting exception to this is Rav Yechezkiel Landau, in his Introduction to *Nodeh B'Yehudah*. Rav Landau named his *seforim* for his parents; *Nodah B'Yehudah* for his father (Yehudah) and *Tzlach*, an abbreviation of *Tzion L'Nefesh Chayah*, for his mother (Chayah). In addition to an appreciation of his parents, his Introduction to *Nodah B'Yehudah* contains a brief but poetic reference to his wife, recognizing her devotion.

wife was so ingrained that public mention would seem to violate the privacy of the relationship. Gedolim could convey their appreciation without putting it on public display.

It is only recently that it has become the style to list "thank-you"s in an Introduction to *seforim*, both in Hebrew and in English works. It would seem that these acknowledgments are an American innovation. My Rebbe, Harav Avrohom Pam *zt"l*, did write a list of acknowledgments at the beginning of his *Atarah LaMelech* and included an appreciation of his Rebbetzin, *she'tichyeh*.

What has brought about this change? Why are acknowledgments suddenly in style? Are we greater *makrei tov* than the generations that preceded us?

■ A CHAPTER OF *NECHEMIAH*

Let us learn a chapter of Nach, as explained by Rav Pam.

Nechemiah arrived in the Land of Israel fifteen years after the second *Beis HaMikdash* had been built. He found a poor and dispirited people who were oppressed and physically attacked by the gentiles who lived in the land. The wall around Jerusalem had been breached in numerous places and its gates had been burnt. Nechemiah immediately set out to rebuild and fortify the wall, to protect the city.

People ridiculed the sight of the Jewish rabbi setting out to rebuild the city wall. They said, "What are the feeble Jews doing? ... Will they revive the stones from the piles of dust? ... Even that which they do build, if a fox comes up to it, he will break their stone wall!" (*Nechemiah* 3:34-35).

Nechemiah pushed forward and successfully rebuilt the wall. The third chapter of Nechemiah contains 32 verses of acknowledgment. In these verses, the families of those who came forward to help Nechemiah are listed by name, with the location of the part of the wall that each family rebuilt.

In the final verse of the chapter, Nechemiah writes, "And so, we built the wall, and half the wall was completed, and the people had the heart to do (the rest)" (ibid. 3:38).

Nechemiah acknowledges by name those who built the first half of the wall. Those who came forward to complete the second half of the wall are not mentioned individually. Why?

Rav Pam explained that those who came later and built the second half of the wall did indeed do something wonderful. But this is not enough of a reason to be acknowledged by name in Nach.

It was those who came at the beginning who deserve to be

acknowledged. These were people who came forward to strengthen a weakened Jewish community; those who felt a sense of history, a realization that they stood at an opportune moment to turn the tide on behalf of their nation. They were not just building a wall; they were fulfilling a mission. These were special people, whose names are therefore spelled out in Nach for eternity.

■ WE, TOO

The Jewish People have suffered much during our lifetime. The Holocaust was followed by the increased dangers of assimilation that met us here, in our new country. Torah communities have flourished, but only after the significant *mesiras nefesh* of the survivors of the death camps. Even in these communities, the struggle continues; a struggle to build holiness on foreign soil and in a foreign culture, a struggle to remain strong in a society that entices us away from our values.

Outside of our few communities, the war for the Jewish soul is intense. The struggles are great. Like Nechemiah, we are disturbed to see a people whose souls are poor and dispirited. Like Nechemiah, we need to build a wall, a protection against the gentile forces that threaten and attack our people. As in Nechemiah's day, there are those who say that it cannot be done.

Nechemiah knew where to build his wall. What of us? How are we to reach out to Jews living in 50 states and beyond?

Our building tool is the printed word, the explosion of Jewish *seforim* and books of all types. These books (and their tape and digital equivalents) reach across the borders of states and countries. They are our long arm, stretched out to revive the Jewish spirit, wherever it may be found.

And like Nechemiah, we acknowledge. We have a sense of mission. Our books are not simply reading material or sources of information. They are the work of individuals who recognize the opportune moment to reach out and build; to help turn the tide on behalf of a nation.

Books have always been the lifeline of the scholar; today they are the lifeline of Jews the world over.

As in the days of Nechemiah, we acknowledge those who help us in our mission.

■ AND SO, I, TOO, ACKNOWLEDGE

The thoughts in this book may be mine, but they were put to paper through the efforts of others. Rabbi Nosson Scherman and

Rabbi Meir Zlotowitz were *zocheh* to begin an "ArtScroll Revolution," creating Jewish books with a new level of excellence and availability. I am honored to become a part of this revolution. I appreciate their perseverance; it was more than a decade ago that they first encouraged me to publish some of the *Navi Shiurim*. My time constraints prevented this from happening. It was Rabbi Yehudah Heimowitz who made this work possible; he authored a major portion of this book. His literary skills made this project happen. A special "thank you" to Rabbi Nissin Wolpin and the *Jewish Observer*; three of these *shiurim* originally appeared in the *JO*. Mrs. Felice Eisner was my editor and contributed much to the literary excellence of this book; her advice was indispensable. Rabbis Avrohom Chaim Young, Dovid Shurin, Gershon Dubin, and Chaim Fuhrer have been kind enough to review portions of the manuscript. Thanks also to Reb Mendy Lustig, for his expert technical help.

My wife served as my senior editor, reviewing and often rewriting sections of the articles. It is a fitting role; the *Navi Shiurim* have always been enhanced by her thoughts, ideas, and gentle (sometimes) critique. May the *Ribbono shel Olam* grant us continued *nachas* from our wonderful children, our extraordinary daughters-in-law, and our beautiful grandchildren.

The *Motza'ei Shabbos Navi Shiur* is more than 20 years old; I have been giving the *Shiur* for the majority of my adult life. I am very indebted to the institutions who've made it happen; to Agudas Yisrael of America for starting the *shiur*; to the Mirrer Yeshivah, which hosted the *shiur* for its first eight years; to Ahi Ezer Congregation, our present hosts, who forgo the income of *Motza'ei Shabbos* affairs to accommodate the *shiur*; and especially to the late beloved Marvin Azrak, long-time president of Ahi Ezer, who was always a source of inspiration. His untimely passing leaves a void to many; may his family find consolation.

The *Navi Shiur* owes much to many individuals, as well. To Rabbi Yosi Spanier, Reb Shimshon Benyamin, and their crew, who've set up the *shiur* for two decades, *kein yirbu*; to Rabbi Menashe Mishon, who has flawlessly managed the video equipment for the hall downstairs; to Dr. Shaul Schwalb, whose vision gave birth to the *Pathways of the Prophets* tapes; to my good friends Reb Ezriel Krumbein, Reb Yosi Stern, Reb Dovid Stern, and Reb Dovid Horowitz, who distribute the tapes on *Motza'ei Shabbos*; to Rabbi Yosi Fisher, who has masterminded the proliferation of the *Navi Shiur* tapes with extraordinary skill and devotion; to my dear sister, Mrs. Chani Fixler, who manages the Navi tape office, giving generously of her considerable talents and energies; to the wonderful Rico Tuson, a *marbitz Torah*, who produces the tapes and CDs; and to everyone's favorite, the highly talented Reb Sholom Lebendorf, who does the signing for the hearing impaired.

Most of all, my thanks to the *Navi Shiur* regulars, who are kind enough to join me each *Motza'ei Shabbos*. It is *you* who have made the *shiur* so special.

Recently, the *Navi Shiur* has taken on a new dimension, with our expansion to other cities via satellite and Web Stream technology. For this I thank TCN and its visionary founder, Reb Moshe Smith, as well as our technical manager, the highly efficient Reb Menachem Hayum, who does everything with a smile. Most of all, I express my appreciation to the many people who join me via these sites; a special "thanks" to our very first satellite site, in the Chicago community, where the *Navi Shiur* was shown (via video tape) even before the new technology; and to my dear friend Rabbi Yehudah Neuhaus, who pioneered the first satellite showing in Eretz Yisrael.

To many, my name has become identified with the *Navi Shiur*. Actually, I do other things, as well. I have the extraordinary *zechus* to teach at the *Beis HaMidrash* of Yeshivah Torah Vodaas. In my classroom, I have met the most wonderful army of young men with shining *middos* and a desire to excel. I have gained from my association with them and I hope to merit the *zechus* to continue.

A special "thank you" to the Yeshivah's executive director, Rabbi Yitzchok Gottdiener, and his office staff, who cheerfully allowed me to use their offices and computers to complete this book. May Hashem reward your *mesiras nefesh* for the Yeshivah by giving success to your dreams for the continued growth of the Yeshivah.

I am also fortunate to serve as the Rov of the Agudas Yisrael of Madison, Zichron Chaim Zvi. Those who learn and daven in our *Beis HaMidrash* span the diverse backgrounds of American Jewry, united in our love of *Klal Yisrael* and our devotion to be true *ovdei Hashem*. My love for our *mispallelim* has been reciprocated. For this, I am eternally grateful. I am especially grateful to those who attend the *shiurim* in shul. I have grown from their questions and insights, much of which ended up as material for *Navi Shiurim*.

There are many individuals who have given — and continue to give — of their time, talents, and resources to make the Agudath Israel of Madison, and its functions, run smoothly. It is their kindness that has allowed me to learn and teach, undistracted. It is difficult to adequately express my deepest feelings of gratitude to them. May I be worthy of their trust and devotion.

I am deeply grateful to my dear friends whose dedications enhance this book and make its publication possible.

Mr. Naftali Mermelstein, *z"l*, always treated me with great love and warmth. He was an extraordinary *ohev Torah* and *mokier Rabbanim*. His generosity helped the Agudah of Madison in its earlier years as the Bachurei minyan, and continued as we grew to our present building. I am gratified that **his wife Ruth** and their children, **Evelyn and Shalom Orkaby, David and Nina, Zvi and Tova,** saw fit to dedicate this book in his memory. May Hashem grant them all long happy years of *nachas* from the beautiful family that was Reb Naftali's pride and joy.

Dr. Meir and Shandee Fuchs have dedicated this book in memory of **his parents, Sam and Helen Fuchs,** *z"l*. It seems that whenever I need help or encouragement in a new project, they are there to help. The family's extraordinary love of Torah and Eretz Yisrael is overshadowed only by their love of fellow Jews. Reb Meir, I am grateful to you for your friendship and kindness. May your parents, from up high, enjoy continued *nachas* from your extraordinary family.

Mr. and Mrs. Michael Hoenig have dedicated this book in memory of his parents, **Dr. Edward and Mrs. Paula Hoenig,** *z"l*. Michael continues to be a source of inspiration to me, both in terms of his enthusiasm for Torah and as the mainstay of the wonderful and loyal Great Neck contingent of the *Navi Shiur*. Michael is a *talmid chacham*/lawyer, who has shown that excellence in the professions is not a contradiction to the ideal of *Toraso ikur u'milachto arai*. The first *yahrtzeit* of Mrs. Hoenig, on Taanis Esther, coincides with the completion of this book. May Michael's love of Torah continue to his generations and serve as a true source of *nachas* to his parents.

I end with my thanks to the *shloshah shutfim b'adam*; to my parents who have raised me with warmth and a love of Torah and Chesed and to my parents-in-law who are my role models in serving *Klal Yisrael* with wisdom and kindness. It was their encouragement that kept me in the Bais HaMidrash for my fifteen years in Kollel and my subsequent years as a Rebbe. And most of all, to my Rebbe, Moreinu HaRav Avraham Pam *zt"l*, who lovingly gave me of his precious time and broad wisdom until his untimely passing. Rav Pam's imprint is on every *shiur* in this book.

I close with a profound sense of gratitude to the *Ribbono shel Olam*, who has shown us His supreme kindness in opening the beauty of Torah to His people.

Yisroel Reisman

13 Adar, 5769

Introduction: Turning Saturday Night Into Motza'ei Shabbos

The *Motza'ei Shabbos Navi Shiur* was born from a desire to increase the *kedushah* of *Motza'ei Shabbos*.

It was 1986. Not many people were learning on *Motza'ei Shabbos*; today's popular father/son learning programs did not yet exist. Rabbi Joshua Silbermintz, the enthusiastic spirit of Pirchei Agudas Yisrael, started a new program. Yeshivah *bachurim* were invited to a night learning seder in the Mirrer Yeshiva in Brooklyn.

Soon, a simultaneous *shiur* for the parents was begun in the Ezras Nashim. This was the origin of the *Navi Shiur*. We have been fortunate to be a part of the new appreciation of *Motza'ei Shabbos*.

Over the years, the *Motza'ei Shabbos Navi Shiur* has grown from the dozen men who sat around the table on that first *Motza'ei Shabbos*. Moshe Smith and his marvelous innovation, TCN, the satellite network system, have allowed the *Navi Shiur* to be broadcast and seen in many cities in the United States and Canada.

Over these two decades, the temptations of the secular world have grown more insidious and pervasive. In many communities, people have responded with a new respect for *Motza'ei Shabbos*. Torah study, classes, and learning programs abound.

Saturday night has been turned into *Motza'ei Shabbos*.

Still, this is only a beginning. Much remains to be done.

> Someone joined the *Navi Shiur*. After a few months, he approached me to express his thanks.
>
> "For the last five years, I've been going to the office every Saturday night. Now, I come to your *shiur* — and then go to the office."
>
> I expressed my appreciation and responded with a question. "In another month or two, Shabbos will end much later. You will not have the time for both the *shiur* and the office. Which will you choose?"

We all face this question, in one form or another. At some point, the glow of Shabbos, the sense of Holiness, seems distant. The working week has begun in earnest. Soon, we will have to make choices.

⌘ *Gehinnom's* Hours of Business

It is our custom to add to the prayers at the end of the *Motza'ei Shabbos* Maariv. The *Tur* (295) explains the reason for this; "The custom to recite *V'yehi noam* and *Kedushah d'sidra* slowly and in a pleasant voice, when Shabbos ends, is so that it should take the Jewish People a bit longer to complete their order [of prayer]. This gives *reshaim* more time before they have to return to *Gehinnom*. For on *Motza'ei Shabbos*, the Guardian of the Spirits calls out, 'Return to *Gehinnom*, for the Jewish People have completed their order [of prayer].'"

The *Yesod V'Shoresh Ha'Avodah* (*Sha'ar* 8, end of Chapter 1) explains that each person's *Gehinnom* depends on his personal behavior in regard to Shabbos.[1] "If a person's soul is in *Gehinnom*, he is taken out every Friday at the time that he was accustomed to begin Shabbos in this world. So too, with adding to Shabbos on *Motza'ei Shabbos*. One who delays [the end of Shabbos, in this world], delays the return to *Gehinnom* ...."

This is a twist to the simple meaning of the *Tur*, which would imply that *Gehinnom* is open for every soul, at the same time.

---

1. This concept is also found in *Noam Migadim* to *Parashas Tzav*.

~§ A *Kabbalistic* Concept

The concept of spirits leaving *Gehinnom* for Shabbos and returning afterwards is a *kabbalistic* concept, beyond our understanding. Yet, the *Tur* is a halachic work, so the concept must fit logically as well.

There are difficulties with the words of the *Tur*. If we wish to end Shabbos later for the benefit of the spirits in heaven, why not simply have a custom to add five (or ten or twenty) additional minutes to the Shabbos? What is the great benefit of the few minutes that are spent saying these paragraphs? In addition, Shabbos actually ends at the beginning of Maariv. An *aveil* removes his shoes after *Borchu* is recited. This marks the end of Shabbos, well before *V'yehi noam*!

~§ A Simpler Understanding

The *Netziv* (*HaEmek Shailoh* 1:18) explains these additions to the *Motza'ei Shabbos* Maariv in a manner that is better understood. *V'yehi noam* and *Kedushah d'sidra* are meant as prayers for the coming week. As we take leave of the Holy Shabbos, we prepare for the workweek. We begin by turning to God with a prayer for success. This is *V'yehi noam*, a prayer that God bless the work of our hands as we prepare to begin the mundane work tasks of the coming week. This prayer is particularly sweet in heaven. As long as these prayers are being offered, the heavenly Attribute of Mercy is dominant and the weekday workings of *Gehinnom* do not begin.

Lekutei Ma'harich (quoting *Mateh Moshe*) adds to this theme of prayer for the coming week. Shabbos protects from *sheidim* and *mazikim*, the damaging spiritual influences of our world. When Shabbos leaves, these dangers are once again real. This is why *V'yehi noam* begins with *Yoshev b'saiser* (*Tehillim* 90), which is a prayer for protection from dangerous spirits.

◆§ A Fuller Understanding

This allows us to read the *Tur* and his *kabbalistic* reason for these prayers in a new light. The *kabbalistic* meaning is really not far from the simple meaning. These *tefillos* do serve to protect us from *Gehinnom* — in a very real way.

It is no secret that there is great spiritual danger in the offices and marketplaces in which we work. It does not take a *kabbalist* to see the *yetzer hara* standing on the streets of America. One does not have to study *Zohar* to realize that the gates of *Gehinnom* are wide-open before us as we set out to earn our livelihood. For six days, the Guardian of the Spirits of *Gehinnom* beckons us to enter his world.

The week must begin with a sense of holiness. We begin with a prayer that God help us avoid the dangerous spirits that entice us to be distant from the Holy Spirit of Shabbos. "Please Hashem, let our weekdays, too, be imbued with holiness. We are in trepidation of the coming week; worried that our behavior during the six 'ordinary days' will not measure up to Your expectations for His Holy People."

Motza'ei Shabbos is special. It is the beginning of a week. Indeed, Shabbos does end with *Borchu*. It is precisely *the first weekday moments* that we wish to imbue with holiness. Our first weekday words are directed to heaven. Our first thoughts are for the protection we need. We can now understand why this prayer is particularly sweet in heaven. As long as these prayers are being offered, the heavenly Attribute of Mercy is dominant and the weekday workings of *Gehinnom* do not begin.

Indeed, this explanation is easily read into the words of the *Arizal* (quoted in *Kaf HaChaim* 295). He explains that we say *V'yehi noam* "to extend the *Tosafos Shabbos*, the addition to the holiness of Shabbos, into all of the days of the week up to the coming Shabbos ... Our intention is to draw this added holiness into creation itself, so that we can survive the six weekdays, until the next Shabbos arrives."

The words of the *Tur* take on added meaning: "... recite *V'yehi noam* and *Kedushah d'sidra* slowly and in a pleasant voice, when Shabbos ends ... so that it should take the Jewish People a bit longer to complete their order [of prayer]. This gives *reshaim* more time before they have to return to *Gehinnom* ...."

If so, we understand that each individual's *Gehinnom* corresponds to his level of preparation. The more effort we put into extending holiness into the coming week, the longer we can withstand the temptations of the *Gehinnom* on Main Street.

◆§ "May the Work of Our Hands Find Favor ..."

Topics at the *Navi Shiur* vary. *Shiurim* may be on Halachah or Hashkafah. Either way, they are culled from the teachings of our Masters, the Great Teachers of Israel. Their lessons need to remain with us when we step out of the *Beis HaMidrash*, so that our feet do not lead us in the wrong direction. We would love to take these teachings into our workweek.

The book you are holding contains some of the most memorable *Motza'ei Shabbos* lessons. Like the *Navi Shiur* itself, the book has a wide variety of Torah lessons.

- **The first section** contains *Hashkafah Shiurim*; classes that deal with the spiritual challenges of everyday life. The emotional and spiritual challenges of the week are daunting. The lessons of our *Ba'alei Mussar* and *Machshavah* are invaluable tools in dealing with these challenges.

- **The second section** contains *Halachah Shiurim*. These lessons help round out a person's *yedios haTorah* by presenting topics that are not usually covered in everyday *sedorim*. We have deliberately chosen topics that are not readily available in English-language publications. I hope that you will be enticed to pursue these topics further.

- **The third section** contains a selection of Imponderables. These *Shiurim* offered questions (and some answers) of general interest, which were designed to generate discussion during the coming week. Judging from the response, the annual Imponderables *shiur* has become a favorite of listeners, just as it is a favorite of their presenter.

Shiurim related directly to the Navi have not been included in this work. This is a bigger job, deserving a work of its own. It is my dream to collect *klalei haTanach* in a comprehensive *sefer*. I pray that *HaKadosh Baruch Hu* will grant me the ability to succeed in this dream.

With a sense of humility and gratitude to the *Ribbono shel Olam*, we present these classes to the public. This is done with the confidence that you will find them interesting and enlightening. But our hope is for more. It is our prayer that this book will serve as a tool for extending the lessons of *Motza'ei Shabbos* into the week that follows. We hope and pray that *Klal Yisrael* will be *zocheh* to a greater attachment to holiness; to more spiritual lives, to be better people.

As always, we begin with a prayer: *V'yehi noam Hashem Elokeinu aleinu, u'maasei yadeinu konenah aleinu, u'maasei yadeinu koneneiyhu* — May Hashem's sweet ways be upon us — may He grant that the work of our hands be proper for us; and may the work of our hands be proper for all.

SECTION I
*Otzar HaMachshavah —
A Treasury of
Jewish Thought*

Prava Galus

We usually associate the term *galus* (exile) with the national exile of *Klal Yisrael*, during which we have been forced to travel from country to country and from continent to continent to atone for the sins that caused the destruction of the *Beis HaMikdash*.

There is another form of *galus*: a personal form of exile. In previous generations, some of the greatest *tzaddikim* would leave their homes and cities to wander from city to city, incognito. In Yiddish, this was called "*pravin galus;*" to "*prava* exile."

Prava is a difficult term to translate. The literal translation would be "to practice" or "to observe," as in observing a custom, but *prava* means much more than that. When a Chassidic master "*pravas*" a *tisch*, he is not eating an ordinary meal in the company of hundreds or thousands of followers. A *tisch* is full of meaning. *Prava* is used in this sense, to practice something with intensity. Similarly, when we say that someone would *prava galus*, we understand that this refers to a practice that is full of profound meaning and extraordinary — even mystical — significance.

This personal *galus* is an experience that is cloaked in mystery. *Tzaddikim* who went into exile did not usually write about it, and since they traveled incognito, very few stories have been recorded about their travels. One exception is Rabbi Moshe Cordavero (known as the *Ramak*), a towering *kabbalist* who lived in Tzefas during the era of the *Arizal*. He wrote a pamphlet recounting his personal exile that took place during 1548 (5308).

Ramak also mentions the concept of voluntary *galus* in his most famous *sefer*, Tomer Devorah,[1] and he attributes the practice to *Zohar's* teaching that a person should exile himself for the sake of Heaven. He adds that the author of the Zohar, Rabbi Shimon bar Yochai, himself practiced a personal *galus*.

The practice of voluntary *galus* is also mentioned by *Rambam* (*Hilchos Teshuvah* 2:4), who writes that it atones for a person's sins. Some commentators write that he is referring to a person who uproots himself from his hometown and moves elsewhere (which can be trying enough!) but others understand that he is referring to the experience of wandering from place to place; *pravin galus*.

Although the concept of *pravin galus* is not well known today, it existed in a cross-section of Jewish communities. Many Chassidic masters took up the practice of *pravin galus*. There are many stories told about the *galus* of the *Ba'al Shem Tov*, and many legends regarding the *galus* of the brothers Rabbi Elimelech of Lizhensk and Rabbi Zishe of Anipoli. Lithuanian Torah leaders also *pravad galus*. The Gaon of Vilna went into *galus* not long after he was first married. He traveled across Europe for five years. His *galus* took him all the way to Berlin, where he had the opportunity to review many original manuscripts. The Gaon was blessed with a phenomenal memory, and he memorized every nuance of the texts. Later, after he had returned to Vilna, he would use this knowledge to help correct the text of the Talmud.

Why?

It is hard for us to fathom how difficult it must have been to *prava galus*. These great *tzaddikim* would wander, without cellular phones — without any means of communicating with their families — and without credit cards. They carried the bare

---

1. The sefer *Tomer Devorah* is discussed in the *shiur* titled "Emulating Hashem."

minimum of provisions needed for survival. The means of transportation were primitive, unreliable, and uncomfortable.

Pravin galus was not only a great physical ordeal; it presented challenges to observing mitzvos as well.

During his years of exile, the Vilna Gaon was once stranded between cities on Erev Purim. He hired a wagon driver to take him to a Jewish village but they arrived late at night, well past the time for *Krias Megillah*. The Vilna Gaon had to wake up ten people and pay them to join him for megillah reading. (Although it is not halachically necessary to read the megillah with a minyan, on Purim, it is the most proper method of fulfilling the mitzvah.)

Think of it! The Vilna Gaon nearly missed the reading of the megillah on Purim! In the course of his travels, the Vilna Gaon must have missed *Krias HaTorah* on days when he could not make it to a city with a Jewish community. His travels must have prevented him from learning as diligently as he would have in Vilna.

When we consider the difficulty and danger involved, the question begs to be asked: why? What great service of God is accomplished by *pravin galus* that would make this enormous sacrifice worthwhile?

What great levels did the *tzaddikim* achieve through their travels, and why couldn't they achieve the same benefits in the comfort of their homes?

I do not think that anyone in our generation is capable of *pravin galus*. Even in previous generations, *galus* was practiced by the select few who were able to achieve great levels through their exile. Yet there is much to be gained from studying this topic, even if we cannot implement it in a practical way.

Let us study the topic.

↘ Three Explanations

We find that three explanations are offered for the practice of a personal *galus*. All three are based on the fact that *galus* breeds humility. We are all more confident when we are in familiar surroundings. A person feels less comfortable in an unfamiliar setting. This humbles a person. *Galus* helps a person behave in a humble manner; it develops the trait of humility. Furthermore, a person who lives as a stranger for an extended period of time, without support from family and friends, stands alone in front of *HaKadosh Baruch Hu*. He literally travels with Hashem.

- **Benefit #1: *Bitachon***

Orchos Tzaddikim (*Sha'ar HaSimchah, Bitachon HaShelishi*) writes that *galus* enables a person to build his *bitachon* (faith) in Hashem.

Imagine traveling hundreds of miles away from home, with nothing but your pajamas and a toothbrush. Picture yourself wandering from one place to the next, not knowing a soul. When you are alone with Hashem, without the people that you would normally rely on for material and emotional support, you learn to rely on Him alone. After a while, this becomes your normal state of mind. Upon returning home, you will continue to place your faith in Him.

Why is this teaching in *Sha'ar HaSimchah* (*The Gate of Happiness*)? *Orchos Tzaddikim* teaches that a person can achieve happiness to the degree that he trains himself to rely on Hashem alone. A person who depends on other people is likely to be disappointed. Human beings are limited. They can help only to the extent that Hashem allows them to. There are events in life that do not go the way a person would like them to, and friends and family are powerless to help. In such times, faith and faith alone will save a person from despondency.[2]

If have trained yourself to recognize the guiding hand of Hashem, you can find happiness under all circumstances.

- **Benefit #2: Conquering Anger**

Rav Tzaddok HaKohen of Lublin *(Tzidkas HaTzaddik* 80) adds a second insight to the practice of *pravin galus*. He explains that *galus* has a very practical benefit: it helps a person conquer anger.

Why do people become angry? Is there a purpose to it? Of course not; anger is an emotional response, not an intelligent one. Anger never benefits the person who is enraged, and is certainly not an effective means of obtaining positive results.

People get angry because they lose control. Someone who is *pravin galus* in unfamiliar territory feels insecure, unsure of where he is going to sleep at night. He does not know how he is going to get to the next village, and where his next meal is coming from. Such a person cannot afford the luxury of a temper tantrum.

Rambam writes that anger is — by and large — a byproduct of conceit. A person who feels that he deserves to have everything done for him will become angry when family and friends do not deliv-

---

2. This theme is discussed in greater length in our *shiur* on *Sha'ar HaSimchah*.

er. When a person is humbled by his inability to care for his needs himself, he acknowledges his constant dependence on Hashem; he learns to suppress, and ultimately conquer, feelings of anger.

■ Benefit #3: Becoming a Chariot for the *Shechinah*

True to form, *Tomer Devorah* (Chapter 9) writes about *galus* in *kabbalistic* terms. He quotes from the *Zohar* that one should wander from place to place for the sake of Heaven, "thereby becoming a chariot upon which *Shechinah* [Divine Presence] — which is in exile together with *Klal Yisrael* — can rest." He adds that a person who goes into *galus* should think, "I am in *galus*, and the *Shechinah* is in *galus*. I am fortunate enough to have the basic implements I need with me, but the *Shechinah* does not even have Its vessels."

Of course, these Gedolim are not suggesting that we all take on the practice of voluntary *galus*. This discussion appears to be academic. We are trying to understand the practice of great Jews who went into *galus* to feel closer to *HaKadosh Baruch Hu*, to work on their *bitachon* and become happier people, to train themselves not to get angry and to be humble, to feel the anguish that the *Shechinah* feels in its exile.

It would seem that *galus* is not an experience available to us ordinary folk.

Or is it?

Pravin Galus in Hong Kong

*I*n his extraordinary *sefer*, *Pele Yoetz* ("The Amazing Advisor"), Rabbi Eliezer Papo offers advice for all time. Although he wrote this work in the 19th century, much of his advice is strikingly relevant today. He advises, for instance, that a person who receives an estimate for remodeling his home should double the figure before the job begins. It seems that contractors have not changed much over the years.

Pravin galus is not for us ordinary folk?

The *Pele Yoetz* offers two important pieces of advice that can enable each of us to tap into this powerful experience.

There are situations in which a person must leave his home for some reason or another. Some people travel to a different country to study Torah; others travel for business or because of family obligations. If you are traveling for any purpose, writes *Pele Yoetz*, you should say, "This trip should be an experience of *pravin galus*."

True, you have planned this trip for personal reasons. You hope to achieve that which you have set out to do. But *Pele Yoetz* recommends that you bear in mind that a Heavenly decree has required you to leave the comfort of your home. You should accept upon yourself the intention that your travels should atone for your sins. "Make sure, however," warns *Pele Yoetz*, "that you guard yourself from engaging in improper behavior."

A business trip is a *nisayon* (challenge). Judaism exists *b'chaburah* — in the support and camaraderie of a community. We need *minyanim*, *chavrusos*, and shuls in which to daven, we need *kashrus* certification that is reliable — none of this is available when you are alone in a faraway city. People who travel on business must often daven in their hotel rooms, or sneak out of meetings to daven Minchah. The wandering Jew finds himself in the supermarket studying the tiny letters on each package in the hopes of finding something with a *hechsher*.

A person feels lonely when he travels. A friend told me that he was once in Hong Kong with a group of Jews, and they were able to form a minyan in their hotel. On Friday night, a fellow poked his head into their makeshift shul, scanned the crowd, and disappeared. A few minutes later he was back, regally adorned in a *bekishe* and *shtreimel*. What happened? He had checked the people at the minyan to make sure that he would feel comfortable in his distinctive *Chassidish* clothing.

Think about it! Ninety-nine percent of the people in the hotel were not Jews. They would still look at him as strange. Yet, because he had his minyan of *Achinu B'nei Yisrael*, it no longer mattered to him. Alone, we are weak, vulnerable, and self-conscious. Together, we find strength.

You may feel weak, says *Pele Yoetz*, but you have an excellent opportunity to get close to Hashem. As the airplane is taxiing down the runway, say to yourself, "I'm *pravin galus*. Wow! Just like the Vilna Gaon." Or, if you are *Chassidish*, you can say, "I am like the brothers Reb Elimelech and Reb Zishe." *Pele Yoetz* recommends that you make a verbal declaration that you are about to go into *galus*. Accept upon yourself the goal of experiencing Hashem's presence in an alien environment, where your usual support system does not exist.

> A Gerrer Chassid came into the *Chiddushei HaRim* (the Gerrer Rebbe in pre-war Poland) to tell the Rebbe that business obligations would take him to Paris for a few weeks.

"I hear that they have extraordinary cigars in Paris," the Rebbe replied. "When you are there, find the best cigars you can, and bring me a box of them."

The Chassid was puzzled by the bizarre request but bid the Rebbe farewell and set out on his journey. After all, we don't question a Rebbe!

Three weeks later, the Chassid returned to the Rebbe with a box of cigars from Belgium.

"Rebbe," he explained, "I was so busy in Paris that I forgot all about the cigars. However, I remembered during the train trip on the way home. I stopped in Belgium and picked up a case of fine cigars. I assure the Rebbe, they are as fine as anything I could have found in Paris!"

The *Chiddushei HaRim* expressed his disappointment.

"Do you think that I need your cigars?! It was my hope that during the three weeks you were in Paris, you would be on the lookout for my cigars. In this way, you would not forget that you have a Rebbe ...."

✦§ Shacharis in Texas: Davening to Hashem

What does a businessman do when he is in a faraway city and there is no minyan? He finds out the local time of sunrise, and he davens *k'vasikin*. (According to many *poskim*, davening *k'vasikin* is equivalent to davening with a minyan.)

I was in Los Angeles for a wedding, and I took the overnight flight back to New York. Hashem has blessed me with the ability to sleep on a plane, and as soon as I settled into my seat, I lapsed into a deep sleep. Halfway through the trip, the pilot awakened us to share some disappointing news: we were having engine trouble, and we were going to make an emergency landing in some small city in Texas that I had never heard of.

I had originally planned to daven in New York, but we were going to be delayed for a while, so I had no choice but to daven in Texas. I had no idea what time sunrise was in Texas. I figured that if I could get my hands on a local newspaper, I could find out the time of sunrise. I walked through the airport in search of a newsstand. But it was three a.m. Not a soul was in sight — let alone an open newsstand.

Left with no other choice, I began to look through the garbage bins in the hopes of finding a discarded newspaper. To my chagrin, every garbage can in that airport had a clean — and empty— garbage bag. I started to walk faster, hoping to intercept the person who was clearing the trash. I got all the way to the other end of the airport, and not a single newspaper was to be found.

I went back to the gate where my fellow passengers were waiting and began to inquire, "Does anyone know what time sunrise is?"

Nowadays, I am sure that someone would pull out a wireless device and produce the desired information within seconds. But this story occurred several years ago, and no one knew when sunrise was. I had no choice but to find a quiet corner of the airport (of which there were many) and estimate the time of davening.

There I was donning my tallis and tefillin in the middle of nowhere, and I learned something new: when you are in some small city in Texas, without another yarmulke in sight, you daven to *HaKadosh Baruch Hu* with greater intensity. You sense the presence of the Creator right at your side, and you feel close to Him. It is a powerful experience.

It can be difficult. People stare at you as you envelop yourself in your tallis and wrap tefillin onto your arm and head, and they wonder if the stress of being delayed has affected your mental health. Then they come over to you and ask, "What are you doing?" and you answer, "Mmm... Uh, uh-uh," as you gesture madly to show them that you can't talk. They walk away, convinced that you are either dumb, or ... well, dumb in a different sense. It is difficult, but if you appreciate the unique challenge and opportunity that you have been given, you can connect to Hashem with a great sense of joy and purpose.

You *prava galus*.

ᓃ No Luggage? Like the Vilna Gaon!

In the course of his travels, the Vilna Gaon once asked his gentile wagon driver to stop at the side of the road so that he could daven. As he was davening *Shemoneh Esrei*, the wagon driver whipped the horse and disappeared in a cloud of dust, taking with him all of the Gaon's meager possessions. He was stranded with absolutely nothing to his name. Nothing, that is, except for his *Shemoneh Esrei*.

Think about this story the next time you travel. You may get a chance to *prava galus*, as the Gaon did. You will land in an airport and wait for your luggage to appear on the carousel. You follow the bags as they revolve upon the carousel until your neck is sore. Then when the last piece of luggage has been removed and your battered suitcase is nowhere in sight, you trudge down endless corridors to the lost-and-found. They tell you that your luggage has gone to Omaha. You are not in Omaha.

How will you react? Will you get angry? No. You will say, "Ahah! That is what happened to the Vilna Gaon. I am *pravin galus* just like him."

That is when you can begin to identify with the Creator. The airline can take everything away from you, but your connection to Hashem stays with you. This is when you take the advice of the *Pele Yoetz*. You will not merely think about the fact that you are in *galus*. You will *say* to yourself, "I am in *galus*, and I want the *Shechinah* to rest on me. I want to be a chariot for the Divine Presence."

Instead of feeling humiliated by your helplessness and dependency, you will come to see it as a way of connecting to Hashem.

ᴇ§ A Jew Is Not Stuck

The story is told of two Chassidim who were traveling to spend *Yamim Noraim* (High Holidays) with the Ba'al Shem Tov. They experienced many mishaps on the way, and were forced to spend Rosh Hashanah in an isolated place where there were no other Jews. They were fortunate enough to have a shofar with them, so they did the best they could to maintain the Yom Tov spirit in lonely and depressing circumstances. When they finally reached the Ba'al Shem Tov, they asked him why they had been denied the opportunity to spend Yom Tov in his presence. "We invested so much time and money in this journey, and we sacrificed the opportunity to spend Yom Tov with our families," they said. "Why did Hashem do this to us?"

"Every location in the world has *nitzotzos* of *kedushah* [sparks of holiness]," explained the Ba'al Shem Tov. "The *Arizal* taught that we must go into exile in order to gather those sparks of holiness, so that every part of the world becomes sanctified.

"That city had *nitzotzos* of *kedushah* since the beginning of time," said the Ba'al Shem Tov, "through performing the mitzvah of shofar in that place, you had the *zechus* of gathering those sparks."

We have to realize that there is purpose in every step of our journey. A person feels lonely and frustrated if he feels that a delay or a redirected flight is a matter of chance. If he thinks, "Why am I here? I shouldn't be here. It is senseless for me to be here," he gets depressed. If you know, however, that you are a "secret agent" sent by God to *prava galus*, then you *prava* as a rebbe *pravas* a *tisch*. You accept the mission of collecting the sparks of holiness wherever you find yourself. You are on a holy mission.

My wife's friend told us that she and her husband were on a plane that made an emergency landing in a strange city. It was Erev Yom Tov, and they realized that there was no way that they could make it home before nightfall. They called their rebbe and asked for advice on how to make Yom Tov in a city without a Jewish community. "What should we do? We are stuck here!" they said.

The rebbe reacted sharply. "*Stuck*?" he exclaimed. "A Jew is never stuck; a Jew is sent. Every morning we recite the *berachah* of *Hameichin mitzadei gaver*. We praise Hashem for directing the steps of man. If you find yourself in a strange city, you were sent there for a purpose. You are not *stuck*."

What about all the *bitul Torah* caused by such side trips? What about all of the *tefillos* we have to daven without minyan? How joyful can a Yom Tov be without friends and family? Shouldn't this depress us?

We have to take a lesson from the Vilna Gaon. If the Vilna Gaon was willing to forgo *tefillah* with a minyan, and he was willing to let his learning suffer for the sake of *galus*, then it must be worthwhile.

◆§ Close to Home; in *Galus* Nonetheless

What about those of us who never travel? What about people who never set foot on a plane? Many people work locally and are always surrounded by fellow Jews. Do they also get a chance to *prava galus*?

Do you ever go to your in-laws for Shabbos? Do you ever have to spend time at the home of a family member with whom you are less than comfortable?

Don't you find yourself in situations in which you feel inconvenienced? If you do, then you also have an opportunity to attain the benefits of *galus*. As we mentioned, the *Pele Yoetz* offers two methods of experiencing *galus*.

We have discussed the first method, tapping into the experience of traveling away from home and accepting the tribulations of *galus*.

Let us study the second strategy of the *Pele Yoetz*. This applies to all of us — traveling salesmen and straphangers alike.

Imagine a winter morning. You leave your warm house to go to shul for davening or *daf yomi*, and it is freezing outside. The wind is howling, and the snow is piling up on the ground. As you trudge to shul, the snow gets into your shoes and melts in your socks. Your socks are now wet and freezing cold, and you face the dilemma that every man faces in this situation: you can suffer the discomfort of wet socks for the rest of the day, or you can go home to change and endure your wife's predictable comment, "I told you to wear boots."

I am not sure which one is worse but either way, you are in an uncomfortable situation.

Or imagine sitting in the *Beis Midrash* late at night, struggling to stay awake to learn a little bit more. You are uncomfortable. You would rather be home, where you have a well-stocked refrigerator and a comfortable recliner.

Accept such situations with love, says the *Pele Yoetz*, and learn or daven with joy. Have in mind that your exile from your home should atone for your sins. You do not have to be the Vilna Gaon who traveled across Europe; you don't even have to be a businessman who travels to faraway city. You can be in shul, two blocks from your own home, and be in *galus*. Any time you forfeit the comforts of home for the purpose of serving Hashem, you are experiencing *galus*.

In fact, *Pele Yoetz* explains that you can be in *galus* in your own home. He writes that in the weeks leading up to Pesach, when your wife sends you out of the kitchen and tells you to eat in the boiler room, you should not complain. Don't say, "These women have such ridiculous *chumros* [stringencies] nowadays."

Wear a big smile on your face, and when your wife asks you why you are smiling, tell her, "*Galus* will atone for my sins!" Then take your meal, head down to the basement, and *prava galus*.

Imagine the benefits of incorporating this attitude into our lives. When we are inconvenienced or uncomfortable, we focus on ourselves. We think to ourselves, "I was walking to shul to daven. Why did Hashem allow the snow to get into my socks? My feet are so cold, I can barely stand. I should have stayed in my cozy, warm bed." Or, "Why am I still sitting here with my *chavrusa*? I should go home and take a hot shower."

If you think that you should not be suffering, then you become frustrated and quit. If you realize that there is purpose, every time you feel inconvenienced you can say to yourself, "I'm *pravin galus*."

Once you begin to think this way, the benefits that can be derived from *galus* will become available to you.

Imagine waiting on line at the DMV (Department of Motor Vehicles) for the second consecutive week. You know that in a few minutes you are going to reach the clerk who is trained to figure out which document you are missing, forcing you to return for a third time.[3]

You are unhappy. You are inconvenienced. Why did Hashem create DMVs anyway!

Rav Tzaddok teaches that *galus* enables us to conquer anger. Every inconvenience in life provides us with the same opportunity. Do you snap at the lady at the DMV, or do you control yourself? Hashem created the DMV for a purpose.

Until now, you would have gotten frustrated and angry. Now you know the trick. You know that Hashem sent you there for a reason. You say, "Me and the Vilna Gaon. We *prava galus*."

And next time you leave your house to come to a *shiur* when it is snowing, don't get upset. You have a golden opportunity! *Tomer Devorah* writes that it is best to walk when *pravin galus*, not to take a horse and carriage. Make it a little bit more difficult for yourself. Don't take your car. Trudge along in the snow and think, "*Galus* atones for my sins."

What do you think about if you feel the snow piling into your shoes? You think about the *Shechinah* and how uncomfortable It is to be displaced.

Tomer Devorah writes that we can make the *galus* experience more profound by minimizing the amount of creature comforts we take with us. We should realize that we have our basic necessities, and the *Shechinah* does not. I don't know about you, but I am not ready to leave my personal items at home. I take my pajamas, a change of clothing, a toothbrush, and maybe a bag of pretzels. Still, there are situations where we would do well to think of the *Tomer Devorah's* words.

---

3. You have to be a New Yorker to appreciate this example. Or is it this way everywhere?

Did you ever rely on a family member to put something important into your suitcase? Did your wife ever tell you, "Don't worry, I'll put it in for you!" and then forget? Do you get upset?

Not anymore! Now you say to yourself, "My wife considers me a *ba'al madrega*. She thinks that I am capable of empathizing with the *Shechinah* by leaving some of my personal possessions at home."

⇜ Every Moment Is Meaningful

The Talmud (*Ta'anis* 24b) relates that Rabbi Chanina ben Dosa, who was famous as a miracle worker, was once walking on the road, and it began to rain. He said to Hashem, "The whole world is in peace, and Chanina is in pain!"

Miraculously, the rain stopped. When he reached home he said, "The whole world is in pain, and Chanina is in peace?"

It began to rain again.

The *kabbalistic* reasons for Rabbi Chanina ben Dosa's behavior are beyond us, but the Talmud goes on to tell us Rav Yosef's reaction to this story. He said, "How effective is the prayer of the *Kohen Gadol*, when there is Rav Chanina ben Dosa?"

The *Mishnah* (*Yoma* 52b) tells us that as the *Kohen Gadol* emerged from the *Kodesh HaKadashim* (Holy of Holies) on Yom Kippur, he would recite a short prayer. What was his prayer?

"*Yehi ratzon milfanecha* — may it be Your will, *shetehei hashanah hazu geshumah* — that there be ample rainfall during this year, *ve'al yikanes lifanecha tefillas ovrei derachim* — and that the prayers of the travelers [who pray that the rain should stop] should not come before You."

When Rav Chanina ben Dosa was the traveler, his prayers were accepted by God. Rav Yosef expressed surprise that the prayers of Rav Chanina Ben Dosa were more potent than the prayers of the *Kohen Gadol* on Yom Kippur.

The *Yitav Lev* (*Parashas Vayishlach*) has a tremendous insight into this Gemara. He writes that there are two types of travelers: there are *ovrei derachim*, and there are *holchei derachim*.

These terms seem synonymous: *ovrei derachim* are those who pass the roads, and *holchei derachim* travel the roads. What is the difference between them?

Ovrei derachim, explains the *Yitav Lev*, are people to whom the trip is meaningless. They need to get to Point B, and they are at Point A, so they must traverse the roads that lead from Point A to Point B. The trip is no more than a means to reach their destination. The trip itself has no inherent value.

Holchei derachim are people who notice Hashem's Hand in each step that they take. As they travel, they feel that Hashem has prepared their footsteps, and that there is meaning to each step of their journey and each experience encountered. Their journey is not merely a means of reaching Point B. It is a journey full of purpose and meaning in itself.

Regarding Yaakov the Torah states, "*V'Yaakov halach l'darko* — Yaakov traveled on his way" (*Bereishis* 32:2). Regarding Eisav it states, *Yaavar na adoni lifnei avdo* — Let my lord [Eisav] pass ahead of his servant [Yaakov]" (ibid., 33:14). Yaakov is a *holeich derech*, and Eisav is an *oveir derech*.

What was the *Kohen Gadol's* prayer on Yom Kippur? "*Ve'al yikanes lifanecha tefillas ovrei derachim* — the prayers of the travelers [who pray that the rain should stop] should not come before You."

The *Kohen Gadol* refers to people who are *ovrei derachim*, to whom the trip has no meaning. They are unworthy of having their prayers answered. Rav Chanina ben Dosa was not an *oveir derech*, he was a *holeich derech*. King David wrote, "*Ashrei temimei derech haholchim beToras Hashem* — Praiseworthy are those whose way is perfect, who walk with the Torah of Hashem" (*Tehillim* 119:1).

An *oveir derech* is unworthy of having his prayers accepted, and the *Kohen Gadol* prays for this. A *holech derech* is not included in the prayer of the *Kohen Gadol*; he deserves to have his prayers accepted.

What a difference! A person to whom the trip is meaningless is an *oveir derech*. *Holchei derachim* live with the feeling that all the drudgery that comes along with daily life is meaningful, and that they can achieve greatness through dealing with it properly.

What do you think about when you find yourself waiting on an endless line at the DMV? For the first twenty minutes you think about your schedule for the day, but what do you do for the next hour? A *holeich derech* thinks, "I should have brought a *sefer* along, but I might as well use the time to think about the *Ribbono shel Olam*."

He thinks of the pain that the *Shechinah* experiences in *galus*. He becomes a chariot for the *Shechinah*.

There are times in life when we think, "*Ribbono shel Olam*, why are you doing this to me?"

My friend's brother had lost his wife to an illness. It is difficult to be a widower with a house full of children, and at a certain point he decided that he must remarry. He had a son in his early twenties who was also trying to find his *bashert*.

When a *shidduch* was suggested to the father for the first time, and he decided to pursue it, his son asked, "How do you go about dating at middle age? It must be so difficult. At my age there is an excitement to dating. It is what I want to be doing at this stage of my life. It must be so hard to go through the process at your age."

"I know," replied the father. "I was wondering how I would approach this ordeal. Then I decided to take a cue from the Torah.

"The Torah says that when Eliezer went to find a wife for Yitzchak, he asked Hashem to give him a sign that would lead him to the right person. When he got to the well, he saw the water coming up towards Rivkah, and he realized that Hashem had sent him his sign.

"I will do the same," concluded the father. "I said to Hashem, 'I don't know how this is going to work. It is going to be so hard to find a second wife. Please send me a sign when the right one comes along.'"

That evening, he phoned his first prospect at a time that had been pre-arranged by the *shadchan*. The woman who picked up the phone sounded very flustered as she said, "I have to apologize. I know that we were planning to speak at 8:30, but I have an emergency. I have little children, and one of them just flushed a toy down the toilet, and it is overflowing. *All the water is coming up toward me.* I can't talk to you now. Please call back in an hour."

Needless to say, he hung up the phone with a big smile on his face. "Is this a sign?" he wondered. They did end up getting married, and that is why I heard the story.

Let us picture the woman at the other end of the receiver. She must have been deeply chagrined at her awkward predicament. Should she describe the nature of the mishap and sound helpless, or should she make some vague excuse and come across as unreliable? What was she thinking when that toilet started to back up? "*Ribbono shel Olam*, why are you doing this to me? Why did this have to happen now, of all times? He will hang up, and I will never hear from him again."

Little did she know what the effect of her mishap would be.

So it is with us all. We are distressed by life's inconveniences and difficulties. We think, "*Ribbono shel Olam*, I am going to a *shiur*, why is the nearest parking space six blocks away from the shul? I only live seven blocks away!"

Do you know why you can't find parking? It is good for you to walk the six blocks. It gives you an opportunity to think about Hashem, to humble yourself before him, and to become a chariot for the *Shechinah*. You can *prava galus*.

When life gets tough, remember the advice of the *Pele Yoetz*. Take those moments of discomfort and transcend them. Elevate them into moments of purpose and of greatness — in which you have a chance to *prava galus*, with dignity and with pride.

Moods: Getting a Hold of Yourself

I'm sure that there are days in your life when things just seem to go your way. On those days, you find yourself davening Shacharis with concentration. You make it home from shul in time to eat a decent breakfast, and when you get to your bus stop the doors are open so that you simply hop aboard and glide to your destination. On such days, you feel that you are going to succeed in all your endeavors, and as the day goes on, your feelings are often substantiated. Your boss will give you an easy time, you will get home from work in record time, and you will even be able to review *daf yomi* en route.

And then there are the days when everything seems to go wrong. You step out of bed and stub your toe. You are in so much pain that you can barely walk, and you get to shul late. You hastily put on your tallis and tefillin and try to catch up, but davening that way seems like just going through the motions. Then you miss the bus and have no choice but to hobble to the train station, your stubbed toe begging for mercy with each step. You develop a pain in the pit of your stomach, because you just *know* that you are going to be hassled at work that day. True to your premonition, the boss will be in a bad mood, all your proposals will be turned down, and your meetings will be delayed or canceled.

Your problems don't end at work. On the way home, you will press the play button on your Walkman and find that the batteries are dead. Or even worse, your child will have switched your *daf yomi* tape for his favorite Uncle Moshe cassette. And yes, those will be the days when you get home, tired and frustrated, and your wife will greet you with, "Oy! Did I ever have a hard day — I couldn't wait for you to get home. Here, take the baby."

If you are like the rest of us, you have had both experiences. Sometimes the good or bad streaks can last a week or even more. Inasmuch as alternating cycles of success and frustration seem to be a fact of life, does the Torah discuss this phenomenon? Does the Torah offer specific guidance for dealing with the cyclical ups and downs of our lives?

Of course it does. Everything is in the Torah. We need only to find it.

⋑ Time To Plant Barley

The Mishnah (*Rosh Hashanah* 16a) tells us that Hashem renders judgment on the next year's crop of grain on Pesach. If we are judged favorably on Pesach, the crops of the coming year will be bountiful; if not, they will fail.

In the Talmudic explanation of this Mishnah, *Abaye* comments that a farmer who sees that his early winter wheat crop is thriving should be sure to plant a barley crop toward the end of the winter. Barley grows quickly and will be ripe before the farmer has to face the next Pesach's judgment. By harvesting barley, the farmer will get another crop into the current year's streak of good fortune.

Left to our own devices, we might assume that a true *ba'al bitachon* need not invest additional effort when he sees his crops doing well. It would seem that the amount of profit that his crops will bring is predetermined, so what will he gain by planting more? *Abaye* is teaching that life sometimes runs in streaks. There are good times, and there are difficult times. When you see things going your way, it may be a heavenly message to *chap arein* — it may be time to invest more effort and to try new things, because you are likely to succeed.

In *Shmuel Aleph* (Ch. 5), we read that Chiram, king of Tyre, sent materials and craftsmen to build a palace for King David. When this happened, "David realized that Hashem had established him as king over Israel and that He had exalted his kingdom for the sake of His people Israel."

What did King David do upon experiencing this level of success?

"David took additional concubines and wives from Jerusalem after his coming from Hebron, and more sons and daughters were born to David. These are the names of the children born to him in Jerusalem: Shammua, Shovav, Nassan, Shlomo" (ibid.)

At first glance, we do not see any correlation between these verses. How is the establishment of David's kingdom related to the fact that he married additional wives and had more children?

The *Ralbag* — one of the early commentators on Tanach — devotes a portion of his commentary to what he calls "*Toaliyos*," lessons, which he derives from the Navi. In these lists, which he places after every few chapters of Navi, he summarizes the practical lessons that can be derived from the words and actions of the prophets. Commenting on these verses, *Ralbag* tells us, "It is worthwhile for a person who sees renewed success in his endeavors to make the most of the good [times] .... When David saw that Hashem had uplifted his kingdom, he immediately married more women, because he thought that the children born at such a time would be more worthy of succeeding him as king than those who had been born at an earlier time. We see that it was so, for the sons born earlier who could have succeeded him were all killed, and Shlomo, who was born from one of these marriages, actually became king."

There are streaks in life. There are good days, and there are bad days. There are opportune moments and there are times that are less auspicious for success. *Rabbeinu Tam* identifies these streaks as *yemei ha'ahavah* and *yemei hasin'ah* — literally, days of love and days of hatred. The Steipler, *zt"l*, quotes the same words from *Rabbeinu Yerucham*, another *Rishon*.

We often think of moodiness as a contemporary weakness. We imagine that in earlier times, people controlled their moods, and at some point during the 20th century, people developed weaker nerves, allowing themselves to be buffeted by their fluctuating emotions. The truth is that moodiness is nothing new — it goes back to the time of the *Rishonim* and beyond.

Michtav M'Eliyahu (Vol. II, pp. 249-250) quotes from *Zohar*, stating that experiencing a good streak may indicate that our lives are being governed by Heavenly Mercy. When we feel besieged by difficulties, it may be that we are being governed by strict Heavenly Justice. In fact, according to the *Zohar*, this is what Shlomo HaMelech meant when he said, "There is a time for everything under the heaven" (*Koheles* 3:1).

In *Parashas Masei*, the Torah enumerates forty-two encampments of the Jewish People during their journey through the Wilderness. The *ba'al korei* often rushes through this portion of the *keriah*, and we rarely focus on the names and the lessons of these encampments. *Chiddushei HaRim* points out that these encampments must have great significance, or they would not have been enumerated by the Torah. He explains that the names of these places allude to the journeys and experiences that we undergo in our lives. Sometimes we camp at *Marah* (bitterness), sometimes we are in *Miskah* (sweetness). At times we are in *Makheilos*, surrounded by friends and well-wishers. At times we feel that we are *B'k'tzei HaMidbar* — lonely and isolated at the edge of the desert. There are times when we reach *Har Sinai*, where it is easy for us to grow spiritually and absorb Torah. But at other times we become mired in *Kivros Hata'avah* — where we struggle with base desires that threaten to pull us down.

Each one of us must journey from one encampment to another, from joy to sadness, from despair to exultation, from rejoicing to mourning. We traverse the full gamut of human experiences, the entire spectrum of moods and emotions, alternating between times of growth and times of stagnation.

◆§ Big Changes; Little Changes

*A*s we saw from the Talmud and from *Ralbag*, when we find ourselves being showered with Heavenly Mercy we must *chap arein*. Strike while the iron is hot!

Someone who fails to appreciate the opportunities of a special moment can make terrible mistakes.

Rav Avrohom Pam would teach this lesson, citing the example of Noach after the Flood. When Noach emerged from the Ark, it was a time of great reconciliation between God and man, a *shas rachamim*. Whatever Noach would have set out to do would have been blessed with unbelievable success. Noach chose to plant a vineyard. He planted, reaped, and pressed grapes in one day, and it even turned into wine. Did you ever get drunk from freshly-squeezed grape juice? This grape juice turned to wine immediately. The moment of blessing was squandered on wine. Unfortunately, that day ended in disgrace. A missed opportunity.

If you find yourself humming happily on the way home from a particularly profitable day at work — *chap arein*. Don't squander your moments of blessing. Use this positive energy to give impetus to your spiritual growth. Commit to another *seder* in learning. Undertake a new *chesed* project. Resolve to use your traveling time more productively by listening to Torah tapes. *Chap arein*.

This is the lesson for the good streaks. The streaks of difficulty are much more challenging. It behooves us to prepare ourselves for the "down" times, the times when things just seem to go wrong.

It is important to clarify that we are not talking about sudden, extreme changes in fortune — when someone suddenly loses his wealth or is struck by a potentially fatal illness. At those times, we are likely to identify the change for what it is. We realize that the "wheel of fortune" has turned, and that we must strengthen our faith in Hashem in order to overcome the challenge.

It is sometimes more difficult to accept the minor frustrations properly: the days when you come home, tired and hungry from a hard day's work, and trip over shoes and briefcases in the front hall. Supper is not ready on time, and you are going to have to wait. You figure that you might as well pitch in, and you bend down to pick up some of the Lego and Matchbox cars that are strewn across the floor. Someone has forgotten to close the door to one of the kitchen cabinets, so as you straighten up, you bang your head. You were in a bad mood to begin with, but this accumulation of additional annoyances threatens to put you over the edge. How can we maintain the perspective needed to cope with the minor travails of our lives?

◈§ Moods Are Normal

The Steipler tells us that we must first identify the problem. Tell yourself that you are in a bad mood, and that it is normal. Bad streaks are not disasters; they are a normal part of life.

The Steipler points out that all of creation has ups and downs. The weather has cycles; the topography of the world has peaks and valleys; the daily cycle has light and darkness. We, too, experience an alternating cycle of ups and downs, highs and lows, peaks and valleys, light and darkness.

If we think that we are the only ones to experience these cycles while the rest of the world coasts along happily, we will surely become depressed. Remember the advice of the Steipler, and it will be much easier to cope. This will help us put things into perspective, and realize that things are not as bad as they seem.

In the early 90s, I met a wonderful young man named Yerachmiel.

Yerachmiel grew up disconnected from his Jewish roots. When he came of age, he joined the U.S. Navy and became a sailor on a nuclear submarine. As the only Jew on the submarine, he was sometimes asked what it means to be a Jew. He had no answer. Yerachmiel decided to visit Eretz Yisrael to find out more about Judaism. A religious Jew approached him at the *Kosel* and struck up a conversation. One thing led to another, and soon Yerachmiel obtained a medical discharge from the Navy and joined a yeshivah in Jerusalem.

Later, Yerachmiel returned to the United States, an observant Jew. Someone had given him my address, and he became our regular Shabbos guest and a favorite of our children. Yerachmiel became a dear friend, an inspiration to my wife and me.

For an entire winter, Yerachmiel spent every other Shabbos at our home. Often, we would learn together on Shabbos afternoon.

A most difficult part of becoming a *ba'al teshuvah* is the struggle to catch up in learning. Intelligent, educated adults see ten- or twelve-year-olds rattling off Mishnayos or Gemara while they struggle to read the words. For many *ba'alei teshuvah*, this is quite depressing, and Yerachmiel was no exception. He did not feel that he was making much progress.

After Pesach, he joined Yeshivah Kol Yaakov in Monsey, to improve his learning skills.

He left for Monsey, and I did not see him for several months. In June, Yerachmiel returned to my home for a Shabbos. During the Shabbos *seudah*, I asked him how things were going at Kol Yaakov. "I love the yeshivah, but I can't say that I have made much progress in my learning," he answered despondently.

When I sat down to learn with him on Shabbos afternoon, I was pleasantly surprised. His learning had improved markedly. So why was he discouraged?

Before Yerachmiel went to Kol Yaakov, he could not read the Rashi alphabet at all. While at Kol Yaakov, he had mastered the Rashi letters. Now he was struggling to fit together the words of Rashi. To him, it was the same struggle — one long, difficult effort to catch up in his learning. When I forced him to recognize how much he had progressed in these few months, he was truly astonished.

In a footnote to *Chayei Olam* (Chapter 6; p. 13), the Steipler writes that when a person becomes depressed, the depression tends to fill his consciousness. It makes no difference how significant or insignificant his problem may be; it is human nature for his negative feelings to overwhelm a person. Depression fills a person entirely, clouding his every thought, feeling, and emotion.

When we identify the "down" periods of life for what they are, we can put things into perspective. We can realize that we are actually making progress, even in such times, and that there are silver linings to the black clouds that seem to hover over our lives.

⋆§ Failure Brings Success

Aside from identifying a bad mood as such, we should also consider a teaching from the *Ba'al Shem Tov*, quoted by Rav Tzaddok HaKohen.

King Shlomo wrote, "*Ki sheva yipol tzaddik v'kam, ureshaim yikashlu b'ra'ah* — even if a righteous person falls [in spiritual matters] seven times, he will keep getting up, but a wicked person will fall once and stay down" (*Mishlei* 24:16).

Ba'al Shem Tov explains that this verse is teaching us a fact of life. In order to become a righteous person, you *must* fall, and fall again, and again — and keep getting up. Through the process of falling and rising again and again, a person becomes a *tzaddik*. Thus, he does not translate the verse, "*even if* a righteous person falls," but simply, "a righteous person falls ...."

Rav Tzaddok HaKohen points out that we see the very same concept in nature. Night comes before day. The inedible peel covers the delicious fruit. Dark storm clouds must fill the skies before we experience the blessing of rain. This is the way the world runs. We have to go through a period of darkness before we see light.

What a message! Falling is necessary for growth! I fall plenty of times; that must mean that I'm ripe for improvement. If we would truly realize this, we'd never be discouraged!

In a powerful letter that we would do well to study and remember, Rav Hutner, *zt"l*, makes this point to one of his students (*Igros Pachad Yitzchak* #128).

Although the *talmid's* letter is not printed, Rav Hutner quotes a portion of it in his response. "I'll never forget the desire I had to succeed, and to keep advancing from one spiritual level to the next," writes the *talmid*. "Now, however, I realize that my dreams have not come true. All hope is lost."

Rav Hutner writes back: "My friend, I am pressing you to my heart, and whispering in your ear. Had your letter described the mitzvos and good deeds you are involved in, I would have said that I received a good letter from you. Now that you chose to write a letter about the pitfalls you face and your spiritual failures, I say that I received a *very* good letter from you."

Imagine the *talmid's* feeling upon reading the response. Discussion of his spiritual failures makes his letter "very good"!?

Rav Hutner points out the underlying mistake that made this *talmid* feel so despondent. He writes:

"There is a terrible sickness among us. When we tell stories of a *gadol*, we only record their later years, when they have already succeeded in becoming *gedolim*, and we make it sound like that they were filled with perfection from birth, rather than it coming from years and years of internal struggles.

"I beg of you — don't picture *gedolim* as people who were born perfect; people who are constantly one with their *yetzer tov*. Rather, realize the greatness that the *gedolim* have achieved is a result of a steady, tenacious war against every base and low inclination.

"Know, that when you feel your *yetzer hara* raging inside of you, it means that you are on par with the greatest *gedolim*.

"Everyone is amazed at the purity of speech of the Chofetz Chaim, but who knows of the battles, struggles, and obstacles, the slumps and regressions that the Chofetz Chaim encountered in his war with the *yetzer hora*?

"Know, however, my dear friend, that your soul is rooted not in the tranquility of the *yetzer tov*, but rather in the battle of the *yetzer tov*.

"The expression, 'Lose a battle and win a war' applies. Certainly you have stumbled and will stumble again, and in many battles you will fall. I promise you, though, that after those losing battles you will emerge victorious .... Lose battles but win wars.

"The wisest of all men said, 'A righteous man falls seven times and rises again' (*Mishlei* 24:16). Fools believe that the intent of this verse is to teach us something remarkable. The righteous man has fallen seven times and yet he rises. But the knowledgeable are aware that the essence of the *tzaddik's* rising is by way of his seven falls.

"'And He saw all that he made and, behold! It was very good.' 'Good, that is the *yetzer tov*. Very good, that is the *yetzer hora*.'"
(*Bereishis Rabbah* 9)

Indeed, only failure brings success.

Moods II: Rav Tzaddok on Failure

Rav Tzaddok HaKohen finds this lesson in the Torah: We read in *Parashas Nasso* that the *nesi'im* were the first to offer private sacrifices in the Mishkan. Why did they receive this privilege?

Earlier, when Moshe called upon the Jews to donate objects for the Mishkan, the *nesi'im* did not bring anything. Instead, they waited to see what others would donate, planning to bring the items that were still missing when all the others had finished donating. The Jewish People donated so generously, however, that the *nesi'im's* offer was totally unnecessary — nothing was left for them to donate. They repented for their arrogance, and Hashem rewarded them by enabling them to bring the *Shoham* and *Miluim* stones.

The *nesi'im* learned their lesson well, and when it came time to inaugurate the Mishkan, they were the first to offer sacrifices.

This is the path of spiritual advancement, says Rav Tzaddok. The earlier failure of the *nesi'im* was their steppingstone to their famous *Korbonos HaNisi'im*. The Torah describes these *Korbonos* in great detail; expressing Hashem's special pleasure with the fruits of their previous failure.

Rav Tzaddok (*Tzidkos HaTzaddik* 49) takes this concept to a level that is positively frightening. Achaz and Chizkiyahu were two kings of *Klal Yisrael*, who, despite being father and son, were absolute opposites. Achaz hated Torah leaders with such a passion that he outlawed teaching Torah to young children, reasoning that if there would be no young scholars, there would eventually be no Torah leaders, either. His son Chizkiyahu brought about national repentance and made Torah study mandatory. The Talmud (*Sanhedrin* 94b) tells us that in Chizkiyahu's times, every man, woman, and child was learned in even the difficult *halachos* of purity and impurity.

It seems somewhat strange that a father and son could be such opposites. Rav Tzaddok attributes this to the very same concept that we have described: that failure is the preparation for success.

In Rav Tzaddok's words, "Through failure one understands that he can excel in that very area. Look at Achaz, who sealed the Torah, holding back young students. He was therefore prepared to have a son like Chizkiyahu who spread Torah study until there wasn't a single *am ha'aretz* ...!"[1]

Imagine! The failures that *Klal Yisrael* experienced during Achaz's days became the springboard for the success they had under Chizkiyahu.

It is hard to understand Rav Tzaddok's teaching. He obviously does not mean to suggest that if someone wants a son like Chizkiyahu, he should follow the example of Achaz. We *can* learn, however, that even when we feel that there is a miniature Achaz inside us, when we feel that we have sunk to levels that are beneath us, we can see this experience as a potential springboard for an amazing future.[2]

⋞§ Prevention

The Talmud (*Moed Kattan* 27b) tells us that a person who cries too much upon the loss of a loved one is preparing himself for another loss — i.e., he will suffer the loss of another loved one. To illustrate this point, the Talmud tells us the story of widow who had seven children. When her oldest child died, she cried incessantly. She would not stop mourning. Rav Huna warned her that she must stop her excessive crying, or she could

---

1. Rav Tzaddok adds, "Therefore, we are taught (*Vayikra Rabbah* 21:5) that a person who sinned should perform a mitzvah with that same limb that was used for sin. This is not only a repair for the earlier sin, but also a *tikkun* for his individual soul, for every person is created to excel in a particular area, unique to his soul ... as we are taught (*Gitten* 43a), a person does not appreciate the Torah's teaching unless he has first stumbled in that [teaching]."
This is also the theme of *Tefillas Zakkah*, which is recited as Yom Kippur begins.

2. The *Sfas Emes* (to *Parashas HaChodesh*) expresses a similar idea regarding Rav Elozor ben Aruch. Rav Elozor ben Aruch was one of the five great disciples of Rav Yochanan ben Zakai (*Avos* Ch. 2). Yet, the Talmud (*Shabbos* 147b) relates that Rav Elozor ben Aruch left the yeshivah for a resort city and subsequently forgot his learning, to the extent that he had difficulty reading a simple verse from the Torah. The *Sfas Emes* explains that this failure was the seed of Rav Elozor ben Aruch's future greatness, as failure can lead to greatness.

start sewing shrouds for her next child. She did not control herself, and, true to Rav Huna's prediction, her second child died. Once again, she began to cry bitterly, day after day. Rav Huna issued the very same warning, and when she did not heed his call to stop crying, her third child died. Tragically, the cycle repeated itself until all seven children had died.

Rav Ahron Kotler *(Mishnas Rav Aharon* 2:17, 3:130) explains the underlying concept of this Gemara.

The problem with this woman is that she lived her life with the feeling that she deserved everything she had; her attitude was that *"es kumpt mir"* — I deserve it. Instead of thanking Hashem and appreciating the seven gifts He had granted her, she felt that she had received the blessing of her own merit. When a person feels he is deserving of something, he will know no consolation when he loses it. This woman's failure was not in her present weeping. It was in her lifelong attitude of entitlement.

As long as our attitude in life is that *es kumpt unz* — we deserve everything we have — we will become easily frustrated when things don't work out according to our expectations.

> A wealthy man once came to complain that his wife was moody and depressed. He could not do much to raise her spirits. He asked me to speak to her to see if I could help her.
>
> The woman expressed her frustrations to me. One of her frustrations was the following: It seems that she was renovating her kitchen. She had seen a certain fixture in someone else's house that she absolutely loved. She decided that she *had* to have that fixture.
>
> "I am so depressed," she cried to me. "I was in every single lighting store in New York City. I can only find it in a different shade. Doesn't it make sense that I'd become depressed?"
>
> It makes sense, indeed.

It is hard to believe that someone would be so distraught over something so minor. This woman had almost everything she wanted, but was frustrated by the one thing she lacked. Why? Because in her mind, she deserved the kitchen fixture that was just right, and she could not get that which she really deserved.

We can prevent ourselves from getting into bad moods, or from overreacting to the minor frustrations of life, by focusing on the fact that Hashem does not owe us anything. Minimizing our sense of entitlement would maximize our level of acceptance, appreciation, and contentment.

⇒§ Damage Control

To sum up: we have the Steipler's advice on identifying bad moods and understanding that they are normal; we learned from the *Ba'al Shem Tov* and Rav Yitzchak Hutner's letter that failure can be a springboard for growth; Rav Aharon taught us that bad moods are fostered by the attitude, "*es kumpt mir.*"

I would like to add three pieces of "bad-mood advice."

#1: Don't make decisions. In another letter, Rav Hutner instructs his *talmid* not to make decisions when he is down. When you are in the grip of a bad mood, don't tell your *chavrusa* (study partner) that you no longer want to learn with him. You will end up regretting it. Don't come home in an irritable state and announce a new policy for the family. You are not rational at such times. The policies enacted when we are down often fall into the category of, "*Gezeirah she'ein rov tzibbur yicholim la'amod bo* — regulations that most people are incapable of following."

The most dangerous words uttered by an irate parent can be "Kids! From now on …!"

Rav Hutner writes that you are guaranteed to make the wrong decisions when your mind is muddled by a bad mood. Accept the fact you are in a bad mood. A *dayan* is not permitted to sit in judgment when he is not in the appropriate state of mind. You, too, should not render judgment or enact new laws when you are not in a calm state of mind (*Igros Pachad Yitzchak* #96).

#2: Keep your mouth closed. Don't be quick to speak. Don't fly off the handle and say things that you will want to take back later on — especially to your nearest and dearest.

There is one story that I often recount when counseling *chasanim*. I was on my way home after *seder*. As I rounded the corner, heading to the bus stop, I noticed a friend of mine standing in the street near the curb. He kept glancing impatiently at his watch, and then toward the traffic coming from the direction of Borough Park. It did not take much genius to figure out what happened. Yehudah, who lived in Borough Park, was waiting for his wife, and (guess what!) she was late.

As I passed him, without breaking stride, I said, "Yehudah, don't blame her, blame Hashem. He made women that way."

I was not trying to give Yehudah *mussar* or advise him, I was just kidding. I was absolutely shocked the next day when Yehudah began to thank me profusely.

Yehudah told me that he was very angry. His wife was late and she was going to hear about it. As she drove up, she was ready for an argument. Yehudah got into the car, shrugged, and said, "Nu, Rabbi Reisman says that it's not your fault. It's Hashem's fault ...."

Think about it. Did Yehudah arrive any later at his destination because he remained silent? No. But he did get there in a pleasant frame of mind, because he kept his mouth closed.

It's hard to do. When we are upset, we feel that we cannot control ourselves. When the pressure mounts, an explosion seems inevitable. But believe me, it is not worth it. The Vilna Gaon writes about a person who remains silent, "He merits the divine light that is unattainable by angels."

#3: Don't shift the blame. When we get into bad moods, we tend to blame others for all our problems. Be honest. You are no less culpable for your difficulties than they are. Take responsibility. Most of our problems are due to our own failings.

The *Arugos HaBosem* once devoted his speech before *Ne'ilah* to the subject of not having *tevios* (complaints) against others. He illustrated his point with the following Chassidic tale.

> There was a Chassidic Rebbe who had a wayward son. He would show up at *tisch* in the 17th-century version of blue jeans. He acted in an inappropriate and obnoxious manner, and he did many *aveiros* publicly. Despite his pain and shame, the Rebbe did not distance his son. On the contrary, he would treat him with great respect, seating him up front in shul and giving him a seat of honor at the *tisch*.
>
> The chassidim couldn't bear it. How could the Rebbe treat his undeserving son so royally? What kind of example did that set? What would other chassidim say? They decided to put an end to this unseemly spectacle. They decided to form a committee of three distinguished chassidim to approach the Rebbe and ask him put a stop to this ridiculous state of affairs.
>
> The committee members hesitated and procrastinated. They simply could not bring themselves to broach the sub-

ject. As the *Yamim Noraim* drew near, the chassidim became more apprehensive than ever. Large crowds would come to the city to be with the Rebbe. His son would be a disgrace to the entire community! The committee knew that it was time to approach the Rebbe.

They headed towards the Rebbe's study, determined to convince him to distance his son, at least for the *Yamim Noraim*. As they stood poised to knock on the door, they heard the Rebbe crying and asking Hashem for forgiveness on their behalf.

"*Ribbono shel Olam*," the Rebbe was saying, "Please forgive my chassidim. I know that not everything is right in the community. I know that Your children act improperly, be it in monetary matters or in how they treat each other. But c, I also have a son who does not act the way I would like him to act, and I do not distance him. I overlook his sins. I hold him close to me. Please, *Ribbono shel Olam*, can't You overlook the sins of Your children? Forgive them and hold them close!"

The committee quietly turned around and went home.

Don't look to blame others. Look at yourself.

By accepting responsibility for our bad moods, we will be able to minimize the damage, bounce back quickly, and use the experience as a catalyst for spiritual growth.

Central Jerusalem

Chazal (*Kiddushin* 69a) tell us that Eretz Yisrael is *gavoha mikol ha'aratzos*, and that the *Beis HaMikdash* was *gavohah mikol Eretz Yisrael*. The simple translation of these words is that Eretz Yisrael is at the highest point of any country in the world, and that the *Beis HaMikdash* is at the highest point of Eretz Yisrael.

Anyone familiar with the topography of the world knows that this is not so. There are mountains all over the world — and even some within Eretz Yisrael — that are much taller than *Har HaBayis*, where the *Beis HaMikdash* stood. How could *Chazal* tell us that it was the highest point in the world?

Chasam Sofer (*Responsa* 2:233) teaches us how to view world geography from a Torah perspective.

When we look at a globe, we see the North Pole at the top. Who decided that the North Pole should be on top? The world is round. Gravity causes each person in the world to feel as if he is on top and that the rest of the world is below him. It is impossible for us to decide which section is the top. *Chasam Sofer* tells us that from a Torah perspective, Jerusalem should appear on top of the globe. Others may consider the North Pole the top of the world, but to a Jew, Jerusalem is the uppermost point in the world.

A similar idea can be applied to a location called "Central Jerusalem," which we hear and read about often in the news. Sometimes there are reports of protests in Central Jerusalem, and in tragic times there are bombings in Central Jerusalem. Where is Central Jerusalem? News reporters seem to think that it is in the vicinity of major hotels or the central bus depot. That may be their Central Jerusalem, but it is not our Central Jerusalem. To a *frum* Jew, Central Jerusalem is the *Kosel*, the yeshivos, and the homes of Rav Elyashiv and other *gedolim* who dwell in Jerusalem. If you go to Meah Shearim to hear a *shiur* from Rav Elyashiv, then you are in Central Jerusalem. If you are on Rechov Yaffo, you are far from Central Jerusalem. In the hearts and minds of Jews, the spiritual fortresses of Jerusalem have always been the center of the world.

In recent years, however, we have occasionally heard *frum Yidden* talking about Jerusalem in a different tone. Some people regard it as a dangerous place, to be avoided.[1] It seems that the deep emotional bond between the Jewish People and Jerusalem needs to be stronger. Let's study the loving statements of *Chazal* regarding Jerusalem and try to reinforce that bond.

~§ Jerusalem: Our Bride

*I*sraelis have a day each year that they call *Yom Yerushalayim*. Religious Jews also have a *Yom Yerushalayim* — each Monday. The *Shir shel Yom* that we say each Monday morning is a song of praise for Jerusalem: "*Gadol Hashem umhullal me'od be'ir Elokeinu har kadsho* — Great is Hashem and much praised, in the city of our God, Mountain of His Holiness. *Yefei nof, m'sos kol ha'aretz* — Fairest of cities, joy of the earth ..." (*Psalms* 48).

The Talmud (*Rosh Hashanah* 26a) relates that *Reish Lakish* once visited a community in which they would call a bride *ninfi*, which he associated with the words *yefei nof*. When we refer to Jerusalem as *yefei nof*, we are calling it the beautiful bride of *Klal Yisrael*.

---

1. This refers to the years that bombings were frequent in Jerusalem.

We know that a certain element of mystery and distance often has a positive influence on a *chasan–kallah* relationship. For generations, the romance between the Jewish People and Jerusalem was strengthened by the city's distance and inaccessibility. When Jerusalem was difficult to reach, there was a certain mystical aura and deep-seated longing that people felt when they mentioned Jerusalem. Nowadays, we are accustomed to having Jerusalem within reach. The mystery is gone. That aspect of the romance is missing. At a time when Jerusalem is in danger — in terms of the security of its citizens and in political terms — it can use the love and support of *Klal Yisrael*. Familiarity has unfortunately done its job, and we are often lax in providing that support.

When a young man is about to get married, we try to provide him with some lessons on how to treat a wife properly. Boys in our community spend most of their lives interacting with other boys. Their primary interaction with girls was back in the days when they would fling mud at them in the bungalow colony — a form of entertainment that they probably should not bring into their marriages. We therefore give *chasanim* some pointers that will help them develop a loving and productive relationship with their *kallahs*. Let us examine some of those pointers to see how they can help us develop a loving relationship with our collective *kallah*, Jerusalem.

↬ Overlooking the Failings

A young man who becomes engaged is convinced that his *kallah* is a good, even a perfect, match. When they are married, they inevitably find out that the match is not so perfect after all. She has some failings. But King Shlomo wrote, "*Al kal peshaim tichaseh ahavah* — love covers all offenses" (*Mishlei* 10:12). No husband talks about his wife's failings. Even before the *chasunah*, a *chasan* does not discuss his *kallah's* mistakes with his parents. The nature of a loving relationship is that the offenses are kept between the couple, not raised as a subject for public discussion.

The same attitude must be applied to Jerusalem.

In counting the miracles that occurred in the *Beis HaMikdash*, the *Mishnah* states, "No one ever said to his fellow, 'The space is insufficient for me to stay overnight in Jerusalem.'"

Chasam Sofer points out that this seems to contradict another one of the miracles listed there. We read that the people stood crowded together in the courtyard of the *Beis Hamikdash*. When it came time to prostrate themselves on the *Bais HaMikdash* floor, miraculously, there was ample space. That miracle seems to indicate that (most of the time) the multitudes were indeed cramped together. It seems obvious that with millions crowded into Jerusalem for the three festivals, they should certainly have felt cramped. How could we say that there was sufficient space for all of *Klal Yisrael* to fit comfortably in Jerusalem?

If we examine the *mishnah* carefully, answers *Chasam Sofer*, we notice that it does not state that there was actually enough space for everyone. It states that "No man ever *said to his fellow*, 'The space is insufficient for me to stay overnight in Jerusalem.'" They *were* cramped; but no one complained. People did not talk that way about Jerusalem. When you asked someone how their visit to Jerusalem went, they did not respond, "Oy, it was so cramped. I wish these people would shower more frequently." Their overwhelming love for the holy city prevented them from denigrating it in any way, even if only to mention that it was too crowded.

Rav Pam often said that it hurt his ears when he heard people talking about Jerusalem in a negative manner. It would bother him when someone would ask his friend, "How was your visit to Jerusalem?" and his friend would respond, "The weather was lousy. It was so rainy."

My wife once asked a neighbor of ours how her Pesach went. "I gained too much weight," she responded.

On a different occasion I asked her how a recent trip she had taken to Eretz Yisrael went. "I had a stomachache the entire time," she said.

Many people gain weight on Pesach, and if you drink the water in Eretz Yisrael, you are likely to get a stomachache. But is that the way you talk about Pesach? That is how you describe a visit to Jerusalem?

Many of us are guilty of this sort of speech in some way or another. Over the years, Jerusalem has had periods in which there were frequent terrorist attacks. During those times I would hear people say, "I'm not letting my son go to Jerusalem. It is too dangerous there." Others seemed to be on an anti-Israel campaign: "You're letting your son go to Eretz Yisrael? What are you, crazy?"

I'm not suggesting that you have to ignore your emotions when it seems dangerous to you. But if you are too "chicken" to send your children to Eretz Yisrael, don't advertise it.

If someone had a brother who had a nervous breakdown and was confined to a psychiatric ward, he would not walk around saying,

"You know what my brother did yesterday? He was totally out of control, and he did some really crazy things!" He would be ashamed, and he would try to hide it as much as possible. When terrible things are happening in Jerusalem, don't walk around talking about it so flippantly. Jerusalem is your *kallah*. It should pain you when her streets are filled with danger.

I traveled to Eretz Yisrael several years ago in the midst of a spate of suicide bombings. A fellow came over to me the day before I left and said, "Here is some *shaliach mitzvah* money. You'll need it." He followed his unsolicited comment with a piece of advice: "Don't go to the *Kosel* on Friday. It is the most dangerous day."

That is the way people talk about the Kosel — and with a smile?! I thought. I went to the *Kosel* on Friday. It was packed with *Yidden* who have the courage to go to the *Kosel* during times of trouble. In fact it was much easier to daven without all the tourists taking their photos.

We must realize that what we hear or read in the news is not an accurate representation of the situation in Eretz Yisrael. In 1948, the *Chazon Ish* (*Igros Chazon Ish,* 1:107) wrote a letter that could have been written in recent years. At the time, the Jews in Eretz Yisrael had been attacked by the Arab nations surrounding them. Jews in the Diaspora thought that those living in Eretz Yisrael were in a panic.

The *Chazon Ish* wrote: "I would like to calm you, to let you know that the situation is not as bad as it is exaggerated in *Chutz La'Aretz*. We are not about to act out of panic or out of stress. We are calm. We know that we must daven, but we reflect upon that need in a logical manner. In terms of emotion, we are calm and composed."

We who live out of Eretz Yisrael are under the impression that Jews there live in constant fear. In reality, the more religious a person in Eretz Yisrael is, the less he feels abandoned by Hashem. The secular Jews are on the verge of packing their bags and heading for America when the security situation is tough. The religious Jews increase their *tefillos*, but they go about their daily lives calmly and with faith in Hashem.

Even in safe times, I occasionally I hear people say, "This year I'm not going to Eretz Yisrael. I would rather go to France or Switzerland."

How do you compare the two? You want to go visit the great *ohavei Yisrael* in France or Switzerland, then do it. But how can you contrast such trips with a visit to Eretz Yisrael?

We have to do *teshuvah* for the way we talk about Jerusalem.

You may think that I am overreacting. Who says that Jerusalem is bothered by the way we talk about her?

Actually, the Talmud says so. In Talmudic times, the person who received the last *aliyah* on Shabbos or Yom Tov was allowed to choose any portion from Navi to read as a *haftarah*, as long as it had some connection to the Torah reading. From a *halachic* standpoint, we may still do so today, although the custom has become to read the *haftaros* printed in the Chumashim. The Talmud (*Megillah* 25b) relates that a man once chose to read a *haftarah* that began with the words, "*Hoda es Yerushalayim es toavosehah* — Inform Jerusalem of her abominations" (*Yechezkel* 16:2). The Talmud states that the *Tanaim* were stunned. "Before you examine Jerusalem's abominations," they said, "examine your mother's abominations."

Their rebuke was extremely harsh. Who would even think of telling someone to inquire into his mother's abominations?

It appears that the *Tanaim* were trying to impart to this man that just as you don't think of talking about the abominations of your family members, you should not think of talking that way about your bride, Jerusalem.

◆§ Being Faithful to Jerusalem

Marriages typically go through happy, loving times, as well as times when things do not go so well. *Rabbeinu Tam* goes as far as writing that there are *yemei ahavah* (days of love) and *yemei sin'ah* (days of hatred). But a marriage is not a relationship that you terminate as soon as things are not going well. You stick with it, and hope for better times.

The same is true of our bride, Jerusalem. We have to be faithful to her no matter what circumstances she finds herself in. How do we remain faithful?

Yeshayah said, "*Al chomosayich Yerushalayim hifkadeti shomrim kol hayom v'chol haleilah* — Upon your walls, O Jerusalem, have I posted guardians, all the day and all the night" (*Yeshayah* 62:6). Simply understood, this refers to guards stationed on the walls to protect it — much as we see soldiers standing guard when we visit Jerusalem today.

Redak writes that the guardians referred to in this verse are the Jewish People in exile. We, who remember Jerusalem constantly and daven for it in *Shemoneh Esrei* and in *Bircas HaMazon*, are the guardians of Jerusalem.

By "standing guard" for Jerusalem, remembering her even when danger lurks in her streets, we show our faithful devotion to her.

Once again you can ask, "Does Jerusalem care whether we remember her? Does she have emotions that are affected when the Jewish People forsake her?"

☙ The *Chasam Sofer* Speaks Up for Jerusalem

The *Chasam Sofer* delivered a eulogy after a terrible earthquake that rocked Tzefas, Teveriah, and Shechem in 1836, killing thousands — including many great Torah scholars — and leaving destruction in its wake.

In his eulogy, which is printed in *Toras Moshe* (end of *Parashas Emor*), *Chasam Sofer* asks a question that we would be incapable of answering: Why? Why did Hashem bring such destruction upon these cities?

Chasam Sofer offers a bone-chilling answer. "*Kin'as Yerushalayim asesah zos* — the envy of Jerusalem caused this to happen," he writes. "The gates of Heaven are in Jerusalem; it is the cite of Har HaMoriah, where Yitzchak was offered as a sacrifice to Hashem and Yaakov slept [and had the Heavenly vision in which Hashem promised Eretz Yisrael to his descendants]. In the last hundred years, however, people have moved out to Tzefas and Teveriah. Jerusalem, Hashem's city, has been forgotten."

If you need any further proof that Jerusalem is our *kallah*, *Chasam Sofer* provides it. Like a jealous woman, Jerusalem felt betrayed when the Jewish People forsook her and took up residence in other cities and made them the centers of Jewish life in Eretz Yisrael. The jealousy of Jerusalem caused destruction to befall the Jewish communities of Eretz Yisrael. When people talk about the danger of living in Jerusalem, Hashem shows us that it can be dangerous elsewhere as well. We have to stand guard when our bride is in trouble, not forsake her in her time of need.

☙ Bring a Gift

very *chasan* must be told to buy his *kallah* gifts that *she* enjoys. I know a young man who came home on his first anniversary and presented his wife with a brand-new cooking implement. His wife was insulted. "What am I, the cook in the house?" she asked. This boy's mother happened to enjoy kitchen gadgets, so that is what his father would buy her when he wanted to please her. But when you are married, you don't buy something you like, or something your mother likes — you have to find out what your wife likes.

Ki m'Zion teitzei Torah ud'var Hashem m'Yerushalayim. Your *kallah*, Jerusalem, likes Torah. She likes spirituality. When you go to visit Jerusalem, don't just go to visit the tourist attractions. Bring a gift. Take a *mesechta* or a *perek* that you have never studied before, and sit down to learn for a couple of hours each day. Find one of the yeshivos in Jerusalem and engross yourself in Torah study. That is what your *kallah* likes; that is what you should bring her.

I have heard people say, "I'm not going to Eretz Yisrael again. I've already seen everything."

You have seen everything? Have you seen all of *Bava Kamma*, *Bava Metzia*, and *Bava Basra*? Have you been to Rav Elyashiv's *shiur*?

What have you seen in Jerusalem — museums with some ancient *avodah zaras*? That is what you travel to Jerusalem to see? Jerusalem wants you to come and learn, to grow spiritually while you are there.

Perhaps you think that I am exaggerating. Perhaps you think that Jerusalem doesn't care why you come and what you do while you are there.

The Talmud tells us otherwise. The Talmud (*Pesachim* 8b) wonders why Hashem didn't place the *Chamei Teveriah* — the hot springs of Tiberias — in Jerusalem, and why Hashem didn't allow the delicious fruit that grows in the north of Eretz Yisrael to grow in Jerusalem. The Talmud answers that Hashem did not want those who journey to Jerusalem for the festivals to say, "It was worth visiting Jerusalem just for these hot baths or just for these fruits."

Piskei Teshuvah (#265) raises a question. The Talmud states that a person who donates money to *tzeddakah* on the condition that his son should recover from an illness is considered to have performed the mitzvah of *tzeddakah* properly. Apparently, we are allowed to have ulterior motives when performing mitzvos. Why couldn't people make the pilgrimage for two reasons — to perform the mitzvah and to enjoy the hot baths or the fruit?

If we look at Jerusalem as a bride, this question poses no difficulty. You can have ulterior motives in most relationships in life, but not in a marriage. Imagine someone saying, "I really like my *kallah*, but it is nice that the family owns a Jacuzzi," or, "She's a great person, and the money in the family also helps." Much as this may be a person's second consideration, it cheapens the relationship.

Jerusalem has no interest in hot baths, in fruit, and certainly not in museums built by secularists who deny the holiness of Jerusalem. Jerusalem wants Torah.

There is a passage in the Talmud that seems to contradict this principle. The Talmud (*Kiddushin* 49b) states that ten measures of beauty came into the world, and nine of them were taken by Jerusalem. If Jerusalem is so beautiful, then doesn't it run the danger of having people visit it to enjoy its beauty?

Ohr Gedalyahu (*Parashas Tazria* pg. 39) states that the beauty of Jerusalem is not in its rising mountains, in its beautiful trees, or even in the *Kosel*. The beauty is displayed on the faces of the people who visit Jerusalem in order to grow spiritually.

We know young men who have gone to study in Jerusalem, and when they return at the end of a *z'man* their faces shine with beauty. It is a beauty that is as indescribable as the beauty of Shabbos candles. Try lighting candles on your silver candlesticks on a Wednesday night. Will they have the special glow of Shabbos candles? They won't even come close! The beauty of Jerusalem appears on the faces of people who go to learn in Jerusalem — the beautiful glow of spiritually. Bring the gift of Torah to your *kallah*, and she'll give you that special glow to take home.

ᴥ§ *Chareidi* Jews at the Movies?

I often have the *zechus* to travel to Eretz Yisrael. I don't understand: On the plane ride to the Holy Land, Orthodox Jews are watching the movies! They look like chassidim, yeshivah *bachurim*, and regular *chareidim*. But they are watching the movies! On the way to Eretz Yisrael?

Dear reader, I know that you don't believe it. You think that I'm exaggerating. Unless you've flown to Eretz Yisrael. In that case, you've seen it with your own eyes.

I know that it is difficult to sit through a long plane flight. But is it more difficult than the trips made by Jews to Eretz Yisrael over the last few hundred years?

Movies. Murder, *z'nus*, and *leitzonus*. Ready to land in the Holy Land!

Is it any wonder that people arrive there devoid of their spiritual senses?

✺ Now — or (Maybe) Never

Finally, the Talmud (*Bava Basra* 75b) warns that Jerusalem in *Mashiach's* time will not be like Jerusalem today. Nowadays, anyone can visit Jerusalem. Just buy a ticket and go. In *Moshiach's* times, Jerusalem will accept visitors by invitation only.

Imagine if a boy is going out with a girl, and he decides that she is not for him. The day after he calls off the courtship, she wins the Powerball lottery for $100 million. If he calls her up and says, "I'm thinking that maybe you *were* the right girl for me," she'll slam down the telephone. If she wasn't good for him when she did not have the money, then she won't allow him to marry her now that she is rich.

Take my advice. Visit your *kallah* now. Does Jerusalem care? Sure she cares. In *sheva berachos* we say, "*Sos tasis v'sagel ha'akarah, bekibutz banehah lesochah besimchah* — Bring intense joy and exultation to the barren one [Jerusalem], by gathering her children into her with joy." Jerusalem wants you to come visit her when times are not so great. If you visit her now and bring a gift, you can be sure that she will invite you back when *Mashiach* comes — may it be speedily, in our days.

My Favorite Segulos

The Torah warns us repeatedly not to serve idols. It is difficult for us to understand why this is necessary. Nach constantly relates the tremendous challenge involving *avodah zarah*. We have to strain to fathom the concept that people once had a great desire to worship inanimate objects or animals, because *Anshei Knesses HaGedolah* abolished that desire and freed us from that temptation.

One of the practices we find mentioned, however, is absolutely horrifying. The Torah warns us several times not to pass our children through fire and not to burn them as sacrifices to idols.

Near the time of the destruction of the first *Beis HaMikdash*, Hashem instructed the prophet Yirmiyahu to go to the Valley of the Son of Hinnom. This valley is not far from the entrance to the *Kosel* that is now called *Sha'ar Ha'Ashpos*. If you want to see the valley today, turn right as you exit *Sha'ar Ha'Ashpos* and travel toward *Har Tzion*. The valley to your left is the Valley of the Son of Hinnom. At the time of the destruction of the *Beis HaMikdash*, this valley was the site of one of the most commonly worshipped idols, *Baal*.

Hashem sent Yirmiyahu to warn the people:

"Behold, I am bringing such evil upon this place, that whoever hears of it, his ears will ring. Because they forsook Me, and estranged this place [from Me], and they burned incense in it to the foreign gods ... and they built the high places of the *Baal*, [at which] *to burn their sons in fire as burnt-offerings to the Baal,* which I never commanded, nor spoke of, nor even considered in My heart" (*Yirmiyahu* 19:3-5).

It is important to remember that the people who lived at the time of the destruction of the *Beis HaMikdash* were not vicious, heartless murderers. *Chazal* tell us that aside from their temptation toward idolatry and several other sins, they were decent people. How, then, could they sacrifice their own children to an idol? What caused them to act with such cruelty?

This seems even more puzzling when we realize that this took place in close proximity to the *Beis HaMikdash*. How could it be that within earshot of the *Kodesh HaKadashim* Jewish children were burnt as offerings to the *Baal*?

Rav Isaac Sher, in his *Leket Sichos Mussar* (Vol. I, p. 375), explains the need for so many admonitions against child sacrifice. In doing so, he reveals an extraordinary insight into human nature.

He begins by explaining a seemingly redundant verse in *Sefer Devarim*.

In *Parashas Va'eschanan*, the Torah states, "You shall not add to the word that I command you" (*Devarim* 4:2). This commandment, which is commonly known as "*bal tosif*," admonishes us not to add to the mitzvos that appear in the Torah.

In *Parashas Re'eh*, just two *parshiyos* later, the Torah states, "The entire word that I command you, that shall you observe to do; you shall not add to it" (ibid. 13:1).

There are occasions in which we derive several mitzvos from one verse, notes Rav Sher, but the Talmud (*Sanhedrin* 34a) tells us that we do not learn the same mitzvah from more than one verse. What does the verse in *Re'eh* teach us that we would not have known from the verse in *Va'eschanan*?

Rav Sher answers that these are two distinct *issurim*. The first verse forbids us from adding onto existing mitzvos. We may not add additional species to the four that the Torah commands us to take on Succos, nor add another *parashah* to the four sections in our tefillin.

In *Parshas Re'eh*, the *bal tosef* refers to something else. There, the Torah warns us not to make up a new mitzvah; one that does not appear in the Torah at all.

This leads to another question. We can understand that a person might think that it is proper to add to an existing mitzvah. A person may feel that he is beautifying the mitzvah by adding to it. The Torah therefore warns that such behavior is forbidden. This explains the first verse.

The second admonition is more difficult. Why would someone want to create his own mitzvah?

Rav Sher explains that this can occur when a person feels guilty for sinning or failing to keep the mitzvos of the Torah. The true way to atone for sins is through *teshuvah*. The *teshuvah* process is long and difficult, however, and it does not always leave a person with an emotional high, a sense of accomplishment. People do not feel that they have repaired the spiritual damage they have inflicted upon their souls simply because they feel regretful for their sins and have resolved not to repeat them. There is an emotional need to do something sensational and drastic in order to make up for their sins — and they dream up a new "mitzvah."

If we read the verses immediately preceding the one in *Re'eh*, we find an example of such behavior. The Torah states, "Beware for yourself lest you seek out the gods, saying, 'How did these nations worship their gods, and even I will do the same.' You shall not do so to Hashem, your God, for everything that is an abomination of Hashem, that He hates, have they done to their gods; *for even their sons and their daughters have they burned in the fire for their gods*" (*Devarim* 12:30-31).

People like to serve Hashem in their own way. Idol worship actually originated as a badly misconstrued way of serving Hashem. The Torah tells us that when people feel an emotional need to compensate for a sin, they will be tempted to create new mitzvos. This helps them feel the spiritual high that they crave.

The Torah prohibits this, admonishing us to stick to God's commandments alone. True spiritually lies in the word of God alone. "The entire word that I command you, that shall you observe to do; you shall not add to it."

Humans are stubborn. When we feel a desire to draw close to Hashem, we realize that this is a positive feeling, a righteous drive. We think of ways to achieve this closeness. We are sure that our ideas are correct, that we know how to do it! We cannot be convinced that these ideas may be wrong.

This self-righteous drive causes man to make spiritual decisions on his own. Once man enters into this new realm, anything is possible. A cycle begins. Create your own mitzvah; feel spiritually close to Hashem; create a mitzvah that gives you a greater high.

In its ultimate form, this attitude leads to the spiritual experience of sacrificing one's own child to this foreign form of god.

This is exactly what happened to Yirmiyahu's generation. They were inherently good people, but they were controlled by their desires and sinned repeatedly. Their feeling of iniquity infused them with an emotional need to compensate for their sins, which led them to burn their own children.

This idea is expressed clearly in Yirmiyahu's prophecy: "They burn their sons in fire as burnt-offerings to the *Baal, which I never commanded, nor spoke of, nor even considered in My heart.*"

Would we ever consider the possibility that idol worship was commanded by, spoken of, or entered the heart of Hashem? Why does the prophet have to emphasize the lack of such a mitzvah?

Yirmiyahu was trying to teach us that *Klal Yisrael* was not trying to anger Hashem, but in their zeal to atone for their sins, they went beyond anything Hashem wants from us. They went beyond the commandments that appear in the Torah, beyond the words that Hashem spoke to the prophets, and beyond things "He considered in His heart."

Rav Elchonon Wasserman (*Kuntras Divrei Sofrim*) explains that there are aspects of Judaism that we know are Hashem's will, even though we have no direct commandment in the Torah or the prophets. The need to perfect our *middos*, our character traits is an example of this. "Things Hashem considered in His heart" refers to this aspect of the service of Hashem. It was this concept that was warped in the eyes of the generation of Yirmayahu.

In *Darash Moshe* (Vol. II), Rav Moshe Feinstein, zt"l, expresses a similar thought. He notes that there were several Jewish kings — Chizkiyah and Yoshiyahu, for instance — who were able to bring about a national *teshuvah* movement. They caused people to stop sinning and abandon their idolatrous ways. When the prophet describes the achievements of these generations, we usually find an exception to the king's success, "*Rak habamos lo saru*" — they could not convince people to stop sacrificing on *bamos*, small altars that people erected in their backyards.

The sin of offering a sacrifice on a *bamah* is not one to dismiss lightly, notes Rav Moshe. It is a Torah prohibition that carries a punishment of death. Why did people stick so obstinately to such a grave sin?

A person can have an overpowering temptation to commit an ordinary sin, explains Rav Moshe, but if he learns some *mussar* or discusses it with his rebbe, he may be able to suppress his desire. One form of temptation can rarely be suppressed — the *yetzer hara* to serve Hashem in a manner that a person himself invented. When Chizkiyah and Yoshiyahu came to reprimand the people for sinning, they were willing to accept the *mussar* and mend their ways.

When the kings tried to prevent them from sacrificing on *bamos*, however, the people would not accept their rebuke. "This is a sin?" they wondered. "I get such a spiritual high from it! When I close my eyes, I can just see the pleasure that my sacrifice causes in Heaven. There is no way that I can give this up."

One of the biggest temptations in this world is to invent methods of serving Hashem. It may be a temptation that affects good people, people who stand on a high spiritual level, but it is a temptation nonetheless, and it is ultimately destructive.

The *Segulah* Craze

Throughout our *galus*, and perhaps to an even greater extent in recent years, we have witnessed a plethora of new ideas emerging — new ways to serve Hashem. Many of these methods come in the forms of *segulos*. Open up any Jewish publication and you'll see advertisements for "Proven *Segulos*." Proven? Did anyone hear of them ten or twenty years ago? Where did they come from?

These are new methods of serving Hashem. It is hard for anyone to speak against the phenomenon, because people really do feel close to Hashem when they engage in *segulos*. Very often, however, it is clear that it is a new-fangled idea. You don't have to go too far back to realize this.

I'm not so old, but I can tell you that twenty or thirty years ago there were few customs associated with Lag Ba'Omer. Now there are new ones every year!

Our generation is plagued by "*Segulah* Sickness." People crave *segulos*. Why? Because *segulos* are easy. They are shortcuts. They do not require us to perfect ourselves, to mend our ways.

It has often been said that it is a shame that Rav Yehudah HaChassid did not write in his *tzava'ah* (will) that people should not steal. There are people who follow every single clause in Rav Yehudah HaChassid's will, with real devotion and zeal. To some of them, the fact that the Torah commands us not to steal does not have the same power! It is relatively easy not to shave or take a haircut on Rosh Chodesh — but fighting the temptation to cheat in business can be difficult.

It is unfortunate, but the craving for closeness to Hashem often leads us to do things that are very far from true service of Hashem.

My opinion on *segulos* comes from my rebbi, Rav Pam, *zt"l*. He held that *segulos* that have no clear source should not be followed at all, and even *segulos* with valid sources should only be followed if there is no ordinary, natural way to help yourself.

Early in our marriage, we had to deal with a medical condition for which there is a *segulah* from *Rabbeinu Bachya*. *Rabbeinu Bachya* was a *Rishon* — not a modern-day *kabbalist*. Friends urged us to try the *segulah*, so I asked Rav Pam about it. Rav Pam asked me if there was a natural way for us to be helped, and I said that there was. "In that case," he responded, "stay away."

Similarly, in a letter in *Kreina D'Igrisah* (Vol. 1, Letter 60), the Steipler Gaon writes to a person who was going through a certain difficulty in life, "*Chas V'Shalom* — God forbid that you go to people who offer *segulos* and the like, for they do not help, they only ruin; they confuse the mind with senseless ideas ...."

Despite the fact that our *Gedolim* are against the proliferation of *segulos*, the interest in them remains. People feel that even if the *segulah* will not help, it won't hurt either. It is difficult to argue with these people, because they truly do feel closer to Hashem when they engage in *segulos*.

৺ If You Can't Beat 'Em, Join 'Em

As the saying goes, "If you can't beat them, join them." If I cannot get people to stop engaging in *segulos*, I might as well jump on the bandwagon, and offer some of my own favorite *segulos*. The type of *segulos* recommended here would be acceptable even according to Rav Pam and the Steipler. (I hope this doesn't make them less attractive to the *segulah* crowd.)

I'll admit that these *segulos* are not the most popular. This is partly because they are not so easy, and also due to the fact that no one has figured out a way to make money from them. Nevertheless, I think that they are worth implementing.

There is one problem with the following *segulos*. One of the main attractions of *segulos* is that they have some element of nonsense — sometimes more, sometimes less — and that element surrounds them with an aura of mysticism. Unfortunately, my *segulos* make too much sense, but with a little bit of imagination, we might be able to make them seem like bona-fide *segulos* for today's times.

Let us define the concept of a *segulah*. A *segulah* is a shortcut, an easy way to get something special. There are *segulos* for health, wealth, good children, and many other things that we all hope to have.

■ Segulah #1: Health and Prosperity

The first *segulah* will grant you an abundance of good health and long life.

Many, many years ago, I was standing at the foot of a mountain in a faraway desert, and I heard Moshe Rabbeinu's voice ring out with an amazing *segulah*. Yes, you were there, too, together with the rest of *Klal Yisrael*. In the *Aseres HaDibros* (Ten Commandments), there is only one mitzvah for which Hashem promises us a specific reward in this world: "Honor your father and your mother, *so that your days will be lengthened on the land that Hashem, your God, gives you*" (*Shemos* 20:12).

We can assume that Hashem is not promising us long life spent in the hospital. I think that it is safe to assume that this means healthy, productive years.

Now it may seem that we all keep this *segulah*. We are nice to our parents. But if Hashem gives us a *segulah*, we have to be sure to perform it properly in order to receive the reward. Let us see if we really honor our parents as we should.

One of the basic requirements of honoring parents is to stand up when they enter a room. Standing up does not mean lifting yourself off your chair in a barely perceptible manner as people do when reciting Hashem's name during *zimun*. I mean standing *all the way up*. On your feet. Do you do that?

Of course, our parents are usually willing to be *mochel* (forgo) this honor, but their forgiveness won't grant us long life. Do the *segulah* right!

What's more — and I'm sorry to bear the bad news — the *Shulchan Aruch* states that you are supposed to honor your in-laws in the same manner.

This does not mean that you have to be like a yo-yo, going up and down each time your parents or in-laws walk in and out of the room.

But when they come into the home for the first time, or if you get to shul before them and they walk in, make sure to stand up.

This is not a difficult mitzvah to perform. Somehow, however, it is not widely practiced. The boys in my *shiur* in yeshivah are of marriageable age; some are already married. I tell them that if they do not rise when their father or father-in-law walks into the room, they are advertising their ignorance. It is a clear Halachah in *Shulchan Aruch*!

Some respond that their fathers-in-law don't realize that they are ignorant, because they themselves don't rise when *their* fathers-in-law enter a room, either. It is a good answer, but don't forget, we are talking about a *segulah* here! Stand up! It is a simple way to show respect, and it will bring you long life.

When your father or father-in-law comes to eat at your house on Shabbos, who sits at the head of the table? Is it right for a young man to sit at the head of the table and have his father or father-in-law at the side of the table? Again, people tell me that they are following the precedent set by their own father or father-in-law, who would sit at the head of the of the table when their father or father-in-law visited. It's a good excuse, but what does that have to do with your mitzvah?

We live in a generation that does not understand the concept of respect. When I get to shul, people often hold the door open for me. I do not expect anyone to do so, but I guess they feel that they should show respect for the Rav of the shul. So what happens? As they hold the door for me, some young men walk inside! Adults have to hold the door for youngsters!?

People occasionally get into a disagreement with their parents. Sometimes — if you can believe this — it even happens with in-laws. They come to talk to me about it, and they insist that they are right. If you get into an argument with your friend and you are correct, you still don't have the right to insult him. But this is not your friend — this is your parent or parent-in-law. *Shulchan Aruch* rules that if a person's parent took his or her wallet and threw it into the ocean, the child may not respond disrespectfully. Who is right in this case? Of course the child is right! The *Shach* says that the child may take the parent to a *din Torah* to recover his money. However, there is no *heter* to treat the parent disrespectfully.

Swallowing your pride and treating parents with respect may be easier for people to accept as a *segulah*, because the mitzvah (on this level) may not seem so rational. Next time you are insulted by something your parents say, don't respond, and don't insult them.

Just tell yourself, "*l'maan ya'arichun yamecha* — so that my days will be lengthened."

When I was first married, I told my wife that I wanted to continue to eat lunch at my parents' house each Friday. I felt that it was not such a fair demand, because Friday is the most hectic day of the week in a Jewish home, but I told her that it would be a worthwhile investment on her part to allow me to go. Why? Because the Torah states that a person who honors his parents merits long life. The time I spend with my parents will hopefully be returned to her, because I will live longer!

Years later, someone showed me that *Rabbeinu Bachya* (*Shemos* 20:12) says this; that the promise of long life is to recompense us for time spent honoring our parents.

■ Segulah #2: Good *Shidduchim*

Another *segulah* that deals with honoring people will help in an area that is perhaps the most *segulah*-ridden area of Jewish life: *shidduchim*. The Talmud (*Shabbos* 22b) states that a person who honors *talmidei chachamim* will have sons-in-law who are *talmidei chachamim*. How many of us show respect towards Torah scholars? We don't insult Torah scholars, but it is not in style to show respect to them, either. But it's a *segulah*! Everyone wants a good son-in-law. Isn't it worthwhile?

When Rav Pam, *zt"l* ,would sit and learn in the *beis midrash* in Torah Vodaas and a *rebbi* or *mashgiach* in the yeshivah would pass his seat, he would always rise a little bit to show respect. Was he obligated to do so? Many of the people he stood for were younger than he, and most were less versed in Torah. Rav Pam stood up anyway, because he felt that they deserved respect.

It is hard to remember to do something that you are not accustomed to doing. How are we going to remember to stand up each time a parent, an in-law, or a Torah scholar walks into the room?

I have a great idea: Tie a red string around your wrist and it will help you remember to show respect!

■ Segulah #3: Success in Spiritual Matters

In a famous letter that the Vilna Gaon wrote to his wife, he writes a *segulah*. It is the only *segulah* mentioned in the letter, so it must be a good one.

"One who closes his mouth in this world," writes the Gaon, "merits to use the *ohr haganuz* [a special Divine light] in the upper worlds that even the angels in Heaven do not merit."

There are situations when it seems that we have an absolute right to speak up and put someone in his or her place. Truly great people are able to keep quiet even in such situations.

In the seventies, I attended Rav Moshe Feinstein's Friday *shiurim* in Mesivta Tifereth Jerusalem. One week, a photographer came to take pictures of Rav Moshe delivering the *shiur*. The man, who was either irreligious or a gentile, had no appreciation for the holiness of a *beis midrash*. He was snapping photos from every angle, dragging his ladder from spot to spot, and causing a disturbance that was distracting those attending the *shiur*. At one point he actually put his ladder on the platform of the *Aron Kodesh*, leaned it onto the *Aron Kodesh*, and climbed up to take a picture. As this was going on, people kept trying to get him to stop, but the photographer was too far removed to understand what was wrong.

When the *shiur* was over we davened Minchah, and he kept snapping away. Finally, as Rav Moshe's grandson escorted him out of the *beis midrash*, Rav Moshe stopped and told his grandson, "Let's pose for him."

"Pose for him?" the grandson asked incredulously. "We have been trying to get him to stop all along!"

Rav Moshe turned to his grandson and said softly, "*Vus vilt ir fun em — er iz ah gedungener* — what do you want from him — he is a hired hand."

Every single person in the room except Rav Moshe was angry at the photographer. I had a sneaking suspicion, in fact, that the only reason that no one threw him out was because each of us was secretly hoping to get a copy of a picture of Rav Moshe in which he was also visible. Only Rav Moshe was great enough to realize that there was no reason to become angry. The man was paid to take pictures, and he was doing his job.

So the third *segulah* is to learn to keep our mouths shut. I know that it is hard. You get angry, and you feel that you have all the right in the world to tell someone off, but remember — it's a *segulah*! You can enjoy the *ohr haganuz* in the World to Come.

As a side benefit, you will find that this saves you time, because when you give in to the temptation and speak harshly (especially to a member of your family), you usually have to spend a lot of time undoing the damage.

How are we going to remember this *segulah*? How are we going to stop ourselves from shooting off our mouths when our blood starts to boil and we feel ready to explode? Perhaps we should all buy muzzles and hang them up in a strategic location in the house to remind us to keep our mouths shut when things get rough. Some people might need one in each room.

I'm sure that visitors will want to know why you have a muzzle hanging in the living room, but when you tell them it is a *segulah* they will understand. When it comes to *segulos*, the more peculiar, the better.

■ Segulah #4: Parnassah

What would a discussion about *segulos* be worth if we do not mention the area in which even the greatest doubters are willing to try *segulos*? I refer, of course, to *segulos* for *parnassah*.

Everyone wishes he had more money. People are willing to try anything that will increase their income.

The best *segulah* for *parnassah* is not to cause pain to those who have less money than you. We all know that there is a concept of *ayin hara* (evil eye). What is an *ayin hara*? If you flaunt all that you can afford at your level of income, and someone feels pain because they cannot afford some of things that you can, they look at you with an *ayin hara*. If you want to keep your *parnassah* and succeed in business, make sure not to flaunt what you have.

Once we are on the subject of money, I can think of another *segulah*. This may not help you earn more money, but it will help you feel comfortable with what you already have.

Over the years, I have come to realize that the people who are most comfortable and generous with their money are not necessarily those who are in the highest income bracket. Many people who have average incomes feel comfortable with their lifestyles, and are happy to contribute to worthy causes. Some wealthier members of our community have a richer lifestyle and really do have difficulty making ends meet. Their income may be greater, but so are their needs.

This happens because our attitude towards money is not governed by what we have, but what we expect and want.

Here's a *segulah* for happiness when it comes to family finances.

Let's consider a typical scenario that plays itself out in many households in our community.

> A man goes to work one day, and his boss calls him in and says, "Mr. Schwartz, I am very impressed with your accom-

plishments this year. I think that you deserve a $20,000 raise."

This happens to people all the time (it really does!). What is the typical reaction to this news? Mr. Schwartz goes home that evening and shares the great news with his wife. One of the most fascinating aspects of money is dreaming up ways to spend it, so after supper, Mr. and Mrs. Schwartz sit down to discuss what to do with the extra money.

Mrs. Schwartz says, "You know, the kitchen is getting a little bit old. The cabinet doors don't close properly, and the stoves and ovens should really be replaced. Maybe we should remodel the kitchen."

Mr. Schwartz agrees that the kitchen might be a good place to spend the money, but then he brings up another possibility. "It is getting harder to start the car in the morning," he says. "I think that it is high time that I give up that old jalopy and replace it with something more respectable for a man of my means."

Mrs. Schwartz nods, but then she suddenly comes up with a third idea. "Why don't we go on that vacation we have been talking about for years?" she asks. "We have never been to Europe. This is a perfect opportunity to get out."

The conversation ends when it is time for Mr. Schwartz to go out to *daf yomi*, with three possible ways to spend the money still up in the air.

What did the Schwartz family just do to themselves? What is the result of this seemingly innocent discussion?

Misery. They have set themselves up to be absolutely miserable. Why? Because they spoke about three things: remodeling the kitchen, getting a new car, and going on vacation. At most, the raise will pay for one of the three. Let's assume that they decide to take the vacation. Each time Mrs. Schwartz walks into her kitchen, she will think to herself, "Look how lousy this kitchen looks. I wish we could remodel."

Each time Mr. Schwartz gets into his car he will think, "Ugh! This car is horrible. I wish we could afford a new car."

Logic dictates that upgrading our lifestyle will make us happier. The truth is that the more money we have, the more we think of ways to spend it, and since we cannot cover *all* of our contemplated lifestyle changes, we end up miserable.

And so, here's my best *segulah*. If you get a raise, come home that evening and don't say a word about it. Deposit it in your bank account. Continue living as you did until then. Nothing will happen if you don't decide how to spend it. Eventually you will have something to do with the extra money, and you'll be much happier in the interim.

When a kollel fellow leaves yeshivah and goes out to work, I tell him, "Enjoy your first paycheck. It will feel like a lot of money. By the time you get the second paycheck, it won't seem like enough. You are going to *need* every penny in your paycheck, and then some."

Don't raise your expectations and your standard of living. There are plenty of people making do with ordinary lifestyles who are much happier than those living in luxury.

Even if you feel that you deserve an upgrade in your standard of living, consider what upgrading will do your children. It will make them need so much more later on in life. If they'll want to study in kollel, supporting them will become so much more burdensome. All their lives, they will have to put up with expenses that they could easily have forgone.

The true *segulah* for happiness in life is to remain at the standard of living that you are comfortable at, even if you can afford more.

How are we going to remember this *segulah*? Take something that represents your ordinary standard of living — a chipped china plate, for instance — and put it somewhere where you will notice it. Perhaps you can put it next to the red string and the muzzle. It will remind you that the food tastes the same, even if the plate you eat it from is chipped.

Let's conclude with a story.

> In 1996, I was in Eretz Yisrael for the first time in many years. I was with a camp that was located outside of Jerusalem. On Tisha B'Av, I decided to go to the *Kosel HaMa'aRavi*. Several boys joined me, and we took a taxi together. In planning the trip, I had failed to take into account the heavy Tisha B'Av traffic. Thousands upon thousands of *Yidden* were streaming to the *Kosel* to daven Minchah at the site of the only remnant of the *Beis HaMikdash*. I realized that there was no way that the taxi would get there before sunset, so we paid the driver, jumped out, and ran to the *Kosel*. As we hurried towards the *Kosel*, I told the boys that sunset was approaching and that we should join the first minyan we would spot that was ready to begin the Torah reading.
>
> As we entered the *Kosel* plaza, we found a Sefardic minyan about to start reading from the Torah. They opened the

fancy silver case that held the *Sefer Torah*, and they called up a *Kohen*. When his *aliyah* was over, they started to look for a *Levi*. They called, "*Levi? Levi?*" and no one answered. I am a *Levi*, and it had been many years since I had an *aliyah* at the *Kosel*. I stepped forward and told the *gabbai* my name. As I was about to start reciting *Barchu*, a fellow who had been standing at the side suddenly jumped forward. The man could not have been religious — he was wearing one of the cardboard *yarmulkahs* that they hand out at the *Kosel*, and he was sporting a T-shirt that showcased his muscular frame.

"*Lo!* (No!)," he shouted. "*Hu lo yachol la'alot — hu Ashkenazi, vezeh Sefer Torah Sefaradit!* (He can't have an *aliyah* — he is an *Ashkenazi*, and this is a Sefardic *Sefer Torah*)."

The man continued to go on and on, insisting that they find a different *Levi*. The man's claim was absolutely ridiculous. The Torah that the Sefardim use is identical to that of the Ashkenazim, except for the casing. He was so insistent (and muscular), however, that I decided that it might be wise to shut my mouth and step away. This was a perfect opportunity to practice the Vilna Gaon's *segulah*.

Later, I spoke to the young men who had accompanied me. I suggested that there was something positive to be learned from that man. He was not a *Levi*. He wasn't trying to take the *aliyah* away from me so that he could have it instead. He had simply seen something that he mistakenly viewed as a breach of tradition, and he could not let it happen. He felt passionately about upholding religious custom, and he was willing to pursue it to the very end. Shouldn't we, who have been educated to evaluate mitzvos and *minhagim* in an authentic and accurate manner, pursue them with at least as much passion as this misguided zealot?

The same can be said for *segulos*. We see people throwing time, money, and energy into nonsensical, sensationalized *segulos* with no sources. We should take a lesson from those people, and pursue the *segulos* that we have mentioned — *segulos* that all the *gedolim* would sanction — with equal persistence and enthusiasm.

Plan B

I once asked Rav Pam how he developed his love for Tanach. He replied with the following story.

When Rav Pam was eleven years old, his father immigrated to the United States in advance of his family, who followed several years later. His father had taken most of his *seforim* with him. He left behind a copy of *Yirmiyah* with the commentary of the *Malbim*, which had just been published at the time.

The eleven-year-old Rav Pam began to study *Yirmiyah*. He saw that the words "*Liber Yirmiyah*" were printed on the top of each page of the *sefer*. He assumed that *liber* was the Yiddish word that means *beloved*. He therefore understood that the title *Liber Yirmiyah* printed on each page was an indication that Yirmiyah admonished and consoled the Jewish People out of love. Rav Pam told me that as he learned through the *sefer*, he could feel Yirmiyah's love for *Klal Yisrael* in each prophecy.

Later, Rav Pam found out that the word *liber* is actually Latin for "book of," and that on each page of that set of Nach were the words,

"*Liber Yehoshua*" "*Liber Shoftim*," and so on. *Liber Yirmiyah* simply meant "Book of Yirmiyah." Still, the effect that this experience had on Rav Pam as an eleven-year-old child remained. Forever after, when he learned Navi, he would identify with the personalities of people mentioned and saw their actions in a very practical sense.[1]

Yehu was one of the personalities that Rav Pam would mention often in his *shmuessen*. If we examine Yehu's rise to power, perhaps we can understand why Rav Pam considered him such an important figure.

First, let us consider a broader issue; we will then return to view Yehu in this light.

⇜ The Greater Luchos

Moshe Rabbeinu received the original set of *Luchos* (Tablets) at Sinai, but broke them when he discovered the Jewish People serving the Golden Calf. Later, a second set of *Luchos* was given to the Jewish People as a symbol of their atonement. Which set of *Luchos* is the greater of the two?

Ibn Ezra (*Shemos* 34:1) quotes the opinion of an unnamed *Gaon* who said that the second set of *Luchos* was greater than the first. *Ibn Ezra* cites seven reasons put forth by this *Gaon* to back up his claim.[2]

> 1. The second set of *Luchos* was stored in the *Aron* (Holy Ark of the Covenant); there is a dispute in the Talmud whether the first set was also stored there as well.
> 2. The second *Luchos* contained the statement, "*L'maan yitav lach* — so that it will be good for you" (*Devarim* 5:16), which is a reference to reward in *Olam Haba* (World to Come); the first set did not.
> 3. Three covenants were forged between Hashem and the Jewish People when the second *Luchos* were presented; with the first set, there were none.

---

1. Rav Pam would comment, with tears in his eyes, "Look at the kings Shaul and Shlomo — tragic figures in Tanach. They started with so much promise, but their reigns ended with such great disappointment!"
He would discuss *Tzidkiyahu HaMelech's* failed reign with similar emotion.

2. Not all printings of *Ibn Ezra* contain all seven reasons.

4. The second *Luchos* were fashioned by Moshe and carried up to Sinai. They were a combination of physical and spiritual matter — similar to the composition of the human body. The first *Luchos* were made of spiritual matter alone, as they came from Heaven.
5. The second *Luchos* were given on Yom Kippur, the holiest day of the Jewish calendar; the first *Luchos* were given on the 17th of Tammuz — an ordinary day.
6. Moshe's face shone when he delivered the second set of *Luchos*; it did not shine when he delivered the first set.
7. *Klal Yisrael* actually received the second set of *Luchos*, but not the first.

Ibn Ezra argues vehemently against this claim, stating that the *Gaon* should be flogged for expressing this view. Specifically, he takes exception to the claim that the second *Luchos* were superior because they were comprised of both physical and spiritual matter. How could anyone suggest, wonders *Ibn Ezra*, that the *Luchos* chiseled by Moshe Rabbeinu could be superior to those produced by Hashem? Clearly, says *Ibn Ezra,* the first *Luchos* were superior.

But a Midrash in *Shemos Rabbah* (46:1) supports the view of the *Gaon*. The Midrash states that Moshe regretted having broken the *Luchos*. Hashem consoled him, "Why do you feel regret? The *Luchos* that you broke contained only the Ten Commandments. I will give you a second set of *Luchos* that will also contain *halachos*, *Midrash*, and *Aggadah*."

Apparently, the second *Luchos* are considered superior. But how do we deal with the question raised by *Ibn Ezra*? How could a set of *Luchos* created by human hands be superior to those created by Hashem?

Beis HaLevi (*Derashos* 18) explains that the *Luchos* affect man's ability to study Torah. The first *Luchos* were so perfect that had they not been broken, we could have studied Torah in a most perfect way. Torah study would have been easy. The *yetzer hara* could not have easily prevented us from learning, and we would never have forgotten anything we learned.

Torah studied from the second set of *Luchos* is acquired with great difficulty. A person studying Torah nowadays can find it very frustrating, and can often become discouraged when he forgets much of what he has learned. It is a challenge to continue learning with vigor and enthusiasm.

Beis HaLevi says that this forgetfulness and difficulty are consequences of studying from the second, man-made *Luchos*.

But the *Beis HaLevi* also reveals a great secret: despite all the difficulty — and because of it — Torah study based on the second *Luchos* is far more meaningful. On a basic level, *Chazal* teach that *l'fum tzara agra* — we are rewarded for mitzvos based on the amount of effort we invest. On a deeper level, when we acquire something with ease, we do not develop an emotional attachment to it. The effort we must invest into Torah study as a result of the first *Luchos* being broken causes us to forge a strong attachment to Torah. The entire concept of *ameilus b'Torah*, as we know it, is a product of the second *Luchos*.

Let us try to imagine the feelings of Moshe Rabbeinu as he was chiseling the second set of *Luchos*. He had broken a set of *Luchos* formed by Hashem, and he was replacing them with a set produced by man. What a disappointment! But the *Beis HaLevi* teaches us that Moshe's *Luchos* were actually superior. It is the imperfection of the man-made *Luchos* that was needed. This assures that the people receiving them will have to work hard to reach levels of greatness. Man's accomplishments will be his own.

Beis HaLevi's explanation regarding the *Luchos* is one that we can apply in our daily lives. We all have had plans, visions, and goals in life. We have invested thought and effort into carefully laying plans that we deemed to be perfect. In real life, however, perfect plans rarely succeed. There are bumps in the road. There are "broken *Luchos*" that require us to reconsider, to come up with an alternate set of plans. Plan B never seems as good as Plan A, but if you roll up your sleeves and follow Plan B with the same zest you had for Plan A, you are likely to succeed.

⸳§ Hashem Runs the World Through Plan B

When Hashem initially brought us into Eretz Yisrael, the plan was for there to be a single kingdom, united under a single king. That was Plan A.

Plan A lasted for less than a century. Two kingdoms developed. Even then, the plan was for this division to last for only thirty-six years. Unfortunately, this plan did not work either.

Our inability to unite and serve Hashem as one nation caused many people to sin. Throughout the era of the first *Beis HaMikdash*, many members of the Ten Tribes worshiped idols because they felt inferior to the two tribes who had the *Beis HaMikdash* in their territory. Nevertheless, Hashem did not insist on returning to Plan A. He did not force the two kingdoms to unite. Rather, He sent Yehu to help the Ten Tribes thrive as a separate kingdom. Yehu was the first (and only) king of the Ten Tribes who was appointed by a Navi, on Hashem's command. Yehu began by eradicating the idols and wiping out the leaders who enticed people to sin. Yehu personified Hashem's willingness to run the world through Plan B. It is this aspect of Yehu's mission that attracted Rav Pam's attention.

When we study world history, we find that Hashem consistently runs the world through Plan B.

Man was originally supposed to live in Gan Eden. Adam sinned and was banished from Gan Eden. Plan B. Ten generations later, man's actions brought destruction upon an immoral world and only Noach's family survived the *Mabul* (Great Flood). What happened when the Flood was over? The sun came out, and it was time for Plan B.

It took ten more generations for Avraham to come along and begin to spread Hashem's Name, thus fulfilling the purpose of creation. Did Hashem's plan call for the nine generations that preceded Avraham to ignore this task? It would not seem so. But that is what happened, and the world settled for Plan B.

Creation itself is rife with Plan B incidents. Rav Pam would point out that in describing the completion of the Six Days of Creation, the Torah states, "And Hashem saw all that He had made, and behold it was *tov me'od* [very good]" (*Bereishis* 1:31). Very good? Not everything seemed to go according to plan in those six days. Hashem commanded the earth to put forth trees that would taste like fruit, but the earth sprouted trees that *produced* fruit, but did not *taste* like fruit. Hashem created two great celestial sources of light, but the moon complained and was diminished. Adam HaRishon certainly did not follow the original plan for mankind. Furthermore, Hashem initially considered a world that runs via *middas hadin,* the attribute of strict judgment. In the end, He diluted the *middas hadin* with Divine Mercy. It seems that almost everything that happened during those six days was executed through Plan B.

Nevertheless, Hashem evaluated those six days as *tov me'od*, wonderful, exceedingly wonderful!

The world was created this way with great wisdom. Hashem could have orchestrated these events differently. Creation itself had to happen in a Plan B manner. We live in a world where things don't go according to plan. And still, it's a world of *tov me'od*.

Life doesn't always work out according to Plan A. As a matter of fact, it rarely follows Plan A. The most successful people are those who can adjust and work with Plan B. It is not easy. It involves disappointment, and an ability to reevaluate and lower one's expectations. But if Hashem could look at a world that was created almost exclusively according to Plan B and call it *tov me'od*, then we must learn to do the same.

I once received the following letter. I hope you relate to it, as I did.

> The ceiling collapsed in my laundry room. For a long time, we had a nice-sized hole in the ceiling. I had two options: hire someone for about $200, or buy two pieces of sheetrock and insulation for $20 and do it myself. Of course, I chose the latter option. Things proceeded nicely, but I lacked a very important instrument that I should buy the next time I do renovations: a level. It's very hard to cut sheetrock without a level — even when I used my son's school ruler.
>
> And so, I finished the job. Or at least I thought I finished the job. I accidentally left a rectangular hole in the ceiling. I have neither the patience nor the strength to go out again, buy, and cut a third piece of sheetrock to cover the hole.
>
> My wife comes in to the laundry room. My wife looks at the hole. I look at the hole. I look at my wife. She looks at me. I know I had better think fast. I look back at the hole, I point to it, and I tell my wife, "There is a *minhag* to leave an *amah al amah* [squared cubit] hole as a *zecher l'churban* [reminder of the destruction of the *Beis HaMikdash*]."
>
> My wife calmly turns to me and says, "I think the whole ceiling is a *zecher l'churban*."

In many homes, this would have been cause for World War III. The wife would say, "Didn't I tell you to pay someone to fix it? Now you had to do all the work, and you'll have to pay someone to remove your sheetrock and then fix it."

But if you are willing to work with Plan B — as this couple was — then you can live with a hole in your ceiling. It is *not* a *zecher l'churban* hole; it is a *shalom bayis* hole — and a very beautiful hole at that.

> Childhood polio had handicapped one of the world's most famous violinists. He walks with braces and crutches. When

he plays at a concert, the journey to the center of the stage is long and slow. Yet his playing transcends his personal challenges.

Once, in the middle of a challenging concerto, one of the strings of his violin snapped, with a loud popping sound. The orchestra stopped abruptly and everyone waited with bated breath to see what would happen. After a brief pause, he set his violin under his chin and signaled to the conductor to begin.

With great brilliance he improvised, modulating and adjusting the melody in a way that compensated for the missing string. The music that emerged was hauntingly beautiful.

When he finished, there was an awed silence, followed by thunderous applause. The violinist silenced the crowd. Then he said, "Sometimes, it is the musician's job to find out how much music he can make with what he has left."

That's Plan B. Strings break. Things don't happen as planned. But Plan B is fine. You can still play beautiful music.

ৰ্ভ Anticlimactic — but ...

When we think of *Mattan Torah* we generally think in terms of the great fanfare associated with the original Revelation at Sinai. We picture millions of Jews standing around Mount Sinai after three days of preparation for this great moment. We try to imagine the lightning that could be heard and the *shofar* blasts that could be seen.

That was the story of the giving of the first *Luchos*.

The *Luchos* that remained with us were the ones we received on the following Yom Kippur. These were given quietly. Hashem descended onto the mountain and had a private meeting with Moshe Rabbeinu, who then brought us the second pair of *Luchos*. *Chazal* teach that it was only this quiet, private *Mattan Torah* that could last.

Our lives follow the same pattern. Plan A is exciting. The first time a person starts to learn, he is able to do so with ease. Later, it becomes difficult. Later, he starts to wonder if his learning is worthwhile. Later, he is plagued by the realization that he forgets much of what he learns. That is the sign that he has moved on to Plan B, to the second set of *Luchos*. The natural tendency is to become depressed and to yearn for the days when learning was easy. A person wishes he could be like Moshe Rabbeinu, who studied from the first *Luchos* and did not suffer from forgetfulness and difficulty in studying Torah.

Shockingly, the *Beis HaLevi* takes the opposite approach. He pities Moshe Rabbeinu. He wonders why Moshe could not study from the second *Luchos* and enjoy the benefits of having to *toil* in Torah study. *Beis HaLevi* considers this difficulty so necessary for growth that he questions how Moshe could retain the Torah he learned without having to toil to acquire it.

Beis HaLevi answers that Moshe *did* suffer through these experiences. *Chazal* teach that Moshe could not retain anything Hashem taught him during the first thirty-nine days at Mount Sinai. Only on day forty, when Hashem presented the Torah to him as a gift, was he able to return and teach *Klal Yisrael*. Plan B.

At the beginning of a school year, children come to school with excitement. They take freshly sharpened pencils out of their brand-new knapsacks, and they are ready to work hard. Did you ever look back at your *meforshim* notebooks from high school? You will see how studious you were on *daf beis*, which you began on the first day of the school year. Each comment from a *meforash* is written carefully, and the margins are clean. As you move on to *daf gimmel*, you may find some doodles on the side of the page. *Daf daled* notes tend to be covered with doodles, and at *daf hei*, the notes trail off considerably.[3]

There is a certain freshness we have at the beginning of a year, a freshness that we can call "*Luchos Rishonos*." But *Luchos Rishonos* don't last. The trick is to succeed with the *Luchos Sheniyos*, to persevere even when it gets difficult to focus on your learning, as the *z'man* progresses.

◈§ Graduating to Real Life

The freshness that we felt at the beginning of school years when we were children joins us as we advance to the various stages in life.

When a couple is first married, they feel unique, and they are excited about sharing their lives with each other. When five or ten or

---

3. This is a reference to the days when *bachurim* actually learned past *daf hei* in *shiur*. May Hashem grant us a return to those *shonim kadmoniyos*.

thirty years go by, the excitement is no longer there. Is that a bad thing? On the contrary — that is when real life begins.

> When my wife and I married, we lived on the ground floor of a two-family house. Our landlords, who were several years older than we were, lived upstairs. They were wonderful, friendly people. Often, when we would come into the house our landlady would open her door upstairs to say hello. Often, she would be dressed in a *tichel* (kerchief) and a housecoat, with a little child pulling at her clothing. Her oldest daughter, who was about five or six at the time, loved to visit us, and when she walked in we could sometimes hear her mother say, "Don't go down. Leave them alone!"
>
> We were the freshly minted couple, walking into a freshly painted apartment with new furniture, and she was the harried housewife, with an apartment that lacked the freshness and had the marks made by the children on her furniture.
>
> It was five years later. By that time, we had purchased a two-family house of our own, and we were renting *our* first-floor apartment to a newlywed couple.
>
> I came home from yeshivah one day and my wife said, "I felt a little bit funny today. Our tenants came into their apartment today, and I was standing at the top of the steps," she said. "Here I was, in a *tichel* and housecoat, hands covered in flour from the *challah* I was baking, with one child in my arms and another clinging to my hem, and there they were, a newlywed couple.
>
> "Only five years have passed," she continued, "and so much has changed."
>
> "That's true," I said, "But which one is better? Which one is firm and solid? Is it the first years, with the fresh paint and new furniture, or is it the time when you have the good fortune of being hassled, of having a demanding family?"

Indeed, life is full of peeling paint and scratched furniture — things that are no longer "just so." But you can be happy as long as you don't cling rigidly to your original expectations.

The following joke targets *shadchanim*, but it is an appropriate parable for our topic.

> Sometime during the 1800s, a *shadchan* visited a wealthy man and said, "I have the perfect *shidduch* for your son."

The man says, "I don't have time to deal with you now. I'm too busy."

"Do you realize who the girl is?" the *shadchan* asks. "She is Rothschild's daughter."

"Oh!" the rich man responds. "Rothschild's daughter? Of course I am interested."

The *shadchan* then goes to visit Rothschild, and says, "I have the perfect *shidduch* for your daughter."

"I don't have time for you *shadchanim*," Rothschild responds.

"But the boy I have in mind is the vice president of the National Bank," the *shadchan* says.

"Well," says Rothschild, "If he is the vice president of the National Bank, then of course I am interested."

The *shadchan* then visits the president of the National Bank and says, "I have a perfect candidate for vice president of the bank."

"Who are you to suggest candidates for vice president?" the CEO replies angrily.

"But the man I have in mind is Rothschild's son-in-law," the *shadchan* persists.

"Rothschild's son-in-law?" says the CEO. "Of course we are interested in having him as vice president of our bank."

The *shadchan* smiles with glee and says, "You see, I can solve all of the problems in the world if people would only be willing to follow my plans."

Somehow, life doesn't always follow our plans — perfect as they are. We have to learn to be happy to follow Plan B.

⋅≪ Seeing the Bright Side with Hindsight

A woman once visited a Rav to discuss her disappointment with her husband. When she had gotten married, she thought that she was marrying a *ben Torah* who would sit and learn all day and would eventually become a great *talmid chacham*. It turned out that he was not suited for full-time Torah study. He had a great heart, and was always doing *chesed* (acts of kindness) for others, but she wanted a *talmid chacham*. She would ridicule him when he would run to help those in need. "They consider you their *shlepper*," she would say. "They take advantage of you."

"Do you know what you did to your husband?" the Rav responded. "You made him into a nothing. You wanted to be like Rachel, Rabbi Akiva's wife. Unfortunately, that was not going to be your lot in life. You could have settled happily into the role of the prophetess Devorah. She was a married to a simple man, Lapidos, who did a lot of *chesed* for others, and she helped him with his *chesed*. Now you are neither of the two. You were not going to be married to a *talmid chacham* either way. But since you ridicule your husband's efforts to help others, he is embarrassed to do *chesed*. You've failed in your mission to be like Devorah."

Sometimes a person envisions a certain *tafkid*, but Hashem has something else in mind. Being married to a *ba'al chesed* may not have been this woman's Plan A. It certainly was not the role that the *rebbetzins* in Bais Yaakov preached about. But accepting Plan B would have enabled her to fulfill her *tafkid*. Be willing to modify the dreams you had during your years in yeshivah or Bais Yaakov. Be happy to fulfill the *tafkid* that suits *you*.

◆§ When There Is Nothing To Do — Do Nothing!

The concept of accepting Plan B was very much a part of Rav Pam's teaching, although he may not have phrased it in those terms.

An incident that illustrates this attitude occurred to a young man who is now one of the distinguished members of the kollel in our yeshivah. At the time, this *bachur* was engaged. Everything seemed perfect. The date for the *chasunah* had already been set, and the invitations had already been printed. One day he received a call from the *kallah's* parents informing him that the engagement was off. "We will send back the engagement ring," they said. "Please don't call."

Understandably, this boy was in a terrible state of confusion. "What should I do?" he asked me. "Should I try to call her behind her parents' back?"

"This is not an issue for me," I responded. "Go around the corner to Rav Pam's house, and ask him what to do."

He went. Half-an-hour later he was back, calm and content. Rav Pam had told him that if the *kallah's* family wanted to break the engagement, it was better that it happened now, not later. "Send back anything you have received from the *kallah*, and don't call her," Rav Pam advised. "*Im yirtzeh Hashem*, you will marry someone else, and you'll have a happy life."

Rav Pam practiced what he preached.

Once, Rav Pam had to take a group of *baalebatim* to a *din Torah* regarding a *tzorech tzibbur*. I knew of this, because Halachah mandates that a *hazmanah* (summons) to a *din Torah* must be sent through a third party. I was the one who delivered the *hazmanos* to the *baaleibatim*. I delivered one *hazmanah*, then a second, and a third.

Some of the *rebbeim* and kollel *yungeleit* in the yeshivah found out about this, and they were incensed. Rav Pam should have to take *baaleibatim* to a *din Torah*? What a chutzpah! They decided that they would protest publicly to protect Rav Pam's honor, and they asked me to join. I told them that Rav Pam would not approve. They felt that as students it was our duty to protect his honor. We decided to quietly write a letter of protest and have the *rebbeim* and kollel *yungeleit* sign it. I would deliver it to the *baaleibatim*.

The letter was written. When I read it, my heart sank. I suspected that Rav Pam would be upset if he found out that this letter was sent. The letter used very harsh terms. I told them that I would write a letter. I wrote what I thought was a very innocent letter. "The entire world comes willingly to Rav Pam for advice," I wrote, "and you ignore him when he asks you to listen to him?"

We were ready to pass the letter around for signatures, but I felt a little guilty taking this step without Rav Pam's knowledge. I went to him and told him that I wanted him to be aware that the *talmidim* had decided to send a letter to protest the *baaleibatim's* behavior.

Rav Pam's response was one of total confusion. "Protest?"

he wondered. "What is there to protest? When *Yidden* have a difference of opinion, they go to a *din Torah*. What is wrong with going to a *din Torah*?"

You can be sure that this was not Rav Pam's Plan A. He certainly had no interest in taking people to a *din Torah*. But Plan B was just fine.

In Rav Pam's later years I would occasionally assist him in dealing with community problems. There were instances in which all of the attempts to solve a problem fell short. Rav Pam would say something that I never heard him say in public: "*Nisht aleh ken men helfen* — not all situations can be helped."

To all others involved in these problems, it seemed imperative that we do *something*. Rav Pam would reason that no solution is better than a poor one. He preferred to live with a problem, rather than to flail hopelessly in a desperate attempt to change things.

◈ A Lesson From an Egg

There are times when the transition from Plan A to Plan B is extremely unpleasant. In such instances, we can take *chizzuk* from the nature — and Halachah — of eggs.

When a chicken lays an egg, you can fry it, cook it, mix it into a cake, and it tastes delicious. But an egg can also turn into a chick. How do you know when a chick is beginning to develop? The Talmud (*Temurah* 31a) states that when an egg begins to rot, it is a sign of an imminent transformation.

As long as an egg tastes good, you can use it for Plan A — breakfast, for instance. When it starts to become acrid, you may be disappointed. In reality though, you will now be able to derive even more benefit from it. It can turn into a chicken, which will eventually provide you with many more eggs. But you see, sometimes things must spoil before they improve.

God designed the world this way. He could have come up with another system for providing us with chickens, without putting eggs through the rotting process. But that is not the nature of *olam hazeh*. Here, things improve by the Plan B process.

Take a lesson from chicken eggs. Next time things don't seem to be working out as well as you would want them to, don't become frustrated or angry. Remember that Plan B may really be Plan A.

Lessons for In-Laws

In recent years I have witnessed some of the nicest people I know becoming parents-in-law. The phenomenon caught me by surprise, because *shvers* and *shviggers* (fathers-in-law and mothers-in-law) are the most-often maligned family members. It seems, however, that *shver* and *shvigger* are not titles that are limited to those with sinister temperaments. Many nice people actually become in-laws! And yet, where there is smoke, there is fire. The in-law jokes that abound did not appear from nowhere. It is true; one of the most difficult relationships is that of people with their in-law children.

When a young couple becomes engaged, they usually enroll in *chasan* and *kallah* classes. Aside from being taught the pertinent halachos of marriage, there are usually lessons on how to maintain a peaceful and productive relationship. I often think that we would do well if we could institute "*Shver* and *Shvigger*" classes for those who are about to be initiated into the role of being in-laws. Let's look at some of the topics that are sure to be part of the curriculum in such classes.

➣ Yehoshafat's Error

*P*erhaps the gravest error ever made in the history of in-laws was the mistake made by King Yehoshafat.

At the time, the Jewish People had been divided between two kingdoms, the northern kingdom of Ten Tribes and Yehudah, the southern kingdom. The Ten Tribes had strayed, falling to idol worship. Yehoshafat hoped that by developing a close relationship with Achav, the king of the Ten Tribes, he could convince them to repent.

This was a mistake. Yehoshafat overestimated the influence he could have on the Ten Tribes. His mistake turned him into the paradigm example of *"Al tischaber l'rasha* — do not associate with a wicked person" (*Avos* 1:7, see *Avos D'Rabbi Nassan*, ibid.).

But Yehoshafat compounded his error. As part of his effort to be *mekarev* the Ten Tribes, he married his son Yehoram to Ataliyahu, the daughter of Achav. Yehoram would later succeed his father as king. Yehoshafat hoped to influence his daughter-in-law, make her righteous, and persuade her to lead her family back to Hashem. Tragic mistake. The outcome of this marriage was the single greatest disaster to strike David's kingdom. After Yehoram died, Ataliyahu wanted the throne for herself. She murdered every single descendant of King David, except for a baby who was spirited away and concealed in the *Kodesh HaKadashim*.

Al tischaber l'rasha is not a mistake that affects every one of us. Some of us rarely — or never — come into contact with wicked people like Achav. But the mistake of trying to influence an in-law child is one that is extremely commonplace. Thankfully, most parents do not have a daughter-in-law like Ataliyahu, but they still suffer from the underlying cause of Yehoshafat's error. They do not recognize that the scope of their influence on their in-law children is limited.

Moreover, parents do not realize that their lack of influence is not an unfortunate fact of life — it *should* be limited. In *Parashas Bereishis*, the Torah states, *"Al kein yaazov ish es aviv v'es imo v'davak b'ishto* — Therefore, a man shall abandon his father and his mother and cling to his wife" (*Bereishis* 2:24). The term *yaazov*, abandon, seems very severe, but the Torah teaches that it is the only way for a marriage to succeed. One of the gravest dangers to marriages is the constant involvement of parents who feel hurt when their children disconnect from them and become close to their spouses. You should be happy when your children abandon you in favor of their spouses. Never try to regain the level of influence you had on them when they were single.

Let us examine some of the most common ills to plague in-law relationships and see if we can develop a Torah perspective on how to serve as in-laws.

◆§ The No-Interference Clause

The first law of in-law relationships is well known: Don't interfere. There is a clear source for this rule from the Torah. When Rivkah was handed over to Eliezer to become Yitzchak's wife, the Torah states in successive verses, "They sent Rivkah," and then, "They blessed Rivkah." They sent her away, and wished her farewell. The Torah is teaching us that there comes a point when we have to say goodbye to our children.

> I once saw a story about a young woman who called her father a few weeks after her wedding. "Daddy," she said in a tear-choked voice, "we just had a terrible fight. I'm coming home."
>
> "You *are* home," the father responded, and hung up.

In our hearts, we realize that this is the correct attitude. In almost all scenarios, it is best not to meddle, and to let a married couple sort things out on their own. We know that it is the correct attitude, but how good are we at following through in daily living?

Do you find yourself saying negative things about your in-law child? Regarding your own child, you are accustomed to saying whatever you want. Your child is yours, and chances are they he or she has gotten used to your rhetoric during the last twenty years or so. If you find yourself saying negative things about your son-in-law or daughter-in-law, however, it is a warning sign. This is not only true about those who call their in-law children crooks or hoodlums. Simple observations about in-law children's incompetence or unrefined behavior can also be dangerous.

The Talmud (*Kesubos* 16b-17a) records a dispute between Beis Shammai and Beis Hillel regarding the mitzvah of rejoicing with a *chasan* and *kallah*. Beis Shammai states we must praise a *kallah* honestly when dancing before her. Beis Hillel says that we should always speak positively about the *kallah*.

According to Beis Hillel, what are you supposed to do if you can't find anything positive to say about the *kallah*? Lie. Beis Hillel — undoubtedly drawing on the words of the popular song — says that we should always say, "*Kallah na'eh v'chassudah* — a beautiful and refined *kallah*."

Beis Hillel draws a parallel from a scenario that is unfortunately quite common nowadays. A fellow walks into shul and tells his friends excitedly about a new car he just bought. "Which model did you buy?" one fellow asks. When he responds, the friend says, "Oy, that model? What a shame. It is a real lemon."

Another friend asks, "How much did you pay?" Already daunted by the first person's denigration, the purchaser reveals the price he paid in a soft voice. "You paid $20,000? You could have gotten it for $18,000."

By the time the fellow leaves shul and gets into the car that he was so excited about, he wishes he had never bought it.

Beis Hillel teaches that this sort of response comes from our negative character traits. If someone is excited about his purchase, you should not dampen his excitement by voicing your honest opinion. Tell him what he wants to hear.

If this is true of inanimate possessions, reasons Beis Hillel, then certainly when you are referring to someone's spouse, you should point out only the praiseworthy qualities, never the faults. Be careful not to over-exaggerate, or everyone will know that you are lying. (A little exaggeration is fine!) Try hard. You should be able to find something nice to say about him or her without obviously exaggerating.

People are sometimes disappointed with a *shidduch*. This usually stems from one of two problems: They either have an over-inflated view of their own child, or they have an under-inflated view of their in-law child — and often a combination of the two. It's hard to tell a person what to think. If you see something that bothers you, you should try to overlook it or rationalize it. Even if you can't, however, you must keep it in the realm of thought, and not voice your negative impression.

I have had instances in which *chasanim* have come to discuss comments their parents have made. The parents told them, "We are happy with the *shidduch*, but we just want you to know what you are getting into," and they went on to make negative observations about the *kallah*. Once a child is engaged — and even before, once they are going out seriously and there is an emotional bond between the young couple — you should verbalize only the positive aspects of your child's prospective spouse.

▰ Friction Is Normal

I once heard a speaker sum up the problem we have with in-law children very well. He said that people are usually able to differentiate between their friends and their enemies. You know that your friends are sensitive to your needs, and that your enemies are not. In-law relationships are unusual in that the person *is* sensitive to your needs, and can nevertheless cause you plenty of grief.

The speaker illustrated his point with a story. An American was visiting Eretz Yisrael, and he needed a sewing needle. He went into a store and asked for a needle, but the storekeeper did not understand English. He tried switching to Yiddish, telling the store owner that he was looking for something that *shtuchs* (pricks), but the man still did not understand. The storekeeper happened to have a Hebrew-English dictionary on hand, and the American customer found the word. "I want *machatim*," he said.

The storekeeper brought him some sewing pins, not needles. "I need *machatim* that *shtuch* on *both* sides," the customer said.

"Those are not called *machatim*," the storekeeper said. "Those are called *machatanim*."

Somehow, even when an in-law intends to help and say nice things, and certainly when they make insensitive comments, it always hurts. It *shtuchs* both ways.

The first time there is friction between a parent and an in-law child, the parent feels that the child-in-law should be able to conform to his in-law's way of life. This is wrong.

When *chasanim* come for advice before they get married, I try to focus on three points, all of which apply to in-law relationships as well:

1. Clichés are probably true. If there are clichés about women being late, I tell *chasanim*, then it is probably because it is normal for them to be late, and it should not bother you. If it is the way of the world for women to be late, don't blame them for it — blame Hashem.

> This lesson applies to in-law relationships in equal measure. If there are dozens of in-law jokes, then there must be some truth to them. In-laws and in-law children often have difficulty getting along. Make peace with it.

2. You are a product of your home. Every person is a product of his or her upbringing, and follows the patterns of behavior that they saw as children. After marriage, these differences have the potential to cause friction between the couple, who've grown up in different homes.

> This, too, causes a lot of friction in in-law relationships. When parents see their in-law children doing things differently, they unfairly look askance and wonder why they cannot follow the mode of behavior that is "normal" in their newfound home. Give your in-law children the space to do things their way.

3. Hashem pairs people with different strengths and weaknesses. One of the most frustrating parts of marriage is that a couple will quickly realize that their spouses are very different from them. The husband may be neat and the wife will be messy, or the wife will be calm and the husband nervous. When I tell this to a young married man, or sometimes even to a newlywed couple, they smile. This reflex indicates that they know exactly what I am talking about, and it feels very good to know that it is normal. If that is the way that it is in every home, they can live with it.

> If you find that your in-law child is different from your child and handles things differently, don't comment on it or get frustrated. It is normal, and they will learn to use their differences to the advantage of their marriage.

Rav Shamshon Raphael Hirsch sums up all these points. He notes that the Talmud derives from the verse *Al kein yaazov ish es aviv v'es imo* that gentiles are prohibited from marrying certain relatives.[1] They must "abandon" family members and find wives from other families.

Although the depth of reasoning behind any given mitzvah is beyond us, Rav Hirsch writes that the fact that we learn two ideas from one verse indicates that the two are interrelated. What does the simple understanding of the verse — i.e., that a person should cling to his wife rather than remain tied to his family — have to do with the prohibition against marrying relatives?

The Torah is hinting to us *why* we should not marry relatives, says Rav Hirsch. The point of marriage is to bring together people who

---

1. Prohibitions regarding Jewish marriages are mentioned separately in the Torah.

are different from each other. Two people who enjoy different tasks, handle problems differently, and have different ways of coping with difficulty are brought together to complement each other. If we were allowed to marry close relatives, husbands and wives would find themselves dealing with issues in exactly the same manner, and it would weaken their chances of leading productive lives. It is good for a husband and wife to deal with issues differently.

This does not mean, of course, that we should look to marry off our children to people with opposing sets of values and behavioral traits. It is important for husband and wife to share goals and to have personalities that will blend cohesively. But there will always be aspects of personality that will differ. Recognize that those differences will strengthen the marriage.

Rav Hirsch's exposition is an amazing insight into the source of in-law problems. If Hashem seeks to pair people who come from homes in which life is handled differently, it should not surprise us that there is potential for friction. When parents see in-law children handling situations differently from the way they would, they should realize that Hashem built the institution that way deliberately. Included in *al kein yaazov ish es aviv v'es imo* is that our in-law children will behave differently from us, and we should not try to influence them into converting to our system of behavior.

When Chavah (Eve) was created, Adam HaRishon said, "*Zos hapa'am etzem mei'atzamei ubasar m'bsari — This time*, it is bone of my bones and flesh of my flesh" (*Bereishis* 2:23). Only once in history — *zos hapa'am* (this time) — was there a *shidduch* between two individuals who were exactly the same, explains *Pardes Yosef*. Because the *shidduch* market was so limited, Hashem made sure that Adam and Chavah remained married to each other. If differences were to have caused a rift between them, it could have posed a great risk to world population. For future generations, however, it would be counterproductive to have people who come from the same home married to each other.

✥ You Are Partial

nother issue that plagues in-law relationships is that parents sometimes feel that there is an unfair balance of workload between their child and the in-law child. Parents complain that their child has been saddled with the responsibility of earning a living, while their in-law child spends all his/her time enjoying life.

This complaint stems from the fact that — whether you realize it or not — you love your child more than you love your in-law child. Logic often dictates otherwise. Your in-law child has given you mostly *nachas*, and you did not have to go through the pain of raising him or her. On an emotional level, however, we are partial to our children. If *shochad*, bribery, "blinds the eyes of the *wise*" (*Devarim* 16:19) — people on Moshe Rabbeinu's level — then we are certainly susceptible to our emotional partiality to our children.

A speaker at a *sheva berachos* once said that when his son came of age, people asked him what kind of girl he was seeking for his son. He would answer with a story.

> He was once traveling to the mountains, and as he was speeding down the highway, he noticed an obviously *frum* woman struggling to change a flat tire. His reflexes were not quick enough to pull over to help, but he felt very guilty for leaving her stranded. He got off the highway at the next exit, drove back down south, got back onto the highway, and pulled over to help her. When he got out of his car he saw that she still had not even managed to get the lug bolts off the flat tire. He told her to stand aside, and then removed the bolts, changed the tire, and replaced the bolts, while the woman expressed her heartfelt appreciation in the background. He picked up the flat tire, placed it into the trunk, and was about to slam the lid, when the woman suddenly called out, "Wait!"
>
> He turned to to her, and she said, "Please close the trunk gently. My husband is sleeping on the back seat."

"I would tell people," said the person speaking at the *sheva berachos*, "that I was looking for that type of girl for my son."

Now for a reality check: Everyone is looking for such a devoted girl, and few are going to find one. It is feasible that you will feel that your in-law child is taking advantage of your son or daughter. The *Ra'avad* hints to us how to handle such feelings.

The *Rambam* (*Hilchos Ishus* 21:9) raises a halachic question. If a woman breaks something while doing housework — a dish, or a vacuum cleaner, for instance — can her husband demand that she pay for it?

The *Rambam* writes that the husband cannot demand that his wife pay for items she damages — but not because he does not have a rightful claim against her. Rather, writes *Rambam*, we do not allow a husband to claim damages against his wife, because this will cause *sholom bayis* problems. The *Rambam's* ruling is certainly understandable. The *chiddush* (novel idea) lies in the words of the *Ra'avad's* comments to this *Rambam*.

Ra'avad argues with *Rambam*. He writes that the husband has no legal claim against his wife for breaks that occur while doing housework. Why? This is based on a law regarding damages of a *sochir*, a hired hand. Halachically, if someone borrows an object from his friend and hires the owner of the object to help him use the object, the owner cannot claim damages against the borrower.

Ra'avad compares a woman doing housework to a borrower who has hired the owner of the object to help him. Since a husband is required to support his wife at all times, writes *Ra'avad*, it is considered as if he is her hired hand, and it is as if he is with her at *all times* — including the time that an object breaks.

Some people will probably consider this a very novel idea. Husbands know that it is our job to earn a livelihood, but we assume that we can fulfill that obligation by working from nine to five. *Ra'avad* teaches that a man's obligation to his wife is constant. Rav Moshe Feinstein (*Dibros Moshe* to *Kiddushin*) explains that a wife is similarly obligated to her husband. The verse reads, *Ish aviv v'imo tera'u*, a man must fear his father and mother. The man is singled out for this obligation, as if to limit a woman's obligation. Indeed, the woman's obligation of *kibbud av v'eim* is limited by the Torah, precisely because she is always obligated to her husband.

If you are concerned that your son is working too hard to support his wife, or vice-versa, remember that *Ra'avad* says that spouses are *obligated* to each other. You can also remind yourself that your emotional bond with your child makes you partial toward him or her, and that you are probably viewing the situation with a certain slant. But even if you cannot come to terms with what you consider to be unfair treatment of your child, verbalizing that feeling will only make matters worse. Why worse?

The Talmud (*Beitzah* 32b) states that there are three people whose lives are not worth living. One of the three is *mi she'ishto mosheles alav* — a man whose wife rules over him.

If a parent feels that his daughter-in-law's control of the household is making his son's life one that is not worth living, it is important to examine the exact wording of the Talmud. The Talmud does not say *mi she'ishto molech alav* — a person whose wife is king over him, but *mi she'ishto **mosheles** alav*. What is the difference between a *melech* and a *mosheil*?

The Gaon of Vilna writes that a *melech* is a king who is accepted by his people, and a *mosheil* is a dictator who forces his rule upon his subjects. Regarding *Klal Yisrael's* relationship with Hashem, the verse states, "*Ki laShem hameluchah* — the kingdom is Hashem's," because we willingly accepted his rule upon us. The nations that did not accept the Torah are subject to His rule by force, so the verse states, "*Umosheil bagoyim*." When *Mashiach* comes, all the nations will accept Hashem's rule upon them; thus the verse states, "*Vehayah Hashem l'**Melech** al kol ha'aretz* – Hashem will be King over all the world."

Chazal said that *mi she'ishto mosheles alav* has a life that is not worth living. Your son may be married to a domineering woman, but if he accepts her rule upon himself and learns to live with it, he will be far better off. If he constantly tells his children that his wife is always right, he is also right by default. If husband and wife are in a constant power struggle, however, then she becomes a *mosheil* over him, and his life is not worth living. Anyone who is privy to a marriage in which both husband and wife insist on "wearing the pants in the family" knows how miserable it can be.

If you feel that you are going to improve your son's life by telling him to assert himself and take control of his home, you may make things worse, far worse. You may succeed in turning him into a person whose wife is *mosheles alav*.

৺ Extend Credit

Finally, we come to one of the most difficult aspects of parenting married children.

What happens when you see your child making a mistake? Parents are trained to correct children when they see them err. If we were to take an honest look at ourselves, we would have to admit that even when our children were young there were instances in which our criticism was less than constructive. We would be better parents if we would learn to look aside and ignore some of our children's mistakes rather than try to correct them each time. But when children get married, correction of their errors must not be a way of life. Children are allowed to make mistakes. They will learn from their mistakes — the same way you learned from yours.

A father once told his son, "You rush too much. Stop rushing!"

"Remember when you were my age?" the son asked. "Didn't you also rush at my age?"

"Yes, you're right" he admitted with a smile.

We forget that we also used to make mistakes. If you see your children making mistakes, as long as they are getting along with each other, they are fine. If you get involved, they will probably get into a fight over it, and their marriage will head for dangerous territory.

When I was in fourth grade, my *rebbi* once turned his back to the class to write something on the blackboard — which is something a *rebbi* should never do — and the boy sitting behind me made a very disrespectful noise. The *rebbi* whirled around, instinctively strode toward me, and gave me three resounding smacks in rapid succession. I guess past experience led him to believe that I was the culprit, but he was wrong. (Honest, it wasn't me!) I didn't say anything, but some other boys cried out, "*Rebbi*, it wasn't him!"

My *rebbi* felt terrible. He had hit me three times for no reason. He handled the situation in an amazing way. He went over to his desk, took out a paper, fashioned a credit card, and wrote, "Credit — 3 Smacks" on it. I was entitled to pull out the credit card the next three times that I deserved corporal punishment, and use the smacks I had received unjustly to pay for future infractions.

Later the same day, I must have misbehaved, for I remember using the credit card. My *rebbi* crossed out the 3 and wrote a 2; leaving me credit for two additional occasions. Unfortunately, I left the credit card in my pants pocket and it went through the washing machine, where it became ruined.

Eventually, though, I settled the score with my *rebbi*. Many years later, I married his daughter. I am probably the only son-in-law in the world with a credit card for two smacks from his father-in-law.

Every father-in-law and mother-in-law should extend credit to their children. Allow them to make mistakes!

Yehoshafat thought that he would be able to make Ataliyahu mend her ways by marrying her to Yehoram. If there is one lesson that we can learn from his mistake, it is that we cannot change our in-law children. The nature of the in-law relationship does not allow for it.

At *sheva berachos,* we ask Hashem to bring joy to the *chasan* and *kallah k'sameicha'cha yetzeercha b'Gan Eden mikedem,* just as He brought joy to Adam and Chavah in Gan Eden on the first day of Creation. What was so special about that time?

Pardas Yosef writes — tongue in cheek, I'm sure — that the joy Adam and Chavah experienced then was so great because there were no *mechutanim* to cause friction between them.

Let's do the same for our married children.

Great Expectations

Yirmiyahu is a tragic figure. He watched in horror as *B'nei Yisrael* catapulted toward disaster, ignoring his words of reproof that could have averted the Churban. How desperately he tried to save them from catastrophe! As time went on, Yirmiyahu's warnings became more ominous. Nobody wanted to hear what he had to say.

As you can imagine, Yirmiyahu was not a popular figure. He was ignored, derided, attacked physically, and thrown into jail.

There is a major turning point that comes early in the Book of *Yirmiyahu*. In the earlier chapters of his book, Yirmiyahu complains bitterly to Hashem. He bemoans his fate when he is humiliated or attacked for carrying Hashem's message.

The last protest of Yirmiyahu appears in Chapter 20, when Pashchur, the chief official in the *Beis HaMikdash*, hit him and then imprisoned him overnight. "You persuaded me, Hashem, and I was persuaded," Yirmiyahu tells Hashem. "You were more forceful than I and You prevailed. I have become a laughingstock all day long, and everyone ridicules me. Whenever I speak to them, I shout. 'Corruption! Robbery!' do I proclaim, for the word of Hashem has become a source of shame and derision to me all day long" (*Yirmiyahu* 20:7-8).

In Chapter 38 we read that Yirmiyahu was thrown into a pit full of mud and left there to die. Although that incident is far worse than the one in Chapter 20, Yirmiyahu does not complain to Hashem. What happened? Why did Yirmiyahu stop complaining?

Rabbi Josef Breuer, in his commentary to *Yirmiyahu*, writes about Yirmiyahu's last complaint: "The prophet has endured the abuse with unshakable calm. He achieved this calm after an arduous struggle that won him a profound insight into the ways of Hashem, and reconciled him to the sacrifices demanded by his life's work. This event was the touchstone, as it were; the test by which Yirmiyahu had to prove himself. He has passed the test."

This verse clearly describes a watershed moment in Yirmiyahu's life. Let us examine this episode, which has powerful implications for each of us in our lives. Let us begin by asking two seemingly unrelated questions.

✥ Why Does He Deserve a Limousine?

*I*n commanding us to give charity to the poor, the Torah tells us to give "*Dei machsoro asher yechsar lo* — His requirement, whatever is lacking to him" (*Devarim* 15:8).

The Talmud (*Kesubos* 67b), cited in *Rashi*, explains these two clauses in contradictory ways. First the Talmud deduces that we are only to give a poor person "his requirement," but we are not required to make him rich. But the Talmud then deduces that we are required to provide him with "whatever is lacking *to him*" — i.e., the luxuries that he was accustomed to having until now. The Talmud explains that if a rich man is used to having a horse and he loses all of his money, we are required to buy him a horse to fulfill this mitzvah properly. If he is accustomed to having servants run before him and announce his arrival, we must provide this service for him.

Aside from the seeming contradiction — if we are not required to make a poor person rich, we certainly don't have to provide him with luxuries — I think that most people find this passage difficult to accept. We can understand the requirement to help a poor person obtain the basic necessities: food, housing, and clothing. A horse, however, is the ancient version of a limousine. If a rich person loses his money, should we be required to provide him with a limousine? *We* don't have limousines; why should he be better off than those who are providing for him? Why must we enable him to maintain the luxurious lifestyle that he was accustomed to? Let him learn to live like the rest of us!

We can pose a similar question on the Talmudic teaching (*Kesubos* 61a) that if a woman is accustomed to one standard of living, and her husband to another, he is required to support her at the higher standard. If the husband comes from a wealthy home, his wife is entitled to that standard of living, even if she comes from a poor home. If the reverse is true and the wife comes from a wealthy family and is accustomed to having maids, he must provide for that need, even if he comes from a poor home.

The Talmud derives this Halachah from the verse, "*Vehi beulas ba'al* — she is a married woman" (*Bereishis* 20:3), which can be rendered homiletically as "*ba'aliyaso shel ba'al, v'lo beyiridaso shel ba'al* — a woman is entitled to the higher standard of living that her husband is accustomed to, but she need not descend if he has a lower standard of living."

I'm sure that all the men are getting nervous, so I will tell you that the *Rema* states that you are only required to live up to your wife's expectations if you can afford it. Whether you can afford it might be a matter of opinion — you will have to argue about that with your wife.

Someone told me that he was dating a girl whose father asked him, "Can you afford to support my daughter at the standard of living she is accustomed to?"

His answer — which I thought was pretty good under the circumstances — was, "I can afford to support her at the standard you had when you were first married."

"You cannot compare your situation to mine," retorted the girl's father. "I had a father-in-law who helped me!"

Indeed, how are we to understand this Halachah? Why must we support our wives at a higher standard of living than we are accustomed to, simply because she was raised that way?

◆§ Drip, Drip

I noticed something many years ago, and have seen this observation confirmed so many times.

Most pain in the world is not the result of objective facts or things that take place. Pain is caused by the expectations that people have. When we feel *agmas nefesh*, mental anguish, over something that happens, it is usually because we expected things to go otherwise. We would lead much happier lives if we would learn to limit our expectations.

The first time this lesson occurred to me was back in my days at the yeshivah dormitory. I always tried to choose the bed closest to the sink, so that I could wash my hands in the morning without walking *daled amos*. One night, as I put my head down on my pillow and tried to fall asleep, I heard the faucet dripping. I tried to ignore it, but I just couldn't. *Drip. Drip*. It was so disturbing, I could not fall asleep. I got up, turned the handle on the faucet as hard as I could, and got back into bed. I settled down, closed my eyes, and there it was again: *Drip. Drip. Drip.*

I tossed and turned much of the night, and the next morning I registered a complaint. It seems that the yeshivah had difficulty allocating money for a rubber washer, because it took quite a while for them to fix it. Finally, it was repaired.

A few nights later, as I was drifting off too sleep, I noticed that it was raining outside. *Drip*, I heard. *Drip, drip, drip*. But somehow, with all of the dripping outdoors, I had no problem falling asleep. Rainfall is soothing. Some people play recordings of rainfall to lull them to sleep. I couldn't understand it. What is the difference between the *drip, drip, drip* of a faucet and the *drip, drip, drip* of rain? Why did one keep me awake and not the other?

The question bothered me. *Now,* I really couldn't fall asleep!

It was then that a profound *chiddush* was revealed to me. I realized that the drip had not been keeping me awake — my expectations had kept me awake. A sink is not supposed to drip. When it did, it annoyed me so much that I could not fall asleep. The sky is supposed to drip, so it did not bother me.

I once mentioned this idea in a *shiur*. A short while later I was in a car with someone who had attended that *shiur*. "Remember when you spoke about the dripping and expectations?" he asked.

"Of course I remember," I responded.

"You helped me," he said.

How did I help him?

It seems that this fellow works very hard during the week. When he comes home from work, he goes out to learn for a few hours. By the time Shabbos comes, he is exhausted. All week long he would look forward to the two hours that he had allotted for sleep on Shabbos afternoon.

Every Shabbos, without fail, he would lie down for his two-hour nap. To his chagrin, he would wake up after half-an-hour. He would spend the next hour and a half tossing and turning, lamenting his lack of sleep. When he heard my *shiur*, he decided that he would simply change his attitude. He would now anticipate waking up after half an hour. Now he lies down for his nap, and when he wakes up after half an hour, he says, "Well, what do you know! Isn't it amazing? Every single week I wake up after thirty minutes!" Then he turns over and falls asleep peacefully for another hour and a half.

As long as he thought that he was not supposed to wake up, it bothered him so much that he could not fall asleep again. As soon as his expectations changed, as soon as he *expected* to wake up in half an hour, he had no *agmas nefesh*, and his insomnia was cured.

ೆ§ My Alternate Routes

As time went by, I began to notice numerous examples of how often — and to what extent — our expectations control our reactions.

I have an unfortunate tendency. When I drive on unfamiliar roads, I inevitably get lost. I miss exits; I make wrong turns; I find myself driving sixty miles an hour on a highway, in the wrong direction …. Suffice it to say that I have much experience in making U-turns and exiting highways in order to reverse directions.

This used to bother me terribly. I remember attending a wedding held at Ateres Avraham in Williamsburg, which was a new wedding hall at the time. As I left the wedding, one of the older *rebbeim* in the yeshivah asked me for a ride. As we discussed the *sugya* we were learning, I drove home. Somehow, I did not realize that Ateres Avraham is not on the same side of the highway as are the older wedding halls. I got onto the BQE as I usually do and drove along for a while, deeply engrossed in our conversation. Soon the *rebbi* turned to me, pointing to a building in the distance. "What's that?" he asked.

"Shea Stadium," I replied.

He was very polite. "That's funny. I don't usually pass Shea Stadium when I come home from a wedding in Williamsburg!"

I was traveling in the wrong direction.

My frustration reached its peak after I attended a wedding in Chicago. I made elaborate plans to get back to yeshivah in time to give *shiur* the following day. Despite that fact that the wedding ended late, I rose early in order to reach the airport in time to daven *k'vasikin*. I then caught an early flight back to New York. I had parked my car at LaGuardia Airport, and it seemed simple enough to retrieve my car and drive to yeshivah in time for the *shiur*.

I left the airport and drove along for a while. Suddenly, I realized that I was in Long Island. I exited and reentered what I thought was the same highway in the opposite direction. Apparently it was not. I drove a bit farther, trying desperately to figure out where I was. Finally I gave up. I pulled out my cell phone and called a friend who is known for his expertise at giving directions. "Help!" I said. "I am near a sign for the 'Pulaski Skyway.' How do I get to yeshivah?"

"How did you get to the Pulaski Skyway?" he asked incredulously.

"Am I still in New York State?" I asked hopefully.

"Look," he said, "You know Manhattan. Follow the signs to Manhattan, and take a route to Brooklyn that you are familiar with."

I was very aggravated. I had gotten up in the wee hours in order to be back in yeshivah on time, and my sense of direction — or lack thereof — was destroying my carefully laid plans. Out of frustration, I asked, "Why do I have to get lost every time I get into the car?"

There was quiet at the other end of the line, and then my friend asked, "Why is that every time I learn a *Maharsha*, I can't understand what he is saying?"

Suddenly, I felt a lot better. Given the choice, I would rather get lost and have the ability to understand the *Maharsha*, than have a great sense of direction without the skill to navigate a *Maharsha*.

Since that day, each time I get lost I say to myself, "What do you know? I'm lost again!"

I still take "alternate routes" pretty often, but my level of frustration has diminished. I have come to accept getting lost as part of the reality of my life.

Weight, Gas Prices, and Health: The Common Denominator

Slowly but surely, it dawned on me that when I meet a person who is upset, it is almost always related to his expectations.

Since my leg injury, I swim at the Sephardic Center a few times each week. There is a scale in the dressing room, and many of my fellow swimmers step onto the scale every day to check their weight. I won't repeat some of the words that they say, but it is always interesting to watch their reactions. One man who weighs in at 200 pounds is very happy. Another man who weighs only 180 pounds is upset. Why? Expectations. The man who now weighs 200 pounds was once 220 pounds. He is very happy that he managed to shed those twenty pounds. The man who weighs 180 was once 170, so he is disappointed.

If you want to see how your own expectations affect your reactions, consider this: just a year or two ago, would you have smiled and sped into a gas station because they were charging $1.89 per gallon? Now $1.89 seems cheap, because we were paying $3.59 or more.

Our expectations rule our emotions in every area of life. Take health as an example. If it would be an accepted fact of life that everyone who reaches the age of seventy automatically loses his eyesight, would it be totally devastating? We wouldn't be happy about it, but we would shrug and say, "It's better than the alternative."

Why do people who lose their eyesight at seventy feel anguished? Isn't it better to be alive, even with minimal vision?

It is all in the expectations. No one expects to lose his eyesight by seventy, so it is considered tragic.

Not only are we affected by our own expectations, but we are affected by the expectation created for us by society. I am certain that people who lived 100 years ago — many of whom did not have indoor plumbing, not to mention dishwashers, cars, and other conveniences that we take for granted — were not less content than we are. The most commonly prescribed drug in America today is Prozac. With all of the luxury and convenience we have, people are unhappy. We are easily frustrated by the many things we lack. We have come to expect too much, and when our expectations are not met, we sink into depression.

If we can learn to limit our expectations, we can lead happier lives.

৺§ Luxury or Necessity?

To go back to our original question, why we are required to provide a formerly rich man with a limousine? Why is he entitled to luxury?

The Torah is revealing one of the great secrets of life. When a person expects to have a limousine in his driveway, it is no longer a luxury. It has become a necessity. It may be nonsensical — who needs a servant to run before him and announce his arrival? — but it can become a necessity. And that is a tragedy. Here is someone who is so poor that he has to accept charity, yet he must have his limousine. That is the power of expectations.

The Torah is teaching us a lesson in how to give *tzeddakah*, but it is also a lesson in how to live our lives. Don't train yourself to live in luxury. When you acquire something that you consider a luxury, it makes you happy for the first week. After that, it becomes a necessity. And when something is a necessity, it won't make you happy anymore.

Don't train yourself to need elaborate *simchos*. The joy that *mechutanim* feel at a wedding is not related to the amount of money that is spent. It is not related to the kind of food that is served, nor is it related to the decor of the hall. There are as many disgruntled *mechutanim* at elaborate weddings as there are at simple, understated affairs — and probably more. How can they be happy if the tablecloths are not the correct shade of blue? "It's so aggravating," they say, as they walk around at their child's wedding with long faces. And they are right — it *is* aggravating, because they expect everything to be perfect.

We are discussing luxuries, but the same applies to small things as well. Many people believe they cannot eat day-old bread. Why handicap yourself? Don't become the type of person who cannot eat day-old bread.

Youngsters are being raised with the inability to use a generic brand of ketchup, or to drive five-year-old cars. How we are handicapping them! Why raise their expectations?

If you want to be happy, learn to expect less.

◃§ Joy? In a Hut, with Water?

The festival of Succos is called *Z'man Simchaseinu* — a time of joy. How should we rejoice? Hashem commands us to leave our homes. Where should we go? To a five-star hotel? Hashem says, "It is a time of joy. Go build a little hut outside, and go live in the hut."

That is going to make us joyful? Tell us to go to a palatial hotel!

The joy on Succos was most palpable at the celebration of *Simchas Beis Hasho'evah*, which was celebrated by pouring water on the Altar in the *Beis HaMikdash*. Water. Not wine, not champagne. Plain water.

The Torah is giving us a message. Living in a simple hut and celebrating the simple things in life, like water, will provide us with true happiness. The simpler our needs, the more modest our expectations, the happier we are.

✎§ Appreciating the Basics

*C*hazal attribute great importance to our concentration during the blessing of *Modim* in *Shemoneh Esrei*, and on the recitation of *Mizmor LeSodah*, which the Shulchan Aruch (51:9) suggests that we sing![1] These are the parts of prayer in which we express our gratitude to Hashem for all that He has granted us. Why? Because if we train ourselves to focus on what we have and to appreciate it, we will be happier people.

An elderly *Yid* came to visit me on Succos, and I asked him what his *succah* looked like in prewar Hungary. As he was describing his *succah*, he mentioned that there was an outhouse in the backyard. "You still had an outhouse?" I asked.

"Yes," he said, "we still had outhouses."

It made me remember something that I read. Several years before World War II, a young lady who was born in the United States married a young man who wanted to move to Lithuania to study Torah in one of the great yeshivos of Lithuania. She wrote of all the hardships she endured: extreme seasickness during the voyage, the freezing winters, and the limited diet. She was able to handle all the difficulties, except for one: the outhouses. When she returned to America, she appreciated indoor plumbing as she never had before.

We don't appreciate the convenience of indoor plumbing nowadays. We expect it, so we don't appreciate it. The only time we pay attention to the convenience of indoor plumbing is when it is clogged and does not work!

Once we are discussing the appreciation we should have for plumbing facilities, how about appreciating our own waste-manage-

---

1. It is interesting to note that of all the parts of the prayer service, it is only *Mizmor L'sodah* which the Shuchan Aruch suggests that we sing. I have heard many parts of the davening being sung — but never this part!!

ment systems? I once heard Rabbi Avigdor Miller *zt"l* lecturing — in his inimitable style — about the appreciation we should have for our ability to expel wastes. He said that when a person relieves himself, he should thank Hashem for that ability. "If you don't believe me," he said, "Ask *him*! [I heard a recording of the lecture, but it is obvious that he was pointing to someone in the audience.] *His* plumbing wasn't working, and he had to call Hatzalah to take him to the hospital and clear out his system."

When we hear about people whose bodies do not function properly, we suddenly realize how thankful we should be. Otherwise, we are handicapped in our ability to appreciate what we have. We just expect too much.

I feel sorry for husbands who buy flowers every Erev Shabbos without fail. After awhile, the flowers become meaningless. They are expected. A person who buys flowers every week for ten years will only hear a comment when he forgets to bring them.

If you want the flowers to be appreciated, change the system. Start buying flowers only on occasion and you will receive an appreciative comment each time you buy them.

The same applies in the reverse. A woman who has supper ready on time every single night will never receive a compliment. A man who is used to having supper on time will come to expect it.

I don't think that we will ever truly appreciate indoor plumbing. It is such a basic fact of life that it is hard to appreciate it. Let us try, however, to appreciate conveniences and objects that we did not have two, five, or ten years ago. We are so accustomed to our laptops that they no longer make us happy! We should work on appreciating them so that we can maintain the happiness we felt when we first acquired them.

⇞§ She's Different

Now we come to our earlier question. Why does a married woman have the right to choose the better of her father's and her husband's lifestyles? Many men consider it a *chok,* similar to the laws of *parah adumah* and *sha'atnez.* Just as we have no way of understanding how and why a *parah adumah* purifies a person and why we cannot wear a garment that contains *sha'atnez,* we cannot understand why a woman is entitled to a superior lifestyle.

Is that what the Torah intended with this Halachah? I don't think so. Let me illustrate what I consider to be the message of this teaching by recounting a conversation that I had with a *chasan*.

> I was approached by a young man in the yeshivah who was to be married in two weeks. He requested tips on maintaining *shalom bayis*. I have had many such requests from *chasanim*, and almost none from married men, who do not seem to need this information.
>
> After thinking for a few moments, I said, "You should be aware that after you are married, there are going to be many differences of opinion between you and your wife. It is normal. You are going to differ on where to go on vacation, on how to renovate the house, on how to spend money, and on many other issues."
>
> "Okay," said the *chasan*. "And what is your advice in handling such situations?"
>
> "No advice," I responded. "I'm just telling you that it will happen."
>
> "What good is it to know that it will happen?" he asked.
>
> "Let me explain," I said. "If you have a wedding in Marina Del Ray in the Bronx, and it takes you an hour to get there, do you feel frustrated?"
>
> "No," he replied. "An hour is pretty reasonable to Marina Del Ray."
>
> "What if you have a wedding in Williamsburg and it takes an hour to get there?" I asked, silently assuming that he does not take the Shea Stadium route.
>
> "Then I would be frustrated," he said. "Williamsburg is no more than a fifteen- or twenty-minute drive from Flatbush."
>
> "What is the difference between the two?" I asked. "It took you an hour to get to each wedding."
>
> "I expect it to take an hour to drive to Marina Del Ray," he reasoned, "but I don't expect it to take an hour to get to Williamsburg."
>
> "Marriage is exactly the same," I said. "It all depends on your expectations. If you expect not to have any differences of opinion with your wife, you will have a great deal of frustration and *agmas nefesh*. If you go into marriage realizing that it is normal to disagree, you will take the disagreements in stride."

In the verse of *vehi be'ulas ba'al*, the Torah is reminding us that our wives are different from us. Just as she is used to a different lifestyle, she sees life differently. If you expect her to be different, you will be able to handle it; if not, you are doomed to unhappiness.

In fact, we can avoid many *shalom bsayis* issues if we learn to adjust our expectations.

> A man once came to me to discuss a situation that he considered very frustrating: his wife was constantly getting parking tickets. "It is one thing if she spends money," he said, "but why does she have to get parking tickets all the time? We fight over it constantly, and I don't want to fight with her. What should I do?"
>
> "How long have you been married?" I asked.
>
> "Ten years," he replied.
>
> "If you have been talking to her about the parking tickets for the last ten years, and the situation has not improved, then it is not going to improve in the next ten years either," I reasoned. "Rather than talk to her about it, just learn to expect it. You get a monthly gas bill, water bill, electric bill, and, although you don't relish paying them, you accept them because they are facts of life. Apply the same attitude to your parking-ticket bill. Open the bill and say, 'What do know? We got a parking ticket!'"

You don't have to be happy about the problems that aggravate you, but if you learn to expect them, you will have much less *agmas nefesh*.

⇝ Spiritual Expectations

Let us now turn to the importance of adjusting expectations in *ruchnius*.

When Yirmiyahu became a prophet, what did he expect? He expected to be like the other prophets of his generation: Yeshayahu, Hoshe'a, and Ovadia. He knew them, and he saw them being honored and respected. He thought that he would be honored and respected, too.

What happened when Yirmiyahu started to prophesy to *Klal Yisrael*? People threw things at him, hit him, and imprisoned him.

What is going on? he must have thought. *This is not the way a prophet should be treated.*

At the beginning of *Sefer Yirmiyahu*, when Yirmiyahu began his career as a prophet, he was bothered by these attacks, until he finally made peace with his situation in life. In Rav Breuer's words, "He achieved this calm after an arduous struggle that won him a profound insight into the ways of God, and reconciled him to the sacrifices demanded by his life's work. This event was a touchstone, a test by which Yirmiyahu had to prove himself."

Yirmiyahu was expecting his life's work to go easily. When it did not go as well as he expected it to, he complained — until the day that he was imprisoned by Pashchur and complained for one last time. That was when he realized that Hashem had not given him an easy job. His job was to prophesy, and to be derided. To prophesy, and to be attacked. To prophesy, and to be thrown into jail. And to keep prophesying nonetheless.

Yirmiyahu won "a profound insight into the ways of God that reconciled him to the sacrifices demanded by his life's work." He realized that his work was to struggle with the people and to admonish them. When he came to this realization, he stopped complaining. Later on (in Chapter 38), when the people went so far that they tried to put him to death, he did not complain, because he had adjusted his expectations.

Did he lower his expectations? You could argue that he did. He realized that he was going to have a difficult life.

I don't think so. I think that he raised his expectations — of himself. He had a job that made him greater than the prophets with whom he was familiar. *Chazal* say that the two greatest prophets were Moshe Rabbeinu and Yirmiyahu, both of whom struggled greatly with their respective generations.

If there is one area of life in which we *must* learn to adjust our expectations, it is the area of spiritual achievement.

We must withstand challenges on a daily basis, but the challenges are different for each of us. Some people have trouble in their personal lives, others in their ability to daven or learn as they feel they should. Some face temptation to earn money illegitimately. When we find ourselves being challenged day after day, we start to get depressed. We feel that we are not making any progress in our spiritual lives.

Yirmiyahu's change of attitude should serve as a guide to us all. Yirmiyahu realized that he had to adjust to the task that Hashem had presented *to him*. We must learn to do the same. If you find it difficult to learn, adjust to it. Realize that it is not always easy to serve Hashem. Expect to be challenged.

Someone in our community told me that when he davened at Rabbi Friedman's shul, where Shabbos morning Shacharis begins at 9 o'clock, he had the habit of arriving at 9:45 each Shabbos. When our shul opened closer to his home, he became a member. We start *Shacharis* at 8:30, and he walks in every Shabbos — without exception — at exactly 9 o'clock. I told him, "I wish Rabbi Friedman could see you now. What changed? You couldn't make it until 9:45 when you davened in his shul!"

What changed? Expectations. We start earlier, so he adjusted his expectations. Until he switched to our shul, he expected to come at 9:45, so he did. Now he expects to be in shul at 9:00, and that is when he arrives. I wish he would adjust his expectations and come at 8:30 (or go back to Rabbi Friedman's shul and come at 9:00!). So you see, behavior is based on expectations.

Rav Pinchus Hirschprung, *zt"l*, was one of the best-known rabbonim in Montreal. When I was sixteen, I visited him with a group of boys, under the auspices of Pirchei. As each boy in the group approached him, he asked, "What *masechta* are you studying, and what *daf*?" As soon as the boy told him the *masechta* and *daf*, he immediately recited the entire *daf* from memory. He could have recited all of the *Rashi*, too. He had memorized all of *Shas*.

After that meeting, I did not see Rav Hirschprung for approximately twenty-fves years. Several years ago, I traveled to Montreal for a wedding at which he officiated. Rav Hirschprung had grown old and frail, and people said his memory was not what it had been. He needed help filling in the *kesubah*. At the *chuppah*, I sat down next to him and told him that I had visited him when I was sixteen, and that he had rattled off the entire *daf* that I was learning.

"My memory is not as good as it was," he said. "But what are you learning?"

I did not want to tell him the *daf*, because I was afraid that he would be upset if he did not remember it, so I told him the *sugya* (topic) I was studying.

"Uh! *Daf tes-zayin!*" he said.

I didn't know what to say, because the *sugya* was actually on *tes-vav*, a page away. I just sat there in silence.

"It's not *tes-zayin*?" he asked, sensing my hesitation.

"Well, it's close," I said.

"Is it *tes-vav*?" he asked.

"Yes," I replied.

He had *agmas nefesh*. He expected himself to know all of *Shas*, and he was upset that he was off by one *daf*.

As a postscript to this story, I must tell you that I was amazed when I got home and took out my Gemara. The *sugya* was on *tes-zayin*. I was wrong. I should go to his *kever* to apologize for causing him unnecessary pain.

Was I upset when I realized that I was wrong? I was happy that I knew which *perek* the *sugya* was in! I don't expect to be able to memorize *Shas*, so I was not upset. He expected more from himself, so he was disappointed when he thought he was wrong.

Don't you see? It's all about expectations.

The Struggle

Each year, as the Yamim Noraim draw near, we look to do *teshuvah*. Many people are under the impression that doing *teshuvah* means that one must become perfectly righteous from that Yom Kippur on. I'm not sure where that definition came from. In my dictionary, the definition of *teshuvah* is "to return." I cannot do *teshuvah* if it means that I have to become a perfect *tzaddik* from now on. I was never a perfect *tzaddik* to begin with, so how can I return to that position?

Do you know what *teshuvah* really means? It means to go back to your original struggle. You have a *yetzer hara* and a *yetzer tov*, and you struggle. With time, there are areas in which the *yetzer hara* overwhelms you, and you get used to behaving in certain ways. It becomes commonplace for you come to shul half-an-hour late. *Teshuvah* does not mean that you decide that you are going to come exactly on time every single week. There came a point during the previous year when you gave up the struggle. The *yetzer hara* won. *Teshuvah* means to go back to the struggle. Sometimes you will win, and sometimes you will lose — but you will be struggling to improve.

I remember R' Moshe Feinstein, *zt"l*, encouraging *bnei Torah* to set higher goals. He wanted yeshivah students to strive to be *gedolim*. He would often point out that the ladder in Yaakov Avinu's dream was situated in Beis El, with the top reaching the heavens and the midpoint being Jerusalem. He would explain that if you try to reach the heavens, you might reach Jerusalem. Shoot for the heavens!

Today, thirty years later, attitudes are different. There are fine young men who think that they are obligated to become *gedolim*, and they become depressed when they don't feel that they are reaching the heavens. We have to explain to them that Hashem does not expect everyone to become the Torah leaders. It is okay to shoot for the heavens and reach halfway. Be what you can be.

What changed? A generation ago, Rav Moshe had to convince us to strive for more. Today, why do we have to convince young men that they are striving for too much!?

One thing changed. Today, we do not know how to struggle. With Hashem's kindness, life has become more convenient and more manageable over the last thirty years. No one expects to struggle anymore. That is fine for the physical world, but it does not work in terms of spiritual growth. If a person does not want to struggle, he cannot become a *talmid chacham*, and certainly not a *gadol*. The disappointment of achieving half of the dream is too painful. We want our dreams to come true, and to come true quickly and easily.

> I once contacted a 9th-grade *rebbi* on behalf of one of his students. Ninth grade is the first year of *mesivta* (high school), and it is one of the formative years in boys' education. This boy's father was concerned because his son could not understand the *meforshim* that his *rebbi* was teaching in *shiur*. I told the *rebbi* that the *shiur* was too difficult for this boy and, perhaps, for many others in his class. The *rebbi's* answer was reassuring. He was an experienced 9th-grade *rebbi*, and he told me that he had one objective in teaching this formative year: he tries to teach the boys that they have to be willing to work hard. Once they are willing to work, he shows them lots of patience and understanding, letting each one grow at his own pace. But first he makes it clear that they will not grow unless they are willing to work. He teaches them that if they do not work hard in *mesivta*, they will not get anywhere. He therefore deliberately overreaches, hoping to teach them the invaluable lessons related to the struggle to achieve.

Yirmiyahu learned that his life would be an arduous struggle, and he accepted that struggle. We have to learn to do the same. If we expect life to be easy, we won't get anywhere. If we expect to struggle and work hard, then we can grow.

✦ Winter's Personality

We are accustomed to hearing that each Yom Tov has its "personality." The month of Nissan represents renewal, Shavuos is a time to recommit to the Torah, Rosh Hashanah and Yom Kippur are times for *teshuvah*, and Succos is a time of joy. What happens when Succos ends? We have six months without any Biblically ordained Yamim Tovim. It would seem that the winter months have no "personality." It seems that when we came out of Egypt, there were lots of reasons to celebrate; but when winter came, the supply of Yamim Tovim had run dry.

Why is this so?

A winter *z'man* in yeshivah is long, with no Yom Tov break. Somehow, Tu B'Shvat just doesn't do it.

It is difficult to imagine what a winter *z'man* was like before Chanukah and Purim came about! How did *bachurim* survive?

The answer is that winter *z'man* also has a personality of its own. We can gain insight into its personality from winter itself. What happens during winter? A farmer plants seeds at the beginning of winter. He makes sure that there is enough water and fertilizer, and he hopes that deep in the ground the seeds are taking root and will eventually produce a bountiful crop. During the winter, however, all he sees is mud.

Winter *z'man* is the same. For a *ben Torah* — whether he is still in yeshivah full time, or he is working and trying to maintain his *sedorim* when he is not at work — winter is a time to plant seeds. You don't become a *talmid chacham* overnight. You don't wake up one morning knowing many *masechtos*. You plant seeds deep inside yourself, and every time you work on your learning, something is happening.

And yes, there are struggles. The farmer goes out from time to time and sees mud, and he is tempted to dig up the seed and see if anything is happening. He knows, however, that he will kill the seed if he digs it up. We have the same temptation. A month or two into the winter *z'man*, we feel less motivated to learn and we start to wonder if our seeds are growing roots. We are tempted to dig up the seed and examine it. *"Are we really growing? Are we stagnating?"* we wonder.

To succeed in a winter *z'man*, we have to expect to work hard. Chazal (*Avos* 5:26) told us, "*Lefum tza'ara agrah* — the reward is in proportion to the exertion." If we do not expect to face difficulties in our service of Hashem, it is very painful when we do encounter challenges. But if we realize beforehand that there will be ups and downs, that there will be times when we will wonder whether we are making progress and there will be times when everything will be muddy, then we can succeed.

It all depends on our expectations.

The one winter "Yom Tov" is Tu B'Shvat. On Tu B'Shvat we celebrate the Rosh Hashanah of trees. What do the trees look like on Tu B'Shvat? They are barren. Deep inside, however, the sap is awakening. The earth is giving forth its blessing to the trees. So too, deep inside a *ben Torah*, something is happening. Seeds are forming, energies are awakening, and soon the fruit is sure to come.

People get depressed — they destroy themselves — because they fail to anticipate the difficulties of winter. Winter is a time of darkness. There are very few hours of daylight. We come home from work or yeshivah when it is dark, and it affects our mood. We must anticipate the darkness and realize the blessing that comes from the difficulty of forcing ourselves out of our warm, comfortable homes and trudging to the *Beis Midrash*. The struggle of staying up late at night and trying to learn, the effort of learning in a standing position to fight off sleep — that is what makes one succeed.

If we can master the lesson that Yirmiyahu learned, if we can adjust our expectations to realize that life is often a struggle, we will be able to handle our difficulties and grow from our challenges.

Emulating Hashem

One of the lesser-known mitzvos in the Torah is mitzvah #611: "*V'halachta b'drachav* — and you shall walk in [Hashem's] ways" (*Devarim* 28:9). Just as Hashem is merciful, we are required to be merciful; just as He is compassionate, righteous, and holy, so must we be. This mitzvah, which governs our interpersonal relationships, is perhaps the most underestimated — and misunderstood — of all 613 *mitzvos*.

Most of us admit that we are lacking in our observance of the *mitzvos* of *bein adam l'Makom* (*mitzvos* between man and God). We know that we do not know *Hilchos Shabbos* so well, and that makes our observance of Shabbos less than perfect. We realize that we do not daven as well as we should. But when it comes to *mitzvos bein adam l'chaveiro* (*mitzvos* that govern interpersonal relationships), we feel quite comfortable with our level of observance. If you were to survey the average person and ask, "Are you merciful? Are you compassionate?" I'm fairly certain that most will respond, "Sure! I'm a nice guy. I help people. I empathize with those in need."

This perception comes from a basic misunderstanding of the mitzvah of *v'halchta b'drachav*. If we would have a mitzvah that required us to emulate our *gedolim* — Rav Moshe Feinstein, Rav Yaakov Kamentzky, the Steipler Gaon, or *yibadel l'chaim tovim*, Rav Elyashiv — we would certainly think, "Impossible! How can I be like those *gedolim*? They are light years beyond me! I could never dream of reaching their exalted levels."

Somehow, when people hear of the mitzvah to emulate Hashem, they think, "Oh, to emulate Hashem — no problem! I can be like Hashem. Hashem is kind, and I am kind. Hashem is nice, and so am I."

We underestimate this mitzvah because the words chosen by *Chazal* have universal appeal. Everyone relates to the idea of being merciful and compassionate. The problem is that each of us interprets those words on his own level. Some define mercy and compassion as helping a neighbor unload heavy packages from his car. To others, being nice means not cutting people off at the entrance to the Brooklyn Bridge.

This is a terrible mistake. The words *Chazal* chose are not subjective. They are not defined by our personal perspectives. There is an objective, definitive way of measuring kindness, compassion, and all other Attributes of Hashem. The mitzvah of *v'halachta b'drachav* requires us to emulate *Hashem's* level of kindness and compassion.

The mitzvah of *v'halachta b'drachav* also enables us to atone for our sins. After the Jews sinned by worshipping the Golden Calf, Hashem taught Moshe the Thirteen Attributes of Divine Mercy. The Gemara (*Rosh Hashanah* 17b) states that Hashem told Moshe, "Any time that *Klal Yisrael* sins, let them perform this order [i.e., the Thirteen Attributes] before Me, and I will forgive them."

Panim Yafos (*Parashas Ki Sisa*) points out that there are two ways to understand the words "perform this order before Me." It can mean that we should emulate Hashem's actions as recorded in the Gemara — i.e., we should wrap ourselves in a tallis and recite the Thirteen Attributes. This would be a form of *tefillah*, of davening for atonement. On a higher level, it can mean that we should follow in Hashem's footsteps and act the way He does — in other words, to fulfill the mitzvah of *v'halachta b'drachav*. But if the compassion and kindness required by this mitzvah are defined by a standard beyond human perception, how do we learn to follow in Hashem's ways?

~§ *Tomer Devorah:*
The Guide to Hashem's Ways

The Sefer Tomer Devorah was written by Rabbi Moshe Kordavero (known as *Ramak*), one of the *Arizal's* greatest disciples. The *Ramak* wrote a set of pamphlets entitled *Shiv'im Temarim* (*70 Palm Trees*), which are introductions to the study of Kabbalah, the hidden portions of the Torah. Most of the *Shiv'im Temarim* are beyond our grasp, but the first one, *Tomer Devorah*, which is a study of the Attributes of Hashem, has become part of *Toras HaNigleh*, the revealed Torah. Rav Yisrael Salanter and his disciples republished *Tomer Devorah* and encouraged people to study it. It has been reprinted recently in an expanded version, with explanations and sources, so that it is now more accessible to the average person.

Those seeking *segulahs* would be interested to know that in his approbation to the second printing of *Tomer Devorah*, the *Shelah* writes that a person who reads the work regularly is guaranteed a place in *Olam Haba* (World to Come). I know that the *segulos* we seek today are not those that require studying a deep *sefer* or emulating Hashem. It is a lot easier to immerse in the *Arizal's* mikvah (ritual bath). You go in, you go out, and you are all set. Unfortunately, life is not that simple. You won't necessarily reach *Olam Haba* by taking a shortcut through the *Arizal's* mikvah. A young man once told his *rosh yeshivah* that he had been to the *Arizal's* mikvah. He mentioned the tradition that one who immerses in that mikvah will not die without doing *teshuvah* (repentance). His *rosh yeshivah* replied, "Then you'll probably live for a very long time."

If you want a guaranteed spot in *Olam Haba*, you are better off immersing yourself in the study of Hashem's Attributes and applying them to your life.

It is impossible to conquer all of Hashem's Attributes at once. We have to examine each *Middah*, understand it, put it into practice, and move on to the next one. Let's begin with the first of the thirteen, as explained in *Tomer Devorah*.

When we think of the Thirteen Attributes, we think of the terms that appear in *Parashas Ki Sisa,* which we recite during *selichos* and in *Tachanun* (according to *nusach Sefard*): *Hashem, Hashem, kel rachum vechanun, erech apayim,* etc.

Tomer Devorah refers to these *middos* in the terms used by the Prophet Michah (*Michah* 7:18-20). You may be familiar with these terms, because we recite them yearly in *Tashlich*: *Mi Kel kamocha, nosei avon, ve'over al pasha*, etc. As you may recall, many *machzorim* and siddurim have the corresponding terms from *Parashas Ki Sisa* superimposed over these words.

Let us see how *Tomer Devorah* explains the first Attribute, *Mi Kel kamocha* (Who is like You, God), which corresponds to the first appearance of the Divine Name in *Parashas Ki Sisa*. Once we see the *Tomer Devorah's* explanation, it will become obvious that the mitzvah of *v'halachta b'drachav* is not so simple.

৺ Empowering the Enemy

Tomer Devorah points out that when a human being sins, it is only by the grace of God that he is able to do so. If he is using his hands to commit a sin, Hashem could easily immobilize his hands and stop him from sinning. As a person eats something that is not kosher, Hashem enables him to chew and swallow each morsel. Hashem does not withhold His kindness from us even when we transgress His commandments; He allows us to think, decide, and act in a manner than runs contrary to His will.

Thus, the mitzvah of *v'halachta b'drachav* requires us to benefit those who hurt us. Are you up to the challenge?

Imagine the following scenario.

> You are the sound engineer at a large public gathering. As you sit there with your hands on the dials, ensuring that the speaker is heard properly, he begins to attack you and your family. As he describes your failings and humiliates your closest family members, you feel the blood rushing to your cheeks, and you can barely restrain yourself from shutting off the microphone. To your relief, the microphone saves you from further humiliation by emitting a piercing shriek that drowns out his diatribe. Would you fix the problem? Would you enable the speaker to continue his attack?

Now, of course you will tell me that in this example you are not required to help him, because he is speaking *lashon hara*. Let's put that aside. Would you have the strength to overcome your personal shame and adjust the dial?

There are people who have wronged us. There are situations in which we have been victimized and humiliated. We are filled with righteous indignation against the sinner and we know with absolute clarity that he is wrong and we are right, in the same way that a person who sins is wrong, and Hashem is right. The mitzvah of *v'halachta b'drachav* requires us to put our feelings aside and seek ways to benefit that person.

How can we learn to emulate Hashem in this manner? It is impossible to train ourselves in one step. I would suggest working on this trait in three stages.

Step one is to heed the Torah's prohibition against revenge. If someone harms you, do not retaliate in kind. Don't mistreat those who mistreat you.

This should be followed by a second step. Remain silent when someone insults you. Even if you do not actively take revenge against one who has wronged you, it is difficult to keep quiet when you are at the receiving end of a verbal attack. (It takes years of marriage to master this feat.)

Even if you have the self-control to remain silent, you will certainly not feel that you must go out of your way to help the offender. The third step, which is certainly the most difficult of all, is to overlook the wrongdoing and continue to benefit the perpetrator as if nothing has happened.

It sounds impossible, but there have been people in recent history who have mastered this trait. Rav Yitzchok Blazer, one of the most famous disciples of Rav Yisrael Salanter, wrote an appreciation of his *rebbi*. One of the outstanding things he writes about his *rebbi* is a description of how Rav Yisrael would not bear a grudge against those who hurt him. He writes that if someone caused Rav Yisrael Salanter any sort of pain, he would immediately find a way to do a favor for that person.

I once spoke about this topic in camp. I advised the boys, "Is your bunkmate giving you a hard time? Do him a favor. Make his bed in the morning! If it happens to be his turn to sweep the floor, grab the broom and do it for him! He will be so confused that he won't know what to do!" This is *v'halachta b'drachav*.

It is hard to overlook other people's failings, especially when you are hurt. Your friends may tell you that you are right, he is wrong, and there is no reason to forgive and forget. If we look at the situation from the perspective of *v'halachta b'drachacav*, we will understand that it is worthwhile and necessary for us to overcome our instinct for revenge.

∽ Be Selfish!

*I*n *Pachad Yitzchak* (*Pesach, Ma'amar* 18), Rav Hutner notes that there are two mitzvos in the Torah governing *mitzvos bein adam l'chaveiro*: *v'ahavta lerei'acha kamocha* (Love your friend as yourself), and *v'halachta b'drachav*, the mitzvah we are now discussing. Both require us to perfect our interpersonal relationships, but there is a basic difference between the two. *Ve'ahavta lerei'acha kamocha* requires us to treat others as we would want to be treated. If Reuven hurts Shimon, the latter might say, "I would not expect to be treated well by others if I treated them the way Reuven treats me, so I do not have to treat him well." According to the principle of *v'ahavta lerei'acha kamocha*, that line of reasoning would seem to be valid.

However, *v'halachta b'drachav* is a mitzvah *bein adam l'Makom*. Your friend may not deserve your friendship. He may have wronged you time and again. Why should you benefit him? Because *you* have the mitzvah of *v'halachta b'drachav*. It is not for his sake — it is for yours. *v'halachta b'drachav* is a selfish reason to be nice to others. Don't think about whether your friend deserves a favor from you — think about whether you deserve to become Godly, to become a greater person.

There are people who walk around feeling bitter because others have wronged them. Who are they hurting? Themselves. There are those who have valid reasons to be bitter but choose to be loving and kind. They are heroic figures — true *ba'alei madreigah*. I know a woman who has been an *agunah* for many years. If anyone has a right to be bitter, she does. Yet she is one of the most loving, understanding, and compassionate people that I have ever met. Someone has sinned against her, and continues to sin against her. His actions are inexcusable, but she does not allow that to affect her relationship with the rest of the world. That is true greatness.

Recently, I went out of town to raise funds for Yeshivah Torah Vodaas. I had given my daily *shiur* in the yeshivah that morning, and then rushed to the airport and caught a midday flight. I spent the entire afternoon visiting offices and homes of the affluent donors of the community, and in the evening I attended a parlor meeting. It was a beautiful event. The people were very kind. They laughed at all of my jokes — exactly the sort of audience a speaker hopes for. By the time I got back to my host's home, it was well past midnight. To be honest, I felt a bit down. I usually spend my entire day in the *beis midrash*, and here I was running around raising funds. I knew that this was what Hashem wanted me to do, but it was still a bit depressing.

I had to rise early for the flight back to New York, but I pulled a *sefer* off the shelf so that I could learn a bit before I went to sleep. The *sefer* happened to be a biography of the Steipler Gaon. I opened it at random, to a description of the Steipler's *hasmadah* (diligence).

I read about the Steipler's total immersion in Torah. He did not stop thinking *Divrei Torah* for a single second, no matter what he was doing. His grandson once saw him engaged in a household repair and rushed forward, "I'll fix it. You can return to your learning."

"No," the Steipler responded. "While I fix things, I am still learning. I am reviewing the *Ketzos* and the *Nesivos*. If you fix it you will waste your time."

The book went on and on about his diligence, describing how he would learn as he walked from place to place and while engaged in the most mundane tasks. If I had been depressed when I began to read, I became more disheartened as I read these stories. I have news for you — maybe I should not admit it, but while engaged in fund-raising, I am not reviewing the *Ketzos* and *Nesivos*.

I thought about it some more and realized that I had no reason to be discouraged. Reading of the Steipler's level of *hasmadah* should inspire us to attain the level that each one of us can reach. Hashem knows who we are. He does not expect each of us to become the Steipler Gaon.

In what way can anyone achieve greatness? Hashem gave us the mitzvah of *v'halachta b'drachav*. With this, we are provided with a way to become great, even if we do not have the intensity to constantly think about Torah. Emulate Hashem. Don't bear grudges. Your level of Torah knowledge does not have to be on the level of the Steipler's; you don't have to have great *yichus* and you don't have to be a great genius. What you must have is the determination to perfect your character, develop self-control, and overlook grievances. Each of us can emulate Hashem, and therefore each and every one of us can achieve greatness.

܀§ "Matat"

There was a person who never died, but went up to Heaven alive. Most people will assume that I am referring to Eliyahu HaNavi, but I am actually referring to a person who was not even Jewish. His name was Chanoch, and he lived several generations before Noach.

The Torah tells us, "Chanoch walked with God; then he was no more, for God had taken him" (*Bereishis* 5:24). *Chazal* explain that Chanoch reached such an exalted level that he had no reason to die. According to an opinion cited in *Tosafos* (*Yevamos* 16b; *Chullin* 60a), Chanoch became an angel referred to as *Matatrun*. According to *Arizal,* for *kabbalistic* reasons, names of angels that do not appear in the Torah or Scripture should not be recited aloud. Although we usually rule in accordance with the revealed Torah, in the case of *Matatrun*, Rav Shlomo Zalman Auerbach ruled that we should not recite his name aloud because he is too exalted to be mentioned by name. This is why this angel is generally referred to with the shortened name "*Matat.*" *Tosafos* also cites an opinion that Chanoch is the angel known as "*Sar Ha'Olam*" (Minister of the World).

The subject of "*Matat,*" is extremely deep — and absolutely fascinating. If you want to learn more about it, you should study an exchange of letters between Rav Dessler and, *yibadel l'chaim,* his son-in-law, Rav Yehoshua Geldzheiler. These letters are printed in the fifth volume of the latter's work, *Kodshei Yehoshua.* I want to share just one of *Matat's* outstanding characteristics, as described in these letters.

There is a cryptic verse describing Moshe Rabbeinu's ascent of Mount Sinai: "To Moses He said, 'Go up to Hashem'" (*Shemos* 24:1). The "He" referred to in this verse seems to be Hashem. The Gemara (*Sanhedrin* 38a) wonders, therefore, why the verse does not read, "To Moses He said, 'Come up to *Me.*'"

The Gemara explains that the pronoun in this verse actually refers to *Matat,* "whose name is the same as his Master's." *Rashi* explains that *Matat* is also referred to as Hashem, and it was he who commanded Moshe to go up to Hashem. This is incredible! *Matat* is known as Hashem?! How can that be?

Ramban adds to our difficulty. He explains that the word "He" in this verse refers to Hashem, and the actual word Hashem, which appears in the Torah as the *shem havayah* (the four-letter, ineffable Name of Hashem), refers to Matat.

How can any other being be referred to by that Name? I don't hope to understand how this is explained in *kabbalistic* terms, but what is the basic understanding of this idea?

We find this astonishing concept elsewhere in the Torah. In *Parashas Vayishlach* (*Bereishis* 33:20), we read that Yaakov set up an altar, and proclaimed "*Kel Elokei Yisrael* (God, the God of Israel)."

It is obvious that Yaakov was not calling the altar a God, so to whom was he referring?

Rashi quotes *Chazal's* alternative explanation of this verse: it was Hashem who referred to Yaakov as *Kel* (God).

How can God's Names ever be conferred on a human?

We mentioned the view of the *Panim Yafos* that performing the order of the Thirteen Attributes means using those attributes in our own lives. When we do so, says the *Panim Yafos*, we are described by those Attributes. Hashem's Name is conferred on angels or humans when they have mastered the Attributes described by those Names.

When people are honored with a *berachah* (blessing) at a *bris* or *chasunah*, a variety of titles can be attached to their names: *Rosh Yeshivah, Rav, Admor*, etc. No one would ever think of conferring the Name of Hashem upon a human being, no matter how great that person is. If we can train ourselves to fulfill the mitzvah of *v'halachta b'drachav*, we will become worthy of having Hashem's Name attached to us in the World to Come, just as Matat did.

◆§ A Figment of the Imagination

This reward certainly makes it worthwhile for us to develop the trait of not bearing grudges. It can motivate us to forgive and forget when others hurt us, just as Hashem does. But I have a basic question on the requirement to emulate Hashem in this manner.

When a person sins against Hashem — let us say that he eats food that is not kosher or desecrates the Shabbos — does he "hurt" Hashem? Of course not! Hashem is not harmed by the actions of mortals. It is no wonder, then, that He can benefit those who violate His laws.

However, when someone insults another person, the victim suffers humiliation. When one steals from another person, the victim suffers a loss. This throws the lesson of *Tomer Devorah* into question. *Tomer Devorah* teaches that we should emulate God by not responding to those who harm us. But the comparison is incorrect! God is not harmed by those who sin against Him, but we are! How can we compare the harm done to us by others to the harm, or lack of harm, committed when someone sins against Hashem?

The answer is simple, yet surprising. The shocking reality is that people do not have the power to harm us. The *Sefer HaChinuch*, in his explanation of the prohibition against revenge, notes that no man can harm another person unless it was ordained that the victim suffer the harm.[1] The *Tomer Devorah* is therefore correct. Just as Hashem loses nothing when others sin against Him, we do not lose anything when others harm us.

I know a person who has many troubles. He was looking for a way to remain happy despite his difficulties. He was told to read the *Sha'ar HaSimchah* of the *Orchos Tzaddikim* each day. Do you know what the *Orchos Tzaddikim* writes? He writes that a person has to remind himself time and again that no one can harm him unless Hashem wills it. "Let man rejoice with the pain or harm which befalls him, for who knows the ultimate good which will result from this ...."

Bitachon is the key to the Gate of Happiness!

The Gemara tells us that a person does not hurt his finger in this world unless it was proclaimed in Heaven. If your friend was able to rob you, perhaps you were supposed to lose the money and he was merely the agent. If you were not meant to lose the money, Hashem will find a way to return it to you. The Gemara tells us that Hashem finds ways to return money that was taken unjustly.

If you can live with the constant awareness that no one can harm you, then you can learn to ignore other people's failures. You will not merely tolerate people who harm you. You will have the strength to benefit them despite the fact that they continue to treat you improperly.

Rav Pam, *zt"l*, would often say that when someone humiliates you, it is the greatest thing that could happen to you. He would quote the Chofetz Chaim as saying, "*Vei iz tzu mir az ich bin an elterer Yid, un keiner iz mir nisht mevayesh* — Woe unto me that I am an elderly Jew, and no one insults me!"

Of all of the difficulties that we can experience in this world, humiliation is the easiest to endure. Humiliation is much easier to handle than monetary loss. It is certainly easier to handle than an illness in the family.

Furthermore, when we feel offended, the insult is often a misunderstanding. Sometimes it is truly a figment of our imagination.

---

1. This is actually a *machlokes Rishonim*. We have followed the opinion of the *Rambam* and *Chinuch* (in their explanation of the prohibition against revenge), which is the opinion of the majority of *Rishonim*. There are *Rishonim* (most notably, the *Alshich*) who maintain that the free will of a human being does allow him to harm others, even if this was not preordained.

Many years ago, one of the members of our shul made a kiddush to celebrate the birth of a daughter, and his father came to participate in the *simchah*. His father is a fine person, an *ehrilche Yid*. However, his mode of dress is more casual and contemporary than the typical garb of our community. After davening, I greeted him, and we walked down to the kiddush together. There were pastries on the table, and I turned to him and said, "*Nu, machts a berachah* (lit., recite a blessing)."

To my surprise, he immediately walked away and took a seat at a different table. I could not understand what was wrong. I asked around and was informed that he was deeply offended. When I had told him "*machts a berachah*," he assumed that because of his attire I was judging him as one who would not recite a *berachah* unless prompted. I went over to him and explained that I had merely used a Yiddish expression that means, "Have a bite to eat." I told him that the expression is used even when addressing a rebbe or a *rosh yeshivah*. I could see that he was skeptical. He thought that I was merely trying to appease him.

To his credit, he called me on *Motza'ei Shabbos* to tell me that he had made inquiries. His Chassidic friends had confirmed that "*machts a berachah*" is, indeed, a common expression. He apologized for the misunderstanding, and we have had a warm relationship ever since.

Let us examine this scenario. I had not intended to embarrass this man, and the people who were standing near us did not hear anything that they would consider degrading. Only one person felt insulted. Yet, as he discovered later, it was all in his imagination.

I have news for you — every embarrassing situation is exactly the same. It is not the words that were said that cause us pain. It is our perception that causes us pain. When people are insulted, they often invoke *Chazal's* teaching that those who embarrass others do not merit a place in the World to Come. It is very important to keep that teaching in mind — so that *you* remember not to hurt other people's feelings. But if someone else insults you, the sweetest revenge is to smile and say, "Thank you." I know that it is hard, but that is what makes you Godly. That is emulating Hashem.

Opening the Gates of Torah Knowledge

I want to tell you the story of a person who was able to remain silent when he had the right to speak up, and the reward he received for it.

Rav Chizkiyahu, author of the *S'dei Chemed*, was blessed with a remarkable memory. Long before the advent of computers, he wrote an encyclopedic digest of Talmudic principles. How did he merit such phenomenal success in Torah study?

> After R' Chizkiyahu married, he studied in "R' Zorach's kollel." R' Zorach was a wealthy man who supported Torah scholars very generously, enabling them to study diligently without worrying about *parnassah* (livelihood). The *S'dei Chemed* was the most outstanding member of that kollel. His diligence and brilliance aroused great jealousy. One person in particular hated the *S'dei Chemed* with such passion that he decided to disgrace the *S'dei Chemed* in a way that would force him to leave town.
>
> R' Zorach had a non-Jewish maid who was responsible for cleaning the *Bais HaMidrash* late each evening, when the members of the kollel had left for the day. The jealous instigator knew that the *S'dei Chemed* stayed in the kollel much later than the others. He approached the maid and promised to pay her a large sum of money if she would accuse the *S'dei Chemed* of indecent behavior toward her.
>
> The woman readily agreed. The next night, shortly after the others left, she came in to clean the kollel room. Suddenly she ran out, screaming and yelling. A crowd quickly gathered, including the *S'dei Chemed's* adversary, who had stayed nearby waiting for the action to begin.
>
> She shrieked in hysteria, sobbing that the *S'dei Chemed* had attacked her. The story began to spread, spurred on by the jealous adversary. The townspeople insisted that Rav Zorach dismiss Rav Chizkiyahu. R' Zorach was not sure what to do. On the one hand, it seemed that that Rav Chizkiyahu was guilty. On the other hand, R' Zorach knew the *S'dei Chemed* well, and he had a hard time believing the rumors. He decided to fire the maid.

Unfortunately, the maid's dismissal did very little to quell the rumors.

A day or two after this incident, the man who had promised to pay her suddenly died. The maid found herself in a terrible predicament. She had no job, and she did not have the money, either. She came to the *S'dei Chemed* and offered to declare the truth publicly, if he would help her get her job back.

At first, the *S'dei Chemed* was tempted to consider her offer. The accusation had caused a great *chillul Hashem*. It would be good to clear his name. Yet, after further thought, he decided that it would cause immeasurable pain to the dead man's wife and family if the truth were revealed. He decided to remain silent.

The *S'dei Chemed* wrote that from the moment he made the decision to remain silent, forgoing the opportunity to prove his innocence, the gates of Torah knowledge opened up for him dramatically, and he was able to study with remarkable clarity.

We would never want be challenged on that level. But when we see the reward of those who remain silent when they are wronged, we realize that it is worthwhile!

When people harm us, it may seem impossible not to retaliate. If we try to remain silent for altruistic reasons, we may not succeed. If people have responded to our kindness with derision, it may seem that we do not have the strength to be gracious. Yet, if we think of ourselves, if we remember that we ourselves can benefit, that we can achieve greatness, perhaps we can have the strength to model our response after the *S'dei Chemed*. Perhaps we, too, can emulate Hashem.

✦§ The Greatest Level: Seeing the Good

The name Chanoch received when he rose to the heavens, *Matat*, is based on an Aramaic form of the root word *shomer*, a guardian.[2] What is he the guardian of?

---

[2]. This is based on *Aruch*; the Targum for *shomer* is *noter*. See also *Malachei Elyon* (by Rav Reuven Margolis), p. 85, n 57.

The Gemara teaches that Matat's eternal mission in Heaven is to record the merits of *Klal Yisrael* (*Chagigah* 15a). He is the one who came to the defense of *Klal Yisrael* and tried to convince Hashem to crown King Chizkiyahu as *Mashiach* (*Sanhedrin* 94a).

Amazing! The ultimate mission of a person in this world — the mission that was given to Chanoch in heaven after he had accomplished all that he could in this world — is to see the good in people; to see the merits of *Klal Yisrael*. A person who merits having Hashem's name attached to him, as Matat does, is someone who can see the good in everyone. He has the ability to benefit, and even to smile at, those who have wronged him.

This is the first of the thirteen levels of *v'halachtah b'drachav*. It seems incredibly difficult to master, but we have to try. If there is one place where we should start, it is in the home. Even if we cannot control ourselves in other relationships, we must learn to treat our family members with love despite their shortcomings. Is there a husband or wife in the world who cannot remember at least a few instances where he or she was mistreated or offended? It is not easy to let it pass.

As you may know, Congress has forced the president to sign a law prohibiting the use of physical duress in the interrogation of possible terrorists. However, the interrogators are allowed to speak harshly to the terrorists. I read recently that one of the interrogators complained that the new approach is not always effective. It seems that a recent detainee, clearly a married man, would respond to the harsh words of his interrogators by murmuring, "Yes, dear, you are right, dear," and dozing off.

A joke? Perhaps. But imagine the level of perfection!

People are not perfect. A natural outgrowth of human imperfection is that no matter how thoughtful a person is, there are times when he is going to do something wrong. You will be hurt sometimes, and it often comes from those you love most. Can you learn to just ignore these moments and continue as if nothing happened? "Yes, dear."

Imagine a world in which Hashem would not allow us to sin. Imagine if each time a person began to sin, he would freeze. We would all be frozen in place, and the world would cease to exist.

Just as the world cannot exist without Hashem's ability to overlook our failings, your marriage, your familial relationships, and your business cannot survive if you cannot overlook the failings of those closest to you.

It is very difficult to learn to forgive and forget, to benefit those who hurt you instead of bearing grudges. It is a trait that can take years to master.

Approximately ten years ago, I gave a *shiur* on *dikduk* (the grammar of *Lashon Kodesh*). *Dikduk* is a subject that some people love and some people hate. After the *shiur*, several people told me that if I ever planned to give another *shiur* on *dikduk*, I should please warn them not to attend. I told them that I would not give another one for at least a decade, for fear of losing the audience.

There are Thirteen Attributes of Hashem. In this essay, we have discussed the first one. It seems that it will take us many years to achieve this level. Shall I wait another decade to discuss about the second attribute? If we allow a decade for each Attribute, we will not get to all of them, even if we reach 120. I don't know when we will be ready to tackle the next trait, but for now, let us try to work on this one. Let's try to overlook other people's failings and see their merits, so that we, too, can have Hashem's Name attached to us for all eternity.

Judging Others

One of the sources for the mitzvah of emulating Hashem[1] is the verse in which Yirmiyahu tells the wicked King Yehoyakim, "If one does justice to the poor and destitute, then it is good; *is this not 'knowing Me'?*" (*Yirmiyahu* 22:16).

Toras Avraham (written by one of the pre-Holocaust *roshei yeshivah* of Slabodka) points out that in this context, "knowing Hashem" does not refer to the philosophical knowledge of Hashem's existence. Rather, it refers to "knowing Hashem" by understanding His Attributes, the ways by which Hashem chooses to reveal Himself to human beings. Yirmiyahu was telling Yehoyakim to learn how Hashem acts, so that he could emulate Him and mirror His justice, kindness, mercy, and righteousness.

A difficult question arises when we view the mitzvah of emulating Hashem from the perspective of this verse in *Yirmiyahu*.

Just two verses later, Yirmiyahu relates a stern prophecy to the King: "Therefore, thus says Hashem concerning Yehoyakim son of Yoshiyahu, King of Judah: They will not lament for him: 'Woe, my

---

1. This is a mitzvah *d'Oraysa*. This was discussed, in depth, in the previous *shiur*, "Emulating Hashem."

brother!' or 'Woe, I was his sister!' They will not lament for him, 'Woe, master,' or 'Woe, his majesty!' With the burial of a donkey will he be buried — dragged and thrown beyond the gates of Jerusalem" (ibid., 22:18-19).

The Talmud (*Sanhedrin* 82a; 104a) tells us a fascinating story regarding Yehoyakim's burial.

> R' Preidah's grandfather lived during the era of the second *Beis HaMikdash,* centuries after the death of Yehoyakim. He was once walking near the gates of Jerusalem, and he found a human skull with the words, "*Zos ve'od acheres*" inscribed on it. He took the skull and buried it. As soon as he finished the burial, the skull resurfaced above ground. He buried it again, and again it resurfaced. "This must be the skull of Yehoyakim," he reasoned, "upon which [the prophet] said, 'With the burial of a donkey will he be buried — dragged and thrown beyond the gates of Jerusalem.'"[2]
>
> *This is the skull of a king,* R' Preidah's grandfather thought. *It is improper for him to suffer such indignity.* He took the skull, wrapped it in a garment, and stored it in his house, in a special box in which he kept his personal possessions.
>
> One day, while cleaning the house, his wife chanced upon this human skull in her husband's box. She ran out of the house and told her neighbor what she had found. Why would her husband save a human skull among his personal items?
>
> "Hmm ..." her neighbor said. "You are his second wife, aren't you? That skull must be that of first wife, whom he simply cannot forget."
>
> The explanation made sense to Mrs. Preidah. It disturbed her to think that her husband was still thinking about his first wife. The more she thought about it, the angrier she became. She lit a big fire and threw the skull into it. When her husband came home and found out what had transpired, he said, "Now I understand. This is the meaning of '*Zos ve'od acheres.*' Not only did Yehoyakim's skull resist burial, but it also suffered the humiliation of cremation."

---

2. People do not bother to dig a deep grave for a deceased donkey. They just put it into a pit and cover it with a little bit of earth. Before long, dogs smell the meat and dig up the grave to eat the donkey. R' Preida's grandfather surmised that Yehoyakim had been condemned to a similar fate — his skull would not remain buried in the ground for any length of time.

We learn from this passage how Yirmiyahu's prophesy came true; Yehoyakim was disgraced posthumously for his wicked behavior. His skull rolled around near the gates of Jerusalem for some 500 years and was then burned.

The appearance of this prophecy immediately following the command to emulate Hashem leads us to consider the following question.

We are commanded to emulate Hashem. Just as Hashem shows kindness to people, even if they have sinned, so should we. We know that Hashem is also *ma'arich af* — He waits for people to repent, and only punishes them for their sins when they do not do *teshuvah*. We look to emulate this as well.

Still, a person is ultimately punished for every sin he committed for which he did not repent. In fact, the Talmud (*Bava Kama* 50b) teaches that it is absolutely wrong for us to say that Hashem allows people to sin without retribution. There is an accounting for each and every deed.

If we are required to emulate Hashem's Attributes, are we also required to emulate Him by punishing others in the manner that He punished Yehoyakim? Is the Attribute of Justice, by punishing those who hurt us, also included in the mitzvah of *v'halachta b'drachav*? Granted, we would have to give them time to repent, but once we determine that there is no hope of repentance, must we punish them?

Furthermore, King David described Hashem as, "*Kel nekamos* — God of vengeance" (*Tehillim* 94:1). If we are supposed to emulate Hashem's Attributes, why does the Torah prohibit us from taking revenge on those who hurt us?

Similarly, we find the term, "*vayichar af*" ascribed to Hashem in several places. There are times that Hashem reacts with the Attribute of Anger. Are there times that we are required to become angry?

◆§ Don't Be Judge and Jury

Maharal (*Sotah* 14a) explains that the mitzvah of *v'halachta b'drachav* applies only to those Attributes that are related to *rachamim*, the mercy and kindness that we are required to extend to others. The mitzvah does not include the requirement to judge or to punish others.

This begs explanation. Why not emulate every *middah* of Hashem?

V'halachta b'drachav certainly sounds like a blanket instruction to follow all of Hashem's attributes.

Maharal explains that we cannot mete out justice as Hashem does. We are unable to judge accurately, as only He can. We simply do not have the tools that would enable us to assess each person's actions, to understand his motivations, or to appreciate his unique situation.

When it comes to *chesed*, it is hard go wrong. Most situations are fairly straightforward. But when it comes to judging others, *emes* is elusive. How easy it is to misjudge a person's actions and intentions! It is more likely than not that we will judge other people unfairly. Therefore, even if we did judge people, we would not be emulating Hashem.

Even the Sanhedrin, which is charged with judging people, is limited by the Torah's guidelines for a Court of Law. Only in the rarest of cases is punitive action actually taken by a Sanhedrin.

When we are angry at someone who has harmed us, it is usually because we are judging that person. When we vent our frustration, we say, "He should have known better," "She's always out to get me," "They never think about others — only about themselves."

Can we really judge who should have known better, whether someone was acting intentionally when he wronged us, or whether he was being selfish?

Now, if you are a teacher, you may be required to judge your students in order to ensure that you are teaching them properly. But otherwise, why judge other people? You may disapprove of the person's actions, but why judge them?

> There is an old Jewish joke about two people who come to a rav with a dispute. One man presents his argument. The rav thinks a moment and says, "You know, you are right." His adversary presents his argument. Again, the rav thinks a bit and says, "You know, you are right."
>
> The rebbetzin, upon overhearing this conversation, calls out to her husband, "They can't both be right!"
>
> The rav thinks for a moment and says, "You, too, are right!"

This story is often told as a joke, but I don't think that it is a joke. I think that it is an ideal.

If the rav had been a *dayan* (Rabbinical court judge) who was called upon to render a halachic ruling regarding a monetary dispute, it would be inappropriate to tell both parties that they are right. But if a person is not a *dayan*, what is wrong with perceiving the validity of each viewpoint? This side is right, and that side is right. Each viewpoint has its merits.

Rav Yitzchak Hutner (*Pachad Yitzchak* to *Rosh Hashanah, Maamar* 31) explains the *Maharal* on a deeper level.

"By its very essence, the act of judgment is not within the power of a human being. The Torah states clearly, 'For the judgment is God's' (*Devarim* 1:17). Who are we to judge other people? Even in the case of a *Din Torah*, in which the *dayanim* must render judgment, the Torah states, 'God stands in the assembly' (*Tehillim* 82:1). It is entirely inappropriate for human beings to render judgment unless they are acting as agents of the Supreme Judge."

Rav Hutner adds that this idea is the basis for an interesting Halachah. True *semichah* (Rabbinic ordination) can be traced all the way back to Moshe Rabbeinu, who was ordained by Hashem. The Talmud teaches us that only a judge who has true *semichah* may judge a case in which there is some sort of penalty. To rule on *Yoreh De'ah* issues — whether a chicken is kosher or *treif*, for instance — one does not need to have *semichah*. To answer a question regarding the permissibility of an action on Shabbos, one does not need *semichah*. To decide a case which could require a *knas* (punitive payment) or in which there is the possibility of *makkos* (lashes) or a death sentence, one must have *semichah* that can be traced back to the *Shechinah*. Why?

The responsibility to determine punishment is not ours, explains Rav Hutner. It is the sole responsibility of Hashem. Only someone whose ordination can be traced all the way back to Hashem can decide who should be punished, because he acts as an agent of Hashem.

V'halachta b'drachav does not apply in the case of punishment, because we are not commanded to judge other people. Hashem is the Creator. Are we expected to emulate Hashem in this regard? Can we create? Of course not! We have no commandment to create, so we do not need to emulate that attribute of Hashem. The same is true regarding judgment. We have no commandment to judge others, so we do not emulate Hashem by judging people.

►§ How To Live Happily

Maharal and Rav Hutner clear us of the obligation to judge people. However, we are *machmir*. We act *lifnim meshuras hadin*! We excel in judging others. We delight in judging others. We are quite active in evaluating people, examining their motives and assessing their level of guilt.

How much anguish we cause ourselves! It happens; people do things that hurt us. Neighbors, friends, relatives, even husbands and wives sometimes cause each other pain. We are angry and disappointed. If this continues, we are in danger of becoming bitter, unhappy people.

Somehow, when the difficulties in life are placed upon us by Hashem — whether it is in the realm of *parnassah*, health, or *shidduchim* — we can be strong and find ways to accept and to cope. However, when pain is inflicted upon us by other people, it is harder to accept because we consider it avoidable.

Let me share a bit of advice. If you want to live a happy, peaceful life, don't judge people.

Let's look at a hypothetical case. You live in a two-family house. Your upstairs neighbor gets up each morning at the crack of dawn. It seems that he just joined the early *daf yomi shiur*, and you have to suffer. As he wakes up early, your sleep is disturbed by the banging, crashing, and thudding overhead. Your complaints do not help.

You have two choices. You can judge him. *That scoundrel,* you can think to yourself. *He deliberately makes as much noise as possible just to make sure that I know he's awake.* You can look at him venomously each time he walks out of his house, surreptitiously examining him to see if he is developing a set of horns to go along with his vicious persona. Do you know what will happen? You will wake up an hour or two before him each morning, and wait with tension and anger for the stomping to begin — while he slumbers peacefully in his bed. You will condemn yourself to a life of misery.

If you want to be happy, don't judge him. Try to discuss the issue calmly. Tell him that you are a light sleeper. Ask him to tiptoe. Suggest a carpet or an area rug. If none of this works, in worst-case scenario, join the same *daf yomi*. But don't judge him.

Suppose you married off a child, and your *mechutanim* are not as generous to the couple as you are. You find yourself shouldering the lion's burden of the expenses and the other side is simply not doing its share. How do you react? If you want to walk around in a miserable mood, judge them. Think, *They are tight-fisted people. I should have known from the shidduch information that I received that they were not nice. I felt bad vibes from the first time I met them ....*

If you want to be happy, simply accept the reality of the situation. You have no idea what is going on in their bank account. Be grateful that you can give, and ignore what they do.

One more example: Your married son doesn't call as often as you would like him to. To make matters worse, when he does finally call, his wife rarely bothers to say hello.

If you want to be miserable, sit down with your spouse and vent. Talk harshly about your son. Talk about how unappreciative and ungrateful he is. That will bring you to one level of misery.

If you really want to become depressed, take your anger one step further. Call your son over to your house, and tell him that his wife is inconsiderate. That will guarantee some truly joyful exchanges. That will really give you peace of mind. Everything will be just wonderful from then on!

You want to be happy? Don't judge people. Just tell yourself, "People make mistakes. What can I do; not everyone is as perfect as I am!"

Rabbi Shimon Diskin, one of the *roshei yeshivah* of Yeshivah Kol Torah, was approached by parents regarding a prospective *shidduch* for their daughter. Their daughter had met a young *talmid* of Kol Torah several times, and everything seemed perfect. The boy had fine character traits, he learned with *hasmadah*, and he was graced with *yiras Shamayim*. What was the issue?

"The boy," complained the girl's father, "does not learn with enough depth for my taste. He covers a lot of ground; he knows many *masechtos*, but only superficially. He cannot answer my questions on the *sugya*. Do you think that we should go through with the *shidduch*?"

"It is a wonderful *shidduch*," replied Rav Diskin, "He is an outstanding young man. Go through with the *shidduch*, but on one condition — that they live far away from you!

"If you are already judging his learning, there is no way that the couple can live near you."

Maharal has taught us that we have no business judging people. Not only is it wrong to judge others, not only is it not constructive, not only does it make us miserable — but it also threatens our ability to get along with others. For your own sake, make the decision. Never judge anyone.

➳ Don't Be an Executioner

There is another important lesson in the juxtaposition of these verses in *Yirmiyahu*. Don't be a judge; neither should you be an executioner.

Many people feel that those who wrong them must suffer the consequences. They can't let anything slide. Some might blame it on *v'halachta b'drachav*. Hashem doesn't permit people to sin without suffering consequences (they reason), so neither should we. Most people don't base it on anything. They simply feel that it is a fair way to behave.

If judging people will make you miserable, you can add to your misery by adding punitive measures. For example, when you finish berating your son about his wife's derelictions, you can ensure that he never talks to you again by adding some kind of punishment. Tell your son, "Until your wife starts calling, we will no longer help you financially." You will get your anger out of your system, and destroy everything you have worked for in the process.

But aside from the practical damage to our relationships that we cause by punishing people, is there something objectively wrong with it? Hashem punishes, so why shouldn't we?

There is a version of *Tomer Devorah* published with a commentary named *V'halachta B'drachav*. The author cites a critical teaching from *Nefesh HaChaim* (*Sha'ar* 1), which also appears in Rav Tzaddok's *Takanas HaShavin*.

It may appear to us that God metes out punishment. This is not really accurate. God never punishes. Period. Hashem fixes. He repairs the damage that our sins have wrought. This may sometimes require pain and difficulty. But there is never punishment for the sake of punishment.

Now don't get me wrong. If a person spends his entire life trying to extract as much physical pleasure from this world as possible and does not spend any time studying Torah, he will not be able to enjoy *Olam Haba*. Our reward in *Olam Haba* will be a form of spiritual pleasure that will eclipse all the physical pleasures of this world, but it can only be appreciated by those who have trained themselves to appreciate it. Those who haven't studied Torah in this world will feel embarrassed in the Next World. It may feel like punishment, but it is not a punishment that will be meted out by the Heavenly Court — it will be a direct consequence of the person's lack of foresight in this world.

Hashem does not punish? What about the difficulties that we experience in this world?

Our suffering in this world is not punishment for the sake of punishment — it is our chance to repair the damage we have done to our souls, so we can be worthy of reward in *Olam Haba*.

Nefesh HaChaim and *Takanas HaShavin* are works of *machshavah*. This novel insight appears appropriate for this type of *sefer*.

Interestingly, the *posek* of our generation, Rav Moshe Feinstein, *zt"l*, (in *Darash Moshe*) proves this idea from a halachic standpoint.

There is a rule in the Talmud that *"Ein onshin min hadin* — we do not punish based on *kal v'chomer (a fortiori* argument)."

Let's say that the Torah considers a certain action, which we will call Action A, to be a sin, and states that a person who commits that sin is punished by receiving lashes. If there is another action — Action B — that is clearly worse than Action A, the logic of *kal vachomer* dictates that it is certainly a sin and should certainly bear the punishment of lashes. Nevertheless, *ein onshin min hadin* teaches us that we may not subject someone guilty of Action B to lashes, because this punishment is derived by a *kal v'chomer.*

What is the logic to this restriction? It certainly seems correct to subject a person guilty of Action B to this punishment. Why should he get off with no punishment at all?

Maharshah explains that the Torah tells us to lash a person who commits Action A only because those lashes will atone for his sin. Action B is a more serious sin and we do not know that lashes are enough to wipe away this sin. The punishment is therefore not given.

Now, if we were to understand that punishments need not be constructive, that they are simply a consequence of a sin, this would make no sense. If Hashem punishes people, then why not subject someone who transgresses Action B to lashes, just to punish him? We see, writes Rav Moshe, that Hashem does not punish for punishment's sake, but only as a means of repairing the sin.

This may sound technical, but let me illustrate this with a story that I remember from my teenage years.

One of my friends in yeshivah received a ticket for going through a red light, but not in the traditional style — he had backed out of a block through a red light.

This fellow had a great idea. He was going to go to traffic court and plead innocent, on the grounds that the law only prohibits going *forward* through a red light. It does not say anywhere that you are not allowed to go through a red light in reverse!

I don't remember what the verdict was, but somehow I doubt that the judge bought his claim. There is no need for a law that prohibits one from backing through a red light, because it is clearly worse than going forward.

Now let's assume that the ticket for going forward through a red light is $250. The law does not prescribe any sort of punitive measures for those caught reversing through a red light, but logic dictates that his ticket should be for a minimum of $250.

If traffic laws were Torah-ordained, we would not be able to punish someone who backs through a red light based on this logic. Heavenly punishments are not deterrents or punitive measures — they are meant to repair, and if they cannot repair the damage, there is no reason to make a person suffer.

We would certainly prohibit people from backing through red lights, but we could not know that the $250 punishment is adequate.

Ironically, the story of King Yehoyakim's skull is another example of this concept. The Mishnah (*Sanhedrin* 90a) lists seven people who have no portion in the World to Come. Three of those people were kings: Yeravam, Achav, and Menasheh. The Talmud (*Sanhedrin* 104a) wonders why Yehoyakim — who was apparently as wicked as the other three — is not listed. Why did he merit a portion in *Olam Haba*?

Let us return to our original question. We cited the burning of Yehoyakim's skull, which certainly seemed like Heavenly punishment to us, and we wondered why *v'halachta b'drachav* does not require us to punish people who hurt us. The Talmud turns our question into an answer. The Talmud states that the indignity Yehoyakim suffered, having his skull languish at the gates of Jerusalem for 500 years and then being burned, atoned for his sins. Hashem did not punish him; He repaired Yehoyakim's sins so that he could merit a portion in the World to Come.

Hashem does not punish. Hashem does not destroy. Hashem does not break. Hashem repairs. What happens when you become not only a judge, but also a punisher? What happens when you are angry at someone and you raise your voice? Or you label them with a less-than-complimentary adjective? Are you repairing? I don't think so.

Go over to someone who has just given his son a lecture in which he degraded his daughter-in-law. Ask him, "Were you repairing the problem?"

What will he answer? "No, but she deserves it."

That is punishing. That's breaking. That's foolish.

Even if you are going to misuse *v'halachta b'drachav* and judge others, don't punish. Your punishment will only cause damage and Hashem doesn't do damage. He repairs.

~§ "I Only Want an Apology"

*P*unishment is not the only method of breaking people and ruining relationships. When people are in a dispute, you will often hear one of them say, "All I want is an apology.

Just apologize."

This happens all the time — a parent will demand an apology from a child or a child-in-law, or a husband from his wife.

Rav Pam often spoke about the foolishness, the destructiveness of this approach. I heard him say time and again that people should not demand a verbal or written apology. He felt that demanding an apology is degrading. It breaks the person; it does not repair the damage.

Let me clarify — Rav Pam was not suggesting that someone who hurt someone else should not apologize. If the wrongdoer had come to him for advice, he would certainly have advised him to apologize. But he did not feel that an apology should be demanded. What do people really mean when they say, "All I want is an apology"?

"All I want is that he should come to me, and blush. Let him feel ashamed. That's all. I don't want anything else."

And when the person does humble himself by apologizing, the person at the receiving end will often say, "That was not a sincere apology. It didn't seem as if he really meant it."

This may seem harsh, but it is what demanding an apology is all about. It breaks; it does not repair.

A good friend of mine is a psychologist. When he began to deal with family issues, he would listen to the couple describe the problem and he would try to figure out who was right. He would put in much effort to convince the one who was wrong to see the matter from the correct perspective. Somehow, he wasn't having much success.

So he became smarter. He realized that it does not matter who is right. He now tries to figure out who is more reasonable about the issues at hand. He now uses his skills and persuasive powers to get the reasonable party to give in.

Is that fair? The spouse who is more reasonable can ask, "Why should I give in? I am right. Let him give in! Why should the obstinate one come out ahead?"

The answer is that therapy is not punishment. It is an attempt to repair a damaged relationship. How do you repair a problem? By finding the approach that is most likely to work. You don't figure out who is right. You figure out who is most capable of eliminating the problem.

The same applies to all of life's problems. Don't punish people. Don't demand apologies. Remember, Hashem does not punish; he repairs. If you want to emulate Hashem, make sure that you are repairing, not breaking.

Judging Others II: Judging Yourself

◄§ Accept Bribes!

What if you can't resist? By nature, you find yourself judging others, and you often feel an urge to punish those who wronged you. If you forget the *Maharal* and decide to blame your urge on *v'halachta b'drachav*, you should at least emulate the way the Heavenly court operates.

Is a judge allowed to take a bribe? Of course not.

Does Hashem accept bribes? The *Talmud* (*Berachos* 20b) states that the angels challenged the Torah's description of Hashem as "the great mighty and awesome God, who does not show favor and who does not accept a bribe" (*Devarim* 10:12). This seems to be contradicted by the verse in *Bircas Kohanim*, through which *Klal Yisrael* is blessed with the Biblical blessing, asking that Hashem favor them (*Bamidbar* 6:26).

Hashem responded, "How can I refuse to favor *Klal Yisrael*? I told them that they should recite *Bircas HaMazon* only when they eat enough food to feel satisfied, and they go beyond the call of duty and *bentch* even when they eat as little as a *k'zayis* or *k'beitzah* [an olive- or egg-sized piece of bread]!"

In other words, Hashem accepts certain types of bribes. He shows favoritism to those who go beyond the call of duty.

Someone told me a joke about a man who comes to the World of Truth and finds a long line to get into Gan Eden. He goes to the back of the line. After a while he becomes impatient. He calls a *malach* (angel) aside and says, "I've been waiting 120 years to get into Gan Eden. I don't want to wait any longer. I'll give you a few dollars to get me to the front of the line."

"How much?" asks the *malach*.

"I'll give you $1,000," says the man.

"$1,000?" asks the *malach* incredulously. "That's nothing!"

The man waits a few more minutes, and the line just does not seem to be moving. He calls the *malach* over to him again and says, "I'll give you $10,000."

"Sorry," says the *malach*. "$10,000 will not get you to the front of the line."

Half an hour later, the man calls the *malach* over once again and says, "I'll give you $100,000."

"Okay," says the *malach*. "For $100,000 I can get you to the front of the line." The man pulls out his checkbook and starts to write out a check for $100,000.

"You want to give me a check?" asks the *malach*. "We don't accept checks up here. In Heaven we only accept *receipts*."

Here's the secret. This is not such a joke. It is true. There are ways of "bribing" the Heavenly Court. Congress passed a law that you have to have a receipt for a donation that exceeds $250. Now you'll have something to do with the receipts. You can't take your money with you, but if you want to bribe Hashem or the *malachim*, ask your children to bury you with your receipts. You can bribe the *Beis Din shel Ma'alah* (Heavenly Court).

How about you? Do you accept bribes?

Let us say that you have a dispute with a long-time friend, a relative, or someone else to whom you should feel indebted. You have valid complaints against them. You have already judged them as guilty. Before you punish them, consider the "bribes" they have given you. Think about the amount of love and kindness they have showered upon you. Think about all the good memories. Why not accept the fond memories as a bribe and forgive the person?

Not only does Hashem accept bribes from the person being judged, Hashem will apply the merits of a person's father and forefathers as well.

How about you? If the defendant comes from a family that you are close to, why not accept the close relationship as a bribe?

Can a person be angry at his husband or wife? After all, your spouse agreed to marry you. Remember how all the others didn't want marry you, and you finally found someone who said *yes*? Shouldn't that serve as a bribe?

The Talmud (*Yevamos* 63a) relates that Rav Chiya had a terrible wife. Did he judge her? Did he punish her? No. Whenever he found something that he knew she would like, he would bring it home for her. He would say, "It is enough that they [i.e., our wives] raise our children and protect us from sin."

Before you punish your wife, remember how many diapers she has changed. Apply them to her account. Accept all her favors as a bribe.

We started with the plan of understanding why *v'halachta b'drachav* does not apply to judging people, but we really come away with a guide to happy living. Don't judge, don't punish — and accept bribes.

≈§ The Last Resort

If these three lessons are not enough, if you find yourself judging, punishing, and unmoved by bribery, there is still something that might help. As a last resort, remember this incredible teaching of the *Ba'al Shem Tov*, which is cited in many Chassidic works.

The *Mishnah* states that on Judgment Day, "*Nifra'in min ha'adam mida'ato v'shelo mida'ato* — they collect from a person, with his knowledge and without his knowledge" (*Avos* 3:20).

What does that mean? A person will either know that they are collecting from him, or he will not know. How can he both know and not-know?

Another question: *Chazal* tell us that on Judgment Day we are going to face a *din v'cheshbon*, a ruling and an accounting. The two aspects of the judgment seem to be listed out of order. Shouldn't *Beis Din shel Ma'alah* first make an accounting and then give forth a ruling?

The *Ba'al Shem Tov* answers these questions by describing what will happen to us during our final judgment.

> We will ascend to the Heavens and they will say, "Ahh! R' Yitzchak, we have been waiting for someone of your stature to come along. We need another *dayan* in the next room. Can you please sit in on the court?"
>
> "Me?" you are going to wonder. "I am not good enough to sit on *Beis Din shel Ma'alah*."

"Sure you are," they will say. "Here, take a tallis, and go to the next room."

You will sit with the other *dayanim*, all ready to act as a judge. What sort of sins are we dealing with in our community? Hopefully, nothing too serious. They will bring a Jew before you and say, "This person double-parked on a Friday afternoon on Avenue J and caused thirty people to suffer. Judge him."

"Double-parked on Avenue J?" you will exclaim. "That's terrible!" You will throw the book at him. You are the judge now, and you can get rid of all the frustration that people caused you in *Olam Hazeh*.

Then they will say, "He also yelled at his wife." As proof, they will play a video of his wife crying, distraught because her husband berated her. You are going to say, "What an awful husband! He deserved to be punished."

Finally, when you are all finished judging, they will tell you, "R' Yitzchak, *atah ha'ish*. The man we are judging is you. Do you remember the time you double-parked on Avenue J? And the time that you raised your voice and made your wife feel bad: Do you remember how distraught she was?"

The final judgment is *mida'ato*, explains the *Ba'al Shem Tov*, because a person chooses his own sentence, but it is *shelo mida'ato*, because he does not realize that he is judging himself.

The *din* will come first: "Double-parking on Avenue J — that's terrible!" Then they will make a *cheshbon* of all the times that we were the guilty party.

There are those who wish to quibble with this point. The little trick that *Beis Din shel Ma'alah* employs will work on everyone, they say, except for those who have heard this *shiur*.

You know the trick. You will come up to *Beis Din shel Ma'alah*, and they will say, "We need a *dayan* in the other room. Can you sit in on the court?"

"Sure," you will say. "I can serve as a *dayan*."

They will send you next door, bring someone in, and say, "This man double-parked on Avenue J on a Friday afternoon."

You will jump to his defense: "He just had to run into a store for a couple of seconds."

"A couple of seconds?" the prosecuting angel will argue. "He left his car double-parked for fifteen minutes."

"All right, a couple of seconds turned into fifteen minutes," you will argue. "It wasn't his fault. Besides, he was doing a mitzvah, getting food for Shabbos. He should be allowed into Gan Eden."

Then they will tell you, "*Atah ha'ish!*"

You will say, "Oh! I'm so surprised! It's good that I just ruled that a person who double-parked is not guilty."

Why do we have to avoid judging people in this world — can't we can just avoid judging them in *Beis Din shel Ma'alah*?

The answer to this question comes from the *Beis HaLevi* (*Parashas Vayigash*), who teaches us the *Ba'al Shem Tov's* concept with a little twist.

The *Beis HaLevi* writes that we don't wait until after 120 to be pulled into a courtroom to judge people. The Talmud (*Shabbos* 127b) tells us, "*Hadan chaveiro l'kaf zechus, danin oso l'kaf zechus* — someone who judges his fellows favorably is judged favorably [in Heaven]."

We won't be able to save ourselves by avoiding judgment in Heaven, says the *Beis HaLevi*. We have to judge people favorably in this world. When you are driving down Avenue J this Friday, and someone double-parks and you can't get by, just remember — you are wearing the tallis. You think you are judging the man who double-parked? You are judging yourself!

When you talk about someone who speaks harshly to his spouse and you judge him, when someone rises early for *daf yomi* and wakes you up and you judge him — who are you judging? You are judging yourself. When you ascend to the Heavens on the Judgment Day, they will replay the judgment you rendered here on earth and they will tell you, "*Atah ha'ish!*"

Some will say that the same objection to the strategy of the *Ba'al Shem Tov* applies to this teaching of the *Beis HaLevi*. You know the secret methods of *Beis Din shel Ma'alah*. Next time you see someone doing something wrong, all you have to do is remember that by condemning him you are condemning yourself, and you will have an easy time on Judgment Day.

The answer is: yes, you know the secret. You know it. But it is not so easy to implement it. The *yetzer hara* does not make it easy. When someone does something wrong to you, it seems impossible to maintain self-control and good judgment. You become annoyed, you feel stressed out, and your guard is down. That is when it becomes crucial to remember this secret and avoid judging others.

Indeed! You do know the secret. Make it work for you.

If all the other reasons not to judge people were insufficient, it seems worthwhile to train ourselves to avoid pronouncing judgment, lest we condemn ourselves on Judgment Day.

Sha'ar HaSimchah

When I visit Eretz Yisrael in the summer, I usually daven and learn at Yeshivas Ohr Same'ach. Towards the end of my recent visit, I was asked to speak in the yeshivah. My topic was *bitachon* (faith).

The theme of my *shmuess* was that the *middah* of *bitachon* can enable us to overcome difficulties and find happiness. I was trying to come up with an appropriate anecdote with which to begin the *shiur*.

> This talk took place on a Tuesday evening. Tuesday morning, is *sponja* day at Ohr Same'ach. After davening, the chairs are raised onto the tables and everyone vacates the *beis midrash* to allow the maintenance men to clean the floors.
>
> I stepped out of the *beis midrash* and returned a short while later to see if the *sponja* was finished. For those of you who have never witnessed the process of *sponja*, it involves sloshing huge quantities of water on the floor, and then forc-

ing the water into a drain with something that looks like a windshield wiper on a stick. It is often difficult to figure out whether you are looking at the room before *sponja* or after, so when I returned, I asked one of the *sponja* men if he was finished.

"*Baruch Hashem*," he responded.

I was surprised, because this man did not seem to be Jewish, let alone religious. Out of curiosity, I asked, "*Mah zeh 'Baruch Hashem'* [What does '*Baruch Hashem*' mean]?"

"When you want to say 'yes' *besimchah* [joyfully]," he responded, "you say, '*Baruch Hashem*.'"

Apparently, this is what he absorbed by simply watching people's faces as they talk. The expression "*Baruch Hashem*" is a phrase that had no meaning to him. But he understood from its context that it is a joyful response. Incredible!

"*Baruch Hashem*" is a phrase that all Jews have on the tip of their tongues. It is an expression of our *bitachon* in Hashem. It is a statement of gratitude and acceptance. And, as the *sponja* man in Ohr Some'ach noticed, faith in Hashem enables us to find happiness in our lives.

When I was a young *bachur* in Yeshivah Torah Vodaas, Rav Pam, zt"l, once saw me learning *Mesillas Yeshorim*. He told me that the *Mesillas Yeshorim* was not appropriate for me at that stage of my life, and he suggested that I learn *Orchos Tzaddikim* instead.

So I began to learn *Orchos Tzaddikim*, and eventually I came to the ninth *sha'ar*, the *Sha'ar HaSimchah* (Gateway to Happiness). The *Orchos Tzaddikim* has a unique approach to living a happy life. He teaches that faith — and faith alone — is the key to happiness. The second half of the *Sha'ar HaSimchah* contains practical strategies for acquiring *bitachon*, for only through *bitachon* can we attain *simchah*. Let us see how these strategies can help us cope with the difficult and painful challenges of our lives.

✥ What Bothers You Most?

The *Mishnah* in *Avos* (4:1) states "*Eizehu ashir? Hasamei'ach b'chelko* — Who is rich? He who is happy with his lot." *Orchos Tzaddikim* explains that a person who is happy with his lot is rich *even if he knows that he is poor,* because he is happy that *Hashem* is his lot. A person who has faith in God's ability to help is always happy.

When I am in Eretz Yisrael, I attend the *shmuessen* of Rav Mordechai Druk, a well known *maggid* in Jerusalem. He often talks about the *Olam HaSheker* (the phony world) in which we live, calling it a massive "bluff," the "bluff" of the *yetzer hara* (evil inclination); the "bluff" that causes us to feel sad.

"Be aware, it is all '*a groiseh* bluff.'"

If we take an honest look at many of the problems that get us down, we will realize that many of these problems are not real. The perceived difficulties are most often an illusion; certainly the perceived seriousness of a situation is always overstated. In fact, our bouts of despondency often originate with the lies of the *yetzer hora*.

Let's take the example of a *bachur* studying in yeshivah. He's depressed because he's not learning well enough. He is frustrated by his inability to achieve the level that he dreams of.

I remember — with some sadness — the ninth-grader who made an appointment to speak to me. He came to the *Beis HaMidrash* at Yeshivah Torah Vodaas at lunchtime, sat down, and with tears in his eyes confessed, "I can't take notes in *shiur*. It just doesn't go."

He was crying over his inability to take notes in *shiur*! I must admit that at first I felt a bit jealous. He was genuinely sad that he could not learn as well as he wanted to. It was really depressing him, and it was extremely difficult to comfort him. What a level! How *chashuv* those tears must have been in the eyes of heaven!

But, of course, he did not see it that way. He saw a world of bluff ....

When I recalled that meeting later on, I realized something strange.

Many people in our generation merit to spend the first thirty years of their lives studying Torah, first in yeshivah and then in kollel. They spend the next thirty years working, trying to earn a livelihood and raise their families.

Typically, then, during the first thirty years there is more *ruchnius* in our lives. We spend more hours each day in direct service of Hashem. During the next thirty years, there is less *ruchnius*. Most of the day is spent in the business world.

The reverse is true when it comes to *gashmius* (materialistic pursuits). When a kollel *yungerman* first gets married, he has very little in the way of *gashmius*. Later, when he leaves the kollel and enters the business world, he will usually attain a higher standard of material comfort.

It would seem logical that, at each stage in life, a person would tend to become depressed over what he lacks most. Doesn't that make sense?

If a kollel *yungerman* were to be sad or depressed, we should assume that this is because he does not have enough money to cover his expenses. Perhaps he feels anxious because he doesn't know what he will do for a living, or because he cannot afford to buy a house. This would be a natural sort of challenge.

On the other hand, if a person is working and feeling sad, we would assume that his depression is because he is not able to spend so much time in the *Beis HaMidrash*. One would expect him to worry about maintaining his relationship with Hashem. He should worry that he is only able to attend a *Daf Yomi shiur* and that he cannot keep good notes, or that his mind wanders, or that he forgets his learning because he has no time to review it.

Yet, most often, the opposite is true! It's truly amazing. Those who are in high school, *beis midrash*, or kollel become depressed because they cannot learn as well as they would want to.

Those who are in the working world, in the second set of thirty years, rarely get depressed over their learning. At that stage of life, people complain that business is tough, they have too many businesses, or that they are worried about their investments. A friend came to me during a stock market crash and told me that he is terribly depressed because he lost three-quarters of a million dollars in the market in one week.

"*Oif mir gezugt* [the same should be said about me]!" I tried to console him. "At least *you* probably have another three-quarters of a million dollars still in the market."

His worries are about the market!

Why is this so? Why are the issues that worry people the opposite of what we would logically expect?

Because it is all "*a groiseh* bluff."

Depression is rarely rooted in reality. It is not based on what is missing in your life. The *yetzer hara* finds the most important factor in your life at any given time — whether it is spirituality or materialism — and makes you feel depressed over your inadequacies in that area. In Jerusalem, where people have so much less than we have here, people are not sad that they do not have cars. They are sad because they want to be closer to Hashem. When people have more assets, they are saddened by problems related to their material possessions.

◆§ The Bluff: Spiritual Dejection

The truth is that anyone who feels anguished about his spiritual failings should feel very fortunate. He is one of the few people in this world who is investing his emotional energy into *ruchnius*. It is precisely in the spiritual arena that it is difficult to experience tangible success. We cannot calculate these gains and losses in the same way that we follow our holdings in the stock market. Hashem evaluates our spiritual successes and failures by a different yardstick. He may value the sincerity of our efforts and the intensity of our struggles *davka* in those areas in which we are frustrated by our lack of progress.

On some level, we are all aware of this, but we rarely stop to think about it. We are in danger of sinking deeper and deeper into frustration and despondency. Why?

It's the "bluff." The *yetzer hara* fools us. Depression is a sign that the *yetzer hara* is hard at work, actively convincing us that things are not going as they should.

When we say *Bircas HaMazon* with a *zimun* we say, "*Boruch she'achalnu mishelo, u'vetovo chayinu* — Blessed is He of Whose we have eaten, and in Whose goodness we live." The Talmud (*Berachos* 50a; also in *Shulchan Aruch, Orach Chaim* 192:1) teaches that a person who says *u'vetuvo chayinu* — in Whose goodness we live — is a *talmid chacham*. A person who says, *u'mituvo chayinu* — from Whose goodness we live — is a fool.

Rashi explains the reason for this. When we say "from Whose goodness," this implies that we have only received a little bit of Hashem's goodness. The words, "in Hashem's goodness," accurately relate that we are able to live only because of Hashem's continuing abundant goodness.

But this seems to be contradicted by another phrase in the siddur. Every Shabbos and Yom Tov we say in *Shemoneh Esrei*, "*Sab'einu mituvecha* — satisfy us from Your goodness." Why is that not considered as if we are diminishing Hashem's goodness? Why is it not imperative to say, "*Sab'einu bituvecha*"?

I saw a beautiful explanation by the grandson of the Chasam Sofer, printed at the end of *Devarim* in the newer editions of the Chasam Sofer. He says that we must look at the context in which we say these words in *Shemoneh Esrei*. The words, "*Sab'einu mituvecha*," immediately follow the words "*v'sein chelkeinu beSorasecha* — grant our share in Your Torah."

Not everyone is expected to become the *gadol hador*. We cannot skip three or four levels at a time and become great overnight. In *ruchnius*, we have to grow one step a time. As long as we are progressing, we should be happy. Each individual asks for his own specific share in Torah. For some, that means learning Chumash. For others it means learning Mishnayos, and for others — Gemara.

When in comes to *ruchnius*, then, the correct phrase is, "*Sab'einu mituvecha* — satisfy us **from** Your goodness," because we cannot receive all of Hashem's goodness when it comes to *ruchnius*. We ask that we be satisfied with our level of spirituality, as long as we are proceeding at our pace.

When that ninth-grader was depressed because he could not learn at the level that he expected, he was making a mistake. He was being unrealistic. It is not constructive to become depressed over *ruchnius*. We have to be satisfied with the amount of potential that Hashem has granted us, and build on it progressively.

✥ Who Wants To Be Rothschild?

If you are in the second thirty years of life, you are probably nodding your head in agreement. You understand the need to settle; to make peace with your level of *ruchnius*. You have tempered your youthful idealism with what you have come to regard (correctly or incorrectly) as the necessary level of realism.

Our previous question about the phrase *mituvecha* can be asked regarding *parnassah* (livelihood) as well. In *Barech Aleinu* — the blessing in the weekday *Shemoneh Esrei* in which we ask Hashem for *parnassah* — we say *v'sabeinu mituvah* (Nusach Sefard) or *mituvecha* (Nusach Ashkenaz). Why *mituvah*?

Apparently, when it comes to *parnassah*, too, we ask Hashem to supply us with our portion, whether that portion is great or small. To feel pain or sadness because we want to have more is phony. It is truly "bluff."

Do you know how phony it is?

If you could switch places with Baron Rothschild — if you could have the ability to go back 250 years and have his fabulous wealth and influence — you would probably jump at the opportunity, right?

Let me tell you how you would live if you switched places with Rothschild. You would have no air-conditioning. None. I'm not talking about in your car — nowhere!

You would also have to forgo indoor plumbing. Now I'm sure that Baron Rothschild had a very cushioned seat in his outhouse, but would you want to switch places with him and have to use an outhouse?

Rothschild traveled in a coach with horses in front of him. Do you remember the last time you caught a whiff of a horse? Would you want to travel constantly with that sort of horsepower?

Can you imagine having to light candles every night? It would take half an hour to light your chandelier! Of course Rothschild had servants do this for him. We, however, flick a single switch, and there is light. We don't need to hire servants!

Today, the average person of modest means is living with many comforts and conveniences that Rothschild never dreamed of. In a very real sense, we are all richer than Rothschild.

Why do we feel that we need more money, more comforts, more and more and more?

Why are there people today who are depressed over their *parnassah* situation? Are we living in adequate physical comfort?

You see, the world really is a phony place; it's a world of bluff.

∼§ Concentrating During *Ashrei*

Last year, before the Yamim Noraim, I took upon myself — together with many members of our shul — to try to recite *Ashrei* three times a day with proper concentration.

It is not as easy as it sounds.

Ashrei is the most important part of *Pesukei D'Zimrah*, and the most important verse in Ashrei is, "*Posei'ach es yadecha, umasbia lechol chai ratzon* — You open up Your hand, and satisfy the desire of every living thing."

Posei'ach es yadecha is so important, that we are obligated to concentrate on these words when reciting them. If a person was daydreaming while reciting *Ashrei*, and woke up at a later point in *Pesukei D'Zimrah*, even during the last part, *Az Yashir*, he must go back. He must repeat *Posei'ach es yadecha* (with *kavannah*) and follow through to the end of *Ashrei*. (Shulchan Aruch, Orach Chaim 51:7; *Mishnah Berurah* §16).

This year I became more realistic. Our resolution for this coming year is to concentrate while reciting *Posei'ach es yadecha*, and to go back to it if we realize that we were daydreaming while reciting this verse.

I don't know if it is just my imagination, but I think I hear people reciting the verse of *Posei'ach es yadecha* out loud — and it sounds as if they are concentrating on the meaning of the words.

When I started to concentrate on these words, I started to think about their meaning. This led to the following question: Does Hashem really satisfy the desires of every living thing? I know people who desire a bigger house, a family, better health, a job ... the list goes on and on. How can we say that Hashem satisfies the desires of all beings?

I found an explanation in the *Me'am Loez* to *Tehillim*, quoting *Ohel Yaakov*, by the Maggid of Dubno. In keeping with his approach, let us illustrate with a parable.

> A man walks into a shoe store and asks for a size-13 shoe.
>
> "Size 13?" the salesperson asks incredulously. "Your foot is no bigger than a 10!"
>
> But the fellow is adamant; he wants a 13. The salesperson decides that there is no point in arguing. He goes to the back and brings out a pair of shoes, size 13. They are way too big. He goes back for a size 12, and then a size 11, and finally a size 10. Even the size 10 turns out to be too big. Size 9 fits perfectly. The customer takes the size 9.
>
> Ask yourself: Did the salesperson satisfy this man's desire? On a superficial level, he did not. The man wanted a size 13, and he got a size 9 instead. But a sensible person understands that what he really wanted was a shoe that fits. His true desire was fulfilled.
>
> In the world of "bluff," he was disappointed. In the real world, he is satisfied.

Posei'ach es yadecha, umasbia lechol chai ratzon. There is a certain *ratzon*, a certain desire, that is the perfect size for you. It fits you just right. If Hashem gave you a certain amount of possessions, your desire should match what you have, because that is what is right for you.

> When the Chofetz Chaim was a young boy, he was once playing with his friends and they decided to play, "If I were Hashem." Each child imagined that he was God and explained how he would improve the world if he were in charge. One boy said that he would give a cow and some chickens to a

poor widow with seven children. Another boy said that he would provide a home for the poor homeless fellow who slept on the street each night.

When the young Yisrael Meir had his turn, he said, "If I were Hashem, I would do everything exactly the way it is done now. If this is the way Hashem has chosen to run the world, then this is the best way for it to be."

Hashem gives each person the amount that fits his personal *ratzon*. Don't allow your *ratzon* to be formed by a world of bluff. We must work hard to adapt our *ratzon* to the real world.

Reb Zisha M'Annapoli was a very poor man. Someone overheard him saying the blessing, "*She'asah li kol tzorki* — Who gives me all that I need," with great fervor.

"But the Rebbe is so poor!" exclaimed the listener. "How can the Rebbe recite this blessing with such enthusiasm? Does the Rebbe really have everything he needs?"

"You don't understand," the Rebbe responded. "Before I was born, Hashem looked at my soul and said, 'What you need, to fulfill your potential, is poverty.' So it seems that my *tzorech*, my need, is poverty. And that, He has given me in full measure!"

This is what *bitachon* can do for us. If we take some time to evaluate our lives properly, we can occasionally see through the mirage that the *yetzer hara* has created for us. Each of us can train himself to think, "Hashem has given me my real *ratzon*; that which I truly need. Everything else that my *yetzer hara* convinces me to 'need' is phony. It is bluff."

◈§ The Tough Ones

Many of life's difficulties are bluff. But not all. There are some that I would call "tough."

There are problems that are very difficult to bear; they seem too hard to overcome. There is nothing imaginary about them; they seem all too real.

We cannot possibly learn to handle all of life's tests in one sitting. If one truly wants to live with the happiness that *bitachon* brings, one must master the entire *Sha'ar HaSimchah*, or at least take the time to read the second half of it on a regular basis. If your issues are too overwhelming to be dismissed as illusions, then you may take comfort in the sixth form of *bitachon* that is listed by the *Orchos Tzaddikim*.

Orchos Tzaddikim writes that a person should have faith in a kind God who does not bestow reward in this fleeting, transient world. This would leave man with less merit in the World to Come.

Each individual should train himself to realize that Hashem is watching over him. Hashem cares about him, protects him, and looks after his needs.

Rav Tzaddok HaKohen of Lublin (*Tzidkas HaTzaddik* #154) writes that an integral part of the obligation to have *emunah* in Hashem is for each person to feel that God wants to have a relationship with him. "Just as one is obligated to believe in God, so, too, he must afterwards learn to believe in himself; to believe that God is involved with his life …."

What happens when you feel that Hashem is punishing you; that He wants to make your life tough?

A long time ago, I heard a speaker quote the *Ramchal* to the effect that there is no such thing as punishment in this world. Any time we are faced with a difficulty in this world, it is really something constructive, a positive development in our lives.

I'll be honest with you. At the time, it struck me as a Chassidishe thought that is meant to raise our spirits when we are down. In truth, though, *Chazal* do refer to *onshim* (punishments). There must be such a thing, right?

A while later I saw that Rav Moshe Feinstein, *zt"l*, writes the very same idea in *Darash Moshe* (Vol. 1, *V'aira*, s.v. *sham tamuah*). Rav Moshe writes in a very technical sense that Hashem does not punish just to punish. He doesn't give us a "*potch* on the hand." Every experience in this world that causes pain or anguish is intended to repair a person's mistakes, to perfect his actions, to make him a better person.

Last year we learned *Maseches Kiddushin* in our shul, and I came across yet another expression of this principle. The Talmud (35a) lists the areas of Torah in which men and women are different, and those in which they are the same. When it comes to punishment, states the Talmud, men and women are equal, because punishment is meant to atone for a person's sins, and both men and women need the opportunity for atonement.

Clearly, then Hashem does not punish us just for punishment's sake. What a refreshing thought for the times when life seems to be tough!

~§ It's All in the Attitude

I thought about this recently, when I visited my father's *kever* (grave), prior to the *Yamim Noraim*. We understand that a *niftar* can hear what is said at a *kever*, and as I prayed in my own words, I began to think about the issues in my life that were bothering me. Suddenly, an interesting memory came to mind.

> As I was walking home from shul one Shabbos afternoon, I passed a young couple out for a walk with their little son. The boy must have been about two years old or so, and he decided to sit down on the sidewalk — as little boys seem to do when their parents take them for a walk on Shabbos. Our community has no *eruv*, and the parents were stuck with a two-year-old who refused to budge. The parents promised an ice cream, they promised a lolly, perhaps they even promised a *potch* ... but to no avail. He simply ignored his parents. (Amazing — two years old and already behaving like a teenager!)
>
> I don't know if what I did was right or wrong, but I decided to help them. I rushed up to the little boy, put on my angriest face, and bellowed, "Why are you crying on my sidewalk? Get off my block!"
>
> You should have seen him move. He scrambled to his feet and ran to his parents, who immediately began to laugh uncontrollably. The boy looked up at his parents with a bewildered look, as if to say, "This mean man wants to bite me, and you're laughing?"

As I stood there at my father's *kever*, I couldn't help but think that my father might just be looking down at me and laughing. *That is what you are crying about?* He might want to say to me. *That's rough? That's tough? That's your job! That is why you are there. You are succeeding; you are doing well despite the difficulty. You have no reason to cry — when you will come up here you will be delighted about it!*

HaKadosh Baruch Hu sees us sitting still and He comes up to us with a "mean face"; He speaks harshly to us: "Why are you crying on my sidewalk?" He jolts us. We have to get up and do something.

It may hurt. It may cause a lot of pain. But how you accept the jolt depends on your attitude. It may not be bluff; it may be tough, but

SHA'AR HASIMCHAH / 163

the experience is a step in a good direction.

Here's a great question. Most of us daven on Erev Rosh Hashanah, five or ten minutes before sunset. There are only a few minutes left to the year. In our prayer for *parnassah* (*Bareich aleinu*) we say, "*Bareich aleinu ... es hashanah hazos v'es kol minei sevuasah l'tovah* — Bless on our behalf ... this year, and all its types of produce, for goodness." Here we are, asking for a blessing for *this year's* income. But there are only minutes remaining to the year!

What do *you* think, when you say these words? Are you asking that your investments in the market suddenly shoot up a few hundred points? But the markets aren't open anymore. Are you thinking, *God, please let the markets miraculously reopen; You have the power to do it!*

I doubt that this is the correct intention for the *Shemoneh Esrei*. What is? The year is up. Why are we asking Hashem to bless the year for us?

I'll tell you what I was thinking during that *Shemoneh Esrei*. I had just come across Rav Shlomo Kluger's explanation of these words. We beseech God, "Hashem, the year is up. Nothing is going to change in terms of the technical success of the year. But Hashem, please let me see this year as a blessed one. Help me appreciate that You have given me a year of blessing."

We ask Hashem for the *Siyata d'Shmaya* (Divine Assistance) to enable us to view the past year with a positive attitude, because our attitude is the only thing that we can change in the last few minutes of the year.

This is a true blessing; it is worthy of our prayers all year round!!!

⇜ Two Ways To Feel Satisfied

Our Rosh Hashanah resolution to recite the blessing of *Posei'ach es yadecha* with concentration has led us to still another understanding of this verse. Earlier, we wondered how we can say that Hashem gives every being what it desires when that does not appear to be true. We shared one explanation, above. The Satmar Rebbe, in *Sefer Divrei Yoel* (*Parashas Nasso*, p. 179), offers another insight.

Hashem commanded us, "And you shall eat, and you shall become satisfied, and you shall bless Hashem, your God" (*Devarim* 8:10).

The Gemara tells us that *Klal Yisrael* accepted upon themselves the obligation to recite *Bircas HaMazon* after eating a olive-size piece of bread, even though this is not enough to become fully satisfied.

The *Zohar* asks a question. Is it so simple to recite blessings when we are not required to do so? There is a concept of a *berachah l'vatalah*; it is forbidden to recite an unnecessary blessing. How can we accept a "stringency" to recite *Bircas HaMazon* when we are not satisfied; isn't this is a leniency in the laws of *berachah l'vatalah*?!

The *Zohar* answers — as explained by the Satmar Rebbe — that a person can feel satisfied because he has eaten a large quantity of food. He is then expected to thank Hashem. However, it is also possible for a person to feel satisfied because of his attitude. When a person has the right attitude, his satisfaction after eating a little can be the same as that of one who has eaten a lot. *Klal Yisrael* has undertaken to reach such a high level that even when we have no more than a *k'zayis* to eat, we should be able to turn to Hashem and say, "*Savati* — I am satisfied." This level of gratitude should be the same as the ordinary person who has eaten much.

The *Bircas HaMazon* is not an issue of *berachah l'vatalah*. It comes from the same sense of gratitude that normally obligates a person in *Bircas HaMazon*.

So, too, in *Ashrei*. When we say that Hashem satisfies the desires of every being, we mean to say that Hashem enables a human being to *feel* that his desires are satisfied, no matter what he has or does not have. He allows us to infuse *bitachon* into our lives so that we can be happy in the most difficult circumstances.

If there is one generation of Jews who should be able to appreciate this idea, it should be ours. Those of my generation need look no further than our parents or grandparents who survived the Holocaust. They experienced horrors that should have left them permanently depressed. And, in truth, the pain never really left them. Somehow, they emerged with an attitude that allowed them to rebuild, and to be happy. They had a firm commitment to trust Hashem despite the fact that they could not fathom His mysterious ways. Without their staunch *bitachon*, we would not be where we are today.

> A few weeks before my father, *a"h*, passed away, my son came home from Eretz Yisrael. I took him to the hospital to visit my father. It was traumatic for my son to see his beloved grandfather in the hospital, and I remember my father trying to comfort him.
>
> "When you see me like this, don't be sad," my father said. "My whole life I was well, I never had to be in a hospital, I

was always strong. My whole life I did not have any problems, and I never had to worry. Hashem was always good to me."

I was thinking — my father never had any troubles!? He lost his parents as a teenager. He was 17 years old when he was transported to Auschwitz. He barely survived the infamous death march. He lost most of his siblings and every one of his ten beloved nieces and nephews. Later in life, he lost a 22-year-old son, and shortly thereafter was treated for Hodgkin's disease. Yet he genuinely felt that he had no problems, that he never had to worry.

It is amazing to see how everything in life is controlled by attitude!

The Brisker *Segulah*

Some difficulties can be pushed away by convincing ourselves that it is bluff. Even those that are tough can put into perspective by a person with *bitachon*.

The Brisker Rav was stuck in Warsaw at the beginning of World War II. The Nazis had already conquered Poland, and they were on every road. The Rav knew that the only way to escape was to reach Vilna, and from there to set out for Eretz Yisrael. Before leaving on the dangerous journey, he told his students of a tradition from his grandfather, the *Beis HaLevi*. A person who is totally focused on the concept that *ein od milvado* (there is none other besides Hashem) will be spared from all harm.

There are several versions to the story behind this tradition, one of which goes something like this:

> One day, the richest man in the *Beis HaLevi's* town knocked on his door and frantically asked him for help. As the richest man in town, he was entrusted with all the *tzeddakah* funds, which he stored in his office together with all of his own money. That morning, the Russian government had sent a detachment of troops to raid every business in town and confiscate their money and valuables.
>
> "*Gevald!*" the man cried to the *Beis HaLevi*. "All my money is there and all the *tzeddakah* money is there too. What should I do?"

The *Beis HaLevi* took the man into his study and closed the door. They stayed there for hours. Finally, the rich man's wife returned and exclaimed happily, "The *berachah* has arrived. We are saved."

"What happened?" he asked.

"The soldiers spent the morning looting the shops in town, going from one to the next. When lunchtime came, they took a break. Before leaving, the Captain took a paintbrush and painted a large white stripe on the door of the next business, the one that was next in line. That was our store. They left to eat.

"When they came back — possibly a bit tipsy from their favorite Russian beverage — the Captain said, 'The one with the white stripe is the last business we raided; let's go to the next one.' And *Baruch Hashem*, our business was spared."

Later on, someone asked the rich man, "What were you and the *Beis HaLevi* doing during all those hours in his study?"

"The *Beis HaLevi* told me to concentrate on the words *ein od milvado*," he responded.

Apparently, the tradition that the Brisker Rav received from his grandfather, the *Beis HaLevi*, originated from *his* grandfather, Rav Chaim of Volozhin.

In *Nefesh HaChaim* (3:12), Rav Chaim of Volozhin writes, "A wonderful *segulah* to remove and disable all harsh judgments, so that they should not have control over us or affect us in any way, is to implant in our hearts the faith that Hashem is the One and Only, and *ein od milvado* — no other forces in the world other than Hashem have any power whatsoever."

It is important to remember that we are quoting from the Soloveitchik family here — who are certainly not known for promulgating all kinds of mystical *segulos*. If the Soloveitchiks recommend this *segulah*, you can be sure that the power of *bitachon* goes beyond all other measures.

The only problem I have with the story of the *Beis HaLevi* is that it has a happy ending. I have nothing against the rich man in the story, but I think that the outcome makes this lesson lose a good part of its impact. *Ein od milvado* is not only successful in situations that have a happy ending. Rav Chaim of Volozhin tells us that it is a wonderful *segulah*, no matter what the outcome is. Sometimes the conclusion is not what we hoped for, but that too is part of *ein od milvado*.

∽§ Surviving the Final Test

*I*n dealing with people, I have found that the most difficult time comes right before the salvation. Just as it gets dark right before it rains, the most difficult tests come right before Hashem's Mercy begins to shine through.

I received a phone call last May or June from a young lady who did not identify herself. She had been dating for nine or ten years and was quite frustrated. She felt the need to make a difference in the world, and she had a plan. Eli Weisel was organizing a contingent of Jews to go to Sudan to help the natives. She felt that Orthodox Jews should also be represented in that group, and nominated herself as their representative.

Her friend insisted that she not make the trip without consulting a Rav first, so she called me to ask if I felt that she should go.

I told her that while her motives were honorable, her idealism was misdirected.

"Your first thought should be to help your own people. If you really want to make a difference," I advised, "go to Eretz Yisrael. I am sure you can find people there who need your help."

She argued with me — I saw that it was difficult for her to change her plans. I was not sure if I had convinced her. We hung up, and as far as I was concerned, that was that.

That August, when I was in Eretz Yisrael, I received a phone call from this young woman, and this time she identified herself. She told me that it had been very hard to reverse her decision to go to Sudan, yet she decided to take my advice. She had come to volunteer in Eretz Yisrael. That wasn't the reason she was calling. She was calling to invite me to her *vort*. She had met a fine young man who was giving a *shiur* at Aish HaTorah, and they were about to get engaged.

∽§ Beyond Bluff, Beyond Tough

*S*ome things are bluff, and some things are tough. Here's the secret. When life is really, really hard to handle, it is not bluff, and it is not tough — it is love.

Shlomo HaMelech writes, "For Hashem admonishes the one He

loves" (*Mishlei* 3:12). The really tough times in life are expressions of Hashem's love for us. It is His way of inviting us to call out to Him, and to develop a closer relationship to Him.

We say *Ashrei* at Minchah. What is the most important verse in *Ashrei* at Minchah?

No, not *Posei'ach es yadecha*. That is the most important verse in *Pisukei D'Zimra*, the morning prayer. Rashi states that *Chazal* chose to include *Ashrei* in Minchah because it contains the verses, "*Karov Hashem lechol koravav, lechol asher yikruHu be'emes* — Hashem is close to all who call upon Him — to all who call upon Him sincerely. *Ritzon Yereyov yaaseh* — He fulfills the desires of those who fear Him." (See *Orach Chaim* #93.)

If you are worried about something, call out to Hashem sincerely. You have no guarantee that your request will be granted, but you have a guarantee that you will feel closer to Hashem. And when you are close to the Creator, the blessing can come on its own.

This is a great challenge. It is very difficult to feel close to Hashem when things do not go well. It is a challenge worthy of those who seek to love *HaKadosh Baruch Hu*.

◆§ The Real World

A fellow leaves this world and comes before the Heavenly Court. The angels bring all his good deeds and place them on one side of the scale, and they place all his sins on the other side of the scale. To his dismay, his sins outweigh his merits. He is terrified.

But wait, hope is not lost! The angels began to place all of his *tzaros*, his difficulties, his pain and suffering on the side of the scale alongside his merits. The man stands there, cheering the angels on, hoping, "More *tzaros*, more *tzaros*."

Sure enough, the scale slowly begins to tilt in the right direction, but it is still a little bit short. Finally they reach the last difficulty he experienced in his life. At a very advanced age, he was walking up the steps to his house, and he fell. As he was tumbling down the steps, however, he managed to catch onto the banister, so that his suffering was diminished. The angels place this *tzarah* on the scale, and lo and behold, it is close, but it doesn't quite make it. His sins still outweigh his good deeds.

The man turns to Hashem and says, "You are an *Av HaRachaman*, a Merciful Father. Couldn't you have let me fall down the whole flight of stairs?"

Which is the *Olam Ha'Emes*, the real world, and which is the *Olam HaSheker*, the world of falsehood?

Rav Avigdor Miller would use this scenario to teach people how to view painful events in their lives with the proper perspective. How about this one:

A man walks into shul for Maariv one night, visibly disturbed about something. The Rav goes over to him after Maariv and asks him what is wrong. The man tells him that he was supposed to fly to Europe that night, and he got stuck in traffic and missed the flight. He could not get onto another flight, and he was stuck in America.

"I have to cancel all of my meetings," the man moans. "I'll ruin my business. Why did this have to happen to me?"

"What would happen," asks the Rav, "if you wake up tomorrow and read in the newspaper that the flight crashed, and all 450 people on board died. What would you do then?"

"I would give a kiddush!" the man exclaims. "I would be delighted that I missed the flight."

"You *rasha*!" the rav responds. "Do 450 people have to die for you to see Hashem's Hand in your life? Do you have to kill 450 people to say 'thank you' to Hashem?

"Do the world a favor. Let those people live, and just see Hashem's Hand in your missed flight."

If we learn to use our *bitachon* to view our lives positively, we can merit to see David HaMelech's words fulfilled in our lives: "One who trusts in Hashem, kindness surrounds him" (*Tehillim* 32:10).

Shalom Bayis for Husbands

My position in life provides me with a unique vantage point from which to observe the challenges of marriage. I am fortunate enough to live in two worlds: I spend a large part of my day in yeshivah with young men who are either engaged, newly married, or actively involved in seeking a life partner. I am also the Rav of a shul whose members have reached a stage of life where they are "pros" at marriage — so to speak. I often find myself involved in discussions that serve as striking studies in contrast. During the course of an average day I find myself counseling those who are naively optimistic about marriage, as well as those who are weary and disillusioned.

As many people know, Rav Pam, *zt"l*, would give a *shmuess* about *shidduchim* each year, on Erev Shabbos *Chayei Sara*. I follow his tradition and give a *shmuess* about dating, in which I repeat much of what our *Rebbi* taught us about proper priorities in looking for a wife. In a typical encounter at yeshivah, I was recently approached by a young man who was bursting to share the wonderful news that he was getting engaged that night.

"I listened to the recording of the *Chayei Sarah shiur* three times," the *chasan*-to-be told me, "I am sure that she is the right one." He was so happy. His face shone with excitement and joy.

In my capacity as rav, on the other hand, I often deal with squabbling adults who simply cannot get along, and it is hard to believe that they were once *chasan* and *kallah*. It often seems as if there are two unrelated categories of people. When does this metamorphosis take place? When — and even more important, why — does an excited *chasan* turn into a frustrated husband?

The answer can be derived from a Midrash.

Yalkut Shimoni asks why Hashem did not create husband and wife as a pair from the start. Why do young people have to go through the dating period, an experience that is often filled with tension and frustration?

The Midrash explains. Hashem saw that men would complain about their wives. Had each person been created together with a spouse, that spouse might be totally unappreciated. A person might think, "I would be better off single." Hashem creates each person alone and has him go through process of seeking a mate so that he will better appreciate marriage. In addition, the courting period enables one to plant seeds for a successful marriage. The problem is that the courtship often ends when marriage begins. When people are dating, they go out and spend time with a person who *might* be their spouse. Then they become engaged, and they continue to go out with the person who is *going to be* their spouse. Suddenly they get married, and the courtship is over. No more going out, no more special time set aside for each other.

Rav Pam would tell newlyweds, "The courtship must continue."

Rav Pam taught that to create happy marriages, we have to keep up the courtship, even when the wedding is but a distant memory.

It would behoove us to examine the courtship period, and learn its lessons well.

The Third Partner

As the destruction of the *Beis HaMikdash* drew near, Hashem told Yirmiyahu, "Do not take for yourself a wife, so that you do not have sons and daughters in this place. For thus said Hashem concerning the sons and daughters who are born in this place, and concerning their mothers who gave birth to them and their fathers who beget them in this land: They will die as victims of diseases" (*Yirmiyahu* 16:2-4).

This prophecy implies that people get married only in order to bear children, and since those children were destined to die, it would be better for them to remain single. Is that true? What about love? What about friendship? What about the joy of having a soul mate? Is raising a family the only reason to get married?

It may not be the *only* reason, but it is clear from many sources that it must be a primary motivation.

Rav Chiya said, "*Ein ishah elah l'banim*" (*Kesubos* 59b). When a man marries, he should do so with the intention of building a family. Love and romance are important tools for building a marriage, but they cannot be the sole purpose of marriage. Moreover, these things alone cannot bring long-term happiness to a married couple.

On a similar note, the Talmud (*Sotah* 17a) tells us, "*Ish v'isha zachu, Shechinah beineihem.*"

The most common interpretation of this passage is that if a man and woman merit (to live in harmony), the Divine Presence comes to rest between them — i.e., marital harmony *causes* the Divine Presence to rest in a home.

The interpretation can be altered ever so slightly to reflect another profound truth: If a man and woman live in harmony, it is *because* the *Shechinah* resides in their home.

A successful marriage must consist of three partners: a man, a woman, and Hashem. If spiritual ideals are paramount to the young couple as they meet and decide to marry, their marriage will have the ability to flourish. If they are primarily motivated by their selfish desires, leaving Hashem out of the equation, their marriage is doomed from the start.

But there are many couples who do make Hashem a partner in their marriage, and yet their relationship leaves something to be desired. That is where Rav Pam's advice comes into the picture: "The courtship must continue."

Let us analyze the primary changes that take place in the transition from *chasan/kallah* to husband/wife. Are all of these changes truly inevitable? If we can identify some of the specific behaviors that enhanced our relationship as *chasan* and *kallah*, perhaps we can avoid some of those losses. Perhaps we can revive some of these practices and breathe fresh life into our marriages.

Every person can think of things that are standard practice for *chasanim* and *kallahs*, but less common among married couples. I made a list of what I consider the most common changes, which, coming from the perspective of one who deals primarily with *chasanim* and husbands, focuses on the male responsibilities. Unfortunately, the list is too long to be tackled at once. You can't give a man a list of ten things to change and hope for any measure of success.

Let us focus on four important changes that happen en route from being a *chasan* to being a husband — and examine how those changes can be avoided. Through this process we can include Hashem as an active partner in our marriages. We can revive the courtship and have it continue throughout our married lives.

■ Change #1: Talking

When a young man and woman meet on a *shidduch* date, how do they spend their time together? They talk. When they get engaged, what do they do as *chasan* and *kallah*? Talk. *Chasanim* and *kallahs* are excited to talk to each other, to explore their goals and ideals, to share every detail of their lives with one another. Somehow, when a man gets married, he stops talking.

Many husbands feel that it is unfair to place the blame for the cessation of communication on their shoulders. "When we were dating, she did most of the talking," they say. That is true — and she is likely to do most of the talking even when you are married. But she can only talk if someone is listening.

The diminishing level of communication is a natural outgrowth of the familiarity that develops in a marriage. When a couple becomes engaged, everything is new. There is so much to share. As *chasan* and *kallah*, they have so much to learn about each other, and they are excited to share their opinions and feelings. The excitement and newness wears off after awhile, and it is only natural that they stop talking. What are a husband and wife supposed to talk about when it seems that everything has already been discussed?

The answer to this question can be derived from the contrast between two *berachos* we say each day.

On one hand we ask, "*Shetargileinu be'Torasecha* — May we become accustomed to your Torah." On the other hand, in *Bircas HaTorah* we say, "*Ha'arev na Hashem Elokeinu es divrei Torasecha b'finu*," asking that the words of Torah become sweet in our mouths. Even when familiarity does not breed contempt, it is difficult for something habitual to be truly sweet. Why do we ask Hashem that we become habituated in Torah? The word *hergel* implies *habit* — something that we do automatically— as if by rote. Is that what we truly want?

When a little child begins to learn the *aleph-beis*, he is very excited. Each new letter is a new accomplishment. We would expect his excitement in *aleph-beis* to diminish as he begins to feel comfortable with the letters. If a ten-year-old is excited about knowing the *aleph-beis*, that is not a good sign about his progress in learning.

After mastering the letters, a child learns how to read. Again there is excitement. He sits with a siddur and reads word by word, enthralled by this new skill. If a twelve-year-old is still exhilarated by the fact that he can read, he will never move on to the next level; that of understanding the meaning of the words. A child advances to a new level only when he becomes accustomed to the previous one. A child who has mastered the study of Chumash will be happy to move on to Mishnayos, and when he is familiar with Mishnayos, he will want to go on to Gemara. Each level of accomplishment must become automatic, so that we can enjoy the sweetness of the next level.

The same principle applies to marriage. The period in which a couple is dating and getting married is new and exciting. They walk around in a dreamy state, feeling unique and special. When they become accustomed to marriage and the excitement wears off, it is time to move to the next level.

What is the next step in the relationship between a man and woman? A strong feeling of partnership. A husband and wife must now become a single unit, building a family, doing mitzvos *together*, and achieving a portion in *Olam Haba together*. The feeling of partnership — the feeling of being united in a common mission, with common goals and ideals — is the true feeling of love that should exist between husband and wife. Building that feeling requires communication. Talk. You cannot be united in your mission if you never take the time to discuss or define the goals of that mission.

A man must be *machshiv* his wife — he has to hold her in high esteem. In *Emes L'Yaakov* (*Parashas Ki Seitzei* 24:1), R' Yaakov Kaminetzky writes that in order to have a good marriage, a man must consider his wife the wisest, the most beautiful, and the best woman in the world. Again: a man must consider his wife *the* wisest, *the* most beautiful, and *the* best woman in the world. And yes, R' Yaakov named his *sefer* "*Emes L'Yaakov* (*Truth* to Yaakov)."

To be fair, R' Yaakov adds — albeit in parentheses — that the same applies to the wife.

Isn't that incredible? Every man should think that his wife is wonderful?

Thankfully, R' Yaakov himself implies that this is a difficult level to attain. "Is it really possible for two separate people to become so united that they will honestly feel that way?" he asks.

In this rhetorical question, R' Yaakov hints at the key to success: unity. Two people who are truly united view one another as the best, the wisest, and the most beautiful. And how can two people become united? Through talking, through the process of real communication.

Men excel at imparting information. They love to remind you of the facts. A man will never forget to tell his wife things like, "There is no more money in the checking account," or, "You parked on the wrong side of the street and we got a ticket."

Yet when it comes to talking about feelings, the most confident man becomes insecure. We are uncomfortable with topics that venture beyond the pragmatic. We want to talk about things that are real — things that can be proven and measured, not those annoying insubstantial things called feelings.

Men often wonder why it is that their wives seem to *kvetch* a lot. Why do women complain so much? It is because their husbands want to limit conversation to the practical, technical stuff of life. If you limit the range of discussion to the practical details of living, your wife will inevitably find something to *kvetch* about. After all, she's been left with no other way to express her feelings! If you are willing to talk about feelings, if you are willing to share thoughts and ideas, you will have engaging conversations, and she will have less of a need to complain.

In order to achieve this goal, the courtship must continue.

A husband and wife must date each other every once in a while. They have to go *out*, just like a couple who is dating. Rosh Chodesh is a woman's Yom Tov. Wouldn't it be nice if we would make a point of going out each Rosh Chodesh?

Women do not understand why it is important to go out. Women don't have to get out to talk. They can talk anywhere, anytime. A man cannot. A man has to get out of his ordinary setting in order to talk about his feelings. Put a man in his natural habitat and his focus will inevitably wander to the bills, tax returns, and tuition forms. If you want your husband to talk, you have to go out. You can go out to eat, or to the botanical gardens — don't worry, you won't meet any other men there, unless they are also out with their wives. Go for a walk or a ride. You can even go to a lounge. Hotel lounges don't limit access to single people. But go *out*.

At the beginning of a *z'man* in yeshivah, *bachurim* are filled with excitement. They come in and "roll up their sleeves," ready to learn diligently, because the days at the beginning of the year seem crucial to the success of the *z'man*. The challenge comes towards the middle of the year. During Teves or Shevat, an absence here or there doesn't seem to make much of a difference. The problem is that one absence here and one absence there cause a person to fall from his level of diligence. If one day doesn't matter, then the next day doesn't matter, either. Before long, the level of commitment felt at the beginning of the *z'man* is gone.

Marriage is the same. At the beginning of a marriage, husband and wife "roll up their sleeves," working hard to make sure that they succeed. They try to figure out ways to make each other happy. They put effort into maintaining their *shalom bayis*. They talk. They communicate.

Then comes the "middle of the *z'man*." At some point during the marriage, there will come a day when you will think, "It is not so important to talk today. We can let one day pass without touching base." If you let one day pass without touching base, you can go the next day without talking, and the next … before long, you aren't communicating at all, and the trouble starts.

Clearly, talk, or the lack thereof, is the greatest change that occurs during the transformation from *chasan* to husband. If your relationship is important to you, and if you want to have the type of partnership that will bring the *Shechinah* into your home, you must make time to talk.

■ Change #2: Spending

If the most significant change in the metamorphosis from *chasan* to husband is in the amount of conversation, there is no doubt that the spending level is a close second.

It never ceases to amaze me. A *chasan* has to buy a bracelet, a ring, then another ring, and a necklace, a watch, *machzorim* — leather-bound, at that — everything that is in the typical engagement-and -marriage-package nowadays. You buy, and buy, and buy. It seems that developing a relationship involves spending.

What happens when you get married? Why do you stop spending money on your wife?

So some men say, "Well, when I got engaged and married, I was spending my father's money. That was easy."

I agree. It is hard to spend your own money, but it must be done. As important as your money may be to you, you must realize that in order to show love, you have to spend money. It might be expensive, but if the courtship is to continue, you have to sacrifice some of your money.

Rav Pam would say that a married person who spends money to please his wife — or a greater challenge, a person who looks the other way and ignores his wife's spending habits — should consider it *hiddur mitzvah,* the beautification of a mitzvah. We spend extra money to have a beautiful *esrog* for Succos. We buy tefillin that cost close to $1000 or more. There are tefillin that cost a few hundred dollars. Why do people spend so much money on tefillin? Because it is a mitzvah that we perform six days a week? *Shalom bayis* is a mitzvah that applies every single day of the year.

You can achieve this mindset only if the Divine Presence rests in your marriage. If you live with the understanding that Hashem is an active partner in your marriage, you will handle the expense of this *hiddur mitzvah* graciously. If not, you will be very unhappy when you have to spend money on your wife.

In a most encouraging prophecy, Hashem says, *"Ve'eirastich li l'olam* — I will betroth you to Me forever" (*Hoshea* 2:21).

There is an obvious problem with this pledge. *Eirusin,* betrothal, is similar to what we consider the state of being engaged. In the Talmudic era, a betrothed woman was considered married in the sense that no one else could marry her, but she lived in her parents' home until the *chupah,* just as an engaged woman does today. Imagine a *chasan* telling his *kallah,* "I plan to be engaged to you forever."

"What do you mean?" the *kallah* would gasp.

"Yeah," the *chasan* replies, "Let's stay engaged. It's a lot of fun. Marriage? Nah, it's not for me."

Why does Hashem pledge to betroth us to Him forever, rather than to marry us (so to speak)?

The *Sefas Emes* explains that the pledge of betrothal is the promise to maintain the freshness of one's love for eternity. When people are engaged, they are willing to sacrifice for one another. They joyfully endure hardship and are willing to move mountains to demonstrate their love and loyalty. In marriage, that willingness eventually fades away. Hashem promises to maintain that freshness forever.

On the very first day that the manna fell in the Wilderness, Moshe relayed Hashem's command to Aharon, "Take one jar and put a full *omer* of manna into it; place it before Hashem for a safekeeping for your generations" (*Shemos* 16:33).

The manna was destined to fall for close to forty years, points out the *Meshech Chochmah.* What was the rush? Why did they have to take manna and put it away on the very first day that it fell? Why couldn't they wait thirty-nine years or so, and collect a portion of manna on one of the last days that it would fall?

When the manna fell for the first time, explains the *Meshech Chochmah*, everyone was astonished and awed. Miraculous food fell from the sky, and it could taste like anything you wanted it. Imagine two little children eating manna on the first day that it fell.

"What are you thinking about?" one asks.

"Pizza and ice cream," his friend responds.

"That's a great idea," says the first little boy. "I'm going to think about that, too."

The first manna that fell was thrillingly miraculous. And the second, and the third. But an unfortunate fact of life is that one can get used to anything, even manna. Thirty-nine years later, no one was excited about the manna.

Hashem didn't just want *Klal Yisrael* to remember the manna, he wanted them to remember the excitement they had when it began to fall. He wanted them to bottle that excitement.

Do you remember your first paycheck or the first time you made a sale? You were undoubtedly excited, and grateful to Hashem for enabling you to succeed. Thirty years later, you don't have that same feeling of gratitude to Hashem when you receive your paycheck. The amount on your current check is much larger than it was then, but the thrill of appreciation is gone. Perhaps you have even kept the first dollar you earned as a memento of that excitement.

Marriage is very much the same. Marriage starts with excitement, with a feeling of uniqueness. If you wish to maintain that feeling, you must continue to invest in your relationship with your wife. Isn't attaining the presence of the *Shechinah* a worthwhile investment?! If you keep this goal in mind, you will not balk at spending time and, yes, money, on your wife. If you truly feel that the two of you are united in the pursuit of a lofty goal, you won't risk a failure in your mission for the sake of a few dollars.

■ Change #3: Behavior

Most men understand that talking and spending are important, and they are willing to admit that they do not fulfill their obligations in those areas. The next item on our list is much more subtle.

Do you remember when you were going out and when you were engaged? Do you remember how much your *kallah* respected you, how she looked up to you? What changed? Why do husbands often feel that their wives don't respect them anymore? Did the wives change, or are the men the ones who changed?

Let's go back to the early days. When boys are dating, they are asked to give names as references. Most boys will give the name of one of the rebbeim in yeshivah, assuming that their rebbi will only share good information about them.

If a girl's family calls up the rebbi and asks him, "Is so-and-so your student?"

"Yes," the rebbi responds. "He comes to my *shiur*. Sometimes."

"How often?" they ask.

"He sometimes comes always," the rebbi responds vaguely.

Even if the information conveyed was true, you are unlikely to give that rebbi as a reference again. Why? He only told the truth.

When a boy is looking for a *shidduch*, he does not want the objective truth to be told. He wants a positive assessment to be conveyed. He wants his positive qualities to be emphasized and his faults downplayed.

Is it not strange? Before you meet a girl, you want her to hear great things about you. When you meet, you are on best behavior. I know that "best behavior" means different things to different boys, but each boy is at *his* best behavior. You dress with care for each date. When you are with her, you watch how you speak, weighing and measuring each word. You work so hard to make a good impression. When you get engaged you try your best to maintain that impression. Then you get married and suddenly you couldn't care less. What happened?

People think that as soon as they get married, it is a mitzvah to expose all of their weaknesses to their wives. Suddenly, all their failings must be displayed. Is it really necessary to divulge all of your inadequacies? Don't you want to maintain her positive regard? You should want to make it easy for her to think of you as *the* wisest, *the* most handsome, and *the* best man in the world, as R' Yaakov suggested she do.

A man should make every effort to ensure that he is worthy of his wife's respect. I'm not suggesting that you lie to your wife — I'm suggesting that you behave in a way that is respectable.

Take the language that you use in your home. If you raise your voice in anger, you lower yourself in your wife's eyes. If you lose control of yourself, you become a less-respectable person. If your wife has an image of you as a person who would never fly into fits of rage, and you strive to maintain that image, are you engaging in falsehood? Certainly not! You are living up to your strengths, rather than caving in to your weaknesses.

Married men should try to live up to the image they maintained during the days of their courtship.

When a young man comes to tell me that he is getting engaged, I wish him *mazel tov* and add, "I hope that your *kallah* merits to be an *eishes talmid chacham* — the wife of *talmid chacham*."

I consider this the best blessing in the world. Doesn't every husband want his wife to look up to him as a learned person?

How can a husband achieve this status in the eyes of his wife? By working hard in order to become truly worthy of that respect.

Let me describe a phenomenon that occurs regularly. A young couple gets married, and after a while they plan their first vacation. What happens? I meet the husband and he tells me of his plans. I always say the same thing: "Your wife should know that when you are on vacation, you go to daven in the morning, and then stay in the *beis midrash* to learn for two hours."

The typical response is, "Yes, my wife wants me to learn. She feels good when I learn."

So I say, "Okay, so are you going to follow my instructions?"

"My wife won't mind" they reply.

"So after davening, are you going to spend two hours in the *Beis Midrash*?" I reiterate.

"Sure, my wife won't have any problem with it," they respond.

Finally I have no choice but to ask directly: "Why do you keep telling me about your wife? I know that she is okay with it. She wants to be an *eishes talmid chacham*. What about you? Are you okay with it?"

They begin to shift uneasily and finally offer a vague, "I'll try," or the famous last words: "I'll learn in the hotel room."

Do you realize what this means? This means that a wife respects her husband more than he respects himself. She understands. She wants to spend time with him, but she married a *ben Torah*. She is willing to give up a few hours of his company in order to be married to a *talmid chacham*. He is not so sure. He cannot live up to her image of him. After a while, the wife will feel that she is married to someone who is not worthy of her respect.

The *Chofetz Chaim*, zt"l, was certainly in favor of *shalom bayis*. Nevertheless, in *Nefutzos Yisrael*, he writes that there are situations in which a husband must take a firm stand. Sometimes a woman wants to take an exotic vacation in a place in which there is no Jewish life and no minyan available. The *Chofetz Chaim* writes that a person should refuse to go on such a trip, even if his wife cries and begs him.

The *Chofetz Chaim* recommends that he remind his wife of a historical precedent. When Chavah begged Adam to eat from the *Eitz*

Hadaas and he succumbed, the results were devastating. "Now too," the husband should say, "you are begging me to take you to an inappropriate location, but I refuse. We can go on vacation, but only to a place where there is Jewish life and minyanim."

When I got married, my father gave me some advice about vacations. He told me not to leave my learning for the middle of the day, when it might be hard for my wife to give up the time together. "Instead, get up early, before davening, and learn for a few hours. At that early hour your wife won't mind, because she is sleeping. After Shacharis, you can tell her that you want to take a nap. Napping is a normal vacation activity. She'll gladly let you take a nap on your vacation."

If you make place for the *Shechinah* in your marriage by making learning and spiritual growth your top priorities, your wife will respect you.

Rav Boruch Epstein (in *Mekor Boruch*) recalls an incident he observed at the home of Rav Chaim Berlin.

> A wealthy man complained about his *sholom bayis* situation.
>
> "At work, everyone shows me respect. They open the door for me, show concern for msy comfort, and listen carefully to whatever I say. Then I go home. It's just not the same. My wife doesn't respect me at all."
>
> Rav Chaim Berlin responded, "Your workers don't respect *you* at all. They respect your money. You are the boss and that is enough to cause them to show respect.
>
> "Your wife, on the other hand, wants a relationship with you, not your money. I know you. You were accustomed to learning several hours a day. Your busy lifestyle has caused those *sedorim* to end. Resume your learning. Return to the *Beis HaMidrash*. Then, your wife will give you the respect that you deserve."
>
> As a footnote, Rav Boruch Epstein writes that he met this husband many years later and that he assured him, "Rav Chaim Berlin's advice worked perfectly!"

You think that it is too late? It is never too late. You can start now — but don't delay. If you begin to behave in a respectable manner, your wife will look up to you. You will regain the positive regard she once had for you.

■ Change #4: Accepting Criticism

The fourth and final topic will undoubtedly be the most unpopular among the men: accepting criticism.

I know that I am not talking to *all* men when I say that you have to be willing to accept criticism — just all *married* men.

It's fascinating that every married man is sure that his wife is *the only* critical one. He rarely hears other wives being critical, but his wife is relentless. If you could hear the conversations that take place in your friend's house, you wouldn't feel like such a martyr. Your relationship is typical in this regard; all women criticize their husbands — and rightfully so.

Why "rightfully so?"

When Hashem created Adam HaRishon and placed him in Gan Eden, He said, "It is not good that man be alone; I will make him an *ezer k'negdo* — a helper corresponding to him" (*Bereishis* 2:18).

In a Gemara (*Yevamos* 63a) that is frequently quoted at *sheva berachos*, our Sages explains that if a man has merit, then his wife is an *ezer*, a helper. If not, then she is *k'negdo* — against him. *Rashi* explains that if a person is not righteous, his wife will oppose him and contradict him.

There seems to be an assumption that a wife has a right to criticize her husband if he is not acting properly, and that she is correct in doing so. Why?

In what may be the most important paragraph — at least for married men — of *Sichos Mussar*, Rav Chaim Shmuelevitz (5732:20) teaches, "One of the great secrets of creation is that a woman was created to be an *ezer k'negdo* to her husband, and it is her responsibility to supervise her husband's actions and make sure that he is on the correct path. A woman is blessed with a strong 'sense of smell,' through which she can sniff out her husband's mistakes, and figure out which actions are appropriate for a man of his level."

Anyone who is married knows that this is true. When are you stung by your wife's criticism? When she is right! But if you become too defensive to accept her constructive criticism, you have a big problem.

The Talmud (*Berachos* 17a) tells us that the promise Hashem made to women is greater than that made to men. *Maharal* explains that it is easier for a woman to merit a share in the World to Come than it is for a man.

Maharal does not write things casually, and he is not pandering to the female vote. Women do not have many of the *nisyonos* (challenges) that men have. They do not have the prohibition of straying after their eyes; they do not have to avoid *bitul Torah*.

Did you ever wonder why little girls have manners, and little boys ... don't? Even at a tender age, there is a bigger *yetzer hara* in males than there is in females.

Chida records the following custom. If two people in shul have *yahrtzeit*, one for his father and the other for his mother, the one who has *yahrtzeit* for his father takes precedence in serving as the *shaliach tzibbur*. I don't know if this custom is still prevalent, but it was in the time of the *Chida*. Is this male chauvinism? Why do we favor the person who lost his father? The *Chida* explains that when you lead the *tefillos* on a person's *yahrtzeit*, you enable that person to avoid the pain of *Gehinnom*. Since it is more likely that a man is in *Gehinnom* than a woman, since the man has a stronger *yetzer hara* and is more likely to have sinned, we give priority to the one who has *yahrtzeit* for his father.

If growth in *Avodas Hashem* is a priority in your life and in your marriage, you should take advantage of your wife's ability to point out your flaws. Put aside your ego and avail yourself of this powerful tool for success. A true *eved Hashem* should have no problem accepting criticism.

Again, let us go back to the early days. When a man is engaged or newly married, he is able to accept criticism from his wife, as long as it is said respectfully. Somehow, as the years go on, instead of viewing a wife's criticism as a tool for growth, husbands typically resent and ignore it. If you don't have the strength to accept your wife's constructive criticism, it will seem that her criticism is malicious and hurtful. It depends on your willingness to accept honest feedback. Believe me, I don't like it when I give a *shiur* that everyone seems to like, and then my wife points out its flaws. But I also know that she is one of the few people willing give me honest feedback and it is worth my while to listen.

> A man is going to an important job interview one morning. He comes home from shul, takes a shower, puts on his suit and tie, and heads for the door. On his way out, he turns to his wife and asks, "How do I look?"
>
> "Well," she says, "Your tie is a little bit crooked."
>
> Will the husband get angry? Will he say, "You're criticizing me again"? Of course not! He will appreciate her honesty. He will even thank her. It is easy to straighten out his tie, and he will make a better impression at the interview.

Now let's examine the identical scenario with one minor difference. This time instead of, "Your tie is crooked," she responds, "Your nose is crooked."

He will be furious and hurt. Such criticism is cruel. What can he do about his crooked nose now? Take a hammer to it?

In reality, wives often point out, "Your tie is crooked" but their husbands hear, "Your nose is crooked." Your wife doesn't necessarily mean it that way. When you were engaged, you weren't so hypersensitive. What happened?

Chazal tell us that a person was born to toil. A person cannot escape this destiny. Praiseworthy is a person who toils in Torah, and woe unto a person whose toils in foolishness. Let us apply that teaching to marriage. Your wife is going to give you advice, and it may come in a manner that seems like criticism. A married man cannot escape this destiny. Praiseworthy are those who listen to constructive criticism, and woe unto those who are offended over nothing.

✑Your Ticket to *Olam Haba*

I'm sure that as you read this essay you are thinking, "Big talker." You are right. I don't claim to be perfect. In fact, my expertise in the field of *shalom bayis* is based on the fact that I face these challenges daily.

There is a beautiful story told about Rav Yosef Chaim Sonnenfeld. In his great humility, Rav Yosef Chaim once told his wife, "When we come to the *Olam HaEmes*, you are going to be very disappointed. People tell you that I am a great Torah scholar, and that I am the *gadol hador*. In the next world, you will find out the truth — I am neither of the above."

"What are you saying?" exclaimed his wife.

"Yes, that is the truth," said Rav Yosef Chaim. "But don't worry. You thought that you were married to the *gadol hador*, and you were *moser nefesh* for the sake of my Torah, so you will undoubtedly merit a great portion in *Olam Haba*."

"That doesn't help," Rebbetzin Sonnenfeld protested. "I don't want to go to an exalted place in *Olam Haba* if you are not there with me."

"I know," responded Rav Yosef Chaim. "That is what I am counting on. They will let me in because your *Olam Haba* will not be complete if I am not with you. I will get in on your merit."

Men would do well if they learned this lesson. Your wife may very well be your ticket to *Olam Haba*.

In *Shir HaShirim*, Shlomo HaMelech allegorically compares the relationship between Hashem and *Klal Yisrael* to that of a husband and wife.

In one verse, he writes, "I have come to my garden, my sister, O bride, I have eaten my honeycomb with my honey" (5:1).

Honeycomb has no taste whatsoever. It is a piece of wax. Why is a man telling his *kallah* that he ate the honeycomb?

Rashi explains that when a person is betrothed or a newlywed, he is willing to eat the honeycomb with the honey. A *chasan* willingly accepts the less-palatable aspects of marriage, because he is so enthralled with this new relationship.

The words "I have come to my garden" describes courtship. If the courtship is to continue, you will have the ability to eat the honeycomb together with the honey. Yes, there will be difficult challenges along the way, but you can prevail. And even if you have failed in the past, even if you are married for fifty years and you have forgotten how to talk, spend, give respect, and accept criticism, it is not too late.

The Talmud (*Kiddushin* 2b) tells us, "*Derech ha'ish l'hachzor acharei ishto.*" It is the responsibility of the man to go out and seek a wife. The same applies here. No matter the state a marriage is in, a husband can turn it around. It is not easy, but it can be done. That which came naturally as a *chasan* can still be achieved now. Remember the four keys that we have spoken about. Train yourself to use them on a daily basis. It will take much effort, but is there any goal in our life that is more important?

May we all merit to have the *Shechinah* rest in our homes.

Shortcuts to Gan Eden

*T*here is a puzzling verse in *Zechariah* (12:11): "On that day [i.e., the day that the *yetzer hara* is destroyed] the eulogizing will become intense in Jerusalem, like the mourning of Hadadrimmon [and the mourning] at the Valley of Megiddon."

At first glance, this verse may not seem puzzling, but if you search through Tanach, you will not find mention of a person by the name of Hadadrimmon. The Talmud (*Megillah* 3a; *Mo'ed Kattan* 28b) quotes Rav Yosef's statement that if we would not have Targum on this verse, we would not know who Hadadrimmon was. The Targum reveals that this verse refers to the death of the wicked King Achav, who was killed by Ben-Haddad. Ben-Haddad is referred to, here, by the nickname Haddadrimon.

Thus the verse in *Zechariah* teaches that the eulogies delivered upon the slaughter of the *yetzer hara* will be equal to those delivered upon the death of Achav, and the Talmud (*Bava Kamma* 17a) describes the great honor accorded to Achav upon his death.

The mourning over the loss of Achav seems misplaced. The prophet states that Achav's wickedness was unparalleled by that of any other person in history: "There had never been anyone like Achav, who sold himself to do what was evil in the eyes of Hashem, as his wife, Ezevel, had incited him. He became very depraved, going after the idols, similar to the actions of the Amorite people, whom Hashem had driven out from before the Children of Israel" (*Melachim Aleph* 21:25-26).

Why would anyone mourn the loss of such an incredibly wicked person?

Tosafos (*Bava Kama* 17a, *s.v. Vehalo*) raises this question, and answers that the righteous people in Achav's times did not eulogize him — only his servants and fellow sinners mourned his loss. We can understand this opinion; even a wicked man would be mourned by his comrades.

The *Maharsha* (*Mo'ed Kattan* 28b) disagrees with *Tosafos*. He maintains that righteous people also eulogized Achav. This is difficult; what sort of eulogy would a righteous person deliver regarding Achav?

Another difficulty emerges from two seemingly contradictory passages. The Mishnah (*Sanhedrin* 90a) states that there are three kings who were so evil that they do not merit a portion in *Olam Haba*, and Achav is one of them. This teaching fits well with our perception of Achav.

But the Talmud (*ibid.* 102b) quoting Rav Nachman, teaches that on his Day of Judgment, Achav's fate was hanging in the balance. The scales of judgment showed equal amounts of merits and sins. Hashem sat in judgment to decide whether he should be punished or not. This is shocking. Could it be that the fate of Achav, the most wicked of men, was hanging in an even balance?

Indeed, Rav Yosef argued vehemently with Rav Nachman. "The prophet describes Achav as someone who excelled in evil," asked Rav Yosef, "and you say that his fate was hanging in balance?"

Rav Yosef explains further, "In truth, Achav was very wicked. But Achav had a positive *middah*. He was a *vatran* with his money, and *talmidei chachamim* benefited from this. He was therefore forgiven for half his sins."

Before we go further, we have to define the term *vatran*, a term — and form of behavior — that has no equivalent in the English language. A *vatran* deals with other people in an easygoing manner. A *vatran* is a person who does not insist on the letter of the law when it comes to his own rights and entitlements. A *vatran* overlooks and forgives offenses against his honor or possessions, and does not feel the need to retaliate against those who hurt him or cause him a loss. Apparently, Achav had this fine *middah*. He was a *vatran*.

This explanation is not satisfying. If we cannot accept the fact that Achav had an equal amount of merits and sins, is it any easier to accept that his *vatranus* in monetary issues caused his fate to hang in an even balance?

A final question: If we do accept that his judgment hung in an even balance, why wasn't he entitled to a portion in *Olam Haba*?

~§ Are Tradeoffs Accepted in Heaven?

*I*t is clear that we need to gain a deeper understanding of Achav. In this way, we can understand why he was mourned by the righteous people of his time. Are we to view him as thoroughly wicked, or as a person with an equal amount of merits and sins?

To do so, we must first examine an interesting question discussed by the *Rishonim* regarding man's Final Judgment in the Heavenly Court.

The average person judged by the *Beis Din shel Maalah* is neither perfectly righteous nor entirely wicked. A decent Jew passes away with many mitzvos to his credit, and — unfortunately — with some *aveiros*. Can a person bargain with the *Beis Din shel Ma'alah*? Can he say, "I know that I deserve to go to *Gehinnom* to be cleansed of my sins. *Gehinnom* does not look so pleasant. Remove some of my mitzvos from my account, in exchange for my *aveiros*. Allow me to avoid *Gehinomm* and go directly to Gan Eden with the remainder of my mitzvos!"

Does this work? Are tradeoffs accepted in Heaven?

In an essay recorded in *Sefer Chassidim* (#605), Rav Nissim Gaon writes that Hashem prefers to have good people leave this world with a clean slate. To achieve this, good people are sometimes made to suffer in this world, to atone for their sins. There are times that causing a particular person to suffer will remove his freewill. In such cases, Hashem does not force the person to atone through suffering, and the person comes to Heaven with sins that remain. Rav Nissim Gaon says that such a person is not punished for his sins. *Beis Din shel Maalah* will cancel these sins by wiping away some of the person's merits to "even out the score."

Thus, Rav Nissim Gaon understands that a person can "opt out" of *Gehinnom* by paying for sins with some of his *mitzvos*.

This concept is supported by *Sefer HaAruch*, (a compendium of Talmudic definitions, written by one of the *Rishonim*). In the entry for "*makifin* — extend credit," *Aruch* cites the Talmudic teaching, "*Ein makifin b'chillul Hashem* — No credit is extended to those who desecrate Hashem's Name."

Aruch explains that the Heavenly Court will not extend credit to a person by allowing him to perform a *mitzvah* that will atone for his desecration of Hashem's Name. From this, one may conclude that if a person sinned in a manner that did not cause a *chillul Hashem*, he would be allowed to use his credit for a mitzvah to atone for the sin.

If this arrangement sounds too good to be true, it is. Many *Rishonim* disagree sharply.

Rambam disagrees with Rav Nissim Gaon. The Mishnah (*Avos* 4:29) states, "Blessed is [Hashem], before Whom there is no iniquity, no forgetfulness, no favoritism, and no acceptance of bribery." *Rambam* is bothered by the need to mention that Hashem does not take bribes. "How would one pay a bribe to Hashem, and what can be offered as a bribe?" he wonders rhetorically.

"This Mishnah actually refers to Hashem's refusal to accept a person's good deeds as a 'bribe,'" says *Rambam*. "If a person has a thousand merits, for instance, and but one sin, Hashem will not remove one of his thousand merits in order to erase the sin. Hashem will first demand retribution for the sin, and only then will He allow the person to be rewarded for his merits."

According to *Rambam*, a person must be cleansed of his sins by experiencing the pain of *Gehinnom*. Each and every sin must be paid for. Only then can a person receive reward for all his merits. The following Midrash reflects this approach. On the verse, "For You repay each man according to his deeds" (*Tehillim* 62:13), *Midrash Shocher Tov* states, "One might think that if a person has ten mitzvos and ten *aveiros*, Hashem would allow them to counterbalance one another. But *HaKadosh Baruch Hu* does not do that; first He punishes for *aveiros*, then He rewards for mitzvos."

So, while Rav Nissim Gaon maintains that there is a shortcut to Gan Eden, which avoids *Gehinnom*, the Rambam disagrees.

A parable can be used to explain Rambam's opinion.

> A person is invited to a grand banquet. His mouth is watering in anticipation of the delicacies that will be served. However, he has a slight problem. His teeth are decayed and he can-

not chew. He must go to a dentist and have his teeth drilled and filled. Only then can he partake of the delicious food at the banquet.

(My apologies to our dentists for comparing their drilling to the experience of *Gehinnom*, but I think that most people will relate.)

A person who sinned has deprived his *neshamah* of the ability to experience Gan Eden. He has destroyed within himself the necessary tools for partaking in the celestial banquet. His *neshamah* must first be "drilled and filled." It must be repaired in *Gehinnom*. Only then does he have the tools to experience and appreciate Gan Eden.

Do most *Rishonim* accept the opinion of *Rambam* or that of Rav Nissim Gaon? *Ramban* (*Devarim* 10:16) cites *Rambam's* teaching and does not argue with it. Considering the detractors, it seems that we cannot rely on the shortcut of trading mitzvos for *aveiros*. It seems that we have no choice but to do *teshuvah* in this world, or we will have to suffer the experience of *Gehinnom, rachmana l'tzlon*.

But Rav Reuven Margulies, in his notes to *Sefer Chassidim, Mekor Chesed*, points out that the Talmud's teaching regarding Achav seems to refute *Rambam's* opinion.

As we have seen, Rav Nachman taught that Achav had an equal number of merits and sins. Rav Yosef argued that a person who was so devoted to evil could not possibly attain such a balance. Rather, said Rav Yosef, since Achav was a *vatran* in monetary matters, half his sins were erased.

Rav Margulies points out that Rav Yosef did not mention *teshuvah*. He does not maintain that Achav repented for idol worship or any of his other considerably evil deeds. Nevertheless, he was able to erase half his sins through this one merit of being a *vatran*. It would seem that the rest of us, who are not as bad as Achav, would certainly be able to use our merits to cancel our sins.

Mekor Chesed seems to prove that Rav Nissim Gaon and the *Aruch* are correct. Why do *Rambam* and *Ramban* maintain that we cannot trade merits for sins? How would they answer this proof?

The answer to this question will provide an extraordinary insight into the story of Achav. It will also help us understand why righteous people spoke at the funeral of Achav, and what they said in their eulogy. We will see that we have much to learn from Achav.

The Shortcut

On several occasions, Rav Pam, *zt"l*, discussed a scenario that is painfully common. We all hope to repent and mend our ways before we die. What if someone dies before he was successful in doing *teshuvah* properly? Can he still avoid *Gehinnom*?

Rav Pam answered that there is a shortcut. The Talmud (*Megillah* 28a; *Bava Kama* 92a) teachs, "*Kol hama'avir al midosav, ma'avirin mimenu kol peshaav* — A person who can overlook wrongdoings against him will have all his sins removed from him."

The trait of *vatranus* is a bona-fide shortcut to Gan Eden, even according to the *Rambam* and *Ramban*. A person who looks aside when others wrong him, whether in monetary affairs or interpersonal matters, has bought himself a ticket into Gan Eden. Let us clarify this point. If you are involved in a dispute in which you are wrong and you do not get angry, that is not called *vatranus*. It is called *yosher*, being just. If you are right and you don't get upset — *that* is called *vatranus*.

The Midrash (*Bamidbar Rabbah* 9:2) offers examples of *vatranus*. If someone spills something in your house, says the Midrash, be a *vatran*. Don't become upset. Or if someone rips your clothing, let it slide. Swallow the anger. Restrain your response. Smile and say that it is really okay.

What self-control! How beautiful a *middah*!

How often do we have the opportunity for *vatranus* in our homes? What happens when someone spills something on *your* table — or, Heaven forbid, in your lap? If you can allow it to slide, you can earn a free pass into Gan Eden. If no one in your house ever spills anything, I feel bad for you. In *my* house I have many opportunities to be *mevater*. If you, too, get the opportunity to be *mevater*, rejoice!

Most of all, says the Midrash, be a *vatran* with your money and your possessions. This is the greatest challenge of all. Parents often face a situation in which an older child in the family hides a treasure — such as a bag of cookies or a package of licorice — in his drawer. A younger sibling raids the cache. The older child comes home — lo and behold — his treasure is gone. Filled with righteous indignation, he screams and yells, "How could he take something from my drawer? It's mine!"

Parents often try to placate the older sibling. "Don't get so upset over a package of licorice," they say. "We'll buy you another package."

"That's not the point," the victim screams. "*My* private space was violated. *My* stuff was looted. Nothing is safe in this house!"

Learned parents have an answer. "Be a *vatran* with your possessions," they say. "Don't get so worked up. It is a shortcut to Gan Eden."

The trouble with preaching this principle to your children is that sometimes the tables are turned. When you face the same challenge — when you blow up because someone encroaches on *your* territory and sabotages *your* possessions, your child might just think, "Don't get so worked up! It's a shortcut to Gan Eden. Why isn't he just *mevater*?"

It is easy to tell your children to be *mevater*, and harder to do when you yourself are wronged.

In *Orchos Yosher*, R' Chaim Kanievsky Shlita has a chapter on *vatranus*. He writes that the ability to overlook is generally a sign of wisdom. A person who remains calm and forgiving when the waiter spills a bowl of hot soup in his lap is usually a wise person. Those people who cannot overlook anything are fools. Have you ever seen an argumentative person loudly standing up for his rights? Did he come across as wise?

∽§ Zeh Lo Chashuv

I would like to share with you a story about a husband and wife I knew well.

She was a paragon of organization who ran their home with incredibly efficiency. She cheerfully cooked and baked for their large family and hosted many guests. Although their home was clean and orderly, her house was a busy place. She was sometimes casual about putting things back in their proper places. When her husband would be impatient and point this out, she would smile and say, "*Zeh lo chashuv* — it is not important."

One summer, the family was vacationing in the country and the husband was working in the city. The wife called him and asked that he bring her a checkbook when he returned to the country. At the end of the week, he was already on the highway when he realized that he had forgotten to take a checkbook. He turned around, went back to their home, got the checkbook, and headed for the country. He handed the checkbook to his wife, and she stuck it into a shopping bag that was hanging on the crib. He was annoyed by the casual way she had tossed aside the checkbook, as if it weren't important. After all, he had gone out of his way to make sure that it was there. He controlled himself and didn't say anything.

Shabbos passed, and another week went by. He came back to the bungalow on the following Thursday. The checkbook was still there, in the shopping bag, hanging on the crib. He was upset. What a *nisayon*! His wife hadn't even used the checkbook! He was going to say something, but then he figured that she would simply respond, "*Zeh lo chashuv*," so he remained silent.

A week later he came up again, and the checkbook was still in the bag. I'm not sure why it bothered him so much. I know many men who would be delighted if their wives didn't touch a checkbook for two weeks. But it bothered him. He restrained himself.

The following week, the husband, who was back in the city, got an emergency call. His wife, who was in the advanced stages of pregnancy, was hemorrhaging and had been rushed to the hospital. He jumped into his car and drove as quickly as he could to meet her. Tragically, by the time he got there she was no longer alive.

When he came back to the bungalow that night, he looked brokenheartedly at the crib. The bag was still there and so was the checkbook. He was glad that, at least, he had remained silent. How right she had been! These things are not worth getting upset about. *Zeh lo chashuv.*

He used the first check to pay the *Chevra Kaddisha* (Burial Society) for the funeral and burial. He then took the shopping bag and wrote on it, "*Zeh lo chashuv*." That bag still hangs in his home.

We get so upset over petty things. Neatness, money, honor — things that really don't matter. We allow pettiness to bother us. Does it really matter? *Zeh lo chashuv*. These things are not important.

How Dare She Eat My Cookies?

R' Hanoch Teller tells the story of a *frum* woman who was waiting for a flight at a New York airport. She went to the airport store and bought a pack of kosher cookies and a newspaper. She sat down to enjoy her snack. The bag of cookies lay on the seat next to her, and she noticed another *frum* woman sitting in the next seat, also reading the paper. As she skimmed through the paper, she reached out and took a cookie from the package. To her surprise, the other woman nonchalantly reached into the bag and took a cookie as well. *That is strange*, she thought. *She didn't even bother asking for permission.*

She continued reading. Soon, she reached into the bag for another cookie. Sure enough, a moment later, the other woman also took a cookie. She could no longer concentrate on her newspaper. She pretended to continue reading, waited a few moments, and took another cookie. Out of the corner of her eye, she watched as the other woman continued reading her paper while taking yet another cookie. *What a chutzpah,* she kept thinking, *she is eating half my cookies.*

This continued, each woman taking a cookie, followed by the other woman. Soon, only one cookie remained. *What would this woman do now? Would she take the last cookie?*

The other woman reached into the bag, took out the cookie, cracked it in half, returned one half to the bag and ate the other half. *Incredible! What messed-up middos this lady has!*

Incensed, she was about to rebuke the cookie thief for her rudeness when a voice on the loudspeaker announced that her flight was beginning to board. The cookies were quickly forgotten as she rushed to get on line. As she reached into her handbag for her boarding pass, her hand brushed against something. She looked down and there, in the recesses of her handbag, was her bag of cookies, untouched. At first she was puzzled. Then she realized. The cookies on the seat were not hers, but belonged to the other woman. *She* was the cookie thief.

She rushed back to apologize. The other woman laughed off the incident, saying that she was on a diet anyway and did not need the calories. *She didn't even mind! Incredible! What wonderful middos this lady has!*

There is a lesson in *limud zechus* (judging others favorably) to be learned from this story, but this is also a story of astounding *vatranus*. The owner of the bag was able to take the last cookie, split it in half, and leave it for a person who had been taking cookie after cookie without permission. That is true *vatranus*. That kind of attitude can get you a free ticket into Gan Eden.

✧ What's Wrong with "*Sheli Sheli*"?

Rav Pam would often illustrate the concept of *vatronus* with a question on a Mishnah. In *Avos* (5:13), we learn that one who says, "*Sheli sheli v'shelcha sheli* — my [possessions] are mine, and yours are mine" is — understandably — a wicked person. But the Mishnah goes on to say that according to some Sages, a person who says, "*Sheli sheli v'shelcha shelcha* — mine is mine and yours is yours" is compared to the people of Sodom.

How are we to understand this? What is wrong with this attitude? Is it wrong to insist that my own possessions are mine, as long as I respect the claim of others to their possessions?!

Rav Pam explained this Mishnah. Being overly zealous in establishing "what's mine is mine" is not a good character trait. It is an attitude that causes people to be *makpid* on their money and on their honor. It is the opposite of *vatranus*.

Hakadosh Baruch Hu wants us to develop the capacity to overlook other people's wrongdoings. We are not to be sticklers in aggressively defending our rights. And as the Talmud teaches, our success in doing so can provide us with a much desired shortcut to Gan Eden.

✧ Back to Achav

It is mind-boggling to consider what Achav almost achieved. Achav — the man who was responsible for importing the worship of *Baal* and *Asheirah* into Eretz Yisrael — almost made it into Gan Eden. Hashem considered forgiving him for his sins. Was he truly a man with an equal amount of merits and sins?

Certainly not, says Rav Yosef. But he was a *vatran* when it came to dealing with others. It is not as if Achav distributed funds to *talmidei chachamim* himself. Among his other horrendous deeds, Achav killed every prophet he could lay his hands on. Nevertheless, the spirit of *vatranus* that he inspired in the Jews of his time enabled *talmidei chachamim* to benefit indirectly from his possessions, and that was enough to atone for half his sins.

Righteous people came to Achav's funeral expecting to see the Torah leaders singing and dancing. But the righteous people of the generation saw reason to mourn. Someone went up to the podium and said, "*Achav vatran b'memono haya* — Achav was generous with his money." What a powerful eulogy. What a lesson for the living!

The *Rambam* writes that we cannot exchange *mitzvos* for *aveiros*. *Mekor Chesed* points out that Achav *was* allowed to exchange mitzvos for *aveiros*.

Does this disprove *Rambam's* opinion? No. *Vatranus* is different. Hashem created a world to benefit mankind. When man achieves a proper level of *vatranus*, he becomes a party to the purpose of Creation; his behavior rises beyond that of a good deed. It mirrors the qualities that Hashem looks for in His people. It is an attitude that builds a calm and peaceful home; a better world.

Ordinary mitzvos do not atone for *aveiros*, but *vatranus* is more. Achav's crimes were too horrendous, and he could not enter Gan Eden despite his *vatranus*.

Certainly, we are not nearly as wicked as Achav was. For us, *vatranus* is the answer. It is the true shortcut to Gan Eden.

Matches Made in Heaven

I am fortunate enough to be in yeshivah, where I come into contact with young *chasanim*. I've watched young men grow from *bachur* to *chasan* to husband. And I've noticed: a funny thing happens on the way back from the *chuppah*.

The script runs something like this. A young man is dating. He meets the right one. He is full of enthusiasm as he tells me, "You know, it's amazing. We're the same. Could you believe it! I loved it in Eretz Yisrael and she loved it! We like similar foods; we have similar hobbies; we even use the same brand of toothpaste!"

Then they get married. They find that they are not so alike after all. They like the same foods, but one likes to eat out while the other likes to stay home. They have similar hobbies, but enjoy them in different ways. They both use the same brand of toothpaste, but one replaces the cap, while the other loses it. (It seems that the *Ribbono shel Olam* uses this crucial factor in determining *shidduchim*: pairing one cap-loser with a cap-replacer.)

Suddenly, things are not so rosy. There are disagreements, then arguments, and the happy couple is not so happy. There are problems and the match made in Heaven is a mismatch!

◆§ The *Chasam Sofer*

A lesson that the *Chasam Sofer* (in *Toras Moshe*) derives from *Parashas Chayei Sarah* stands out as crucial appreciation of the difficulties that normal people experience. These are sound words of advice to anyone who identifies with this young couple.

Eliezer proposes that Rivkah marry Yitzchak. In response, Lavan says, "*Mei'Hashem yatza hadavar* — this marriage is Divinely ordained. *Lo nuchal dabeir eilecha ra oh tov* — there is nothing we can say, neither bad nor good."

Chasam Sofer asks: It was understood that Rivkah would marry Yitzchak. Certainly, no person would say anything bad about a *shidduch* once he realized that it was a done deal. But why not say something good? After all, if the *shidduch* was going to happen anyway, why not offer a positive assessment of it?

Chasam Sofer answers that the Torah (through Lavan) is teaching us a lesson regarding marriage. We often harbor the misconception that to make a good marriage, it is crucial that both partners be identical, that they be as similar as possible. But this is not true. In a successful marriage, it is important that there be differences between the two partners, as well. If two people are exactly the same, what benefit is there in marriage? Instead of one six-foot person, marriage would give you twelve feet of that person. He is the same; nothing has changed. Marriage would not bring any fundamental improvement to a human being.

On the other hand, if the two are different, there is a great advantage. They will disagree, they will argue, they will discuss ... and ultimately, they will come to a decision regarding their course in life. The decision will be well-thought-out. It will be the result of much analysis and deliberation. And it will result in a well-planned life. When two people with differences join together to form a single home, there are going to be disagreements. How wonderful!

"*Lo nuchal dabeir eilecha ra oh tov* — there is nothing we can say, neither bad nor good."

The *tov*, says the *Chasam Sofer*, is not always *tov*, and the *ra* is not always *ra*. Differences between husband and wife may seem to be *ra*, but they are not actually so. These differences may in fact be the greatest *tov* in the life of the couple.

Chasam Sofer gives one example of this idea, an example with which many couples would easily identify. Often (*very* often), one partner in marriage is a *pazron*, a person who is quick to spend money, while the other is a *kamtzan*, reluctant to incur expenses. They often disagree on how their finances should be run. How fortunate they are! Imagine if they were both *pazranim*, impulsive spenders: the house would come to economic ruin. No money would be saved. If both would be *kamtzanim*, reluctant to part with their money, the house could not be a happy place. It is because they are different — one is a *kamtzan* and the other a *pazran* — that they will disagree and their constructive dialogue will bring them to a proper, happy medium.

The *Chasam Sofer* says: "Problems? Not at all. This *is* a match made in Heaven, a perfect *shidduch*! That's precisely the benefit of marriage!"

⋧ Afraid of Disagreements?

Perhaps we can better appreciate this by referring to the *chavrusa* relationship. Two young men are studying together, trying to appreciate the depth of a *sugya*. The Gemara introduces a concept that can be understood two ways. Each *chavrusa* pauses to mull over the two possibilities.

Occasionally you have *chavrusos* who will generally agree. They understand the Gemara in a similar manner. They read the Gemara, express their understanding, and move on. Across the study hall, there are two other young men who are studying together. They come to same *sugya*. One expresses his understanding. The other disagrees. They begin arguing. One cites a source to support his approach; the other presents a logical counter-argument. Look — they're fighting!

Which pair of *chavrusos* is ideal? Which will have a better chance of fully understanding the *sugya*? The pair that agrees? Or the pair that disagrees? Which will pursue the truth? Which is more likely to become complacent and move on without much thought or depth?

You get the picture. We know that the best *chavrusa* is the one who disagrees, providing that he disagrees on the issue with intellectual honesty, and with the willingness to yield when disproven, realizing that he is really the winner. Now he has arrived at the truth. This is what a good *chavrusa* is all about.

The *sugyos* of life deserve the same scrutiny!

Disagreements are important tools in a good, constructive dialogue. They are an integral part of marriage. No wonder couples so often disagree!

✺ In-Laws

I had heard that in-laws sometimes do damage to a marriage. It's something I could never understand. Which parents would destroy a child's marriage?

Often, it's exactly the same story. When their child and his/her wife/husband have disagreements, the parents suffer from their failure to learn this *Chasam Sofer*. They fail to realize that disagreements are a healthy part of marriage. They observe disagreements and feel for their child. They forget that young people can disagree; when there is a willingness to listen with mutual respect, these are good signs. Yes, your *tatelle* can learn to work things out without you! The problem is the *parents'* insecurity.

Accept differences; that's the lesson of the *Chasam Sofer*. It's a lesson for *shanah rishonah*, the first year of marriage, and a lesson for all subsequent years of marriage.

✺ A Deeper Appreciation

Rabbi Chaim Shmulevitz takes this lesson a gigantic step further. In *Sichos Mussar* (5732:20), he refers to a "*sod gadol be'yetzira*," what he calls "a great secret of creation." "A woman is created to be helpful to her husband, and as a result of this responsibility, she is endowed with the ability (*chush ha're'ach*) to sense the truth regarding the manner in which her husband conducts himself, in relation to his spiritual status."

He explains that a woman's ability to disagree with her husband regarding his conduct — and to be correct in her contention — is a gift *to the husband* from the *Ribbono shel Olam*.

The Gemara relates that Rav Chanina ben Tradyon, one of the ten *harugei malchus* (Torah giants martyred by the Romans), was punished because he pronounced Hashem's Name as it is spelled, something that is normally done only in the *Beis HaMikdash*. When the Romans took him to be killed, his wife was defiled as well. The

Gemara relates that Rav Chanina ben Tradyon was punished for pronouncing Hashem's Name[1] publicly. His wife was punished for not preventing him from doing so. How incredible! Rav Chanina was a *gadol hador*, the leader of his generation, a *posek* (halachic authority) for his people. He held that he was permitted to pronounce Hashem's Name. Wouldn't it be expected that his wife accept his ruling? How could she be faulted for failing to correct him?

Rabbi Chaim Shmulevitz presents this question, and concludes that even if a man is a *gadol hador*, his wife's ability to sense his failings rises to correspond to his level. Thus, his wife did indeed have the ability to sense his error and to correct him, yet did not do so.

What men often see as a hindrance, as a burden, is actually a gift of the highest order!

How tragic it is when people turn the great gifts of marriage into problems. The very potential for disagreement and constructive criticism that marriage offers should be appreciated and utilized with great joy.

If we understand that it is inherent in marriage to have disagreements, to build from differences — and, yes, to accept criticism — then we can be building upwards, all of our lives.

◆§ Ishto Mosheles Alav

The Gemara (*Beitzah* 32) teaches "There are three whose lives are not lives." One of the three is *mi she'ishto mosheles alav*, a man whose wife rules over him.

Using the *Chasam Sofer*'s idea, we can understand this Gemara in a new light. First, a lesson regarding the word *mosheles*.

The Gaon of Vilna teaches that there are two Hebrew words for a monarch: *melech*, king, and *mosheil*, ruler. There is a fundamental difference between the two.

A *melech* is a king who is willingly accepted by his subjects as their leader. His commands are followed happily. A *mosheil* rules by force, against the desire of his subjects.

The Gaon illustrates this using the following verses. *Ki laShem hamelucha u'mosheil ba'goyim*, the Jewish People have accepted

---

1. This refers to the *Shem Havayeh*, a name which is not normally pronounced as it is spelled (except in the *Bais HaMikdash*).

Hashem's rule willingly (thus, the word *hamelucha*), but the idolater does not accept Hashem's dictates. To him, Hashem is a *mosheil*.[2]

Returning to our subject, *mi she'ishto mosheles alav*, a man whose wife rules over him, lives a tough life, indeed. This is because his wife's opinions cause him anger and aggravation; he feels threatened by her. She has become a *mosheil*. Sad, indeed. A couple should never have a *memshala* relationship. The home should have an atmosphere of *malchus*, where the royal couple rules jointly, and disagreements that arise are cause for fruitful discussion and joyful growth.

◆§ Don't Drop the Egg!

Couples sometimes complain that they are bickering all the time. Their lives feel like one long disagreement. When did this begin?

We can usually trace this back to the first time their disagreement turned personal. He said something. She disagreed. He was insulted (it happens) and responded angrily (bad idea). She responded in kind (worse idea). The disagreement could have been a purposeful constructive discussion. Instead, the "discussion" (if it can be called that) turned into a matter of pride. Everyone loses.

Don't let it happen to you! Treasure your disagreements. See them as something constructive (your tie is crooked), not something spiteful (your nose is crooked). Don't lose this valuable benefit of marriage.

A 17th-century anecdote illustrates our point so well:

> A widow lived with her three children in dire poverty. One day, the widow came home with an egg. The children were overjoyed. They had not eaten an egg in weeks!
>
> "No," their mother said. "We are not going to eat this egg."
>
> To the disappointed children she explained. "We are going to take our egg to our neighbor's farm and place it under his hen. It ten days, it will hatch, and we will have a chicken."
>
> The children cheered. They had not eaten chicken in months!
>
> "No," the widow explained. "We will not eat the chicken."
>
> "We will let the chicken grow, and soon she will lay eggs.

---

2. This explains another verse. "*V'hayah Hashem l'melech al kol ha'aretz*. On that day God will be King over all the Earth." Only when *Mashiach* comes will all accept Hashem's rule willingly.

Those eggs will hatch, more chicks will be born, and before we know it we will have dozens of chickens and hundreds of eggs!"

The children were ecstatic. Their mother kept on dreaming aloud ....

"We won't eat those chickens, either. We will sell them and save until we have enough money to buy a cow. We will have milk from the cow. Then, the cow will have calves. Pretty soon, we'll have eggs and chickens, and milk and meat ...."

In their excitement, the family was jumping for joy, imagining their bright future. In her excitement, the widow stretched out her arm joyfully ... and dropped the egg!

The room became quiet, as the family stood there, gazing sadly at the cracked egg, and with it their shattered hope for the future.

In life, there are many dropped eggs. The wonderful blessing of harmonious disagreement (that means disagreeing and still getting along!), is an egg that gives blessing ... if it is not dropped.

We would do well to internalize the *Chasam Sofer*'s message. Having a disagreement does not mean that a marriage is a failure. It makes growth possible. It can make a home better than it was before.

Yes, intelligent people can have different opinions.

And so, the next time you and your wife view a matter differently, declare with appreciation, "*Baruch Hashem*, this is a marriage made in heaven!"

From the Yeshivah to the Workplace

It was the very last time that I had the privilege of hearing Rabbi Yaakov Kamenetsky, *zt"l*, speak in Mesivta Torah Vodaath. The gathering, sponsored by Torah Umesorah, was for young men who were ready to leave the yeshivah and were willing to consider positions in *chinuch* or *rabbanus* out of town. When word got out that Reb Yaakov was going to speak, the *beis hamidrash* quickly filled up with a few hundred *bnei Torah* of all ages, most of whom (myself included) were not contemplating leaving the yeshivah.

Reb Yaakov surveyed the crowd and then spoke. His words (to the best of my recollection) were brief: "I was told that this would be a gathering of *talmidim* who are ready to leave the yeshivah to earn a livelihood. In fact, I see many *talmidim* who plan to remain in yeshivah. I have prepared an address for those ready to go out into the world; those who are not at this stage should not hear my words.

"Instead, let me tell you a *Dvar Torah* on this week's *parashah*. Afterwards, those who are indeed considering leaving yeshivah may accompany me upstairs to a classroom, where we can speak privately."

With these words, Reb Yaakov conveyed an important message. Torah is a guide to all aspects of a person's life; *ki heim chayeinu*. Yet, just as there are many facets to life, so too are there many facets to Torah. Those facets of Torah that guide a person when he is exposed to the secular society around him are not the same as those that guide a *talmid* through his sheltered years in yeshivah. Nor are the guiding principles of our yeshivah years enough to ensure success when the time comes to leave yeshivah.

◈§ The Yeshivah of Shem and Eiver

This message is spelled out more clearly in Reb Yaakov's commentary on *Parashas Vayeitzei*, in his *sefer, Emes L'Yaakov*:

Yaaaov Avinu, still a bachelor at the age of sixty-three, is sent by his father to the house of Lavan to find his *shidduch*. On the way to Lavan's house, Yaakov stops to study at the *beis hamidrash* of Shem and Eiver — and remains there for fourteen years! After sixty-three years of study under the guidance of his father Yitzchak, why did Yaakov see it as imperative for him to delay his marriage by stopping to study under Shem and Eiver?

Here, too, Reb Yaakov explains that there are two aspects to Torah: First is the Torah of the house of Yitzchak, which is geared to the student who has the luxury of living in a sheltered environment, protected by the *koslei beis hamidrash*. Second is the Torah as experienced in the house of Lavan, the secular world.

After sixty-three years, Yaakov was leaving this yeshivah to be exposed to the dangers of the house of Lavan. To prepare for this, he needed to master the second aspect of Torah, the Torah of Shem and Eiver. Shem and Eiver had lived among corrupt societies — Shem, during the generation of the Flood; Eiver, during the sinful *Dor Haflagah*. Both survived their exposure to these surroundings with their personal integrity intact. Thus, the Torah of Shem and Eiver focuses on withstanding outside influences. For sixty-three years, Yaakov had had no need to study Torah in this way. Upon leaving his father's home, Yaakov knew that he could not expose himself to the pernicious influences of Lavan without proper preparation.

In our yeshivah years, we are fortunate to study the Torah of Yitzchak. We spend these years maturing in a controlled environment. The debased society around us seems distant. It is later, when leaving the *beis hamidrash,* that the Torah of Shem and Eiver must be absorbed. When a *talmid* fails to realize this, he will find himself thrust into a society that is far worse than the house of Lavan; and he will face a challenge for which he is ill-prepared.

In my years in yeshivah, I have seen many *talmidim* come and go. In general, our yeshivah is successful in preparing its *talmidim* for life after *beis hamidrash*. Yet, I often see a *talmid* who had excelled in the yeshivah, but who falters badly when he is no longer sheltered. These *talmidim* may have mastered the Torah of Yitzchak, but have failed in the Torah of Shem and Eiver.

I am delighted to note that the reverse is also true. Many *talmidim* who did not stand out during their yeshivah years nevertheless emerge as outstanding *bnei Torah* after leaving the yeshivah. Their dedication to Torah and Torah values, despite the harsh demands of the business and professional world, is extraordinary. They have mastered the Torah of Shem and Eiver.

This discrepancy has bothered me. Why was it that some *talmidim* fall when exposed to the outside influences, while others thrive despite this exposure?

Dr. Asch's Experiment

A psychologist named Asch conducted an experiment on a college campus, and his results shed light on our question.[1]

> Dr. Asch called seven students into a classroom and told them that they were the subjects of an experiment. Actually, however, six of the students were planted there; only the seventh student was the subject of the experiment.
>
> On the blackboard, two parallel lines were drawn. One was ten inches long; the other, twelve. The lines were close enough so that their relative size should have been obvious.
>
> The students were told that this was a test of their perception. They were asked to carefully examine the board and then decide which line was longer. The six students who had

---

1. This experiment is cited, in part, by Rabbi Aryeh Kaplan in *Encounters* (Moznaim, 1990) pp. 69-70.

been planted were asked to answer first. One after another, each stated confidently that the ten-inch line was longer than the twelve-inch line. Then, the seventh student was asked the same question. In sixty percent of the cases, the student would respond that the ten-inch line was longer!

In the other forty percent of the cases, when the subject would answer that the twelve-inch line was longer, the other six students would argue with him and cajole him to correct his obvious "mistake." Under this pressure, an additional thirty percent would concede that the ten-inch line was indeed longer than the twelve-inch line!

This study revealed that under social pressure, ninety percent of people could be influenced to agree that a ten-inch line is longer than a twelve-inch line! This shows the degree to which a person is influenced by those around him, even in cases where a person has no personal attachment to those people.

Most people are sure that they would not have been fooled, if they had been subject to this test. But is this really so? The subjects of these tests were college students and professors, intelligent people, yet their judgment was easily manipulated by the social pressures of the classroom. It is interesting to note that a few years ago this experiment was replicated in Bais Yaakov Academy in Flatbush. The results were virtually identical to those reported by Dr. Asch.

In fact, we are all subjects of this test — in real life. Every young man or woman who steps out into a secular environment to become part of the workforce is put to this test. People around them will insist that wrong is right, that dark is light and that night is day. The corrupt society tears away at the person, day after day. How can a person resist these pressures?

◆§ The Experiment, Part II

r. Asch's experiment was followed up by another, similar experiment.

Here, seven students were again called into a classroom and shown the same two lines.

This time, only five students were planted, so that the remaining two students were the subject of the experiment.

Here again, the first five students would state with certainty that the ten-inch line was longer than the twelve-inch line. The remaining students were then asked their opinion.

The results of this study are revealing. In this experiment, when an individual answered that the twelve-inch line was longer, he had a second person to back him up. In this case, the individual could not be convinced to change his mind. No amount of ridicule would cause him to waiver from the truth.

This is our answer. A young man or woman who leaves yeshivah must remain attached to his spiritual source in a real and active way. This connection will help him withstand the onslaught of secular values (or anti-values) and moral corruption that abound in today's business and professional world.

↦ Staying Connected

I have maintained a personal connection with many young men after they've left yeshivah. In analyzing the difference between those who feel that they have retained (or improved on) their spiritual level and those who feel that they have not, one common denominator stands out. Those who remained attached to a source of spirituality are best equipped to handle the challenges they face.

This "source" may be in one of many forms. For some, it is an active attachment to a *rosh yeshivah* or a *chavrusa*. For others, it is the *beis hamidrash* where they daven and learn. For some, it is the participation in *Daf Yomi* that gives them this sense of attachment.

Incredible though it may sound, too many *talmidim*-turned-professionals have none of these. Their attachment to their yeshivah is through the checkbook only (if that!); their local shul is only a place to catch a minyan, a place to which they've developed no attachment; and when I inquire regarding *chavrusos*, they tell me of their impending plans to start a *seder* with a friend. All too often these plans remain pending — on a permanent basis.

✡ The Entropy Principle

*T*he scientific principle of entropy maintains that a system, when left unguided, will have an "irreversible tendency towards increasing disorder and inertness."[2]

Simply put, this principle states that chaos and disorder are the natural result of any action or reaction. When a windowpane breaks, it does not break into smaller, usable squares of glass. Instead, the window shatters in a chaotic way, creating non-useful slivers of glass. Only when there is a guiding hand that controls the breakup of a pane of glass will it break into smaller and useful fragments. (This is one of the problems that scientists concede regarding their theory of evolution. Big explosions do not leave useful creations. When two cars collide head-on, we do not find that they've melted into a limousine. Only a guiding hand causes a "big bang" to yield a constructive and useful product.)

The entropy principle applies to the spiritual world as well. The Torah often compares life to goodness and death to evil, as in the verse, "*See, I have placed before you today life and goodness, death and evil ... choose life*" (*Devarim* 30:15).

Rabbi Yitzchak Hutner, *zt"l*, explained the analogy of life and death to good and evil (*Pachad Yitzchak* to *Rosh Hashanah* 8:4). A basic requirement for life is a constant source of sustenance and nourishment, without which life could not continue. This is not true of death. The state of death continues without active involvement from any outside source. This is a passive condition, which requires no guiding hand.

The same is true in regard to good and evil. Like life, goodness must be sustained on a constant basis. Even if one attains a level of righteousness, he cannot expect to remain on that level unless he infuses himself with constant sustenance — no matter what one has already achieved.

Evil, on the other hand, does not require this constant infusion. Evil, like death, is a passive state. When there is no spiritual sustenance, when a person ignores his spiritual self, his lifeblood of rectitude slowly seeps away. Entropy has taken hold. It is a natural consequence for the soul to fall into a state of chaos and disorder.

This is the challenge of the *ben Torah* who has embarked on a secular career. He must continue nourishing his soul or he risks los-

---

2. Quoted from RD Encyclopedia Dictionary.

ing the achievements of his yeshivah years. Like life itself, spirituality cannot continue without constant sustenance.

Entropy sets in when there is no guiding hand. It is the job of a *ben Torah*-turned-professional to ensure that he continues to control his life, that his spiritual self has guidance and direction. This is achieved by the connection he maintains to a source of spirituality, whether via his *rosh yeshivah*, his *chavrusa*, or his local *beis hamidrash*. It is this connection and this connection alone that ensures continued growth in the post-yeshivah years.

The *Kuntzenmachers*

The Vilna Goan spent his later days in his personal *beis hamidrash* in Vilna, in the constant study of Torah. He once asked the famed Dubner Maggid to visit him and offer him words of *mussar*. Although he was reluctant at first (what *mussar* could one prescribe to the *Gra*?!), the Dubner Maggid accepted the invitation.

When he visited the *Gra*, he said, "Is it a big *kuntz*[3] to be a Vilna Gaon when you stay locked up in your room, unexposed to outside influences? The simple tailors, butchers, and tradesmen of Vilna who are exposed to the compromising values of the world and nevertheless retain their Jewish identity, they are the true *kuntzenmachers* of Vilna!"

The *Gra* was not impressed. His response was simply, "The Torah does not command Jews to be *kuntzenmachers*."

And yet, our *talmidim* are faced with the formidable task of managing the trick, of being *kuntzenmachers* in a world of values far lower than any the Dubner Maggid could have fancied in the furthest stretch of his imagination. To maintain a level of spirituality despite the crude society around him, an active Torah connection is needed. For anyone to imagine that he is capable of maintaining his spiritual integrity without great effort is to be self-deceiving.

---

3. *Kuntz* is a Yiddish expression for a trick, used here to refer to an unusual accomplishment. A *kuntzenmacher* (lit., trickster) is a person who can pull off unusual feats.

~§ Too Loosely Affiliated

A ben Torah leaves yeshivah to begin a career. He is exposed to the secular world for the first time. For many years, he has pursued spiritual delights. He has studied Torah, heard *mussar*, and been involved in his own personal soul-searching. He has excelled in the Torah of Yitzchak. But he has not prepared himself for the transition, for the exposure he is about to endure. What happens when he goes out into the world?

The late Rabbi Shlomo Zalman Braun related an anecdote that reflects the experience of an unprepared *ben Torah*.

> A farmer had two horses, which he used to pull his wagon and help earn his livelihood. One night a thief stole into the farmer's barn to steal the horses. The thief first took one horse, then returned for the other. The farmer was alerted to the noise in the barn and went out to investigate. He arrived at the barn just as the thief was preparing to steal the second horse.
>
> The thief sensed that he was cornered. Thinking quickly, he went into the empty stable where the stolen horse had been, and squatted down on all fours. The farmer entered the barn and discovered, to his amazement, that a man was standing in place of his horse!
>
> The farmer asked the man who he was. He was astonished when the man replied that he was actually his faithful horse: "I was an evil person in my previous life. Hashem decreed that I return to this world in a *gilgul*, as your horse. For many years, I labored for you. Tonight, the Heavenly Courts decreed that my time was up, that I had redeemed myself; tonight I changed back to Berel, my human self."
>
> The farmer was amazed. A miracle had occurred in his own farm! Hadn't his horse changed to this man before his very eyes? The farmer expressed his gratitude to his "horse," even giving him a few dollars with which to begin his new life, and sent him on his way.
>
> The next morning the farmer, still marveling at the miraculous events of the previous night, set out for the market to purchase a second horse.
>
> The farmer arrived at the market and examined the horses that were available for sale. One horse looked strangely

familiar. The farmer checked the horse carefully. Yes, there could be no mistake about it, this was his old horse!

The farmer sighed and patted the horse on its back. "Oy, Reb Berel. You're out in the world for one day, *un shoin viter a ferd* [and you're already back to being a horse]!"

≈§ The Challenge

Our community can be proud of its yeshivah graduates in all areas of life. We have lawyers, accountants, businessmen, and doctors who are true *talmidei chachamim*. We can hold our heads up high.

Yet we must seek to expand on our success. We must ensure that every one of us retains his spiritual integrity even in post-yeshivah days. This can be done only by keeping that spiritual connection intact, ensuring that every *ben Torah* retain his lifeline to his yeshivah days.

This is our challenge.

The Longest Berachah

A Jew recites one hundred *berachos* each day. The longest of all the *berachos* is the *berachah* of *Yotzer Ohr*, which we recite as part of Shacharis. We certainly understand that the *longest berachah* composed by the *Anshei Knessess HaGedolah* must have great significance. What is this *berachah* about?

Yotzer Ohr begins with praise to Hashem for creating night and day and providing us with light. Important enough. The *berachah* then shifts into a description of the Heavenly angels and records their daily song of praise. This is *not* easy to understand. *Berachos* are always so concise. Why a long *shpiel* over the angels?

There is a phrase that is recited by the *chazzan* — and an extra measure of zest is usually applied on Shabbos mornings: "*kulam ahuvim, kulam berurim, kulam giborim, kulam kedoshim,*" the *chazzan* trills melodiously, praising the Heavenly angels.[1]

---

1. I often wonder if the singing *chazzan* has any idea what he is saying. What *does* a *chazzan* think when he says, with great gusto, "*kulam ahuvim* ... the angels are all beloved"? Why does this matter? How is this an important part of our prayer?

At *kabalas Shabbos* I hear *chazzanim* chant with cheerful melody and great joy, "*arbaim shanah akut bedor, ve'omar am to'ei leivav heim.*" These words describe Hashem's anger at the Jewish People in the *Midbar*. "For I have sworn in My anger that they will never come to My land," sung so cheerfully. Makes you think twice about that tune.

These words are not difficult to translate — the angels are beloved, flawless, mighty, and holy. But why do we list their attributes in davening? Furthermore, why are the angels praised for those characteristics? Angels do not have free choice. Hashem created them exactly the way they are, and they deserve no praise for what they do.

More questions arise when we examine this *berachah*. Consider the words, "*Vechulam mekablim aleihem ol malchus Shamayim zeh m'zeh* — they all accept upon themselves the yoke of Heaven's sovereignty from one another."

Why do angels need to accept the yoke of Heaven upon themselves? Humans can perform mitzvos or *aveiros*. When a human accepts the yoke of heaven, he commits himself to doing the will of Hashem by performing mitzvos and avoiding *aveiros*. Angels do not have the ability to sin, nor are they commanded to perform mitzvos. What does it mean for an angel to accept the yoke of Heaven?

The *berachah* then shifts gears once more as we return to praising Hashem: "*ki Hu levado marom v'Kadosh, po'el gevuros* ...." How does one segment flow into the next?

The designation of *Yotzer Ohr* as the first *berachah* of *Krias Shema* warrants explanation as well. How do the themes of this *berachah* correlate to *Krias Shema*?

In short: the words of the *berachah* are not difficult to follow. The meaning of the *berachah* is different. We say this every day; shouldn't we understand its profound meaning?

✢§ One Source for Everything

*S*hema is the declaration of our belief in *one* Almighty God. We understand that Hashem's Oneness transcends everything. One God controls all, the good and the evil, the joy and the pain, the light and the darkness.

Heretics in Talmudic times took this mixture of good and bad as a sign that there was more than one god. "The god who created light could not have created darkness," they insisted.

Yotzer Ohr is a preparation for *Shema*. It declares our belief in One God. The Gemara (*Berachos* 11b) instructs us to declare the praises of day, even at night, and those of night even by day, in the first *berachah* of *Shema*.

The light and darkness mentioned in *Yotzer Ohr* do not refer to physical light and darkness. They refer to the illumination of joy and celebration as light, and to the disappointments of pain and suffering as darkness. (Indeed, in the entire book of *Tehillim*, the words *night* and *darkness* are never used in the physical sense.[2] They are always a reference to the darker, more difficult, periods of life.)

↪§ Angels: Representations of God's Will

What is an angel? We imagine angels as creatures, as they are described by the prophets. Since we cannot fathom formless beings, the prophets describe angels in physical terms.

There is another understanding of the angels. *Rambam* (*Yisodei HaTorah* 2:3, *Moreh Nevuchim* 1:49; see also *Shelah, Asarah Mamaros*, p. 33a, and Rav Tzaddok in *Sichas Malachim* 13a) explains that an angel is actually a representation of God's Will. Raphael represents Hashem's Will that a person be healed. Gavriel is the name for His plan to discipline. Michoel is His message of blessing to the Jewish People. Every angel is an expression of God's Will to do a specific task.

Some angels are created through the Divine Attribute of Kindness, and descend to bring blessing to the world. Others are expressions of the Attribute of Strict Justice; they come to challenge people and bring difficulty into the world. It would seem that these angels would be opposing forces; the angels who come to bestow warmth, light, and happiness would oppose those who bring tragedy, illness, and pain. They seem to have opposing missions.

What do we say in *Yotzer Ohr*? *Kulam ahuvim, kulam berurim, kulam giborim, kulam kedoshim*. They are all equal. They are all beloved, flawless, mighty, and holy. There is no imperfection in their missions; no contradiction, no inconsistency.

How can that be? How can we say that an angel who comes to mete out Heavenly Justice is beloved? We immediately explain: *Kulam osim be'eimah uv'yirah retzon Konam* — they are all sent to perform the Will of their Creator. Whether an angel is sent to bring blessing or pain, joy or difficulty, he represents the Will of Hashem. Every angel represents the Will of the One God, the *Hashem Echod*.

---

2. With the exception of 121:6; although there, too, the reference is to God's presence during times of difficulty.

When we declare that the angels accept the yoke of heaven upon themselves, we are not praising them for accepting that yoke. As we pointed out, they have no free choice and no inclination to do otherwise. Rather, we proclaim that no angel challenges the Will of Hashem. All angels, for good and for bad, are His messengers.

These are difficult passages to recite once we realize what we are saying. It must be hard for a person lying in a hospital bed to say "*kulam ahuvim* — they are all beloved." But the recognition that good and bad come from the same source is a profound message, precisely to the person in the hospital bed. This message deserves to be the longest *berachah* in the *siddur*. It requires an extended moment of reflection. And it deserves our attention as we recite these words every day.

> Rav Michoel Ber Weissmandel, *zt"l*, had a family before World War II, and they were killed by the Nazis *ym"s*. After the war he built a new family in the United States. He had five sons who were murdered in the concentration camps, and he had another five children born in the United States. After the war, at the *bris* of his fifth child, Rav Michoel Ber rose to speak. "*Nekadesh es Shimcha ba'olam* — I pray that my five sons should sanctify Hashem's Name in this world, *kesheim shem-akdishim Oso b'shmei marom* — in the same manner that my five sons who are looking down from Heaven sanctify His Name, *vekaru zeh el zeh ve'amar* — let them call out to each other and urge each other to say, *Kadosh! Kadosh! Kadosh!*"

This was a personal *Tzidduk HaDin*, a moving moment, recited at a *bris*. Our understanding, however, sheds new light on the words of this *gadol hador*. Rav Michoel Ber was speaking of the *profound meaning* of the words of the angels. There exist *malachei chavalah* (angels of destruction) who brought the Holocaust upon our nation. There is *Eliyahu Malach HaBris*, the symbol of joy of a family blessed with a newborn boy. As hard as it may be for us to appreciate, these are all messengers of the One God, sent on different parts of one master mission. The angels sanctify His Name together by fulfilling their missions. Our life's mission is to emulate the angels, to sanctify His Name under all circumstances.

❧ A Perfect Segue

The sanctification of Hashem's Name at all times — in times of joy and times of pain alike — is the theme of the first *berachah* of *Krias Shema*. How does this connect to *Shema*?

In his *tzava'ah* (ethical will), Rabbi Yisrael Lifshitz (author of *Tiferes Yisrael* on Mishnayos) instructs his children to have the following thoughts when reciting *Shema*: *Shema Yisrael* — Hear, O Israel; *Hashem* — God of Mercy, who provides us with happiness in life; *Elokeinu* — and God of Justice, who challenges us in life; *Hashem Echad* — are One and the same.

The *Mussar* masters would say that a person cannot begin to work on *emunah* and *bitachon* during times of tragedy. It takes great strength to live a life focused on *emunah* and *bitachon*. When the going is good, when things are running smoothly, this is the time to prepare for life's challenges. When a person finds himself in a hospital bed, it is too late to begin working on faith. When someone loses his job, it is not the moment to teach him that everything Hashem does is for the best. This attitude must be learned and absorbed before a person's moment of challenge arrives.

Shema and its *berachos* are the daily training session for a *baal bitachon*. We begin *birchos Krias Shema* by recognizing that all angels — those that we want to meet, and those that we would prefer not to encounter — are messengers from Hashem. All come on the same mission. They are all beloved, flawless, mighty, and holy. We then close our eyes in concentration and solemnly proclaim the *Shema*, affirming our faith in a God of Justice who is also the God of Mercy.

It is a lot to think about — especially on a weekday morning when the *chazzan* often speeds through the davening. It sometimes seems as though the *chazzan* is being held back by some invisible gate, and that *Borchu* is the signal to start running. If you listen closely you may even hear that he is out of breath — just like a racehorse.

Slow down! It takes an extra minute to think as you recite the words. "*Kulam ahuvim* — they are all beloved. *Kulam giborim* — they are all mighty.*" How *Klal Yisrael* suffers in *galus* from displays of Heavenly might! But "*kulam osim retzon Konam* — they are all fulfilling Hashem's Will."

Take the time to recite this *berachah* with concentration, every day, and you will be well prepared to handle the challenges of life.

⚜ An Angelic Dispute

Let us study the second half of *Yotzer Ohr*. The verses *"Kadosh, kadosh, kadosh..."* and *"Baruch kavod ..."* are the songs of the angels in Heaven. We recite these as part of *Yotzer Ohr* and repeat them in *Kedushah* (during the *chazzan's* repetition of *Shemoneh Esrei*).³

Let's take a closer look at the words recited by the angels. The verse *Kadosh, kadosh* is from *Yeshayah* (6:3). The prophet describes a vision in which he saw angels called *Seraphim* surrounding Hashem, declaring, *"Kadosh, kadosh, kadosh, Hashem Tzevakos, melo chal ha'aretz Kevodo* — Holy, holy, holy is Hashem, Master of the Legions, the world is filled with His Glory." This is why we mention, in *Kedushah,* that this verse comes from **sarfei kodesh**.⁴

The words *"Baruch kevod ..."* appear in a different book of Tanach. Yechezkel saw groups of angels called *Ofanim* and *Chayos HaKodesh,* and heard them sing, *"Baruch kevod Hashem m'mikomo* — Blessed is Hashem's Name in Its place." This is why we refer to these angels in *Kedushah, "v'haOfanim v'Chayos HaKodesh."*

These angels are actually arguing with each other.⁵

The *Seraphim* declare, *"Melo chol ha'aretz Kevodo* — Hashem's Glory fills the world." They maintain that Hashem's Presence can be

---

3. There are significant halachic differences between these verses as they are recited in *Yotzer Ohr* and in *Kedushah*. We are allowed to recite *Yotzer Ohr* while sitting — indeed, some authorities maintain that it is preferable to sit while saying this *berachah*. We are permitted to say these words without a minyan. *Kedushah* must be recited standing, and with a minyan. Why?

Rabbeinu Yonah to *Berachos* 21b explains that in *Bircas Krias Shema* we are "telling the story" of the angels' recitation of *Kedushah* in Heaven. We do not have to rise to tell a story, and we do not need a *minyan*. In *Kedushah,* we ourselves are sanctifying Hashem's Name with words borrowed from the angels. Thus we begin *Kedushah* with an introductory statement, *Nekadesh es Shimcha ba'olam k'sheim shemakdishim Oso b'shemi marom.* (In nusach Sefard: *Nakdishach vena'aritzach kenoam siach sod sarfei kodesh.*) Loosely translated, this means: Let us sanctify Hashem as the angels do in Heaven. Since we are the ones sanctifying Hashem's name in *Kedushah,* we must rise to our feet, and we must have a minyan.

4. In *Nusach Sefard* this statement appears in the daily *Kedushah* and in *Kedushah* for Shabbos morning; in *Nusach Ashkenaz* it appears in *Kedushah* for Shabbos Mussaf.

5. Rav Schwab, in his *Iyun Tefillah,* explains the dispute between these groups of angels. The explanation presented here differs from that of Rav Schwab in one major point. The reason for this is beyond the scope of this work.

clearly felt everywhere in the world. This is a song of *gilui Panim*, a paean of praise to God, whose Presence can be easily sensed in this world.

What happens in Heaven after the *Seraphim* make that declaration?

Other angels dispute the statement of the *Seraphim*.

"*HaOfanim veChayos Hakodesh bera'ash gadol misnas'im leumas haSeraphim le'umasam* — the *Ofanim* and *Chayos HaKodesh* with great tumult raise themselves *against* the *Seraphim*; opposing them; *meshabechim veom'rim* — they give praise, saying: *Boruch kevod Hashem m'mikomo* — Blessed is the Glory of Hashem from His Place."

This is a song of *hester Panim*. The *Ofanim* and *Chayos HaKodesh* insist that we cannot detect the Presence of Hashem everywhere in the world, because He is concealed from us.

The dispute regarding *hester Panim* is the theme of the *berachah* of *Yotzer Ohr*. *Gilui Panim* refers to times in which Hashem displays His love and concern for us openly, when we see the God of Mercy. *Hester Panim* refers to times when Hashem conceals Himself and appears to be "ignoring" us in times of need, when we sense a God of Strict Justice.

↱ The Shabbos Additions to *Kedushah*

On Shabbos, we make significant additions to *Kedushah*. If we understand the dispute between the song of the *Seraphim* and that of the *Ofanim* and *Chayos HaKodesh*, we can understand the depth of these prayers.

During Shacharis on Shabbos morning, we follow the verse of *Kadosh, kadosh* with the words, "*Az bekol ra'ash gado l...,*" which is a description of the *Ofanim* and *Chayos HaKodesh* rising to dispute the sanctification of the *gilui Panim* sung by the *Seraphim*. During Mussaf we add, "*Kevodo malei olam* — [Hashem's] Glory fills the world, *Meshar'sav shoalim zeh lazeh* — His servants ask one another, *ayeih mekom Kevodo l'hareetzo* — Where is the place of His Glory, so that we may serve Him" which are words of praise to Hashem.

When we recite the verse, "*Baruch kevod Hashem mimekomo,*" — the verse of *hester Panim* — we follow with prayer, not praise. In

Shacharis we say, "*M'mekomecha malkeinu sofia*. We beg Hashem, "Please appear to us from Your hiding place." During Mussaf we add, "*M'mekomo Hu yifen b'rachamav le'amo* — from His place (of hiding), may He turn in His mercy to His nation."

Once we appreciate the difference between the praise of *gilui Panim* and that of *hester Panim*, the reason for the words that follow those praises is obvious. *Gilui Panim* refers to times of joy, times when the Heavenly Mercy is visible. During such times, we praise Hashem. We see that *Kevodo malei olam* — His Glory fills the world.

During times of *hester Panim*, we are in pain; we are experiencing difficulties. When we have to strain to see Hashem's Presence in the world, we add a prayer that He make His Presence visible.

This is our greatest challenge. The angels are in dispute. Some see a world of *gilui Panim;* others see a world of *hester Panim*. Each group of angels sees it one way. And we, ordinary humans, are expected to perceive that both realities exist together. There are times of *gilui Panim*, when we take pride in the accomplishments of *Klal Yisrael*. We get together for a *Siyum HaShas* and see myriads joining to bring glory to Hashem, and we can see *Kadosh, kadosh, kadosh … melo chol ha'aretz Kevodo* — Hashem's Glory fills the world. But there are times when we read distressing news from Eretz Yisrael and we feel the pain of the *hester Panim*. We cry out, "*Masei timloch b'Zion* — When will You reign in Zion? "*Ve'eineinu sir'ena malchusecha*." We want to see Your kingdom, Hashem." Angels cannot perceive both realities, but we must. And we therefore praise Hashem as *le'umasam Yotzer ohr u'vorei choshech* — the Creator of light and darkness.

At night, *Bircas Krias Shema* appears in the *berachah* of *Ma'ariv Aravim*, alluding to the same theme. We declare, "*besvunah meshaneh itim …* — In His wisdom, He switches the times, changes the seasons, and sets the stars in their heavenly constellations, according to His will." We shift between alternating periods of good and bad, joy and struggle; from times of *gilui Panim* to times of *hester Panim*.

On a superficial level, these are *berachos* of praise for Hashem. In reality, they are the story of the human experience in *olam hazeh*.

How do we conclude this *berachah* ? By reminding ourselves that Hashem alone is the *Po'el gevuros,* the One who acts with strength. He is the *Ba'al milchamos*. He is the one who controls wars. But He is also *zore'a tzedakos, matzmiach yeshuos*, and *borei refuos*. He sows kindness, provides salvation, and creates cures. All from the same loving God.

What a beautiful *berachah!* What a great way to prepare for the declaration of Hashem's sovereignty in *Shema*. Now if only I could get the *chazzan* to allow me enough time to think about it ...

◆§ Greatness in Times of Tragedy

A discussion of painful times would be incomplete without one final observation.

How much do we know about Mesushelach? Not much. He was a great man — *Rashi* states that the *Mabul* was postponed in his honor — but we do not know much about him.

How much do we know about Noach? We know all about him. We know that he lived through the *Mabul* and rebuilt the world afterwards.

Can you tell me anything about Gad, son of Yaakov Avinu? How about Zevulun? They were some of the greatest people who ever lived. Their greatness is beyond the scope of our imagination. Yet we know very little about them.

Can you tell me about Yosef? You know all about Yosef. He was sold into slavery by his brothers when he was seventeen years old, and despite being tormented by a wicked temptress, he remained as pure as he was in his father's home.

Why are we able to describe the greatness of Noach and Yosef, but not that of Mesushelach, Gad, and Zevulun?

One of the secrets of the world is that greatness is achieved during times of *hester Panim*, not in times of *gilui Panim*. Noach and Yosef lived lives of *hester Panim* experiences. The others did not. Noach and Yosef achieved a level of greatness unmatched by those who lived in the *gilui Panim* dimension.

When you go to a funeral and people eulogize the *niftar* (deceased), which aspect of his life do they usually focus on? By and large, they focus on how strong his faith was during his illness or during other difficult times. What do I know about my grandfather? I know that he was here in America when it was difficult to keep Shabbos, but that he remained strong in his convictions — despite getting fired every week. Were those times of *gilui Panim*, or times of *hester Panim?* Clearly, *hester Panim*.

Given the choice, we would all opt for a smooth and easy existence. But when does the opportunity for growth present itself? During the difficulties and crises of our lives. The times that we struggle to overcome pain and suffering are the times that we can achieve greatness.

I had a long-standing question on an idea that appears in *Tomer Devorah*. *Chazal* tell us that *ba'alei teshuvah* are able to attain a level of closeness to Hashem that is unattainable for the perfectly righteous. Since we are required to emulate Hashem, reasons the *Tomer Devorah*, we should relate to those who wronged us in the same manner as Hashem relates to *ba'alei teshuvah*. If your friend hurt you and then comes to make up, your closeness to that friend should surpass your relationship to those who never harmed you.

I was always bothered by the comparison. When someone sins against Hashem, Hashem is not "hurt" by that person. He is surely disappointed by the person's inability to refrain from sin. But He is not affected by it.

Imagine that someone has broken your windows in the middle of a cold winter night. You spend half the night boarding up the windows, and half the day dealing with the bureaucracy of an insurance claim — you have been hurt and inconvenienced. Now that person comes and says, "I'm sorry, I want to make peace with you." How can you feel closer to this fellow than to your dearest friend who has never slackened in his loyalty and devotion to you?

If the *Tomer Devorah* presented this as a great level that we should strive to attain, I would understand it. But how can he compare it to the case of someone sinning against Hashem, as if there is no difference between the two?

I realized, however, that this question only bothers those who have not incorporated the concept of the *berachah* of *Yotzer Ohr* in their lives.

If you have survived the ordeal of being hurt by a friend and you are able to forgive and forget, you have grown immeasurably from that experience. True, he caused you pain and difficulty, but difficulty is good. You don't ask for difficulties. You pray each morning that you not be challenged. But if you were tested and you passed the test — as evidenced by your willingness to forgive your friend — then you have become greater. Despite your friend's unworthy intentions, he has enabled you to grow. Shouldn't you value him more than you do friends who have not impacted your growth?

The *Nesivos*, in the introduction to his commentary on Megillas Esther, makes this point regarding Haman. Haman was one of the most evil adversaries the Jewish nation ever faced. He tried to annihilate our entire nation — men, women, and children. Nevertheless, the Talmud states that on Purim, we are to drink to the point at which we can say *baruch Haman* — blessed is Haman. Why?

The *Nesivos* writes that despite Haman's intentions, he left our nation with a great gift. As a result of the salvation in the Purim story, the Jewish People were able to attain the joyful reacceptance of the Torah. The *Nesivos* compares this to a person who comes to harm you, but accidentally gives you a million dollars instead. You would probably find it difficult to be angry at him.

Baruch Haman means that despite an adversary's negative intentions, we must appreciate the fact that his actions may in fact be beneficial.

> An American told Rav Chaim Kanievsky that a relative of his had insulted him publicly. "I can't look at the person," the man said. "But he is a close relative, and I can't avoid him either. What should I do?"
>
> "He insulted you *publicly*?" Rav Chaim asked.
>
> "Yes," the man responded.
>
> "Was it in front of ten people?"
>
> "Yes."
>
> "Wonderful!" Rav Chaim exclaimed. "Being insulted publicly is a *segulah* for wealth."
>
> Members of Rav Chaim's family were standing nearby. They began to shower the startled visitor with *mazal tov* wishes for his newfound wealth.
>
> One collector took the opportunity to give the man a card with his contact information. "*Al tishkach oti* [don't forget me]," he begged.
>
> The fellow was taken aback. Here he was, still smarting from his public humiliation, and everyone was blessing him for his good fortune!

I don't know whether the man became rich. One who is skeptical about the promised benefits will probably remain angry at the person who insulted him. But if one who is insulted knows *for a fact* that he will become rich, he will no longer be upset at the person who offended him.

When we incorporate the idea of *Yotzer Ohr* into our lives, we realize that the wealth does not need to be physical. If we can withstand an insult and later accept the offender into our lives, we have thereby attained a precious level of greatness. That greatness is worth millions.

✥ Developing Immunity

We would all like to lead smooth and comfortable lives. We are not thrilled when there are bumps in the road. We do not wish to be challenged through experiences of pain and suffering. However, there are times in each of our lives when Hashem determines that we need to be challenged. In painful times of *hester Panim*, we should cry out to Hashem. But when we look back at those times, we will see that we have grown from those experiences.

> There was a *yungerman* from our yeshivah who had a truly exceptional baby. He did not tell anyone, because he did not want to cause an *ayin hara*, but his baby was every parent's dream. He never cried, he was never sick, and he slept well at night. When the baby was 1½ years old, he became sick for the first time. His parents took him to the doctor, who placed him on antibiotics. That night he took a turn for the worse. He was rushed to the hospital, where he died.
>
> This baby was obviously a very holy *neshamah*. When his *tafkid* was completed, he was called back to Heaven. But in natural terms, why did this happen?
>
> The doctor explained that the baby was affected so drastically by the illness because he had never been sick before. A baby who is ill at a young age slowly builds up immunity that enables him to withstand infection. This baby had never been sick, so he had no immunity.

If you are never sick, if life is always perfect, then you are vulnerable. When Hashem challenges you, He is enabling you to develop your strengths.

If at times you experience suffering and pain, if you find yourself struggling, turn to the longest *berachah*. You will realize that a loving Hashem is giving you an opportunity for growth, a chance to achieve greatness.

Together with all of God's angels, we whisper, *Baruch shem kevod malchuso l'olam va'ed,* blessed is the name of His glorious kingdom for eternity.

Israel at War

Today, *Klal Yisrael* finds itself once again in a *matzav* of *sakanah,* a time of danger. Today, *Klal Yisrael* is once again at war and our sons, *Yiddishe kinder*, are in danger. Let us not be deceived by the fact that they are wearing army fatigues and that they have big tanks behind them. They are soft, kind, Jewish youngsters who are showing a brave face. They are pressed into situations they don't want; into situations that we don't wish on our youth. They are afraid and we share their fear. They are in tremendous danger.

For us in the United States, concerned though we are, our lives go on. Everything around us looks the same as it did a week ago, the same as it did yesterday. We all want to feel, we want to do, but we struggle to have a proper focus. We want to have the attitude of seeing *Klal Yisrael's* concerns rather than our own, but we find it difficult.

I am not here to give new *aitzos* (advice). Our time-honored *aitzos* of improving in Torah, *tefillah*, and *gemilas chasadim* are known to all of us. It is the focus that is difficult. It is hard for us be as motivated as we know we should be; to react with the proper intensity.

~§ Think of the *Harugei Lod*

*I*n 1973, during the Yom Kippur War, Rav Chaim Shmuelevitz spoke to *talmidim* of the Mirrer Yeshivah. Let us study the points mentioned by Rav Chaim Shmuelevitz during that period of great danger.[1] Let his words motivate and inspire us to focus in the coming days on proper davening and concern for *Klal Yisrael*.

In his first *shmuess*, Rav Chaim makes a point he calls a "*hakdamah*," an introduction to the topic. The Gemara (*Bava Basra* 10b) speaks about the *Harugei Lod*. The Jewish community in Lod was accused of killing the king's child. The king was determined to take revenge. The entire community was in grave danger. Then, two individuals came forward. Although they were totally innocent of the crime, they confessed to it so that the Jewish community would be saved. The king took out his fury on them and they were tortured to death. The community was saved.

The Gemara says about the *Harugei Lod*: "*Ayn kol birya yachol la'amod b'mechitzason* — no creature can approach their lofty spot [in *Olam Habah*]." They have an extraordinary *zechus*, an extraordinary place in Gan Eden. Why? Because they were *moser nefesh* to save a Jewish community.

Rav Chaim quoted this Gemara, and added, "*V'cheyn ani omer al eileh shemosrim nafsham ba'avur hatzalason* — so, too, do I say regarding those who are now giving their lives for our rescue."

He tells his *talmidim*, "This is the way you should think about the soldiers who are fighting and risking their lives for *Klal Yisrael*. Our obligation to daven for them is very great."

When you get up to daven for the situation in Eretz Yisrael and for the safety of the soldiers, picture the *Harugei Lod*. It is an image of bravery and suffering. An image of caring about the *tzibbur*. It is an image that should rip us up inside. It should instill in us an awakening, a *hisorrerus*.

I once asked Rav Moshe, *z"tl*, a *sheilah* on behalf of a *talmid* of the yeshivah, whose mother was undergoing a very dangerous surgery. I had brought this *talmid* to Rav Moshe to ask for a *berachah* for his mother. The surgery was scheduled for ten or eleven o'clock that morning and I asked Rav Moshe whether it was appropriate to take a minyan of *bachurim* from the *Beis HaMidrash* to say *Tehillim* in a classroom during *seder*. He said that it was appropriate, despite the

---

1. These *shmuessen* were printed in the 5760 edition of *Sichos Mussar*.

fact that these *bachurim* would be pulled away from their learning. "*Der choleh darf dem un der choleh darf dem* — the patient needs both types of *zechus*." Learning is one type of medicine and *Tehillim* is another type of medicine.

I then asked Rav Moshe, "For how long should we say *Tehillim*?"

Rav Moshe replied, "For the amount of time that people are still thinking about the meaning of the words they are saying." Unfortunately, this is usually not very long.

We are going to be saying *Tehillim* in the coming days. Tehillim without *kavanah* is also *Tehillim*. Still, it doesn't approach the power of *Tehillim* with *kavanah*. To think about the meaning of the words that we say requires a *hisorrerus*. Perhaps if we picture the *Harugei Lod*, it will awaken within us the ability to do what we have to do. This is *our Mesiras Nefesh*, straining to concentrate and focus.

✦§ Think of Iyov

Another powerful image brought by Rav Chaim in these *shmuessen* is the image of Iyov. What does Iyov have to do with the Yom Kippur War or the current situation?

When Paroh declared "*Havah nischakma lo* — let us plan against [the Jewish People]," there were three advisors present. They were Bilam, Iyov, and Yisro. Bilam, who concurred with Paroh, was later killed. Yisro, who protested, merited having his descendants sit on the Sanhedrin. Iyov, who remained silent, was punished through *yissurim*, terrible suffering.

Iyov didn't *do* anything wrong. His misdeed was his silence. *Klal Yisrael* was in danger and he was silent. For his silence, he was punished with terrible suffering. Dare we be silent as the Jewish People are once again in danger?

Rav Chaim points out that had Iyov spoken up, it would not have helped. Yisro did protest and it didn't help; he had to run away. So why was Iyov punished for his silence?

The *Ba'alei Mussar* answer, "*Oib es tut vei, shreit men* — when a person feels pain, he screams."

One must raise his voice, even if it doesn't help; certainly if it does. Had Iyov felt the pain of *Klal Yisrael*, he would have raised his voice. We, who are in pain over today's situation, must raise our voices in prayer. And it must be a *tefillah me'omek halev* — a prayer from the depth of our hearts.

As you prepare to daven, stop a moment and think of Iyov.

Chazal tell us that Eretz Yisrael is acquired through suffering. We know stories of people who experienced difficulties upon arriving in Eretz Yisrael. Today's sufferings are an extension of this pain, as millions of *Acheinu Bnei Yisrael* have returned to Eretz Yisrael.

What can a person do to avoid the suffering of *Kinyan Eretz Yisrael*?

Chazal tell us *adam l'omol nolad* — a person was born to toil. It is the Heavenly Decree that a human being must work hard and experience difficulties in this world. *Zochoh: amolo baTorah* — if a person is worthy, then his toil is in Torah. If he breaks a sweat, if he can't fall asleep, if he struggles because he worries about his learning, if he worries about a difficult question in learning — that is his toil. No other toil is needed. *Lo zachah ...* — if he is not worthy, his toil, his worry, his struggles will come from somewhere else.

This is what we are taught, "*Talmidei chachamim marbin shalom ba'olam* — Torah scholars bring peace to the world." They are involved in the battle of Torah. There is the battle of arguing with a *chavrusa*, of getting into a dispute about learning. That is one type of Torah battle.

There is also a second type of Torah battle that applies to all of us, and that is the battle against the *yetzer hara*. To learn, to get up early to learn, to be on time for learning, to add minutes to learning; this is also *milchamta shel Torah* — the Torah battle. The more that a person struggles for Torah, the more that *talmidei chachamim marbin shalom b'olam*, the fewer the need for *milchamos* on the battlefront.

We realize that this war will not change our lives overnight. Still, *chas v'shalom* to be silent like Iyov. Our davening should be different, the learning should be different.

You have a regular learning *seder*. *B'shaas milchamah*, should it remain the same? Add a few minutes to the *seder*. Do a bit more! *Chalilah*, to be silent like *Iyov*!

We have the image of *Harugei Lod* and the image of Iyov before us.

⥉ Think of Chushim Ben Dan

Rav Chaim gives us a third image: that of Chushim the son of Dan. When the *shevatim* arrived at the *Me'oras HaMachpela* to bury Yaakov, Esav halted the burial proceedings by contesting his brother's right to be buried there.

The *shevatim* argued. They pleaded. Esav refused. The *shevatim* sent Naftali to run to *Mitzrayim* to bring the necessary document of proof. And they waited.

Chushim the son of Dan was deaf. He had no idea what was happening. He saw that his grandfather's funeral was delayed. He was struck with horror. "*Abba d'abba mutal bi'bizayon* — It is disrespectful to make my grandfather wait [to be buried]." Bang! He knocked off the head of Esav. The funeral was completed without delay.

Yehudah was stronger than Chushim. Why didn't *he* kill Esav? What was unique about Chushim?

Everyone else had become gradually accustomed to the situation. They watched the negotiations with Esav and slowly became accustomed to the idea that the burial may be delayed. Chushim had no idea what was going on. He heard of his grandfather's indignity with shock. He was *nisragesh*. He felt the *hergesh*, the emotion, the shock. He reacted in a powerful way.

We have become gradually accustomed to many things. We have become complacent. We have heard of Jewish boys davening alongside their tanks. The tragedy of the image! To us, it almost seems normal, even beautiful. How unfortunate! Is this normal; Jewish boys with guns over their shoulders? A *ben Avraham, Yitzchak*, and *Yaakov* sits in a tank that can *chas v'shalom* turn into an incinerator from which one cannot escape!

Sadly, when a person becomes too accustomed to a situation, it no longer moves him.

This is not limited to the idea of Jewish boys being in danger. We have become too accustomed to something else.

We do not adequately appreciate the fact that Jews are living in Eretz Yisrael. We don't realize that the *gedolim* of a hundred years ago never dreamt that there would be a million *Yidden* in Eretz Yisrael. Did the *Chidushei HaRim* dream that there would be a Gerrer Chassidus of this size in Jerusalem? Perhaps he did, *b'ruach kodsho*, by divine inspiration, but *b'derech hateva*, in a natural way, it could never be anticipated!

It is true that most of the *Yidden* in Eretz Yisrael are not religious. But the fact that they are in Eretz Yisrael is a *berachah*. Nonreligious Jews in America are assimilating and disappearing, *rachmana l'tzlan*. In Eretz Yisrael, at least the non-religious Jews know that they are Jewish! They know *lashon hakodesh*. When Moshiach comes, he will set up yeshivos to teach the millions of Jews who have no connection. At least those in Eretz Yisrael will know the *aleph beis*, the Hebrew language.

If your *zeide* who lived in Europe would hear that you have the choice to travel to Eretz Yisrael or to any other place in the world, he would not dream that it would be a question. That Jews have to think to make a choice whether to spend Pesach in a hotel in Eretz Yisrael or in a hotel in Europe is absurd. Is it a question where one should go?

We take Eretz Yisrael for granted. If we truly appreciated Eretz Yisrael, if it were more dear to us, the worries, the problems, the *tzaros* that exist would touch us more deeply. We have to develop the attitude of a Chushim ben Dan.

The Kuzari complains that when we daven for Eretz Yisrael, it is without feeling, it is "like the chirping of a bird." It is without love, without yearning, without a true *hergesh* for Eretz Yisrael. We once had that *hergesh*, but we lost it because of Hashem's kindness in making Eretz Yisrael so available.

And so, *HaKadosh Baruch Hu* places Eretz Yisrael in danger. When something is held at arm's length, you want it more. A time of a *tzarah* must be used to bring out the missing *hergesh*.

Let us not become complacent — not about the *berachah* of Eretz Yisrael nor about the danger that we are facing. Let us not become so accustomed to the situation that we lose the emotion, that we stop feeling. Remember Chushim ben Dan. Before we begin *Shemoneh Esrei*, let us pause for a moment to think about *Harugei Lod*, Iyov, and Chushim ben Dan.

✥ Think of Queen Esther

There is a fourth figure. Rav Chaim asks us to remember Esther HaMalkah.

Esther tells Mordechai that she is prepared to risk her life for *Klal Yisrael*. "*Tzumu alai sheloshes yamim* — Fast for me for three consecutive days."

Rav Chaim makes an incredible point. The Rambam writes (*Pirush HaMishnayos, Yuma* 8) that we are forbidden to violate the Shabbos to save a life through a *segulah*, anything that works in a supernatural way. It is only permissible to violate the Shabbos for something that will save a person *b'derech hateva*.

Esther asked the *Yidden* to fast for three days. We know that this fast took place on Pesach. The Jews of Shushan did not eat matzah on the *seder* night. They also violated the mitzvah of *simchas Yom*

Tov. They violated two Biblical commandments. They would have been forbidden to do this for a *segulah*. Rav Chaim says, we see that a *tefillah mei'umka d'liba* — a prayer from the depth of the heart — is considered a natural force of salvation in this world. Hashem put this into nature, that *tefillah* for *Klal Yisrael* helps.

I don't know what *gedolei Yisrael* will suggest that we do differently during this period of danger. I imagine that our generation does not grow from fasting the way that *Klal Yisrael* once did. Presumably, there were also those in the time of Esther who were unable to fast, for whom it would have been dangerous. So, they probably fasted as much as they could, *kol echad l'fi madregaso uk'fi kochaso* — each according to his ability and energy.

In a time of danger, we, too, should act in this way, each according to his ability. Deny yourself some type of pleasure — some sweets, some ice cream. In some way, each of us should emulate the *tzumu alai*. It does not have to be something that causes pain, but it should be something meaningful. If you are not stringent about *chalav Yisrael*, for the duration of the war you should be. Limit your entertainment. If you go to stadiums, to basketball or hockey games, this is a time to refrain. Thousands of *Yidden* are in harms' way. We are not going to change our lives totally, but some kind of *tzumu alai* is called for.

✺§ Rav Pam's Thoughts

Let me share Rav Pam's words during a similar time of danger. He said that those who seek to harm us can be compared to the frogs in Egypt during the *makkah* of *tzifardaya*. As you know, the Egyptians hit the frogs. Each time they hit a frog, it turned into two and then two became four and four became eight, and so they multiplied and multiplied and multiplied. Hitting them accomplished nothing positive for the Egyptians, but simply increased their suffering.

The fact is that, although we are required to engage in *hishtadlus*, to do whatever we can to fight back against our enemies to protect ourselves, when a terrorist is killed, two more appear. If we kill four hundred, four thousand, even forty thousand, what have we gained? What does that do for us? Tomorrow there will be eighty thousand!

Killing our enemies is not going to save the day. Finally, Paroh realized the same thing. So what did he do? He called for Moshe and pleaded, "Pray for me, and the frogs will be removed from me and my nation!"

You want to get rid of the frogs? Daven! Only *tefillah* will do it.

Our salvation too, is not with the tanks, but with our prayers.

For a long time, the government struggled with suicide bombers on buses in Jerusalem. There was no logical way to stop it. Attempts were made; there was *hishtadlus*. Finally, *Baruch Hashem*, it quieted down. Why? Can someone tell me why it stopped? It wasn't anything political and it wasn't anything military. *Klal Yisrael* davened and it stopped. People talk about political solutions, military solutions. At the end of the day, it is up to us, those who beseech Hashem.

◆§ A Time To Cry

I heard a precious *vort* related to *Parashas Vayechi*. When Yosef reveals himself to his brothers, he falls upon Binyamin's neck, weeping. Binyamin wept upon Yosef's neck. *Chazal* tell us that Yosef cried over the vision of the destruction of the two *Mikdashos* that would be in the territory of Binyamin. Binyamin cried about the destruction of the *Mishkan* at Shiloh that would take place in the territory of Yosef.

Why did each one cry over his brother's loss and not over his own? Why didn't each brother cry about the destruction that would take place within his own boundaries as well? The answer is an important lesson. When the destruction is in your own boundaries, roll up your sleeves and work — do your *hishtadlus*. When the *tzarah* is in someone else's land — weep!

Those in Eretz Yisrael must do their *hishtadlus* as well as daven. For those of us in America, our only *hishtadlus* is to cry out, to shed a tear, to weep!

> In 1967, an American *bachur* was learning in the *shiur* of Rav Nochum in the Mirrer Yeshivah. As it became apparent that there would be a war, he asked Rav Nochum whether to return to the States. Rav Nochum said "Stay here. If you go back to the States, you will lose an opportunity to *shteig*."
>
> His parents compelled him to return to America. *Baruch Hashem*, in June of 1967 there was an incredible *yeshuah*, the likes of which we hope will be repeated in our time. When

this *bachur* returned to Rav Nochum, he apologized and said, "Please know that I continued to *shteig*. I went to yeshivah in America every day and I kept up with whatever you were learning in Eretz Yisrael."

Reb Nochum replied, "No! I didn't mean *shteiging* from the Gemara. I meant *shteiging* from the air raid sirens, *shteiging* from the fear of death; using that to bring you closer to the *Ribbono shel Olam*. That is the precious opportunity that you missed."

Ais tzarah he l'Yaakov; it is a time of danger. It is our hope and *tefillah* that the *yeshuah* will come quickly. But we hope and pray for more; that we will *shteig* from the situation, that we will have *kavanah* in our davening, that "*sim shalom*" will mean something in our S*hemoneh Esrei*, today and tomorrow.

In *Shemoneh Esrei*, the *berachah* "*Re'eh Nah*" refers to difficulties within the Galus.[2] Here, we should insert a prayer for success in the war in Eretz Yisrael. Take your siddur and insert a little piece of paper at "*Re'eh Nah*," so that even if you daydream, you will wake up when you get to this *berachah*.

Insert a prayer — "Anna Hashem hagen al acheinu Bnei Yisrael sh'b'Eretz Yisrael, u'befrat be'dorom Eretz Yisrael, v'hanilchamim b'Uzzah — We beseech you, Hashem, protect our brothers, the *Bnei Yisrael*, in Eretz Yisrael, especially those in the communities in the south and those doing battle in Gaza." Add these words, or use your own words, preferably in *lashon hakodesh*.

The *yeshuah* will come. The danger will pass. Let us be proud to look back and feel that we, like Rav Nochum, grew from the experience.

---

2. Rashi, *Megillah* 17b.

SECTION II
*Otzar HaHalachah —
A Treasury of Jewish Law*

The Great Siddur Controversy

The most used *sefer* in a Jewish home is the siddur. The *nusach* of our siddur has been greatly enhanced by the contributions of an 18th-century genius, Rav Zalman Henna, whose name is barely recognized, except in more scholarly circles.

In 1704, the *Siddur Derech Siach HaSadeh* was published in Vilna. This publication was the result of the great efforts of two men, Rav Ezriel and his son Rav Eliyahu. This was to be *the* definitive siddur for Ashkenazic Jewry. A great amount of effort was put into correcting some of the errors that had appeared in the earliest printed siddurim, and which had been copied into later printings. Grammatical errors were corrected, as well. New innovations in this Siddur included the marking of each *shva na* with a notation over the letter, so that reader could read the word correctly, even if he was unfamiliar with the rules for identifying the *shva na*. This innovation remains as the standard for all siddurim, to this day. Where issues were unclear, *Gedolei Torah* had been contacted to ensure that this Siddur would be error-free.

Rav Shlomo Zalman of Hanau, Germany (known as Rav Zalman Henna), was born in 1687. He was a young man at the time that the

Vilna siddur was printed. He was already known for his genius, and for his great knowledge of the rules of *dikduk*. His initial work on the rules of *dikduk*, entitled *Binyan Shlomo*, was written when he was only twenty years old. A diverse group of Torah giants, including the *Noda B'Yehudah* (1:74 and in his approbation to the *Kunteres HaSagos*), Rav Yitzchak Elchonon Spector (*Ein Yitzchak* 27:1), and the *Pri Megadim* (*Aishel Avraham* 7:1) would later refer to Rav Zalman Henna as the "*medakdaik hagadol*," the great man of *dikduk*.

However, he was a man of strong opinions and a sharp pen, particularly in the areas of his expertise. This made him a controversial figure.

In 1708, in the city of Frankfurt, Rav Zalman Henna published *Binyan Shlomo* and *Beis Tefillah,* his version of the corrected Siddur. In these works, he takes exception to *Siddur Derech Siach HaSadeh* on over one hundred points.[1] Later, in 1725, Rav Zalman Henna expanded his corrections in another work, *Shaarei Tefillah* (*Gates of Prayer*). This work contained 326 corrections of *Siddur Derech Siach HaSadeh* (this was in addition to the corrections that initially appeared in his earlier works, and had already been incorporated into the second edition of the Siddur)!

One could easily understand the hard feelings this engendered, given that the *Siddur Derech Siach HaSadeh* had been hailed as the first fully corrected version of the Siddur. The sharp words of attack in *Binyan Shlomo* did not help the matter (he refers to Reb Ezriel and Reb Eliyahu as "*Av u'bino she'naflu l'bor* ...," "a father and son who fell into a pit ...").

In fact, many of Rav Zalman Henna's corrections were accepted and later incorporated into subsequent editions of *Siddur Derech Siach HaSadeh*. Indeed, Rav Zalman Henna would wonder how he could be so vehemently criticized, given that so many of his corrections became the standard Siddur text. In fact, it was the sharp tone of debate regarding these other corrections that fed a great controversy.

In *Binyan Shlomo*, Rav Zalman Henna writes sharply against earlier Torah giants.[2] This becomes even more inappropriate when we

---

1. Rav Zalman Henna writes that he first met with Reb Eliyahu, presenting his corrections and offering to withhold publication if the criticisms could be answered. He expresses outrage at Rav Eliyahu's denial that this meeting took place.
[See also "*Shva Na* and Aramaic Words," in which Rav Zalman Henna is quoted regarding the pronunciation of Kaddish.]

2. Regarding *Abarbenel*: "With this, you can understand that the *Abarbenel's* words are nullified and gone, to be mentioned no longer (*lo sheririn v'lo kayamin*)."

consider that he was only twenty years old at the time. The introduction to the recently reprinted *Luach Eresh* contains a collection of his sharp quotes "against thirty different great men."

Rav Zalman Henna would later explain that he never intended to disparage these great men of Israel in a personal way. Rather, he was speaking in the heat of the great battle he was waging to correct the prayer book for all time.

In subsequent printings of *Binyan Shlomo*, Rav Zalman Henna would add a "*daf hisnatzlus*," expressing regret over the sharp tone of his comments (see following page).

This did nothing to quiet the controversy. The *Siddur Derech Siach HaSadeh* reprimanded Rav Zalman Henna harshly. "Although [Rav Zalman Henna] printed a letter of apology, asking forgiveness from each of these great men, as was decreed upon him by the leaders of the community of Frankfurt am Main, he deserves to be banned for the tone of the letter of apology ...."

To illustrate the sharp tone of the controversy, I quote from the introduction to the second printing of *Siddur Derech Siach HaSadeh*: "A new *sefer* on *dikduk* was recently printed, entitled *Binyan Shlomo*. I prefer to call it *Churban Shlomo*, because he speaks sharply, without cause, using words that are sharp as a sword, speaking incorrectly against the giants of *dikduk*, such as the *Redak*, *Ibn Ezra*, and *Rashi*; and against later experts whose pinky is wider than his loins ...."

In *Shaarei Tefillah*, Rav Zalman Henna responds; "This is Torah, and any man is permitted to examine and search for the truth. The *Chavos Yair* writes that one may write, regarding an earlier author, that he erred, since the author is human and will invariably make some mistakes. As Aristotle said, 'I love Plato, I love Socrates, but I love the truth above all."[3]

Regarding *Ibn Ezra*: "I cannot imagine how the wise *Ibn Ezra* could err so ..." and, "He speaks without thinking."

Regarding *Siach Yitzchak*: "Don't concern yourself with these words of his, for there is no flavor to them at all."

3. One cannot help but wonder how Rav Zalman Henna imagined that quoting Aristotle (which had sparked enormous controversies in earlier generations) would somehow contribute to quieting the dispute!

[In his defense, in should be pointed out that this phrase is found in Rabbinic literature. *Chavos Yair* (#9), after mentioning this quotation, cites four earlier Rabbinic sources for it. This also appears in *Teshuvos HaRaavad* #38.]

> **אמר** המחבר הנה כתבתי בלשוני בתשובתי אשר הגנתי על התוספים
> והרבתי מלין ונגעתי בכבוד חכמים (אך לא מרד ומעל
> עשיתי זאת ולא עלתה על דעתי שום מחשבת און או פיגול לבזות חכמים
> בעלה רק כתבווכתי להלהיב כפי המעיין ולהעיר אזני השומע בלמודים)
> על כן באתי לבקש מהם מחילה :

> **על** אשר דן יצחק אברבנאל כתבתי בלא בדעת ידבר ודבריו לא בהשכל ,
> ובמקום אחר כתבתי עליו הנה זאת בלחתה מפלת חסרון ידיעתו
> שלא ירד לסוף דעת הנביא , וכל זה יצא מאתי כסוגה היודע שלפני הטליט
> ומשתעע פני לפניו ומתבקש מחילה מעצמותיו הקדושים ובטוח אני בחכמת
> וחסידות אשר שלח לי האדון על דברים כאלה :

> **על** חכם אבן עזרא כתבתי לא בכן ברוחב דעתו / ובמקום אחר
> ומתעצר ואין כח / ובמקום אחר והשתמישת' מקרא מלא' ולא
> היה לי להפריו על מדותי להליבי פי נגד החכם ההוא אשר קטנו עבה
> ממתני / אף כי חמתו עמדה לי : שלא יהיו הדברים כאלה מצד חסרון
> ידיעתי כי שוגג אני לפלפעה :

> **על** הרב רבינו דוד קמחי כתבתי לפעמים ולא דק / או לא דק לקמחי
> או וקמחא טחינא טחין / או אובקים מיש ואוסיף קמחי / בודק
> עוונותי הוא אלא שיצאו דברים כאלה מפי, שרף לי מרי ושל עובי וחטאת
> מכופר :

> **המדקדק** רבי אלי׳ בחור כתבתי לפעמים בדבריו לא בחרתי ,
> או וטעמו כריר חלמות , או אלי׳ וקין בו , ואף הוא יענה וישמר
> שלחתי :

> **על** הרב בעל שיח יצחק כתבתי לפעמים לומי מדרים לשי שיח , אף
> והרבה שיחה , או וכל השומע יצחק , וכדומה ל ה פגעתי בכבוד
> הרב אף כי קלותי לדבר כנגדו בחמתי כי עשיתי וכבוד הרב במקומו מונח
> במעלה העליונה ידע ולא איפפת לי וחלילה לי מהחדל לבקש מחילה
> מעצמותיו הקדושים ורב שמחל על כבודו כבודו מחול :

> **על** שאל המחברים כאשר הגנתי עליהם והודעתי רוחי במלין בפיד
> מה יעד הכי עומד ומתחרט על דברים כאלה ובגניחות מי יבין
> לכן זמותי בל יעבור פי לדבר עוד כדברים האלה והאל יכפר בעדי :

The "daf hisnatzlus," page of apology, which Rav Zalman Henna added to the second printing of Binyan Shlomo, *in response to accusations that he wrote disrespectfully regarding earlier gedolim. The first and last paragraphs are general in nature; the middle paragraphs mention the offending statements regarding Abarbenel, Ibn Ezra, Redak, Rav Eliyahu Bahur, and Siach Yitzchak, and asks forgiveness.*

܀§ Enter Rav Yaakov Emden

*U*ltimately, another genius of the time would step into the debate. Rav Yaakov Emden (eleven years his junior), would become an adversary of Rav Zalman Henna, arguing with many of his corrections. Rav Yaakov Emden had a sharp style of debate, which matched the style of Rav Zalman Henna. This made for a very colorful controversy, which lasted throughout their lives. In a meeting between the two great men (as described in greater detail, below) Rav Zalman Henna attempted to resolve some of the issues. The different versions of this meeting given by each of these men are a sign of the intensity of the debate.

It was this controversy that ultimately led Rav Yaakov Emden to publish *his* corrected version of the Siddur. In his Siddur, Rav Yaakov Emden mentions Rav Zalman Henna by name only in the Introduction, in regard to their dispute regarding the punctuation of the words *Arvis* and *Shacharis*. There he complains about the *Siddur Shaarei Tefillah*, commenting, "It should have been named *Tzarei Tefillah* [*Pains of Prayer*]"!

Thus, the *Rav Yaakov Emden Siddur* came into existence only because of this controversy. It remains a major part of the standard Jewish library, to this day.[4]

A generation later, the effects of this great battle still reverberated in the Jewish community. In 1784, an attempt was made to settle the issues raised by Rav Zalman Henna. A *Kunteres HaSagos* (written by Rav Mordechai Disseldorf) appeared, with the approbation of the *Noda B'Yehudah*. In his introductory letter, the *Noda B'Yehudah* praises the genius of Rav Zalman Henna, but follows this with the observation, "In his great zealousness against those who preceded him, [Rav Zalman Henna] changed many things, some deliberately, some caused by the error of a quick mind. He found it easy to come up with new rules, which are not found in the earlier works of *dikduk*. Therefore, despite his outstanding genius in this field, one cannot rely on his new [rules]."

Earlier, in 1733, Rav Yaakov Emden, (in the Introduction to *Lechem Shamayim* on *Zeraim*), had offered an identical criticism

---

4. It is important to note that the popular version of the *Rav Yaakov Emden Siddur* contains portions that were not part of the original Siddur. This version contains numerous grammatical errors (see, for example, *Klalei Tamei HaMikra*, p. 140). Recently, an original version of the *Rav Yaakov Emden Siddur* was published by his descendants.

of Rav Zalman Henna.[5] However, his language is far harsher. In the first mishnah of *Berachos*, Rav Yaakov Emden disagrees with Rav Zalman Henna regarding the proper punctuation of the word *eivarim*. Rav Zalman Henna places a *chataf patach* under the letter *aleph*, while Rav Yaakov Emden maintains that a *tzeirei* is correct.

Rav Yaakov Emden writes, "Do not confuse your tongue or rush your heart in disagreement before God, as was the practice of [Rav Zalman Henna], who rushes to amend and edit the ancient, long-trusted texts .... Do not pay attention to him; do not listen to him in any of the places where he looks to introduce new ideas ...."

We cannot help but stand in admiration of these great leaders of yesteryear, to whom a dispute over the simplest vowels of the Talmud meant so much. The heat of the dispute should spark our interest. It should kindle a flame within us to study the Siddur.

Let us learn, together, some of the actual points of dispute, leaving the rhetoric aside.

ঋ§ A Point of Dispute

In the Introduction to *Kunteres HaSagos*, Rav Mordechai Disseldorf gives an overview of their dispute.

Our Siddur is based on the books of Tanach. Many sections are taken directly from Tanach. Others, written over the generations, may appear to be completely new phrases. In fact, as *Avudraham* (and other works on the Siddur) demonstrates clearly, the authors of the Siddur were fluent in Tanach and constantly used Tanach phrases in expressing the various prayers and *piyutim*.

Often, phrases have no clear source in Tanach. There are numerous words in the Siddur that have no precedents in *Sifrei Kodesh*. Reb Ezriel and Reb Eliyahu treated these as new words and punctuated them by comparing them to other words having a similar structure.

Rav Zalman Henna disagreed with this approach. He held that every Hebrew word must be based on a Scriptural source. In his genius, he was able to find a basis for almost every word in the Siddur. To do so, it was often necessary to create *chiddushim*, which

---

5. Later, in the Introduction to *Shaarei Tefillah*, Rav Zalman Henna expressed regret on this point. "It was the youth in me and the flow of the language that swept me. Don't hold me guilty for this; rather, it would be better if you would attribute this to my great effort to establish the truth, to the best of my ability."

often resulted in changes to the punctuation of the word.

Reb Ezriel was much more reluctant to change the accepted punctuation than Rav Zalman Henna was.

Let us see some examples of this.

- **Sha'ah** (hour[6]): This word, which appears often in the Siddur, has no clear precedent in Tanach. Reb Ezriel punctuates *sha'ah* with a double *kamatz* by comparing the word form to other words with a similar form, such as *ra'ah* (evil) or *ta'ah (erred)*.

Rav Zalman Henna agreed with the punctuation, but explained the word differently. He maintained that this word comes from the Hebrew word *na'a* (spelled *nun-ayin-hei*), which refers to movement. Here, the *shin* is a prefix (and the root letter *nun* falls away). In this interpretation, the word refers to an hour as a period of time in which the heavenly bodies show movement.

This dispute has practical significance when the word *sha'ah* is attached to another word, as in the words "*sha'as rachamim.*"

Reb Ezriel, following his line of thinking, compares this to *ra'ah* and *ta'ah*. When these words are attached to another word, the first letter retains its *kamatz* (as in *ra'as Haman* or *ta'us akum*). Here, too, *Siddur Derech Siach HaSadeh* had "*sha'as rachamim.*"

Rav Zalman Henna disagreed, and maintained that the *shin* should be punctuated with a *shva*, "*Sh'as rachamim.*"

- **Chai Olamim** ("Life-Giver of the world"[7]: This expression appears in the *Baruch She'amar* and *Yishtabach* prayers). Reb Ezriel refers to the word as a new expression ("*bittui chadosh*") and places a *patach* under the letter *ches*.

Rav Zalman Henna disagrees and points out that the expression already appears in Tanach (albeit in a slightly different context), and is punctuated with a *tzeirei*, as in "*Chey Paroh*" or "*Chey nafshecha.*"

---

6. Sometimes this refers to a sixty-minute period. Often, it is a general reference to a period of time; and not necessarily sixty minutes. *Chasam Sofer* (O.C. 199) offers a rule for this. When *sha'ah* appears as a halachic term, it refers to a sixty-minute hour. When it is used as part of a story or general statement (e.g., "*Yeish koneh olamo b'sha'ah achas*") it refers to a brief period of time [See also *HaZ'manim B'Halachah*, p. 102.].

7. The correct definition of *olamim* is not relevant to this discussion. Still, it is difficult to present this translation without pointing out that many *Rishonim* prefer translating *olamim* as a reference to time rather than space, hence "the Eternal Life-Giver." Rav S. R. Hirsch prefers this approach, translating *Adon Olam* as the "Eternal Master."

Rav Yaakov Emden would later defend the earlier version[8] (in *Luach Eresh* and again in *She'los Yaavetz* 141).

■ **Shacharis, Arvis**: These words refer to the morning and evening prayers, respectively. *Siddur Derech Siach HaSadeh* viewed these as new words, and they were punctuated with a *kamatz* under the second letter of the word.

Rav Zalman Henna, following his strict doctrine of finding Scriptural sources for every word, argues that these words are no more than extensions of the word *shachar* (morning) and *erev* (evening). The similar word *achar* is found in Tanach in the extended version, as *achris*, with a *shva* under the second letter. The words *Shacharis* and *Arvis* should, therefore, also take a *shva* under the second letter.

■ **Kid'ai** (spelled *kof-daled-aleph-yud*): Rav Yaakov Emden (*Lechem Shamayim* 1:4), punctuates this word with a *patach* under the *kof*. He compares this word to the more familiar *gabbai* or *zachai*.

Rav Zalman Henna once again disagrees, accusing Rav Yaakov Emden of creating a new word. He argues that this word already appears, in a slightly different form, in *Megillas Esther* (1:18), "*kid'ai bizayon va'ketzef*," with a *shva* under the *kof*.

ᴥ§ In Our Siddurim

*T*here are variations in *nusach* that remain in our Siddurim to this day. Some popular Siddurim follow Rav Zalman Henna, while others follow Rav Yaakov Emden (although Siddurim are often inconsistent in their choice of opinion). These include the following (in each case Rav Zalman Henna's opinion is presented second).

---

8. He maintained that words taking a *patach* in the root form (such as *yad*, *dag*, or *dam*) often change to a *zeirei* when attached to the word that follows (as in *yidei Moshe*, *dagei hayam*, or *dimei achicha*). *Chey HaShem* takes a *tzeirei* only because it is attached to the following word. When standing itself, the original *patach* is correct. So, too, *chai olamim* is not an attached word; rather, it is a description of Hashem as *chai*, the Life-Giver) and should take a *patach*.

In *Shaarei Tefillah* 52, Rav Zalman Henna appears to agree with the grammatical rule expressed by Rav Yaakov Emden. However, he maintains that this is an attached verb, and the *tzeirei* is therefore correct. (See *Tosafos Yom Tov*, at the end of *Tamid*).

- In *Birchas Krias Shema*: *Tisbarach tzureinu* (with a *patach* under the *reish*) or *Tisbareich tzureinu* (with a *tzeirei*).

- In **Kaddish**: *Yisgadal v'yiskadash* or *Yisgadeil v'yiskadeish*.

- The *berachah* on wine: *borei pri hagefen* or *hagofen*. (*Gofen* is more common in Tanach, as in *Shoftim* 9, *Yeshaya* 24, and *Hoshaya* 14.)

- The *berachah* for **Shabbos candle-lighting**: *l'hadlik ner shel Shabbos* or should the word *shel* be left out, "as it is not commonly used in the Hebrew language."

- During *Yamim Noraim*: *zochreinu l'chayim* or *zochreinu lachayim*. ("I wrote a separate pamphlet regarding this issue," *Shaarei Tefillah* 86 and 106.)

- *She'hakol nihiyeh b'divoro*: The dispute involves one of the most common *berachos*. This blessing, which is made on most foods, ends with the words *she'hakol nihiya b'divoro* (all came to be, through His word). Or is it *she'hakol nihiyeh b'divoro* (all comes to be, through His word).

  Rav Zalman Henna maintains that individuals who recite the former version of this blessing are guilty of heresy. After all, aren't they referring to God's control of creation in the past tense, as something that existed only in the past? He therefore insists on the present tense of the word, *she'hakol nihiyeh b'divoro*.[9]

  Rav Yaakov Emden (*She'elos Yaavetz*, 1:94) strongly rejects this opinion.[10]

- *Birchos HaShachar*: The dispute regarding the correct tense of the blessings extended to a number of the morning blessings, as well.

---

9. This is actually an earlier dispute; see *Magan Avraham* 204:14 and 167:8

10. "Are all blessings identical? Some are in past tense, such as *asher bara* and *asher yatzar* .... Do not be concerned with the silly words [of Rav Zalman Henna], who is confused and quick to answer, who speaks harshly without cause, for these rabbis don't know what they are saying. The disciples of Rav Zalman Henna are fools, just like him [*shotim kamoso*] ...."

It is interesting to note that Rav Yaakov Emden finds no grammatical reason to reject Rav Zalman Henna's position. He simply maintains that there is no adequate reason to change the current practice, which was to say *she'hakol nihiya b'divoro*.

Rav Zalman Henna, following his position that *berachos* should be recited in the present tense, accepts the following version for two of the everyday *Birchos HaShachar*, *She'Osah lee kol tzorki* and *Hameichin mitzadei gaver*. The earlier Siddur had these in past tense.

In is quite confusing to note that our Siddurim are totally inconsistent, mixing the past and present versions from one *berachah* to the next.[11]

■ ***Shiur*** **or** ***Shey-ure?*** The word *shiur* means "a measure," but is also used to refer to a Torah lecture. In the yeshivah world, the common pronunciation is *shiur* (with a *cheerik* under the *shin*). In many Bais Yaakov circles, this word is pronounced *shey-ure* (with a *tzeirei* under the *shin*).

It is interesting to note that this, too, was a dispute between Reb Ezriel (who favored *shey-ure*) and Rav Zalman Henna (*shiur*).[12]

↝§ The Protagonists Meet

*I*n his initial diatribe against Rav Zalman Henna (in *Lechem Shamayim*), Rav Yaakov Emden did not mention his name. He referred to him only as, "the one who is confused and rushed to answer."

Rav Zalman Henna understood that the critique was aimed at him, and responded by publishing *Tzohar HaTeivah*. The last section, *Michseh HaTeivah*, directly answers the complaints of Rav Yaakov Emden, although Rav Zalman Henna, too, does not mention his adversary by name.

Rav Zalman Henna had been told (by "*magidei emes* — trustworthy people") that Rav Yaakov Emden had written a book, *Luach*

---

11. Rav Shimon Schwab, in *Iyunei Tefillah*, defends the custom of Frankfurt am Main in this regard.

12. In *Shaarei Tefillah* (#17), Rav Zalman Henna reports that in the third edition of *Siddur Derech Siach HaSadeh* the punctuation was changed to conform to his view. The Introduction to this third edition once again contains a sharp personal attack on Rav Zalman Henna for "breaching age-old barriers that were founded by our eldest leaders." Rav Zalman Henna expresses amazement at the attack, "given that they themselves conceded, without shame," to many of his points.

Eresh,[13] in which he sums up his disagreements with Rav Zalman Henna,[14] and presents arguments in support of his opinions.

In 1730, Rav Zalman Henna was living in Amsterdam. Soon, he heard that Rav Yaakov Emden was visiting the city. Rav Zalman Henna set out to meet him. His description of their meeting appears in, *Michseh HaTeivah*.

"This honored man came to town. As soon as I heard the news, I joyously rushed to greet him. I begged him to show me some of his critique, for perhaps his words are correct. If this were so, I would be prepared to admit the truth loudly and clearly ....

"I tell you the truth; this man denied [writing a critique], and he told me that it never entered his mind to write anything of the sort .... I begged him, pointing out that his behavior is not worthy of intelligent people, for we prefer truth. He did not reply to this argument."

The meeting soon turned away from the general theme of their differences and focused on a new dispute — regarding the correct pronunciation of a word in the *U'va L'Zion* prayer.

Rav Yaakov Emden maintains that the Aramic word is "*u'nitalasni*" (the *sof* without a *dageish* and with a *shva* under it). Rav Zalman Henna disagreed, punctuating the word, "*u'nitaltani*" (the *sof* with a *dageish* and with a *patach* under it).[15]

It is mind-boggling that here, at *the* meeting of the decade, they would focus on the *dikduk* of one particular word!

Rav Yaakov Emden's version of their meeting is alluded to in *Luach Eresh* #469, as explained in the Introduction to the recently reprinted *Luach Eresh* (p. 37). At their meeting, Rav Zalman Henna was accused by Rav Yaakov Emden of forging his (Reb Yaakov Emden's) father's *haskomah* to *Shaarei Tefillah*. Rav Zalman Henna ignored the accusation.

This also appears as a note near the end of Rav Yaakov Emden's *Lechem Nikudim*. He maintains that he did present Rav Zalman Henna with arguments, for which Rav Zalman Henna had no response.

---

13. The word *eresh* is related to the phrase "*areshes sifoseinu*" in the davening of the *Yamim Noraim*. It is strange to hear the title of this book mispronounced by many (as *Luach Eres*).

14. It is interesting to note that Rav Yaakov Emden actually *agrees* with Rav Zalman Henna in approximately a third of his corrections.

15. It is interesting that both versions still appear in different versions of the Siddur. *Ma'aseh Rav* (of the *Gra*) #52 pronounces the word with a *sof* (without a *dageish*).

The Story Behind the Story

Rav Yaakov Emden apparently denied the existence of *Luach Eresh*. Yet we know that he *did* print the *sefer* and that it is a record of his disagreements with Rav Zalman Henna (although it contains numerous points in which he agrees, as well). Why, then, did he deny its existence?

Rav Yaakov Emden was in his early thirties at the time of their meeting. *Luach Eresh* was not published until 1769, over thirty years later, and only seven years before Rav Yaakov Emden's passing. Rav Yaakov Emden was telling the truth when he denied the existence of this *sefer*. At the time, he apparently saw these as his personal notes, "… which I wrote in my sharp days of youth, when my youthful blood was boiling within me."

Many decades later, he would explain (at the end of the first section of *Luach Eresh*), that these notes were forty years old and that it had never been his intention to publish the *Luach Eresh*.

He goes on to introduce *Luach Eresh* as a compilation that had been written "when I first saw the *Siddur Beis Tefillah*, because my soul was embittered by the excessive chutzpah and raw nerve that could allow a man to publish a terrible forgery and clear lie, to present forged *haskamos* … in the name of my father and teacher the Gaon, zt"l."

What caused Rav Yaakov Emden to change his mind and publish this work?

By his later years, Rav Yaakov Emden had been embroiled in a number of other disputes, most notably his condemnation and subsequent dispute with Rav Yonoson Eibschitz. This dispute would rock the Jewish communities of Europe and result in numerous personal attacks against Rav Yaakov Emden.

By now, Rav Yaakov Emden had many detractors. They pointed to his earlier disputes with Rav Zalman Henna as a sign of his brashness and tendency to quarrel.[16] *Luach Eresh* was published as an attempt to quiet these critics by proving that the criticism of Rav Zalman Henna was correct and not without cause.

In hindsight, it is difficult to understand how this could, in fact, dispel the quarrel-prone image of Rav Yaakov Emden. On the contrary,

---

16. Rav Yaakov Emden writes, "Those who stand up against me, hating me for no reason …, maintain that I am a controversial person, pointing to my dispute with the *midakdek*. I will tell the truth; their words are partially true. I was, and will continue to be, a man who argues with all those who stand up against us."

most people are not adequately learned to decide on areas of grammatical dispute, even using *Luach Eresh*. To them, this was nothing more than a new presentation of old arguments.

Torah scholars, however, view *Luach Eresh* as a wonderful source of information and are grateful that it was published.

Luach Eresh was out of print for a long time. Rav Zalman Henna's *Sharei Tefillah*, too, is unavailable.[17] The recent republication (in 2001) of *Luach Eresh* is a tremendous service. *Luach Eresh* has been reset in a clear type and published, together with Rav Zalman Henna's *Sharei Tefillah*, sections of his *Beis Tefillah* and *Michseh LaTeivah*, in one 600-page volume. This volume also presents a reset edition of Rav Mordechai Disseldorf's *Likutei HaSagos* (with the approbation of the *Noda B'Yehudah*) against Rav Zalman Henna's *seforim*. Also included are other selections from Rav Yaakov Emden's works and from his responsa regarding the dispute. The editors have also added an introduction and footnotes to *Shaarei Tefillah*, highlighting the areas of dispute.

Today there is an opportunity to obtain this wonderful *sefer*, which is unlikely to remain available for long.[18]

~§ The *Tam Elyon* Controversy

*R*av Zalman Henna's penchant for controversy took on other forms as well. His critical analysis of the Siddur extended to other shul issues. He took issue with various Jewish customs, which he viewed as erroneous.

---

17. I have had access, in the *Masmidim Beis HaMidrash* of Camp Agudah, to all of Rav Zalman Henna's works. The *seforim* located there are hand-bound copies of the original works.

18. It is important to note that this new publication is overly critical of Rav Zalman Henna, on a personal level. The brief biography of Rav Zalman Henna (which appears in the Introduction, p. 29) describes him as an elementary-school *dikduk* teacher who wandered from town to town, "never serving as a rabbi, nor did he ever become a *talmid chacham*." It "credits" him with teaching *maskilim*. This is in contradiction to Torah greats who showed Rav Zalman Henna great respect, even when disagreeing with him.

Shaarei Tefillah contains notations by the publisher, often in sharp tones, and always in criticism of Rav Zalman Henna. In one place, a note to *Shaarei Tefillah* states simply, "*Sheker hu*" ("This is a lie").

For example, it is customary to read the *Aseres HaDibros* from the Torah with a unique set of *trop*. This is known as *tam elyon*, the higher cantillations (as opposed to the regular *trop* for these *pesukim*, as they appear in our Chumash, known as *tam tachtone*, the lower cantillations).

This had been an issue of dispute a century earlier,[19] but it was Rav Zalman Henna who penned the sharpest comments regarding the issue.

In his genius, Rav Zalman Henna had deciphered the code for the *trop* in the Torah. If he was presented with any *pasuk* and given the place of the *esnachta* (a cantillation mark denoting a pause) and *sof posuk*, he could fill in the remaining *trop*. He did this by understanding the *trop* system.[20]

He realized that the sole difference between *tam elyon* and *tam tachtone* is that *tam elyon* renders each of the ten *dibros* as a single *pasuk*, illogically creating an enormous *pasuk* out of the long *dibros*, while creating two-word *pesukim* out of the shortest. All other *trop* differences are simply outgrowths of this change. This explanation has been accepted as accurate (S. A. HaRav and *Beur Halachah* 494).

Rav Zalman Henna argued that the regular *trop* was the only correct system by which to read these *pesukim*. The Gemara forbids the separation of *pesukim* of Tanach in any way other than that presented in the Torah. Thus, the *tam elyon*, by separating the *pesukim* differently, is actually a forbidden method of reading the Torah!

Most importantly, Rav Zalman Henna points out that there is no early source for *tam elyon*. If there is a source for this custom, why was it ignored by the Talmud and *Rishonim*?

Rav Zalman Henna therefore concluded that this is a relatively new custom, and that we would be better off returning to the original *minhag Yisrael*, abolishing the practice of *tam elyon*.

Rav Yaakov Emden took issue with this conclusion, as well. In *Luach Eresh* (#462), he defends *tam elyon*, and writes in anger, "Youngsters seek to tell us what to do, criticizing harshly without

---

19. This had been a dispute between the *Sefer Ohr Torah* and the *Teshuvos Massas Binyomin* in the 16th century. See also *Chasam Sofer* Y.D. 260 and *K'tzeras HaOmer*, which appears as an appendix in the new printing of *Luach Eresh*.

20. Rav Yaakov Emden did concede that Rav Zalman Henna's analysis of the *trop* system was correct. In our own generation, Rav Yaakov Kaminetsky was known to have mastered this wisdom. (Rav Zalman Henna, in this discussion, offers a partial description of this system of cantillations.)

cause, in haughtiness, to set Halachah for future generations, by uprooting the past ...."

Prayers for *Yiras Shamayim*

Most of the areas of dispute were disagreements regarding *dikduk* and the *mesorah*. On occasion, though, these disputes spilled over into *hashkofah* (religious thought) issues, as well.

Near the beginning of the morning prayer, we recite a list of fifteen *berachos*. The final *berachah* is the longest of the set, and ends with a prayer that includes the request, "*v'kof ess yitzraynu l'hishtabed Loch*," "compel our [Evil] Inclination to be subservient to You."

Rav Zalman Henna (in *Shaarei Tefillah*) explained that the word *v'kof* comes from the root word *k'feeyah*, to compel. The correct expression of this word, in this sentence formulation, is *u'kafay*, and Rav Zalman Henna therefore changed the word to reflect its correct grammatical form. In this Rav Zalman Henna was following the opinion that a person may pray for his *Yiras Shamayim*.

Rav Yaakov Emden (in *Luach Eresh* 22) disagreed with Rav Zalman Henna.

He argued that man is responsible for his actions, and that Hashem does not "compel" the Evil Inclination in any way. Still, we find that man can pray for help in this battle, as the Gemara states elsewhere (in *Kiddushin* 30b and *Succah* 52b) that without Hashem's help, the battle against the Evil Inclination could not be successful.

He therefore maintains that the word *v'kof* is correct, but that it does not mean "to compel." Rather, it comes from the root word *kof*, to bend, as in "*kof oznicha l'shmoa*," "bend your ears to listen."[21]

Later, in our discussion of "Prayers for *Yiras Shamayim*," we will study this dispute further.

---

21. See Rav Shimon Schwab in *Iyun Tefillah*, his commentary to the Siddur (p. 54), who presents a novel understanding of this prayer.

～§ Fruits of These Controversies

*T*hese controversies could easily have been a dull issue, of interest only to scholars. Most people are not particularly attracted to disputes regarding *dikduk*. Appreciating the significance of an extra *patach* or *tzeirei* is not everyone's first priority.

Yet, this dispute caught the attention of two generations of *talmidei chachamim*. It was the remarkable personalities who were involved and their intense interest in clarifying the issues of dispute that made these issues newsworthy.

We can guess that the entire European Jewish community had a greater level of interest in davening properly because of the renewed scrutiny of the Siddur. Awareness of the importance of proper pronunciation must have been raised by the image of these great personalities arguing with such intensity regarding these matters.

Rav Zalman Henna suffered much as a result of these disputes. He would be accused of forging the approbations to his *seforim*, most notably, the approbation of *Chacham Tzvi* to *Shaarei Tefillah*. *Chacham Tzvi* was the father of Rav Yaakov Emden!

In their disputes, it was Rav Zalman Henna's position that often involved changes to the accepted version of the Siddur. This position never sits well with us, traditional Jews, who hold the tradition of generations past to be most correct, and allow change only if a past practice can be proven to be in error.

Rav Zalman Henna would argue, again and again, that it was *he* who was safeguarding the ancient tradition, by weeding out the changes that later generations had erroneously made in the daily prayer book.

Add to this Rav Zalman Henna's opposition to various Jewish customs, and the volatile level of the debate is readily understandable.

Still, after the dust had settled and the dispute had passed into history, we find that the majority of Rav Zalman Henna's corrections (including virtually every one cited in this *shiur*[22]) are found in our Siddur. It is amazing that the persistence of the two sides in the debate accomplished what each side wanted most: the establishment of a universal text and punctuation for all Ashkenazic siddurim.

The Introduction to the recently reprinted *Luach Eresh* contains a short biography of Rav Zalman Henna, which is highly critical of him.

---

22. *Shiur*, not *shey-ure*!

Yet even there (pp. 30-31), Rav Zalman Henna's detractors concede, "His *Sefer Shaarei Tefillah* and his *Siddur Beis Tefillah* made a great impact and influenced many to change the language of their prayer …. Many of the ideas that are presented in Rav Zalman Henna's *seforim* have found their way into the *poskim*."

We can safely say, with the benefit of hindsight, that this could never have been accomplished without the intense level of debate that the controversy brought to bear.[23]

In my mind's eye, I picture Rav Yaakov Emden and Rav Zalman Henna in Gan Eden, arm in arm, in friendly embrace.

On second thought, I would picture them in the *Mesivta d'Rakea*, the Great *Beis HaMidrash* in Heaven, debating the laws of our Holy Tongue in a more animated manner than ever!

Epilogue

When discussing this topic at our Shabbos table, I was taken aback by the reaction of one of my guests.

"What? Over this they had an argument? *Chey olamim* or *Chai olamim*; does it really make a difference?"

Unfortunately this attitude is all too commonplace.

> A gentleman was leading the prayers on Rosh Chodesh. In the second paragraph of *Hallel*, he ignored a comma, erroneously reading, "*Hayom ra'ah, vayanos haYarden*" ("The sea saw, and the Jordan River fled").
>
> The Rabbi could not restrain himself at the ignorance and approached him afterwards, saying, "How could you say, 'The sea saw, and the Jordan River fled'? It makes no sense! If it was the sea that saw, why was it the Jordan River that fled?"
>
> The man responded with a second grammatical error, which, comically, made sense out of his first error.
>
> "I was thinking of that, until I realized that the *Hallel* prayer itself asks the question in the next line, "*Ma licha hayom ki sanuss haYarden*," "What happened to you, the sea, that the Jordan River fled?"

---

23. Other issues involving Rav Zalman Henna discussed in this volume appear in "The Tenuah Kallah Controversy," "*Dikduk* for Aramaic Words" and "Ben Asher and Ben Naftali."

The *Noda B'Yehudah* had not yet been born when the dispute involving Rav Zalman Henna first erupted. In his generation, though, he wrote regarding the dispute (in an introductory letter to *Kunteres HaSagos*). He explained that our prayer is in place of the service in the *Beis HaMikdash*. There, before an animal was offered for sacrifice, it was inspected for blemishes that might render it unfit as a sacrifice. The Gemara relates that one of the blemishes that Jews consider enough to invalidate an animal is *niv sifasayim*, a blemish on the lip. The Gemara makes the point that this is something that the non-Jewish world could not appreciate as a blemish.

In prayer, too, *niv sifasayim*, incorrect expressions of the lip, render our prayers unworthy of being a proper service before Hashem. We see this service, the prayers that emanate from our lips, as something requiring perfection. It is excellence and precision in prayer that give the prayers the power to fly heavenward and appear at the Heavenly Throne.

It is this excellence that is inspired by the story of Rav Zalman Henna.

Prayers for Yiras Shamayim

There is a great philosophical debate regarding the propriety of praying for success in serving Hashem. Does Hashem respond to a person's prayer to achieve *Yiras Shamayim*, Fear of Heaven, or that he succeed in doing *teshuvah*? Or, perhaps these achievements are a person's own responsibility, his task in this world, and Hashem therefore leaves this to man's free will. If so, prayer should not cause Hashem to influence man's free will.

As we shall see, this question takes on two forms. First, whether prayer can help for another person's *Yiras Shamayim*; and, if not, whether it helps to pray for one's own *Yiras Shamayim*.

⇜§ Rav Meir and Beruria

The Gemara (*Berachos* 10a) relates that Jewish criminals were terrorizing Rabbi Meir. In response, Rabbi Meir prayed that they die. His wife, Beruria, overheard Rabbi Meir's prayer.

She argued that Hashem does not desire the death of evildoers and that it was more appropriate to pray that they return to the ways of the Torah. Rabbi Meir accepted her argument. Henceforth, he prayed that they repent and live.

Maharsha questions this Gemara. He argues that it is not possible to pray successfully for another human being to repent, since this is subject to his choices and Hashem does not interfere with man's free will.[1] Still, *Maharsha* holds that it *is* appropriate for a person to pray for his own *Yiras Shamayim*.

Later, on Daf 28b, *Maharsha* restates his position. There, the Gemara relates the story of Rav Shimon bar Yochai's last minutes on this world. On his deathbed, he said to his disciples, "May it be His will that your Fear of Heaven be as great as your fear of man." This appears to be a prayer for his students' *Yiras Shamayim*.

Here, once again, *Maharsha* rejects the idea that one man can pray for another person's spiritual success. He therefore explains that Rav Shimon bar Yochai's words were intended as instructions to his disciples, rather than as a prayer to Hashem.

Igros Moshe (O.C. 4:40:13) accepts the *Maharsha's* opinion that prayer cannot affect another person's *Yiras Shamayim*. However, Rav Moshe maintains that prayer can have an indirect effect. A person can pray that his friend be saved from *nisyonos*, situations that would test his *Yiras Shamayim*; or that his friend come into circumstances that would influence him to choose to draw closer to Hashem, such as falling under the influence of a teacher or a good friend. These prayers work!

Ben Yehoyada (*Berachos* 10a) disagrees with the *Maharsha*. He maintains that Rabbi Meir accepted Beruria's opinion that a person may pray for another's spiritual success and that such prayers are appropriate.

Chazon Ish (end of *Taharos*) apparently follows this view and understands these Gemaros by their simple meaning.

He explains, "Hashem has given man free will, but one person can compel another to serve Hashem, whether by forcing him or by convincing him. This does not violate the doctrine of free will, since these actions are taken by man's choice, and all Jews are as one person."

---

1. *Minchas Elozor* (in *Divrei Torah* 2:46) maintains that Rabbi Meir understood this, and that he changed his prayer only out of respect for his wife. In fact, he knew that the prayer would not be answered.

Chazon Ish therefore reasons that prayer, too, is a manner by which free will can be influenced.[2]

ೞ A Third Opinion

Rav Aron Leib Shteinman, *Shlita*,[3] offered an innovative solution to this issue.

We know that once a person sins, it becomes easier for him to sin again. If he committed a particular sin numerous times, it becomes even more difficult for him to resist that temptation in the future. Thus, his original state of free will is altered by his actions. Where he originally could have resisted temptation with a lesser effort, his repeated offenses make it more difficult for him to choose to resist the *yetzer hara*.

The Gemara describes this as "*naa'seh lo k'heter* — actions begin to seem permissible" to a person who sins repeatedly. His free will to resist temptation has been altered. The next time that this particular temptation comes his way, the *yetzer hara* will have the upper hand.

Our prayers work to abolish this change, to move a person back to his original state of free will. In this way, prayer for another person's spiritual state does accomplish much. Still, these prayers do not violate our principle of free will, since the individual still finds himself in a position where he must utilize his free will to avoid sin.

ೞ Rav Dessler and *Nekudas HaBechirah*

Rav Eliyahu Dessler, in his classic *Michtav M'Eliyahu*, establishes a principle he calls "*Nekudas HaBechirah*," the point of free will. This principle maintains that each

---

2. A *nusach haTefillah*, a prayer, is circulating, which is attributed to the *Chazon Ish*. This prayer, designed to be inserted to the fifth *berachah* of *Shemoneh Esrei* (the prayer for penitence), reads, in part, "Remove all of the impediments that prevent him from Torah study, and place before him circumstances that will return him to the study of Torah."

The language of this *tefillah* mirrors the approach of *Igros Moshe* regarding these prayers.

3. *M'pi hashmua*.

individual is actually tested and judged regarding his actions in a limited area; what Rav Dessler calls "the point of free will," in his service of Hashem. This is explained as follows.

There are areas in which the *nisayon* or temptation to sin simply does not exist. This might include the temptation to eat pork, for someone who was raised in a traditional Jewish home; or the temptation to murder, for an even-tempered person. These temptations are said to be below the individual's *Nekudas HaBechirah*, point of free will. Man receives no reward for withstanding this type of sin.[4]

On the other hand, there are areas that are above an individual's *Nekudas HaBechirah*, areas where perfection is not expected, and sometimes is not possible. This includes (for most people) the sin of *bitul Torah*, the ideal of not wasting a single moment that could have been productively used for Torah study; or the commandments related to proper Shabbos observance, for a Jew who just learned of Shabbos for the first time. Man receives no punishment for failing in these areas.

There is a point of free will that corresponds to a person's standing in life and in his service of Hashem. It is here that man's great struggle for growth takes place. It is here that man is tested and that there is a concept of reward and punishment for his actions.

Michtav M'Eliyahu employs this concept throughout his writings to resolve various issues of *Hashkafah*, Jewish thought.[5]

---

4. A person who was previously on a lower level of *Nikudas HaBechirah*, but raised himself to a point where his old temptations no longer tempt him, continues to be rewarded for this accomplishment. (See Rav Dessler's letter on the topic, printed at the end of Volume 5 of *Michtav M'Eliyahu*.)

5. Often, the failure to appreciate one's *Nekudas HaBechirah* leads a person to failure and depression.

There are many yeshivah *bachurim* who truly desire greatness in their service of Hashem in general and in their Torah study in particular. In our time, where Torah scholarship is available to every young man, the *yetzer hara* seeks to derail the growth of a young man by convincing him that his accomplishments in learning are minimal. The young man looks at others more advanced than he, those who have better memories or a quicker grasp of *pilpul*. This thought process is dangerous. The resulting depression can cause the yeshivah *bachur* to forsake his learning entirely.

The *yetzer hara* works with the tool of *sheker*. Most often, the young man *is* successful in serving Hashem. His desire to expend his energies and to dedicate his life to Hashem and his Torah is a total desire. It is precisely those individuals with these sterling character traits and desires who are in danger of this attack of the *yetzer hara*. People who are satisfied with mediocrity and a tasteless service of Hashem are not susceptible to this attack, because they don't care enough to become depressed. Those with fire in their souls feel the pain of inadequacy with which they are challenged. Their souls have achieved man's most important obligation, to know Hashem

Michtav M'Eliyahu (3:47 and 4:271) understands the words of Beruria, based on this concept. "Man cannot affect the *bechirah* of another individual. However, man can affect another person's *Nekudas HaBechirah*."[6]

Beruria argued that Rabbi Meir should be praying that the *Nekudas HaBechirah* of his neighbors be raised, so that they would no longer be tempted to terrorize *talmidei chachamim*. This would affect their free will in regard to this particular sin, by raising their *Nekudas HaBechirah* to a different level. However, this is not inconsistent with the principle of free will, since these people would still be facing the struggle of *bechirah* at their new level. These people would receive no reward for having overcome this temptation, since it was not they, but Rabbi Meir, who accomplished this.

So too, anyone who prays for the spiritual success of another person can be successful in raising that person's *Nekudas HaBechirah*, his point of struggle. This accomplishes much. It brings about a *ree'bouy k'vod Shamayim,* an increased honor of Heaven, in that fewer sins are being committed. It raises the overall level of observance in a community and could serve as an inspiration to others. It does *not*, however, affect the reward and punishment of the individual, unless he himself has made the necessary choice to improve his service of Hashem.

---

and to thirst for greatness in His service. The recognition that one has achieved this should bring them to joy and ecstasy!

The ability to reject these arguments of the *yetzer hara* often lies in an appreciation of *Nekudas HaBechirah*. As *Mesillas Yeshorim* teaches in the first words of his epic *sefer*, "Man is obligated to recognize *his* obligation in *his* world."

The *yetzer hara* is tempting the yeshivah *bachur* to ignore his obligation and to look at others. The lie inherent in this attitude should be obvious. Is success in spirituality judged by comparison to others? Would a young man be better off in surroundings of inferior Torah scholarship?

To this young man, I say, "People only feel pain regarding issues that are close to them. Rejoice because, in a world that is filled with jealousy for material goods, your soul cares only about Torah. Guard your *Nekudas HaBechirah*. Challenge yourself to be better today than you were yesterday, without using the barometer of your surroundings. The Mishnah teaches, '*Hevei boreiach min hakavod ... sof kavod lavo,*' when one runs from honor, he can be sure that the honor will ultimately come."

This does not refer exclusively to honor from outside sources, but to one's own self-esteem, as well. Be calm about your need for satisfaction, *sipuk*, and at the end, it will come!

6. This type of prayer for others is successful only when made *lishmah*, for no ulterior motive. This is the message of the Gemara (*Chagigah* 15a), that the prayer of Avuyah regarding his son Elisha was unsuccessful, because it was not offered for the proper reason (*Michtav M'Eliyahu*, Vol. 4, p. 271).

By giving the matter proper thought, we realize that the opinion of Rav Aron Leib Shteinman, quoted earlier, is similar to that of Rav Dessler. Prayer for another's spiritual growth is possible, providing that it does not deprive the individual of free will in the future.

◆§ "Compel Our *Yetzer Hara* ...." Rav Zalman Henna and Rav Yaakov Emden

*E*arlier, we discussed the great controversies regarding the siddur, which involved numerous disputes between two 18th-century Torah giants, Rav Yaakov Emden and Rav Zalman Henna.

Our present debate, too, has a source in the siddur and is the subject of a dispute between Rav Zalman Henna and Rav Yaakov Emden.

Near the beginning of the morning prayer, we recite a list of fifteen *berachos*. The final *berachah* is the longest of the set, and ends with a prayer which includes the request, "*v'kof ess yitzraynu l'hishtabed Loch*," "compel our [Evil] Inclination to be subservient to You."

Rav Zalman Henna (in *Shaarei Tefillah*) explained that the word *v'kof* comes from the root word *k'feeyah*, to compel. The correct expression of this word, in this sentence formulation, is *u'kafay*, and Rav Zalman Henna therefore changed this word in his Siddur, to reflect its correct grammatical form. In this, Rav Zalman Henna was following the opinion of all the aforementioned authorities, who agreed that a person can pray for his own spiritual success.[7]

Rav Yaakov Emden (*Luach Eresh* #22) disagreed with Rav Zalman Henna.

He argued that man is responsible for his actions, and that Hashem does not "compel" the Evil Inclination in any way. Still,

---

7. This prayer appears in the plural form, "*compel our yetzer hara*," implying that this prayer works for others, as well. As we have seen, this approach is rejected by *Maharsha*, who understands that man may pray for his own spiritual growth, but not for the growth of others.

In fact, virtually all of our prayers are in the plural form. In *Shemoneh Esrei* we ask, "Return us, our Father, to Your Torah and bring us close, our King, to Your service." *Maharsha* specifically concedes that this is appropriate, "where he includes himself in the prayer for others."

we find that man can pray for help in this battle, as the Gemara states elsewhere (*Kiddushin* 30b and *Succah* 52b), that without Hashem's help, the battle against the Evil Inclination could not be successful.

He therefore maintains that the word *v'kof* is correct, but that it does not mean "to compel." Rather, it comes from the root word *kof*, to bend, as in "*kof oznicha l'shmoa* — bend your ears to listen."[8]

In this disagreement, Rav Yaakov Emden is arguing *against* the ability of prayer to drastically affect a person's spiritual growth.

It is interesting to find that Rav Yaakov Emden found himself on the opposite side of the issue in another dispute, in which he argues *for* this type of prayer.

In his *Mor U'ketziah* (46), Rav Yaakov Emden quotes a note of *Ateres Zekeinim*, which is printed alongside the *Shulchan Aruch* (O.C. 46). This note advises that the prayer, "*v'kof ess yitzraynu l'hishtabed Loch*," should not be said, since *Yiras Shamayim* is not in the hands of Heaven.

Rav Yaakov Emden, in his usual sharp manner, rejects the words of the *Ateres Zekeinim*.

"I was amazed that words like these could find their way into print. Isn't anyone supervising ...."

He cites *Berachos* 17a, stating that *Rava* would end his prayers with the request, "May it be Your will that I not sin again," an expression we use in the *Viduei* prayers of Yom Kippur.[9] We also find that Moshe Rabbeinu prayed on behalf of his disciple Yehoshua, "May Hashem rescue you from [joining in the evil] plans of the *miraglim* [spies]," and that Avraham prayed on behalf of Yishmael.[10]

Rav Yaakov Emden therefore restates the position he had taken in his dispute with Rav Zalman Henna, that man can pray for help in serving Hashem, as the Gemara states elsewhere (*Kiddushin* 30b and *Succah* 52b) that without Hashem's help, the battle against the Evil Inclination could not be successful.

---

8. See Rav Shimon Schwab, in *Iyun Tefillah*, his commentary to the Siddur (p. 54), who presents a novel understanding of this prayer.

9. The language of this prayer, "May it be Your will that I not sin again," seems particularly strange. Isn't it already Hashem's will that we not sin? In *Shemoneh Esrei*, we refer to Hashem as *Rotzeh B'Teshuvah*, He Who desires repentance. Hashem always desires that man achieve perfection.

10. Another source for this position is in the *U'va L'Zion* prayer, "May (Hashem) open our heart to His Torah, and imbue our heart with love and awe of Him so that we may do His will and serve Him."

This prayer is therefore proper, because it is only a request for Hashem's help in this battle, not a prayer that Hashem totally compel the *yetzer hara*, as Rav Zalman Henna had maintained.

It is interesting that the *Ateres Zekeinim* mentioned in *Mor U'Ketziah* does *not* appear in our print of the *Shulchan Aruch*. On the contrary, a note of *Ateres Zekeinim* (to O.C. 47) advises that one pray for his descendant's spiritual success, which is consistent with Rav Yaakov Emden's opinion.

◈§ A Practical Suggestion

We pray three times a day. Undoubtedly, we have our personal needs in mind, and those of our friends and relatives. But which needs come to mind?

Typically, it is the need for *parnassah* and for health that are forefront in our prayers. Should this be so? Does it make sense that we focus on the needs of this transient world while ignoring the greater needs of our souls?

Shemoneh Esrei begins with a request for wisdom, insight, and knowledge. This is an important prayer, worthy of being first on our list of requests. However, most people give it little thought. This is because most people feel that they have just the right amount of intelligence. Few people, if any, think of themselves as fools. Clearly, they are not all right.

Success in Torah study requires a great deal of *siyata d'Shmaya*, help from Above. We should be begging for increased wisdom, insight, and knowledge! Why not request it from He who provides it!

The second *berachah* is a request for *teshuvah*. Are we so comfortable in our success in serving Hashem that this is not the primary focus of our daily prayer? Is it only the non-observant who seek to be masters of *teshuvah*?

We all wish to draw closer to Hashem. Prayer works to achieve this. Let us increase our awareness of our true needs, focusing our prayers on these most important aspects of our lives.

Rav Zalman Henna & the Tenuah Kallah Controversy

The original *Complete ArtScroll Siddur* contains the following statement at the end of the Preface, under the heading, "Hebrew Grammar." "In identifying a *shva na*, we follow the Vilna Gaon[1] and Rabbi Yaakov Emden."

Most people do not know the meaning of this sentence and are not aware of the great controversy alluded to by this simple statement. *Dikduk* experts still argue about this opinion of "the Vilna

---

1. The allusion to the Vilna Gaon regarding this matter is itself a matter of controversy. We have no clear source for the Gaon's opinion on this matter. This reference is actually to the disciples of the Gaon, who sided with Rabbi Yaakov Emden in this dispute. Specifically, Rav Chaim ben R'Yehudah, the *ba'al korei* at the *Beis HaMidrash* of Rav Menachem Mendel of Shklov, quotes Rav Menachem Mendel as rejecting Rav Zalman Henna's *tenuah kallah*. (See *Ha'aros al Talmud Bavli Lashon Ivri*, quoted in the excellent abridged rules of *dikduk* in the Introduction to *Tikkun Korim — Simonim*.)

Rav Menachem Mendel of Shklov was one of the most famous disciples of the Gaon and is known for leading the group of disciples who moved to the Land of Israel.

The author of the *Siddur HaGra* (in his Introduction, pp. 9-10) also disputes Rav Zalman Henna's opinion. This is also the view of a third disciple of the Gaon, Rav Yechezkiel Feivel, the Vilna Dayan, in his *Toldas HaAdam* (p. 47).

Gaon and Rav Yaakov Emden." Even today, there are some who do not accept the designation of *shva na* that the *ArtScroll Siddur* has chosen to follow. Let us attempt to understand the issue at its most basic level.

Rav Shlomo Zalman was born in the German city of Hanau, near Frankfurt am Main, in 1687. He was a towering 18th-century genius who specialized in the rules of *dikduk*. Earlier, in our study of the Siddur, we have discussed this colorful personality and his contribution to the Siddur. Here, we will examine his single most-controversial innovation, the *tenuah kallah*.

The *tenuah kallah* controversy can be presented on many levels. I will take the liberty of presenting it in its simplest form. Although this many incur the displeasure of *dikduk* experts, they are not the ones in need of this explanation (and are free to correspond their disapproval, as I imagine they will).

֍ The Problem

This controversy revolves around two of the most basic rules of *dikduk*, which come into conflict in a great number of instances.

■ **Rule One:** A *shva* that follows a *tenuah ketanah*[2] **is a *shva nach*.** There are five basic rules for designating the status of a *shva*. One of these rules[3] is based on the vowel of the letter which precedes the *shva*. If the vowel is a *tenuah gedolah*, one of the five major vowels, the *shva* that follows is a *shva na*. If it is a *tenuah ketanah*, the *shva* that follows is a *shva nach*.

■ **Rule Two:** A *Beged Kefes* letter which follows a *shva nach* receives a *dageish*. We will see that the six *Beged Kefes* letters (*beis, gimmel, daled, chof, pei,* and *sof*) take a *dageish* when they appear at the beginning of a word. This is also true when they follow a *shva*

---

2. The five minor vowels are *patach, segol, koobutz, cheerik katan* (i.e., without the *yud*), and *kamatz katan*. The five major vowels are the *cheerik gadol* (*cheerik* followed by the letter *yud*), *shooruk* (which appears in the *vov* form), *tzeirei, cholum,* and *kamatz*. This will be discussed later, in the "Rules of *Dikduk.*"

3. The other four rules for designating a *shva na* appear in "*Dikduk* for Aramaic Words."

nach, and therefore begin a new syllable, after the slight pause of the *shva nach*.

These rules come into conflict in various words. Let us use, as examples, words that appear in *Krias Shema*.

The word *malchuso* (His kingdom), has a *shva* under the letter *lamed*. On the one hand, this should be designated as a *shva nach*, because it follows a *tenuah ketanah* (the *patach* under the letter *mem*). On the other hand, the fact that the letter *chof* that follows does not have a *dageish*, indicates that the *shva* is a *shva na*.

Which rule takes precedence, the rule indicated by the preceding letter or that indicated by the following letter?

The word *eschem* (you, plural) has a *shva* under the letter *sof*. On the one hand, this should be designated as a *shva nach*, because it follows a *tenuah ketanah* (the *segol* under the letter *aleph*). On the other hand, the fact that the letter *chof* that follows does not have a *dageish* indicates that the *shva* is a *shva na*.

Again, which rule takes precedence? How is the *shva* designated?

Other examples include the words *livavchem* (your hearts), *kanfei* (the corners of), and *yedchem* (your hands). All of these words contain the vowel *shva*, with the same contradictory indications.[4]

✥ What Is a *Tenuah Kallah*?

*I*t is quite common for there to be exceptions to rules of *dikduk*. Rav Yaakov Emden (*Migdal Oz*, pp 83: "Is there a single rule in *dikduk* that has no exception?") viewed this, too, as an exception to the regular rules of *dikduk*. He accepted that the *shva* is a *shva nach*, and that the lack of a *dageish* in the letter that follows must be attributed to an exception in the rules of designating the *dageish*.

Rav Zalman Henna ridiculed this approach. In his *Tzohar LaTeivah* (#17), he argues that something can only be designated as an exception if it is found on rare occasion. "We find this ["exception"]

---

4. Any Hebrew plural noun that begins with a *shva* will fall under this discussion. This includes words such as *milachim* (kings), *dirachim* (roads), *bigadim* (clothing), *zinovos* (tails), and *kinofayim* (wings). These words become *malchi*, *darchei*, *bigdei*, *zanvei*, and *kanfei*, respectively. All of these words contain a *shva*, sandwiched between a *tenuah ketanah* and a letter without a *dageish*.

in the thousands, even tens of thousands. Rules cannot work where the exceptions are more common than the rules!"

Rav Zalman Henna, therefore, sought a single point of similarity in these thousands of "exceptions," seeking to find a single rule that could solve this riddle, making them exceptions no longer.

Rav Zalman Henna came to the conclusion that there is a separate vowel category that is neither *tenuah gedolah*, nor *tenuah ketanah*. The vowels in this category are replacement vowels that take the place of the original root vowel.

For example, the imperative (command) form of the verb instructing someone to write is *ksov*. In plural form (instructing many people to write), this becomes *kisvu*, beginning with a *cheerik*, a *tenuah ketanah*. This *cheerik* is a replacement vowel, in that it replaces the *shva* that was under the *kof* in the root word, *ksov*. This replacement vowel belongs to this separate class of vowels.

Rav Zalman Henna gave this type of vowel a new name, calling it a "*tenuah kallah*," a "light vowel." He maintained that a *shva* that follows a *tenuah kallah* (as in *kisvu*, under the *sof*) is a *shva na*. This explains why the next letter that follows this *shva* (in *kisvu*, the letter *veis*) does not have a *dageish*.

Returning to our examples that appear in *Krias Shema*, the word *malchuso* begins with the *patach* vowel, which would appear to be a *tenuah ketanah*. In fact, this *patach* is a replacement vowel, in that it replaces the *segol* that is under the letter *mem* in the root word *melech*. It is therefore a *tenuah kallah*. The *shva* that follows is, therefore, a *shva na*.[5]

As a *bachur*, I once asked Rav Pam, *zt"l*, why the word *eschem* does not have a *dageish* in the *chof*.

Rav Pam explained that, based on its root form, the word should actually be *oschem* (with a *cholem* on the first letter), since the sin-

---

5. In many of these cases, the *tenuah kallah* actually replaces a *shva*. In the examples mentioned in the previous footnote, the root word begins with a *shva*. In the adapted form, these words have a *shva* under the *second* letter of the word, as in *malchei, darchei, bigdei*, etc.

If we were to allow the vowelization of the first letter to remain as in the root word, it would remain a *shva* and be followed by a *shva*. This would mean that the adapted word would begin with two consecutive *shva* vowels. No Hebrew word can begin with two *shva* vowels, as this is difficult to pronounce.

In these cases, the first letter receives a replacement vowel (so that *malchei* and *darchei* begin with a *patach*, and *bigdei* begins with a *cheerik*). Before this change, the *shva* that follows would have been a *shva na* (since it had no previous vowel on which to rest) and it remains a *shva na*, according to Rav Zalman Henna (*Dikduk Sifoseinu* Lesson 22).

gular form of this word is *osicha*, with a *cholem*. The replacement *segol* is therefore a replacement vowel, a *tenuah kallah*. The *shva* that follows a *tenuah kallah* is a *shva na*. The *chof* that follows has no *dageish*, since it follows a *shva na*. This is all in line with the approach of Rav Zalman Henna.

✎§ After a Prefix

In Hebrew, the word "and" is written as a letter *vuv* prefix. This normally is vowelized with a *shva*. This is very common. Often, the *vuv* has a different vowel, sometimes a *cheerik*, at other times a *shurik*.

Rav Zalman Henna viewed this *cheerik/shurik* as a replacement vowel, and maintained that the *tenuah kallah* rule should apply here, as well. This changes the *shva* that follows to a *shva na*.

There are numerous examples of this in *Krias Shema*. In the first paragraph alone, this replacement vowel appears five times (in the words *u'vilechticha*, *u'vikumecha*, *u'kishartom*, *u'chisavtom*, and *u'vishaarecha*[6]).

In these cases, most of the popular siddurim indicate that the *shva* is a *shva nach*; those who follow Rav Zalman Henna would pronounce this as a *shva na*.

✎§ Not Everyone Agreed

Many disagreed with Rav Zalman Henna. When Rav Zalman Henna's opinion on this matter was published, he had already been embroiled in a great controversy regarding other aspects of the siddur. He had been accused of creating *chiddushim*, novel ideas, regarding the Hebrew language, at the expense of the opinions of early giants of the Jewish People.

The *Noda B'Yehudah* (in his introduction to *Kunteres HaSagos*), after praising Rav Zalman Henna's wisdom, makes the general state-

---

6. A sixth word, *u'vishochvicha* would be included in this list. However, in this case, all siddurim present this as a *shva na*. This is because the *vuv* has a *meseg* (minor accent). The *shva* which follows therefore is a *shva na* even if one rejects Rav Zalman Henna's rule.

ment that, "despite the fact that he is extraordinary in his wisdom regarding this, he should not be relied on in areas where he creates novel ideas (*"al ma she'chideish"*)."

The concept of the *tenuah kallah*, a new set of vowels, was seen as another example of his penchant for creativity and brazen disregard of the need for earlier sources. His new *tenuah kallah* rule, was, therefore, dismissed by many.[7]

In his defense, it must be pointed out that Rav Zalman Henna, himself, conceded that the term *tenuah kallah* was his own innovation. "To these vowels, I have attached the name *tenuah kallah*."

However, he maintained that the underlining theme was not new, but merely an analysis of the way our *mesorah* has always presented these words.

✌ What Do We Do Today?

There are no situations in which the *tenuah kallah* rule actually impacts a word in a way that would change its meaning. Still, we desire to read words correctly, particularly in *Krias Shema*, where the Shulchan Aruch implores us to pronounce the *shva na* and *nach* correctly. There are as many as eighteen places in *Krias Shema* where this controversy affects pronunciation (see facing page).

Halachah l'ma'aseh, do we accept Rav Zalman Henna's *tenuah kallah*?

Some follow the opinion of Rav Zalman Henna. I have been fortunate to spend my life in Yeshivah Torah Vodaath. Our yeshivah is fortunate enough to have had three *Roshei Yeshivah* known for their expertise in the rules of *dikduk*. It is our understanding that all three (Rav Yaakov Kamenetsky, *zt"l*; Rav Avroham Pam, *zt"l*; and, *yibadel l'chayim*, Rav Yisrael Belsky, *Shlita*), accept the opinion of Rav Zalman Henna and recite the *shva* that follows a *tenuah kallah* as a *shva na*.

They are not alone in this regard. The *Otzar HaTefillos Siddur*, the siddurim of Chabad and the *Siddur Chasam Sofer* follow Rav Zalman

---

7. *Kunteres HaSagos* 128 (p. 347, in the new edition of *Luach Eresh*), as well as Rav Yaakov Emden, as cited earlier. Some ridiculed the *tenuah kallah* by paraphrasing a Talmudic expression, calling it a "*kallah na'ah v'chashudah*" (*Migdal Oz*).

> שְׁמַע | יִשְׂרָאֵל, ה', | אֱלֹקֵינוּ, ה', | אֶחָד.
> בָּרוּךְ שֵׁם כְּבוֹד מַ**ל**כוּתוֹ לְעוֹלָם וָעֶד.
>
> וְאָהַבְתָּ אֵת ה' | אֱלֹקֶיךָ, בְּכָל | לְבָבְךָ, וּבְכָל נַפְשְׁךָ, וּ**ב**ְכָל מְאֹדֶךָ. וְהָיוּ הַדְּבָרִים הָאֵלֶּה, אֲשֶׁר | אָנֹכִי מְצַוְּךָ הַיּוֹם, עַל | לְבָבֶךָ. וְשִׁנַּנְתָּם לְבָנֶיךָ, וְדִבַּרְתָּ בָּם, בְּשִׁבְתְּךָ בְּבֵיתֶךָ, וּ**ב**ְלֶכְתְּךָ בַדֶּרֶךְ, וּבְשָׁכְבְּךָ, וּ**ב**ְקוּמֶךָ. וּ**ק**ְשַׁרְתָּם לְאוֹת | עַל יָדֶךָ, וְהָיוּ לְטֹטָפֹת בֵּין | עֵינֶיךָ. וּ**כ**ְתַבְתָּם | עַל מְזוּזוֹת בֵּיתֶךָ וּבִ**שׁ**ְעָרֶיךָ.
>
> וְהָיָה אִם שָׁמֹעַ תִּשְׁמְעוּ אֶל מִצְוֹתַי, אֲשֶׁר | אָנֹכִי מְצַוֶּה | אֶ**ת**ְכֶם הַיּוֹם, לְאַהֲבָה אֶת ה' | אֱלֹקֵיכֶם וּלְעָבְדוֹ, בְּכָל | לְ**ב**ַבְכֶם וּבְכָל נַפְשְׁכֶם. וְנָתַתִּי מְטַר | אַרְצְכֶם בְּעִתּוֹ, יוֹרֶה וּמַלְקוֹשׁ, וְאָסַפְתָּ דְגָנֶךָ וְתִירֹשְׁךָ וְיִצְהָרֶךָ. וְנָתַתִּי | עֵשֶׂב | בְּשָׂדְךָ לִ**ב**ְהֶמְתֶּךָ, וְאָכַלְתָּ וְשָׂבָעְתָּ. הִשָּׁמְרוּ לָכֶם פֶּן יִפְתֶּה לְ**ב**ַבְכֶם, וְסַרְתֶּם וַעֲבַדְתֶּם | אֱלֹהִים | אֲחֵרִים | וְהִשְׁתַּחֲוִיתֶם לָהֶם. וְחָרָה | אַף ה' | בָּכֶם, וְעָצַר | אֶת הַשָּׁמַיִם | וְלֹא יִהְיֶה מָטָר, וְהָאֲדָמָה לֹא תִתֵּן אֶת יְבוּלָהּ, וַאֲבַדְתֶּם | מְהֵרָה מֵעַל הָאָרֶץ הַטֹּבָה | אֲשֶׁר | ה' | נֹתֵן לָכֶם. וְשַׂמְתֶּם | אֶת דְּבָרַי | אֵלֶּה עַל | לְ**ב**ַבְכֶם וְעַל נַפְשְׁכֶם, וּ**ק**ְשַׁרְתֶּם | אֹתָם לְאוֹת | עַל יֶ**ד**ְכֶם, וְהָיוּ לְטוֹטָפֹת בֵּין | עֵינֵיכֶם. וְלִמַּדְתֶּם | אֹתָם | אֶת בְּנֵיכֶם לְדַבֵּר בָּם, בְּשִׁבְתְּךָ בְּבֵיתֶךָ, וּ**ב**ְלֶכְתְּךָ בַדֶּרֶךְ, וּבְשָׁכְבְּךָ, וּ**ב**ְקוּמֶךָ. וּ**כ**ְתַבְתָּם | עַל מְזוּזוֹת בֵּיתֶךָ וּבִ**שׁ**ְעָרֶיךָ. לְמַעַן | יִרְבּוּ | יְמֵיכֶם וִימֵי בְנֵיכֶם | עַל הָאֲדָמָה | אֲשֶׁר נִשְׁבַּע | ה' לַאֲבֹתֵיכֶם לָתֵת לָהֶם, כִּימֵי הַשָּׁמַיִם | עַל הָאָרֶץ.
>
> וַיֹּאמֶר | ה' | אֶל מֹשֶׁה לֵּאמֹר. דַּבֵּר | אֶל בְּנֵי | יִשְׂרָאֵל וְאָמַרְתָּ אֲלֵהֶם, וְעָשׂוּ לָהֶם צִיצִת עַל כַּנְפֵי בִגְדֵיהֶם לְדֹרֹתָם, וְנָתְנוּ | עַל צִיצִת הַכָּנָף פְּתִיל תְּכֵלֶת. וְהָיָה לָכֶם לְצִיצִת, וּ**ר**ְאִיתֶם | אֹתוֹ וּ**ז**ְכַרְתֶּם | אֶת כָּל מִצְוֹת | ה', וַעֲשִׂיתֶם | אֹתָם, וְלֹא תָתוּרוּ | אַחֲרֵי לְ**ב**ַבְכֶם וְאַחֲרֵי | עֵינֵיכֶם, אֲשֶׁר אַתֶּם זֹנִים | אַחֲרֵיהֶם. לְמַעַן תִּזְכְּרוּ וַעֲשִׂיתֶם | אֶת כָּל מִצְוֹתָי, וִהְיִיתֶם קְדֹשִׁים לֵאלֹקֵיכֶם. אֲנִי ה' | אֱלֹקֵיכֶם, אֲשֶׁר הוֹצֵאתִי | אֶ**ת**ְכֶם | מֵאֶרֶץ מִצְרַיִם, לִהְיוֹת לָכֶם לֵאלֹקִים, אֲנִי | ה' | אֱלֹקֵיכֶם.

The letters in boldface have a shva vowel. These are all subjects of the tenuah kallah dispute. They would be pronounced as a shva na according to Rav Zalman Henna and as a shva nach according to Rav Yaakov Emden.

Henna. This is also accepted (without mention of a dissenting opinion) in *Dikduk Sifoseinu*, a short *sefer* on *dikduk*, which Rav Pam had lent me to study.

This is also reported to appear in the *Kitzur Klalei HaDikduk* of Rav Zalman of Salant.⁸

The *Kitzur Shulchan Aruch* (58:4) appears to assume that this is the mainstream opinion. In discussing the blessing on the smell of herbs, *borei isvei bisamim*, the *Kitzur* explains that the word *isvei* is punctuated with "a *cheerik* under the letter *ayin*, and the letter *beis* is soft [i.e., without a *dageish*], because the *cheerik* is a *tenuah kallah*."

The punctuation of *isvei* is not the issue. It is the explanation of the *Kitzur Shulchan Aruch* in referring to the *tenuah kallah* that indicates that he understood that the *tenuah kallah* was an accepted concept. This also appears in the preface to *Kesses HaSofer* (*Klalei Dikduk* 2:42).

The Introduction to the *Pri Migadim* on *Shulchan Aruch* contains letters that the *Pri Migadim* wrote to Rav Akiva Binyamin, a scholar who taught young children. Near the beginning of the second letter, he writes that a teacher is responsible to teach his young students *dikduk*. He writes, in part, "*Tzohar LaTeivah* should be taught while they are young." Although we cannot assume that *Pri Migadim* agreed with every ruling in *Tzohar LaTeivah*, the *tenuah kallah* is certainly the most famous part of the *sefer*. The endorsement of the book, without mention of exception, certainly indicates its acceptance.

Many disagree: The *Siddur HaGra Ishei Yisrael* rejects the *tenuah kallah*. The Introduction to this siddur (pp. 9-10), cites *Ibn Ezra* (*Bereishis* 37, *v'tzari*) and *Redak* (in his *m'chlol*, p. 153) who appear to disagree with Rav Zalman Henna's rule.⁹ This also appears to be the opinion of *Meiri* in his *Kiryas Sofer* (*Shaar Kriyas Shva*).

As mentioned earlier, the *ArtScroll Siddur* does not follow Rav Zalman Henna. This is the opinion followed by most siddurim today. Therefore, you will usually find these *shva* vowels appearing as *shva nach*.

Many contemporary grammarians have stated that the custom is not to follow Rav Zalman Henna in regard to the *tenuah kallah*. This includes the late Rav Yehudah Aryeh Guttman, *zt"l*, in *Klalei Tamei HaMikra* (p. 24) and, *yibadel l'chayim*, Rav Sroya Duvlitsky, *Shlita*, in his approbations to *Kunteres HaTomas HaMilim* and to *Luach Eresh*.

---

8. As quoted in the Introduction to *Luach Eresh*. I've never seen this *sefer*.

9. Quoted in note 204 to the reprinted *Shaarei Tefillah*, as it appears in the new *Luach Eresh*.

Today, this appears to be the majority opinion, although it is hard to declare a "majority" in areas where few have expertise.[10]

Thus, today, almost three hundred years after this controversy first began, there remains a divergence of opinion on this matter.

---

10. The *Beis Yosef* (O. C. 61, s.v. *u'tzarich*) discusses the pronunciation of the word *u'zichartem*. The Tur had warned that a person who recites *Krias Shema* must be careful to pronounce the *z* sound of *tizkiru*, so that it not be read as *tiskiru*, which has an improper meaning.

The *Beis Yosef* (quoting *Redak*) asks why the same admonition was not made in regard to the word *u'zichartem*, where the same mispronunciation can occur. The wording of the answer is not entirely clear. Some have understood the answer to be based on the pronunciation of *u'zichartem* as a word with a *shva na* on the letter *zayin*. The strong *shva na* sound would make a mispronunciation of this word unlikely. This would place *Beis Yosef* in accord with the opinion of Rav Zalman Henna. (Those who disagree would place a *shva nach* under the *zayin* of this word.)

The ambiguous language of *Beis Yosef* is not clear on this point. (It should be remembered that *Redak*, the source for this *Beis Yosef*, does not appear to agree with Rav Zalman Henna.)

Astronomy for Beginners

"Rav Shimon bar Nachmeini said, in the name of Rav Yonoson, from where do we learn that one is commanded to calculate the seasons and constellations? From this, which is said, 'Guard this and accomplish it, for it is your wisdom and understanding in the eyes of the nations.'

"Which wisdom is in the eyes of the nations? This is the calculation of the cycles and the constellations."

(Shabbos 75a)

The *Rishonim* take this Gemara literally, understanding that there is a specific mitzvah to study astronomy. Some count this as a separate Biblical commandment (*BeHag*, *Sefer Yirayim* 60, *Semag* 47, *Semak* 103). Others disagree and maintain that this is a *mitzvah d'Rabbanan* (*Rambam* and *Ramban* in *Shoresh Aleph* of *Sefer HaMitzvos*).

Studying astronomy, as it pertains to Torah is, of course, certainly a *mitzvah d'Oraysa* of Talmud Torah.[1] This dispute involves a *second*

---

1. "Know that Shmuel's calculation for the seasons is considered Torah, as are the 29½ days, 44 minutes, and one *cheilek* mentioned in the Gemara" (*Chazon Ish* 138:4).

mitzvah, which relates specifically to the study of astronomy.

The *Chazon Ish* had great expertise in the study of astronomy. His essays on the topic are unrivaled in their level of scholarship, compared to that of any other of the contemporary *seforim*. After the study of *kiddush haChodesh,* the *Chazon Ish* would take the papers on which he had made his mathematical calculations and place them in *shaimos*. He explained that these calculations had the *kedushah* of *Divrei Torah* (Rav Chaim Kanievsky, in his Introduction to *Shekel HaKodesh*).

Whether we follow the opinion that this mitzvah is *d'Oraysa* or that it is *d'Rabbanan*, this mitzvah is certainly one of the most widely ignored mitzvos.

Today one has to know just a little bit to appear to be an expert in the field. This is because others know so little!

Let us begin by studying some practical points, the "just a little bit." Hopefully, this will whet the appetite to pursue a fuller understanding of the wonders of God's heavens.

✥ Using the Moon to Determine *Mizrach*

Here's a neat trick that requires only a minimum of knowledge, but puts you at great advantage.

You are at a wedding, and after the *chuppah,* the guests prepare to daven Maariv. As they gather, there is confusion as to which direction is east, the direction we face during our prayers. You say, "Let's just go outside and look at the moon, and we'll see which direction is the east."

People will think that you are joking. When you step back a moment later and confidently assured them that a particular direction is the eastern direction, they will be amazed. They will see you as an expert in astronomy.

I know this is so, because this has happened to me, on numerous occasions.

An expert? Nothing could be further from the truth. This observation is based on facts that everyone knows, but that few people realize they know. So, if knowing this simple trick makes you an expert, I invite you all to share my "expertise." It should take approximately two minutes of reading time.

We know that the sun, moon, and stars all move across the sky, rising in the east and setting in the west.[2] At night, when you observe the moon in the sky, it is slowly moving from east to west.

The moon usually appears as a crescent. A portion of the moon is lit up, while the second part of the moon appears dark. Let's review what we already know regarding this crescent that we observe in the sky.

Where is the moon's light coming from? This is an easy question to answer. We all know that the moon is actually reflecting the light it receives from the sun.

Where is the sun during the first half of the night? Again, we all know that it has set in the west, and is below the western horizon.

Which half of the moon would be lit up, the eastern half or the western half?

Again, using the information we all know, we can easily conclude that the sun's light, which is coming from the west, would illuminate the western side of the moon. The eastern half of the moon, which is facing away from the sun, is not receiving its light.

Thus, the lit portion of the crescent is always facing the west. The hollow of the crescent, the dark part, is always facing east.

To daven facing *mizrach*, we simply face the direction toward which the dark side of the moon is facing. Isn't this simple!

A word of caution is in order: This trick will generally work on the first fourteen days of a Hebrew month. On the fifteenth day, when there is a full moon, there is no crescent by which to determine the direction of the sun. After the fifteenth day of the month, the moon is farther in the eastern sky and is getting its light from the rising sun. The crescent will then face the east![3]

Still, most weddings take place during the first half of the Hebrew month and the trick will usually work to determine *mizrach*, the easterly direction.[4]

---

2. Isn't it amazing that all of these heavenly bodies move across our sky in the same direction! Actually, it's not amazing at all. You see, it is the Earth that is turning from west to east, making the sun, moon, and stars appear to move across the sky at approximately the same speed. (Wherever you will observe a difference in the movement of heavenly bodies, this is caused by the independent motion of the sun, moon, and planets.)

3. This method will not work during the last quarter of the month, when the moon is not visible during the first half of the night; moonrise is then after midnight.

4. Below, we will learn that the moon's orbit is not in a straight line, from east to west. In the Northern Hemisphere, the moon actually crosses the sky in an arc, moving from east to west across the southern sky. If so, we are not actually facing due east

Remember, of course, that these "tricks" will not work on a cloudy night, when the moon is not visible.

✺ Finding the Moon for *Kiddush Levanah*

Once a month, usually on *Motza'ei Shabbos*, we step out of the shul to say the *Kiddush Levanah* prayer. As people step out, they scan the sky, searching for the moon, so that the prayer may be said. Most often, people search the sky in all directions. They have no clue as to which direction to look (with the obvious exclusion of downward).

But you — you will search cluelessly no longer! Here's the "just a little bit" of information that will make you appear very knowledgeable.

Both the sun and the moon rise in the eastern sky, then travel across the sky to the west, where they set. Neither the sun nor the moon actually makes its path across the center of the sky.[5] They always travel in an arc, crossing towards the west, in the southern half of the sky.

This is what the verse means when it teaches, "And the sun rises and the sun sets, then to its [original] place it rushes, there it rises again. It goes toward the south and veers toward the north" (*Koheles* 1:5-6). This refers to the fact that in the first half of the day the sun travels west, but at an angle toward the south. In the second half of the day, the sun, which is now in the south, continues to travel to the west, but its path completes an arc by moving in a northerly direction, back towards the center of the sky.

---

when praying in the direction of the moon's crescent. Still, *Chazal* did not require that the prayers be said facing due east. The Gemara allows, even recommends, that a person turn slightly during the *Shemoneh Esrei* (to the left, to request *parnassah*; to the right, to pray for wisdom) this slight deviation has no practical effect as regards the direction of our prayer.

5. At the Equator, the moon does travel across the center of the sky. We in Eretz Yisrael, the United States, and Europe live in the Northern Hemisphere. Here, the tilt of the Earth's axis causes the moon to travel in an arc across the southern sky. To those in South Africa, parts of South America, and Australia, the reverse is true. The angle of the Earth causes the moon to travel from east to west, across the northern half of the sky.

When stepping out for *Kiddush Levanah*, never ever look for the moon in the northern half of the sky. It is never there! For example, our shul is on the southern side of Avenue S, in Brooklyn. As people step out of the shul, month after month, for *Kiddush Levanah*, the moon is always on the shul's side of the avenue. It is never across the street, above Avenue R!

It amazes me that people who recite *Kiddush Levanah* in the same shul, month after month, can step out and search the northern sky for the moon. Don't they realize that this never happens?

Now that we are familiar with the daily orbit of the sun and moon, let us see some other applications of this knowledge.

The Hebrew word for north is *tzafone*, which also means "hidden." Ramban explains the reason for this name, in line with our discussion. The sun and moon can appear in the east, west, or southern sections of the sky, but are "hidden" from the northern section of the sky, as we have explained.

The Hebrew word for south is *darom*. This is also related to our discussion. "*Darom*" is a contraction of "*dar rom*," meaning, "the high one dwells (here)"; i.e., the sun and moon "live" in the southern section of the sky.[6]

In the *Beis HaMikdash*, the Menorah stood on the southern side of the Temple Sanctuary. On Chanukah, when the menorah is lit in shul, it too is placed on the southern side of the shul. Why is this so?

The menorah is a source of light. It therefore belongs on the southern side, where Hashem placed the light sources, which he created to serve man. When davening *Shemoneh Esrei*, we face the east, toward Eretz Yisrael. The Gemara advises that one who is praying for wisdom should angle himself towards the south. This, too, is because this is the direction that represents light (*Bnei Yissoschar, Chodesh Kislev/Teves* 2 and 27).[7]

---

6. *Ramban* (*Shemos* 26:18) and *Rabbeinu Bachya* (*Devarim* 3:27). All references here are to the sky as seen in the Northern Hemisphere, where Eretz Yisrael is located. In the Southern Hemisphere, the sun and moon travel in the northern sky.

7. There is another application of this discussion. As any architect will tell you, when designing a home, windows are positioned for southern exposure so that they receive the direct daytime light of the sun. Windows that face north will not get direct sunlight.

◆§ Where in the Southern Sky Is the Moon?

We now know to search the southern sky for the moon. But where in the southern sky should we be looking to find the moon?

This depends on the day of the Hebrew month. At the beginning of the month, the moon is setting right behind the sun, in the west. As the month progresses, the moon falls behind the sun. After seven days, the moon is in the center of the sky at sunset. At fourteen days (the last day for *Kiddush Levanah*), the moon is rising in the east at the time that the sun is setting.

Typically, *Kiddush Levanah* takes place after Maariv, usually in the first hour or two after sunset. In the first days of the month, look for the moon in the southwest part of the sky. As the month progresses, you will find the moon more toward the center of the east-west path and more to the south. By the middle of the month, you will find the moon still in the southern sky, but more to the east, from where it rises.

With a minimal amount of practice, you can get accustomed to this simple and consistent monthly cycle.[8] Then you will be able to predict the approximate position of the moon, even as you are still indoors, just beginning to make your way out of the shul.

(Practice this one first, before beginning to show off your expertise!)

---

8. You will notice a variation in the spot that the moon rises and sets, as well as in the moon's path (which typically varies by as much as 10°).

The primary reason for the change in the point of moonrise is that the length of nighttime varies. In the winter, it gets dark earlier, making the moon visible at an earlier time. In the summer, the reverse is true. The nights are shorter and the moon first becomes visible at a later point in its orbit.

The Gemara (*Rosh HaShanah* 25a), based on a verse in *Tehillim*, observes, "The sun knows its path, the moon doesn't know its path"; i.e., its path is less predictable.

Or, in the words of Rabban Gamliel (ibid.), "I have received a tradition from my ancestors; sometimes [the moon] travels a long route, sometimes it travels a short route."

◆§ Predicting the Second Adar

Another simple piece of knowledge involves the timing of the 13-month leap years in the Jewish calendar. Most people are aware that the calendar has a 19-year cycle, with seven leap years in every 19. Memorizing which years are the leap years seems to be beyond the intellect of most human beings.

Actually, it couldn't be simpler.

You need to remember only the number eight. This is because the calendar provides for a leap year in years 3, 6, 8, 11, 14, 17, and 19 of each cycle. Or, to put it simply, every third year is a leap year, with the exception of year number eight (remember eight!), where a leap year occurs after only two years. After that, the cycle again reverts to every three years (11, 14, and 17). Year 19 is again a leap year, after two years, but this is easy to remember, because it is the final year of the cycle.

Let us practice applying this information by using it to predict a bar mitzvah date. If a child is born in the second Adar of year number three, his parents may be wondering if his bar mitzvah year will be during a leap year. Of course they have no clue, since their home calendar does not run thirteen years.

You, however, can confidently answer their question almost instantly. The child was born in the third year of the cycle. Add thirteen years and you realize that his bar mitzvah will take place in year 16, not a leap year.

You turn to the child's parents after a moment of thought and inform them, with confidence, that the bar mitzvah will *not* take place in a leap year. Your friends think that you must be a genius, having calculated the following thirteen years without even using a calculator! Don't tell them how truly easy it is!

Of course, had the son been born in year 6, the answer would be different. In this case, the bar mitzvah, in year 19, would take place in a leap year.

There is one catch. How are you supposed to know which year of the cycle it is at the present time?

The answer, again, is quite simple. Divide the present year (for example, the year 5769) by 19. The remainder indicates the year of the present cycle. (In our example, the year 5769, divided by 19, leaves a remainder of 12. This means that it is year 12 of the cycle, not a leap year. Boys born this year will have their bar mitzvah thirteen years later, in the sixth year of the next cycle, which *is* a leap year.)

Once again, we see that a minimal amount of knowledge goes a long way, due to the general ignorance regarding these simple issues.

Here's a way to remember this (or any other short piece of information): The next time that you are standing with people, perhaps at a wedding or dinner, share this information with them. Tell them about the 19-year cycle and the fact that bar mitzvah years can easily be predicted. It does not really matter if the person with whom you are sharing this information is interested or not. As a matter of fact, it doesn't matter if he is awake or sleeping. Your primary purpose, in sharing this with others, is to review it yourself. Do this as often as possible. It is a wonderful trick, and you will usually find that people really are interested in picking up these fascinating pieces of information.

⇨§ Figuring the *Molad*

The moon travels around the Earth in a monthly cycle. The month, in the Hebrew calendar, begins with the birth of the new moon. We call this the *molad*, the birth.

Every month, on the Shabbos before Rosh Chodesh, we announce the *molad* in shul. How to we calculate the *molad*? We don't. We take out a calendar and read the *molad* from there.

It once happened that I was away for the summer. It was the Shabbos before Rosh Chodesh. As we prepared for Mussaf, we realized that we had no current calendar. We only had the shul calendar from the previous summer. This contained last summer's *molad* times, but not the times for the present summer. What to do?

Here again, you can save the day by calculating the present *molad* from the year before. This takes a few minutes, but here, once again, you can seem like an expert. It only takes a small amount of information and a few minutes of practice.

How long is the lunar month? We all know that the Hebrew months alternate between 29-day months and months containing 30 days. Thus, it is fairly obvious that the lunar month contains 29½ days.

The Gemara (*Rosh HaShanah* 25a) gives the precise length of a lunar month, which is the time from *molad* to *molad*, as 29½ days,

44 minutes and one *cheilek*.⁹

To calculate the *molad* of a given month, we simply add this number to the previous month's *molad*. This is not as complicated as it may seem.

The week of the *molad* is known without calculation, because we know that it is on the week of Rosh Chodesh. Thus, the 29½ days can be figured by deducting 28 days (because these are exactly four weeks and would have no effect on figuring the day of the *molad*), and leaving 1½ days and 44 minutes and one *cheilek* for calculation. This becomes quite easy.

Let us take an example: Last month's *molad* was on Tuesday morning, at 7:30 and five *chalakim*. The next month's *molad* is on Wednesday evening (i.e., 1½ days later), at 8:14 and six *chalakim* (i.e., adding 44 minutes and one *cheilek*). Simple enough!

Now, let's try calculating for a year later. Admittedly, this is more difficult, but not much more difficult. After all, we can multiply 1½ days by 12, giving us 18. Since 14 days are exactly two weeks, we need only use the four-day remainder for our calculation.

Let us go back to our example. The *molad* of Tammuz was on Tuesday morning, at 7:30 and five *chalakim*. We are now a year later, and we wish to calculate this year's Tammuz *molad*. We begin by adding four days, thereby pushing the *molad* to Shabbos morning, at 7:30:5 *chalakim*.

We must still add twelve months' worth of minutes and *chalakim*, i.e., twelve times 44 minutes and one *chailek*. The *chailek* part is easy, since twelve months have twelve *chalakim*; this pushes the following year's *molad* forward by twelve *chalakim*, to 7:30:17 *chalakim*.

The most difficult calculation remains. Add 12 times 44 minutes. We can do this in two ways. The accountant's method requires a calculator and is not an option on Shabbos. The yeshivah *bachur's* method would be to round the 44 minutes to 45, making it three-quarters of an hour. Over twelve months, this comes to three-quar-

---

9. *Chazal* did not use the second (one-sixtieth of a minute) as a measure of time. Instead, they used the *cheilek*, which is one-eighteenth of a minute, or three-and-a-third seconds. There are 1,080 *chalukim* in an hour.

Rambam (*Kiddush HaChodesh* 6:2) explains: "Why was the hour divided into this number [of *chalakim*]? Because this number can be divided in half and into quarters and eighths, and into thirds, sixths, and ninths, and into fifths and tenths." It is therefore a handy number for calculations.

(Were it not for this *Rambam*, one might assume that this division of time was used because the *cheilek* allows for a precise expression of the *molad*.)

ters of twelve hours, or nine hours. Add nine hours to our calculation and you come to Shabbos afternoon, at 4:30:17. Then deduct the twelve minutes (which were added to round off the 44 minutes to 45 minutes), and — presto — you have the exact *molad* at 4:18:17![10]

I admit that this is not such an easy calculation. However, it is well worth the satisfaction that comes when you've calculated the *molad*, announced it, and then had the pleasure of having someone come running into the shul, with a newspaper, declaring the *molad* at exactly the time you've calculated!

Here's a shortcut for this calculation. If your shul has a set of *Tur*, you need not bother going through the complicated math. Simply take a look at the *Tur* (O.C. 427), where he has already made the calculation for figuring a *molad*, based on the *molad* of the same month in the previous year. After completing the mathematical computations, he concludes, "add to the [previous year's] *molad*, 4-8-876 [i.e., four days, eight hours and 876 *chalakim*]."

One word of caution is in order. In leap years, thirteen months will have passed from the Tammuz *molad* of one year to the Tammuz *molad* of the following year. In this case, don't forget to add a thirteenth month to your calculation, or you'll be off in your computation.

↜ A Challenging Question

Here's a great question, which will challenge even individuals with knowledge of Talmudic astronomy.

The *molad* is the moment that the new lunar month begins. Astronomically, this takes place when the moon passes the sun in the sky during its monthly orbit. At the moment of the *molad*, the sun and moon are in the same part of the sky. The sun is shining on the far side of the moon. The dark side of the moon is facing Earth.

A solar eclipse takes place when the moon passes in front of the sun, thus blocking the sun's rays.[11] This should occur at the moment

---

10. If the *chalakim* were to total eighteen or more, convert the eighteen *chalakim* to an additional minute. The shul announcement should never count more than seventeen *chalakim*.

11. The sun is actually 400 times larger than the moon. How can the small moon block the entire ball of the sun? The sun is 400 times more distant from the Earth than the

of the *molad*, since the *molad* is precisely this moment. An eclipse does not happen every month. This is because the moon does not pass directly in front of the sun each month. The moon usually passes above or below the sun. Still, whenever the eclipse does occur, it should be at the *molad*.

In fact, this is not so. Although a solar eclipse will always occur near the time that is announced as the *molad*, it is not precisely that time. It is usually off by many hours!¹² Why is this so?

Rambam (*Hil. Kiddush HaChodesh* 6:1 and 3) resolves the question. *Rambam* refers to our *molad* calculation as "the average cycle." The moon does not travel in a perfect circle around the Earth. Its path is elliptical; the lunar month is therefore not precisely the same every month. The Gemara's calculation of 29½ days, 44 minutes, and one *cheilik* is therefore only the *average* lunar cycle. The actual lunar month will vary. Thus, the *molad* announced in shul reflects this average cycle and does not represent the actual moment of the *molad*! Try telling that to the gabbai who announces the *molad* in shul!¹³

Why, then, do we use the average *molad*, rather than the actual *molad*?

Chazon Ish (in *Kunetres Yud Ches Shaos* #12) explains that our calendar is set based on the average *molad*. This is permitted by

---

moon. (The moon is almost 240,000 miles away; the sun is over 93 million miles away.) Thus, the ball of the moon appears to us exactly as large in the sky as the sun.

12. The *Navi Shiur* on this topic took place in December of 2000, after a week in which an eclipse had taken place on Monday morning. The *molad* had been announced as 3:29 a.m. Tuesday morning! Seven hours of the discrepancy can be attributed to the fact that we announce the *molad* based on Yerushalayim time. Thus, 3:29 a.m. is Yerushalayim time, which is 8:29 p.m. New York time. The difference between the announced *molad* and the eclipse was still more than twelve hours!

13. One wonders why such a basic piece of information is not well known.

Our studies center on the Mishnah and Gemara. During most of the era that these were written, the new month was declared based on the testimony of witnesses. During this period, the precise astronomic calculations were gathered in the *Sod Halbur*, a book of secrets regarding these calculations. This was kept secret by the Sanhedrin, so that they could catch witnesses who were presenting false testimony. [*Chazon Ish* 138:4 and Rav Chaim Kanievsky (*Shekel HaKodesh, beur Halachah* to beginning of *Perek* 10) ask why the solar calculations, which are part of *Sod Halbur*, were kept secret. They appear to have no bearing on the monthly testimony regarding the moon.]

Rambam writes (*Kiddush HaChodesh* 11:4), "*Sod Halbur* was known to the wise men, but not taught to everyone ...."

It is this deliberate vagueness that has remained with us to this day.

Torah law (*Halachah LeMoshe MiSinai*), which allows for Rosh Chodesh to be determined by use of the average lunar cycle. When the declaration of the new month was dependant on the testimony of witnesses, the actual *molad* calculation was reckoned. After the Sanhedrin was dissolved and the use of testimony came to an end, the *Chachamim* were concerned for the weakness of future generations in making proper calculations. They therefore elected to use this option, choosing to determine future Rosh Chodesh days based on the average *molad* cycle. Thus, we are correct in using this *molad* calculation in our shuls' announcements.[14]

The Steady State Theory

A final difficulty involves the verse mentioned in the Gemara with which we began. "'Guard this and accomplish it, for it is your wisdom and understanding in the eyes of the nations.' Which wisdom is in the eyes of the nations? This is the calculation of the cycles and the constellations" (*Shabbos* 75a).

What has happened? Where is the Jewish wisdom regarding astronomy? Today, we hardly stand out in this area of knowledge. But this Gemara is based on a verse that is eternal. This should mean that our knowledge of the heavens should continue today.

I would suggest a contemporary understanding of this verse.

What is the origin of the world? How did matter, energy, and life originate? For a believing Jew, this is hardly an issue. We know that Hashem, the great Creator, put everything in place.

Contemporary science generally dismisses our faith. How does it explain the origin of the universe? For centuries, from Aristotle to Einstein, science subscribed to the "Steady State" theory, or, in the words of Aristotle, "the world was always here" — *olam kadmone*.

It was only the Torah that taught that the world started at a specific moment, a "beginning." Science dismissed this. How could there be a beginning without a Great Beginner?

---

14. Even in Talmudic times, the Gemara reports use of this *molad* calculation, perhaps because it is very useful in making long-term calculations. Rav Chaim Kanievsky, in *Shekel HaKodesh* (6:5), explains that the average *molad* cycle was useful in calculating the monthly *molad* as well (see also *L'horos Nosson* 7:28-30).

Then a scientist named Hubble came along. He proved, by observation, that the galaxies are all speeding away from each other at tremendous speeds. We know that there is nothing in space that would cause the galaxies to change course. Hubble therefore concluded that the galaxies have been following their course for all time. Because the stars are speeding away from each other, Hubble was forced to conclude that they all started at a single spot; the spot from which their path originated. The beginning.

With this Hubble proved that there was, indeed, a beginning. Albert Einstein, who had originally disputed Hubble's theory, ultimately conceded.[15] Gradually, scientists changed their view of the origin of the universe. Today, all reputable scientists accept Hubble's conclusion. The "Steady State" theory has been replaced by the "Big Bang" theory. This accepts that there is a point of origin from which all matter began. This is not to say that science has accepted the Torah's version of the issue. A great deal of time and money is being spent to find an alternative version; to figure how there could have been a Big Bang without orchestration by the Big Banger!

For over two thousand years, man believed in idols and saw the heavenly bodies as gods. It was only the believing Jew who taught that the sun, moon, and stars were only servants of a great Creator. Then, suddenly, the desire for belief in *avodah zorah* vanished. Modern man abandoned his old beliefs. The planets were no longer gods, but part of an orderly world. Of all ancient accounts of God's Creation, only the Torah remained.

Mankind became divided. Many non-Jews embraced the Torah's vision of Creation, building new religions upon the Torah account. Others continued to deny the Torah's account. For them, a new explanation was needed. This brought about the Steady State theory, the belief in the eternity of the physical world, *olam kadmone*. Only those who believed in the Torah remained unflinchingly convinced of its belief in a beginning.

Today, in our century, the heavens have born witness to our belief. Masses of scientists, and their followers, have quietly abandoned a basic tenet of their science. Without shame or apology, they switched to belief in a beginning.

We believed in it, unflinchingly, all along. In this, we understand that the Gemara does apply to our day as well, "Guard this and

---

15. As recently as 1959, the *Scientific American Journal* reported that two-thirds of scientists believed in the Steady State theory. Fifty years earlier, the percentage was closer to 95 percent!

accomplish it, for it is your wisdom and understanding in the eyes of the nations. Which wisdom is in the eyes of the nations? This is the calculation of the cycles and the constellations."

By the Dawn's Early Light

◈§ The Sun and *Alos Hashachar*[1]

Rav Zutra bar Tuvia said, in the name of Rav, "One who is capable of calculating the cycles and constellations and refuses to do so, is not worthy of mention."

Rav Yehoshua bar Pazi said, in the name of Rav Yehoshua ben Levi, in the name of Bar Kapara, "In regards to one who is capable of calculating the cycles and constellations and refuses to do so, the verse states, '*And they do not examine God's creation, nor look at His handiwork.*'"

(*Shabbos* 75a)

For centuries, human beings lived with an eye on the motion of the heavenly bodies. The sun, moon, stars, and planets were used to tell time and to keep track of the calendar. The

---

1. Much has been written regarding the topic presented here. I do not pretend to offer a final *psak* on the issue. Rather, it is my hope to acquaint the listeners (and now, the readers) with the significant issues involved. The reader is referred to the numerous excellent *seforim* recently published on the topics related to *z'manim*.

Jewish People stood out as experts in the field of astronomy. Even as a superstitious world ascribed all types of theories to the complicated heavenly cycles, the Jewish People calculated, with incredible precision, the science of the heavens.

"For this is your wisdom and understanding in the eyes of the nations."

How things have changed! Today, we use watches to tell time and pre-printed calendars to keep track of the months. We look for the moon only once a month, for *Kiddush Levanah*!

Yet the fact remains that much of Jewish law is based on the movement of the heavenly bodies. Despite the fact that we get our information from calendars and time charts, we understand that this all must fit with the astronomical facts upon which these are based.

Let us see some of the more difficult aspects of astronomy as it impacts Halachah, thereby fulfilling the calling of the Torah, to "*examine God's creation and to look at His handiwork.*"

⋑ When Does Day Begin?

Conventional calendars post times for sunrise and sunset. However, these are not the moments that day begins and ends.

In the view of Halachah, the moment that day begins is at *alos hashachar*, dawn. Some of us remember elementary-school Rebbeim, teaching in Yiddish, who translated *alos hashachar* as the "appearance of '*der morgenshterin*,'" the morning star. This is totally inaccurate. There is no "dawn star" that announces morning.[2] *Beur Halachah* (89:1) was apparently aware of this error, as he begins his discussion by dismissing the idea of a morning star as incorrect.

Alos hashachar, dawn, is the time that the sun's light begins to appear on the eastern horizon. "If one prayed after dawn, when the eastern sky is lit, he has satisfied his obligation"[3] (*Shulchan Aruch*,

---

2. Venus, the "morning star," is mentioned in *Yerushalmi* (*Berachos* 1:1 and *Yoma* 3:2), where R' Yosi bei R' Boon teaches that it is *not* an indication of morning, because it rises at different times of the early morning.

3. There is a difference of opinion regarding the precise meaning of these words.

■ *Pri Chadash* and *Magen Avrahom* (89:2 and 3) understand that this refers to the moment that the first rays of light appear on the eastern horizon. S.A. HaRav follows this opinion.

O.C. 89:1). Virtually all daytime mitzvos may be performed after *alos hashachar*. (The earliest time for tallis and tefillin is later, after *mi'sheyakere*.)

◆§ How Do We Calculate *Alos*?

The Gemara (*Pesachim* 94a) teaches that there is a period of *daled meelin* from *alos hashachar*, dawn, to sunrise. There is also a corresponding *daled meelin* from sunset until *tzeis hakochavim*.

How does this translate into minutes? What is the amount of time between *alos hashachar* and sunrise?

This is an issue with which I have struggled for a long time. On the evening before a fast day, people are always asking for the *sof z'man achilah*, the latest time that one may eat in the morning. In our shul we typically announce the time, which is *alos hashachar*. The issue of calculating *alos* is therefore very real, *Halachah l'ma'aseh*.

Let us study the two methods of setting a time for *alos hashachar*.

■ **A constant time span:** Some calendars set dawn by using a set number of minutes before sunrise. This appears to be the opinion of *Beur Halachah* (89), who sets the time of dawn at 72 minutes before sunrise. Traditionally, this is the consensus for *daled meelin*, estimating one *mil* as 18 minutes. Other calendars use a constant 90-minute time span. This would follow the opinion that a *mil* is 22½ minutes.

■ **A varying time span:** There are many calendars that follow a different view. They argue that there cannot be a constant time for *alos hashachar*. The amount of time between dawn and sunrise varies, depending on the line of latitude on the globe. The further north one goes, the greater the time between dawn and sunrise. Thus, an

---

■ *Eliyahu Rabbah* and *Gra* require that the eastern sky be lit up. The second opinion would place dawn a few minutes later. The *Derech HaChaim*, *Magen Giborim*, and *Aruch HaShulchan* follow this opinion.

■ *Beur Halachah* (89) brings both opinions and rules that they both be followed (each opinion is followed, where it presents a stringency). *Beur Halachah* further estimates *alos hashachar* at 72 minutes, according to the *Magen Avraham*. The second opinion would place dawn a few minutes later.

The difference between these opinions is relatively minor and is not addressed in our discussion, above.

amount of time (*daled meelin*) that was mentioned for one location is not accurate for a different location.

Furthermore, even at one spot, the amount of time between dawn and sunrise varies, depending on the time of year. During the spring and summer, as the days become longer and there is a change in the angle of the tilt of the Earth toward the sun, the amount of time between dawn and sunrise increases. Astronomically, this is certainly correct.

According to this view, there is no constant time span between dawn and sunrise. These calendars set *alos hashachar* based on astronomical criteria. When using this method, the time between *alos hashachar* and sunrise tends to be greater than 72 minutes.

↭ A Strange World!

Forty years ago, most calendars followed the first opinion.[4] *Bnei Torah*, the world over, are familiar with the *z'man Krias Shema*, and the fact that there are two *z'manim*; an earlier *z'man*, based on the opinion of *Rabbeinu Tam* and a later *z'man*, based on the *Gra* and Geonim. Every calendar we saw, all the years, placed these *z'manim* as 36 minutes apart. The *z'man Krias Shema* signs, which have become a regular feature of shuls all over the world, have a 36-minute difference between the two *z'manim*. This is only true if one follows the 72-minute *z'man* for *alos hashachar*![5]

---

4. As my generation grew up here in the USA, we knew of no other method for calculating *alos hashachar*. See *HaZimanim B'Halachah*, in which numerous old calendars are reproduced, to show that there were many societies that followed the varying time span method throughout the generations.

5. Let us review the basis for the two *z'manim*. All agree that *Krias Shema* must be recited in the first three hours of the day, or in the first quarter of the day. They differ in the method used to measure this quarter of a day.

The *Gra*, following the opinion of the Geonim, measures *z'man Krias Shema* as one-quarter of the time between sunrise and sunset. When the day is exactly 12 hours long, the *z'man Krias Shema* would be exactly three hours after sunrise. According to this opinion, our discussion regarding *alos hashachar* has no bearing on *z'man Krias Shema*.

Rabbeinu Tam measures *z'man Krias Shema* as one-quarter of the time between *alos hashachar* and *tzeis hakochavim*. The disagreement regarding *alos hashachar* has a great impact on this opinion.

■ **If we go with the constant time span method**, we accept the Gemara's statement that *alos hashachar* is 72 minutes before sunrise and that *tzeis hakochavim* is

Clearly then, the 72-minute calculation has been the norm for as long as we can remember.

Today, the trend is shifting dramatically towards the second method of establishing *alos hashachar.* More and more calendars (as well as the digital information sites) use the sliding time span in determining *alos hashachar.*

Who is right? I believe it is fair to say that most rabbonim follow the first view, while most calendar printers follow the second view.[6] While most people would prefer to follow the opinion of their rabbonim (and the *Beur Halachah*), the calendar printers and website managers are in control of the flow of information! The average Jew is loyal to his calendar and assumes that it reflects the accepted opinion. Unfortunately, this is no longer true.

Let us examine the substance of the dispute.

---

72 minutes after sunset. This adds 144 minutes to the day. A day that has 12 hours from sunrise to sunset would now be considered a day of fourteen hours and twenty-four minutes (12 hours plus 144 minutes). To figure the *z'man Krias* Shema, we use one-quarter of the day, which would now be three hours and thirty-six minutes. If we calculate three hours and thirty-six minutes beginning with *alos hashachar,* we would establish the *z'man* as two hours and twenty-four minutes after sunrise. This is 36 minutes earlier than the *z'man* of the *Gra* and Gaonim.

■ **If we go with the varying time span method,** as *Minchas Kohen* maintains, *alos hashachar* is *not* always 72 minutes before sunrise. If so, the aforementioned calculation is totally incorrect. The total number of minutes in the day would be more than 144 and the starting point for the calculation would be earlier. This results in an earlier *z'man Krias Shema,* often well over 30 minutes earlier!

It is abundantly clear that the world in which generations of *Bnei Torah* were raised did not follow the opinion of the *Minchas Kohen,* even in regard to the *mitzvah d'Oraysa* of *Krias Shema.*

[It should be pointed out that even in the yeshivah world, which follows the *z'manim* of the *Gra,* we follow the *chumrah* of *Rabbeinu Tam's z'man* as regards *mitzvos d'Oraysa.* Thus, we wait for *tzeis hakochavim* before ending Shabbos and Yom Tov, and we recite *Krias Shema,* to accommodate the earlier *z'man.* (See *Ohr Gedalyahu,* fn to *Bamdibar,* p. 153, that Rav Aaron Kotler, even while still in Kletzk, instructed his students to recite *Krias Shema* before the *Rabbeinu Tam z'man.*)]

6. This is not meant to disparage the rabbanim who follow the second view. Theirs is certainly a legitimate *shitah,* and the calendar makers have chosen to follow their opinion. This is merely an observation that the calendars do not reflect the opinion of the majority of *poskim* in our communities.

ᵴ Astronomical Facts

*T*he issue at the center of this dispute is a significant one. On the one hand, it is hard to dispute the fact that all earlier sources, beginning with the Gemara, give set times for dawn, dusk, and twilight (*bein hashemashos*). For example, we find in *Shulchan Aruch* (O.C. 261:2), "The time of *bein hashemashos* is three-quarters of a *mil* before nightfall, which is the amount of time it would take to walk 1,500 *amos.*"

On the other hand, it is impossible to deny astronomical facts. *Alos hashachar*, by its very definition, is a time based on the light on the horizon. It is simply not true that the light on the horizon is the same every day, at 72 minutes before sunrise. Certainly, ancient man, who had no clock and no method of measuring time backwards (i.e., of figuring the number of minutes *before* sunrise), determined *alos hashachar* by the light on the horizon.

This argument is not a new one.

An early *Acharon*, the *sefer Minchas Kohen* (2:3, also quoted in *Beur Halachah* 261:2, s.v. *sheh'hoo*) already protested the use of a constant time span. His protest was based on four arguments. First, that the 72-minute time span did not hold true, as observed in his community; second, that the time varies from winter to summer; third, that the Gemara (*Shabbos* 35b) indicates that expertise is required to figure nightfall and that this would not be true if the time span is constant.[7] Fourth, that the *Rambam*, in his Commentary to the Mishnah, *Berachos* 1:1, clearly requires a varying time span (*sha'os z'maniyos*).

Minchas Kohen therefore rules that a varying time span be used. It should be pointed out that *Minchas Kohen* himself does not rely on this opinion to establish leniencies in Halachah; he rules that the stringency of both views be followed (*Beur Halachah*).

The most compelling argument is that astronomical facts do not bear out the possibility of a constant *z'man*.

There is a second factor to be considered in support of this approach.

Regarding nightfall, we also find a time span that is set by the Gemara in terms of *daled meelin*. This is the source of the opinion of

---

7. This can be answered if we realize that the Gemara was referring to a time when clocks did not exist. Measuring time was then more difficult. As a matter of fact, in those days, it may have been easier to determine nightfall by looking at the stars, rather than by trying to figure a constant seventy-two minutes!

Rabbeinu Tam, that night begins 72 minutes after sunset.

Here, in regard to nightfall, we find numerous *poskim* who have pointed out that darkness, both in Eretz Yisrael and in most cities in the Exile, is well before 72 minutes. Although there are many who continue to follow the 72-minute time,[8] "because it came from the mouth of *Rabbeinu Tam*," this is viewed as a *chumrah* (*Igros Moshe* O.C. 4:6).

As a matter of Halachah, earlier *z'manim* have been accepted based on the observed darkness. In the New York area, opinions range from 45 to 60 minutes; most yeshivah circles follow Rav Moshe Feinstein's *z'man* (*Igros Moshe* O.C. 4:62) of 50 minutes.

If we can accept that the *daled meelin* mentioned for nightfall is not a constant time, we should be consistent and accept that the morning time, too, varies from place to place.

After a careful study of these issues, I came to the initial conclusion that the arguments of the *Minchas Kohen* could not be ignored, particularly because the *Gra* (O.C. 261, Y.D. 262) follows this opinion. This creates a stringency regarding the *sof z'man achilah*, the latest time that one may eat before the morning of a fast day. Still, I reasoned, better to fast a little longer than to risk violating the fast by eating after the morning light had already appeared in the eastern sky.

◆§ On Second Thought

After further reflection, though, I realized that this could not be.

The source of the time of *alos hashachar* is the aforementioned Gemara, *Pesachim* 94a. There, we learn that there is a period of *daled meelin* from *alos hashachar*, dawn, to sunrise. The Gemara also mentions a corresponding *daled meelin* from sunset until *tzeis hakochavim*. Thus, the Gemara accepted that the time

---

8. On the fourth of Nissan 5724 (1964), there was a meeting of the Chassidic leaders of American Jewry. The Chassidic communities in the United States were then just coming into their own, and it was necessary to establish a uniform time for *Motza'ei Shabbos*. Fifty Chassidic *gedolim* (including Rav Yonasan Shteif and the Admorim of Satmar, Bobov, Chust, Bluzev, and Pupa) agreed to use the 72-minute span as a set time for nightfall. It is possible that they recognized the fact that the time for darkness fluctuates, but accepted 72 minutes as a standard because it is always after nightfall in these communities (*Igros Moshe* 4:62).

span between *alos hashachar* and sunrise was precisely equal to the time span between sunset and *tzeis hakochavim*!

The new calendars have things in the reverse order! Their *z'manim*, measured by the varying time span, place *alos hashachar* at more than 72 minutes before sunrise; while estimating *tzeis hakochavim* at less than 72 minutes after sunset. This is certainly incorrect.[9] [10]

I realized that this issue requires further examination.[11]

---

9. **Added difficulties:** Upon further examination, the question becomes stronger for the following reason.

Tzeis hakochavim, according to the Gemara, occurs when three average-size stars are visible in the night sky (*Shabbos* 35b). It is sometimes difficult to be certain what constitutes "average-size stars." We therefore follow Rabbeinu Yonah and wait for three small stars to be visible (O.C. 235 and 293), except as regards the end of a fast day, when we follow the Gemara (*Rama* 562).

It therefore turns out that the times posted for *Motza'ei Shabbos* include the added minutes of Rabbeinu Yonah's *chumrah*. The morning time span, which is unrelated to the size of visible stars, has no such *chumrah*. The span between sunset and *tzeis hakochavim* should therefore be longer than the span from *alos hashachar* to sunrise! Here, too, the calendars have it the reverse!

10. The Gemara establishes *bein hashemoshos*, a twilight period between day and night. *Chasam Sofer* (notes to O.C. 89) offers the innovative suggestion that the morning schedule, too, should include a *bein hashemoshos* period of three-quarters of a *mil,* after *alos hashachar*, which is twilight — neither night nor day. This opinion could help resolve the difficulty mentioned here (this may well have been the reason for the *Chasam Sofer's* opinion); however, this opinion was not accepted by any of the other *poskim*.

11. **Another difficulty:** Others have argued that the *Minchas Kohen's* approach would change the time of *chatzos*, midday. The popular understanding of *chatzos* places it halfway between the beginning of day (*alos hashachar*) and the end of the day (*tzeis hakochavim*). According to *Minchas Kohen*, these two *z'manim* are not equidistant from sunset and sunrise. If so, the midday times on the calendars that follow this opinion are incorrect!

In fact, this argument is incorrect. *Chatzos* is not based on the clock. It is the time that the sun, in its daily orbit, reaches its southernmost point in the sky and prepares to enter the western half of the sky. This is clear from the Gemara's numerous references to midday as the time before the shadows begin to fall toward the east. This does coincide with the time halfway between sunrise and sunset, but is not affected by the *alos hashachar* designation.

(See the letter of Rav Sroya Duvlinsky, *Shlita*, printed in the second edition of *Yisrael V'Haz'manim*, p. 1000, where this point is made: "*Chatzos* is a physical fact, not a calculation.")

❧ England, 1968

*I*n 1968, the British government decided to extend Daylight Savings Time into the winter months. This meant that the time of sunrise would be an hour later than it had been according to Standard Time. This created a serious hardship for observant Jews, who did not have sufficient time to daven Shacharis before leaving to their jobs. The January 1st sunrise, which had taken place at 8:05 a.m., now took place at 9:05 a.m.!

At the time, the English communities used the 72-minute time for *alos hashachar.* Rav Meir Posen, *Shlita,* a respected English *gadol,* published a pamphlet entitled *Kunteres HaNeshef* (*Rules of Dawn*), in which he argued in support of the opinion of *Minchas Kohen,* and pointed out that this was the opinion of the *Gra* and S.A. Harav (in his *Siddur*), as well.[12] He sought to show that this was the logical opinion and that it could be followed.

This would establish *alos hashachar* earlier in the morning, giving people more time to daven Shacharis. He further argued that, at the very least, this is an opinion that could be relied upon *b'shaas hadichak,* a time of great need. Members of the London *Bdatz* concurred, and an announcement was issued, informing people of this ruling.

At the time, Rav Chanoch Dov Padawa, *zt"l,* was the respected *posek* of the English community. He disagreed with Rav Posen's pamphlet, and published a series of letters explaining his opposition.

Rav Padawa argued that the opinion of the *Minchas Kohen* could not be followed; that generations of Jews had already established a consensus by designating *alos hashachar* using the constant time method; and that the new method of establishing the time according to *Minchas Kohen* had no halachic basis. The London *Bdatz* retracted its announcement.

Rav Padawa's arguments have been republished in *Cheishev HaAiphod,* his collected Responsa, 142-144. He presents two primary arguments, one based on the *poskim,* the second based on the *minhag,* custom.

---

12. This is also the opinion of *Kitzei HaMateh,* in the commentary to *Mateh Efraim* 602:8.
Minchas Elazor 1:23 and 69 also follows this opinion, although he is bothered by the fact that the Gemara refers only to constant hours. He resolves this by suggesting that this may be the case in Eretz Yisrael and Bavel (to which the Gemara refers), but that in Europe the times vary between winter and summer. In fact, we know that the time varies in Eretz Yisrael and Bavel, as well, as the *Gra* (O.C. 261) writes clearly.

First, that the "simple reading of the language of the *poskim*, from whose words we live, is that the hours are constant hours," and that four *poskim* who saw the words of the *Minchas Kohen* rejected his argument. He cites *Pri Magadim* (O.C. 261:9), *Derech HaChaim*, laws of *hadlakas neiros*: 3, *Machatzis HaShekel* 235:3, and *Birkei Yosef* (O.C. 261). The *Chida* (author of *Birkei Yosef*), in particular, was known for his worldly knowledge, as well as his halachic expertise.[13]

He further points out that *Minchas Kohen*, himself, expresses reservations regarding his opinion.

Secondly, he points out that the custom was always to use constant hours. He recalls that "every child, boy or girl, in Europe" knew the *z'manim*, based on a set time, in regard to the end of the day. The same should hold true for the morning.

The difficulties with this opinion lie in the astronomical truth of a shifting time for dawn. Rav Padawa argues that while these facts are true, they are simply not enough of a reason to change a Halachah that has been established for generations. Earlier generations, too, noted this shift, but retained the practice of using a constant *z'man* to determine *alos*.

In addition, Rav Padawa points out that the astronomical facts do not support the *Minchas Kohen's* use of *shaos z'maniyos* to establish *alos hashachar*. The morning light does not vary at all based on *shaos z'maniyos*![14]

There is a final point, perhaps most significant of all. The *Sefer Z'manim K'Hilchosom* quotes a letter of the *Chofetz Chaim* that was originally printed in *Sefer Avnei Shoham*. He writes, in part, "It is an established custom among the Jewish People that even in the summer months such as Tammuz, we only wait *daled meelin* on *Motza'ei Shabbos*, and the *z'man* is not based on *shaos z'maniyos*."

Thus, the *Chofetz Chaim* endorsed the approach of Rav Padawa, even in regard to nightfall.

---

13. This is also the opinion of Rav Yaakov Emden, in *Siddur Yaavetz* (Laws of Erev Shabbos #28). Rav Yaakov Emden, too, was a *gadol* who was known for his understanding of the sciences as they relate to Torah.

14. The morning light does vary in relation to the length of the day. However, it cannot be accurately measured in terms of *shaos z'maniyos*.

⇜ An Additional Problem

We have pointed out two difficulties with the varying time span method. First, the *z'manim* on these calendars are inconsistent with the Gemara in *Pesachim*, which teaches that the span from *alos hashachar* to sunrise is equal to the time from sunset to *tzeis hakochavim*. Second, this was not the normal practice of the *poskim* throughout the generations.

There is an added difficulty. Even if we were to accept the arguments of the *Minchas Kohen* and accept the idea of a varying time span, we would not know how to establish that time. On what basis do we set *alos*? How can we know, with any certainty, what the precise moment of *alos hashachar* would be, according to this opinion? Is the Gemara's *daled meelin* a maximum time? Is it the average time? Is it a minimum amount of time?

Calendars that follow *Minchas Kohen* use an angle below the horizon as the set point of *alos*, reasoning that the light on the horizon would be the same every day when the sun reaches this point. The difficulty lies in knowing which angle to use. Different calendars use angles varying from 16.1° to 19° below the horizon.

The 16.1° angle is widely used. This is based on the angle of the sun at 72 minutes before sunrise, in Yerushalayim, on the equinox. This assumes that the Gemara, which is referring to Yerushalayim, means to set *daled meelin* as the time for *alos hashachar*, on the equinox day. This is a logical assumption, since the equinox represents the average day of the year.

This, however, appears to be inconsistent with the statements of *Rishonim*. *Tosafos* (*Pesachim* 11b, s.v. *echod*[15]) and *Chidushei HaRan* (ibid.) appear to understand that the time between *alos hashachar* and sunrise is a constant time. They bring the Gemara in *Pesachim* 94b as proof that the time between *alos hashachar* and sunrise is never less than an hour. The only possibility for *Minchas Kohen* to explain *Tosafos* and *Ran*, in line with his opinion, would be to explain that the Gemara in *Pesachim* is referring to a minimum time between *alos hashachar* and sunrise. The assumption that the Gemara is presenting the *average* day seems inconsistent with these *Rishonim*.

---

15. *Tosafos*' reference to "*hei meelin*" is a printer's error, and should read "*daled meelin*." *Tosafos* follows the opinion that each *mil* is 22½ minutes (*Gra* in *Shnos Eliyahu* to *Berachos*, 2a).

∽§ A London Problem

There appears to be one additional problem with the varying time method for *alos hashachar*. This method accepts that it is day once the sun is within 16.1° of the horizon. However, in London (and points north), the sun does not descend lower than 16.1° below the horizon for the entire week of June 3rd through June 8th. According to the opinion of *Minchas Kohen*, it is day for the entire week in these cities.

Much has been written regarding the status of the Arctic Circle, where the sun does not set for many months. The halachic ramification of this has been debated for a long time. This type of discussion always takes on a surreal, almost science-fiction-like feel, in that none of us have ever really contemplated a Jewish community in the Arctic circle. The discussion typically includes the opinion that the weekday remains the same as long as the sun does not set, and the opposing opinion is that every twenty-four hours does begin a new day.

However, according to those who use a varying time method, this discussion is very much *l'ma'aseh*! In London, too, it is day all week![16]

It would appear that all those who discussed this issue, and the London community that has never been concerned with it, did not hold that it applies to these Jewish cities! It would seem that these *poskim* did not even view this as a possibility.

∽§ The *Rambam's* Opinion

The strongest proof offered by the *Minchas Kohen* is from the *Rambam's* Commentary to the Mishnah. Here, we have a *Rishon* with a clear opinion regarding this dispute! Indeed, our translation of the *Rambam*, as printed in our Shas, defines *alos hashachar* as, "when the rays of light shine forth in the southern sky, one and one-fifth hours, in *shaos z'maniyos*, before sunrise."

This contradicts our custom, which uses constant hours, and is a source for the opinion of the *Minchas Kohen*.

---

16. Our question is relevant to those who follow *Rabbeinu Tam* and require darkness to declare night. Those who follow the Geonim and the *Gra* would hold that sunset (followed by *bein hashemashos*) marks the end of the day. Presumably, they would hold that night and *alos hashachar* of the following day occur simultaneously.

However, in *Birkei Yosef* the *Chida* presents a different version of this Rambam. Here, the *Rambam* reads, "*shaos shavos*," constant hours. This was apparently the version of the Rambam that was used by *Tosafos Chadashim* on *Berachos*, quoting *Beis Dovid*. The new translation of the Rambam's Commentary, by Rav Kapach, also has this version.

Rambam's Commentary to the Mishnah was originally written in Arabic. Our version is a translation into Hebrew, which the Rambam did not write. This would explain the discrepancy in different editions of the *Rambam*, as different translators apparently had different understandings of the *Rambam's* intent in the original Arabic. Indeed, the meaning of the original Arabic words used by the *Rambam* is apparently ambiguous, and remains the subject of disagreement (see *Ohr HaMeir*, p. 156, and the *Moriah Journal*, *Teves* 5756).

~§ What To Do?

Having considered these arguments against a varying time span, I returned to my original position, the opinion of my Rebbe, the position of the *Beur Halachah,* to use constant hours. The time for the beginning of the fast day is announced in our shul as 72 minutes before sunrise. I've come to realize that this is also the opinion of most *poskim* in our community.

Then, someone donated an electronic, computer-driven digital clock to our shul. The clock, unfortunately, never learned the *Cheishev HaAiphod*. It does not follow the opinion of my *Rebbe* or of most *poskim* in Flatbush.

It was programmed by a calendar maker, not by a rav.

Worse, it even presents the time for earliest tallis and tefillin (*mi'sheyakeer*) as a varying time. This ignores the *Pri Megadim* (58:2), *Kaf HaChaim* (18:18, referring to *Minhag Yerushalayim*), and *Igros Moshe* (O.C. 4:6), all of whom give a constant *z'man* for earliest tallis and tefillin.[17]

I find myself imploring the *mispallelim* to ignore the electronic clock (despite the fact that it is driven by computer).

Of course, all this confuses my *mispallelim*. Fortunately, they are a bright enough crew to understand: Computers are not always right.

---

17. At 66, 60, and 35 minutes before sunrise, respectively.

✑ A Final Word

I have defended the practice of using the constant-hours method to establish *alos hashachar*. I know that I haven't answered all the questions on the topic. The difficulties still disturb me, but in the same way that Rav Akiva Eiger's questions on the Gemara perplex me. The *Halachah l'ma'aseh* seems clear.[18]

Still, to reassure those who are disturbed by the difficulties, I borrow a quotation from the *Rambam* (*Hilchos Kiddush HaChodesh* 11:5), written in regard to other astronomic calculations. I take these words of the *Rambam* and apply them to the teachings of the Gemara, which was *Rambam* by many *gedolim* to establish the set *daled meelin* for *alos hashachar*.

"If a wise man, Jew or gentile, will study the Greek calculations that I have used in regard to the moon's orbit, and he will see a miscalculation in my work; he will think that I missed something, and that my calculations are off.

"Do not allow this thought to enter your mind! If we have ignored anything, it is because we know, with mathematical precision, and with absolute proofs, that it does not matter ...."

---

18. This difference of opinion is a leniency only in regard to the *mitzvah d'Rabbanan* of fasting on a *Taanis Tzibbur*. It presents a stringency in regard to performing other *mitzvos hayom*, such as davening.

The only area in which our conclusion presents a leniency in regard to a *mitzvah d'Oraysa* is in regard to the *z'man* for saying *Krias Shema* in the morning. As we explained earlier (see footnote 20), the *Minchas Kohen* would have an earlier time for *Rabbeinu Tam's z'man Krias Shema*. As regards this *d'Oraysa*, it is indeed proper to satisfy all opinions and observe the earlier *z'man*, in line with the *Minchas Kohen*.

The Moon and the Molad

*H*ere is another topic that perplexes me. In this case, there are issues of *Halachah l'ma'aseh*, which will remain unresolved. It is my hope that others will reflect on these thoughts and provide me with sources for guidance on these issues.

Let us begin by understanding how the *molad* time is determined. A discussion of Halachah can only begin after this is properly understood.

◆§ What Is the *Molad*?

*T*he *molad* is the time that the new moon first appears. This can be explained either astronomically or in practical terms.

Astronomically, we begin by observing the sun as it sets in the western sky. Where is the moon at this time? This varies, depending on the date of the lunar month. At the beginning of a Hebrew month, the moon is setting right behind the sun. The following night, the moon can again be seen setting behind the sun, but this time, it is farther behind (approximately 12° behind).[1] Each subsequent evening, the moon falls farther behind the sun. Two weeks later, the moon has fallen so far behind the setting sun (by almost 180°, or half the heavenly sphere), that it begins rising in the east at sunset. This is why the moon is a "full moon;" the side that is facing Earth is also facing the sun. Two weeks later, the moon has fallen farther behind (another 180°). It is now in front of the sun, so that it rises and sets during the day, setting right before the sun. The moon, which is now in the sky only during the day, is not visible, due to the powerful light of the sun, which makes the moon's light unnoticeable.[2]

The *molad* occurs when the sun, which is now following the moon in the sky, overtakes it. This is the *molad*, conjunction, the moment that the moon and sun are aligned in the sky. The sun will now begin to set before the moon, meaning that the new lunar month has begun.

For an individual who is not familiar with this, I recommend a simple method of becoming familiar with the moon's monthly rotation. Each night, at the same time, in the same place (for example, after Maariv), look at the moon for a minute or two. Observe where in the sky it is, and its distance from the western horizon (where it will set). If you do this for a while, you will soon be able to predict the moon's spot in the heavens!

---

1. The heavenly sphere is divided into 360 degrees, which form a complete circle. To our eyes, we see the moon making one complete revolution in the heavens each month, until it returns to set right behind the sun. Since it travels 360° in 29½ days, this means that it travels approximately 12° per day.

[It is interesting to note that, astronomically, the moon orbits the Earth once every 27 days. This means that an observer watching from outer space would see the moon circle the Earth every 27 days (rather than the 29½-day lunar month, to which we are accustomed!).

However, the Earth itself is also moving in space, orbiting the sun once a year, or 360° a year. Each month the Earth therefore moves 1/12 of a revolution, or 30°. Therefore, although it seems to us that the sun is in the same spot in the sky every month, this is not actually so. (This can be demonstrated by noting that the sun has moved, in relation to the stars behind it, by 30° each month, making a complete 360° rotation, each year.) This impacts the appearance of the moon by 1/12 of a month, or 2½ days. The moon therefore *appears* to reach the same spot in the sky every 29½ days.]

2. People will remember occasionally seeing the moon on the horizon during the day. This occurs only in mid-month, when the sun is in the west (at sunset) and the moon is in the east, which is darkened because of the distance from the sun. Thus, a daytime moon is always a full moon. At the end of the month, the moon is a slim crescent and is not visible as it sets before the sun in the well-lit western sky.

For those less attuned to observing the moon's movement in the heavens, there is a simpler, more practical way of watching for the *molad*. At the beginning of the month, the moon is a slim crescent, with the lit side of the moon facing west. As the month progresses, the moon becomes fuller. After two weeks, there is a full moon. Subsequently, the moon becomes slimmer, with a crescent that faces east. The crescent becomes slimmer and slimmer until it disappears. The *molad* occurs when the moon reappears, with a slim crescent, which again faces the west.

◆§ When Is the *Molad*?

Sunrise occurs once at each point in the globe. Thus, when the sun rises in Yerushalayim at 5:30 a.m., sunrise has not yet occurred in New York. There, the sun will rise seven hours later. In California, the sun will rise three hours later than in New York.

This is *not* true in regard to the *molad*.[3] The *molad*, like an eclipse, is an astronomical event; it occurs at one precise moment each month. This is the moment that the moon passes between the Earth and sun in the heavens.[4]

This moment can be expressed in different ways. The moment of the *molad* may be expressed as 9:05 a.m. in Yerushalayim, 2:05 a.m. in New York, or 11:05 p.m. in California. Which time is announced in shul?

The time that we announce is the same the world over. Wherever we are, we announce the *molad* based on Yerushalayim time. Therefore, if we were to announce the *molad* as 9:05 a.m., it would mean that the *molad* is taking place at 2:05 a.m. New York time.

The Gemara (*Rosh HaShanah* 25a) gives the precise time for a lunar month, which is the time from *molad* to *molad*, as 29½ days and 793 *chalakim* (which is equal to 44 minutes and one *cheilek*).[5]

---

3. As explained in *Binyan Zion* 1:42, *Chazon Ish*, *Kunteres Yud Ches Shaos*, and by Rav Henkin in *Eidus L'Yisrael*. [The words of *Tiferes Yisrael*, in his Introduction to *Moed* (*Shivelei D'Rokeya* 1:3) regarding this, are puzzling.]

4. Thus, a solar eclipse should always take place at the *molad* (we have discussed this in "Astronomy for Beginners").

5. *Chazal* did not use the second ($1/60$ of a minute) as a measure of time. Instead, they used the *cheilek*, which is $1/18$ of a minute, or 3⅓ seconds. There are 1,080 *chalukim* in an hour.

Every month, we calculate the next month's *molad* by adding 29½ days and 793 *chalakim* to the *molad* of the previous month.

₰ The Calculation

I was traveling to a wedding and I knew that I'd be spending a significant amount of time at the airport. I asked another one of the *talmidei hayeshivah* (who was also flying to the wedding) to bring a calculator, a pen, and lots of paper to the airport. After checking in, we sat down to a challenging project: to calculate the next month's *molad*, based on the original *molad* of the first year of Creation. We would go back 5,768 years, calculating the *molad* for more than 71,000 months, until we reached the coming Rosh Chodesh. Would our calculations verify the *molad* time for the coming month (Cheshvon) that is printed on our calendars?

To begin, we had to know the precise time of the original *molad* in the first month of the first year of Creation. From there, we could calculate forward, by adding 29½ days and 793 *chalakim* per month. Understandably, I was unable to find a calendar for the first year of Creation. How were we to know where to begin?

Fortunately, the time of the first *molad* is known. Both the *Rambam* (*Kiddush HaChodesh* 6:8) and *Tosafos* to *Rosh HaShanah* 8a (*s.v. l'tikufas*) set the *molad* of Tishrei, in the first year of creation, at Monday, five hours and 204 *chalakim* into the day. This is known by the mnemonic *b'harad* (i.e., *beis* – Monday, *hei* – 5 hours, *reish daled* – 204 *chalakim*).[6]

We now set out to add the *molad* for each month of 5,768 years to come to our current month. This is not as complicated as it first

---

6. Any thinking person should immediately reject this! How can it be that the first *molad* was on a Monday? The Torah clearly teaches that the sun, moon, and other heavenly bodies were not created until Wednesday!

Creation began on the 25th day of Elul. Six days later, on the first of Tishrei (the sixth day of Creation), man was created. On that Friday, the first *molad* took place. However, this was the second year of creation, since the first five days occurred in the previous year. (This is known as *Cheshbon Tohu*, and is explained in "The Mystery of the Missing Years.")

In order to calculate accurately, we must imagine Tishrei of Year One (a month that never existed, since Year One began on the 25th of Elul). We calculate backwards twelve months from Friday, the first of Tishrei of Year Two (when the first actual *molad* took place), to Tishrei of Year One. This results in the *b'harad* time for the first *molad* (*Shekel HaKodesh* 6:21). We can now use this *molad* to calculate forward.

seems. We know that every 19-year cycle contains 7 leap years. This means that every 19 years are comprised of 235 months (19 years times 12 months, plus 7 leap-year months). We could calculate the 19-year cycle once, and then use it 303 times to come to year 5757. This would leave us with only the last 10 years and 1 month to add to the calculation. This follows the directions of the *Rambam* (*Hilchos Kiddush HaChodesh* 7:14). To make it easier, the *Rambam* has already calculated the 19-year cycle for us.

We began our calculations, always reckoning twice to avoid mathematical mistakes. After considerable effort, we came to our conclusion. The next *molad* would fall on the following Thursday, 23 hours, 10 minutes, and 1 *cheilek* into the day. Translating the 23 hours into our time, we were hoping to find the posted *molad* at 11:10 p.m. and one *cheilek*.

Next, we looked at the calendar. At first we were disappointed. We had the correct day and the correct number of minutes and *chalakim*. However, the time was 5:10 p.m.! Why were we 6 hours off?

Of course, upon reflection we realized that we were right. Twenty-three hours, as mentioned in Chazal, refers to a 23-hour period from the beginning of the day, i.e., sunset the previous night. This is the equivalent of 6 p.m., making the 23-hour time 5 p.m. The method works!

If ever you are stuck somewhere without a calendar, this is the correct way of calculating the *molad*. (It would be easier to remember to bring a calendar.)

◆§ The Difficulties

*H*aving expended great effort into calculating the *molad*, I now had a greater appreciation of it. Reflecting on our efforts, I thought about what we had done. I soon realized that there appear to be some difficulties with our *molad* system. Even more troubling, these difficulties do present practical halachic issues.

The Top of the Hour

When does the hour begin? We understand that each hour begins when the clock hits the top of the hour. All over the world, clocks point to the top of the hour at precisely the same moment. What criterion was used to determine the moment for the top of the hour? Is this based on an astronomical calculation?

The designation of the top of the hour, as we know it, was agreed to by an international treaty in 1884, which created Standard Time.[7] Before this agreement, there was no uniform beginning for an hour. At each location the clocks would be set, usually by starting the hour at noon[8] on the equinox (the day when both night and day are equal). In subsequent days, the time of sunrise would change, so that sunrise did not continue to take place at the beginning of an hour. Still, this method of setting the clock seemed most reasonable. This method did, however, cause some confusion. Sunrise does not take place at the same time everywhere. Different locations, therefore, had clocks with different moments for the top of the hour. Watches that were set in one city were not accurate in other cities.[9] This led to the international agreement for designating the beginning of the hour in a uniform manner across the globe (based on the top of the hour at the equinox in Greenwich, England). Today, wherever you may be, the clock strikes the top of the hour at the same moment.

This international agreement is a matter of convenience and has no astronomical basis. This agreement certainly did not exist in Year One of Creation (when Man himself was not yet created!).

---

7. It was many years before the different countries actually implemented this system. Calendars from years after 1884 may therefore still reflect the old system. Rav Tikutsinsky's calendar, from the early 20th century, is printed in his *sefer*, *Bein HaShemashos*. This contains separate columns for each time method.

8. This refers to the astronomical noon, when the sun reaches its southernmost position in the midday sky. This is why our clock system begins counting the first hour at midday (or midnight) rather than at dawn.

9. This is why it was standard for each city to have a clock in a prominent location in town, usually on a tall building. Visitors to the area had to be made aware of the correct time in that city, since the time was different than in the city which the visitor had left. Today, with Standard Time, the steeple clock has become no more than a decoration.

[The term "o'clock," for the top of the hour owes its origin to this period, when the top of the hour at each location was "of the clock."]

In Haifa, before the 1884 treaty was accepted, the top of the hour was 20 minutes earlier, based on the equinox time in Haifa. In Yerushalayim, it was 21 minutes earlier; in Tzefas, it had been 22 minutes earlier. Even after 1884, the Ottoman Empire in general and the residents of Eretz Yisrael in particular were not quick to accept the new Standard Time. As recently as 1925, time schedules in Eretz Yisrael were printed with two columns, one for Eretz Yisrael Time and one for Standard Time.[10]

This affects other areas of Halachah.[11] For example, many Chassidim follow the custom that does not allow them to begin the Shabbos meal between 6 and 7 o'clock on Friday night. This custom dates back to the time of *Maharil* and is mentioned in *Magen Avraham* 271:1. This custom originates before 1884 and is therefore based on the old clock. It is interesting that many Chassidim in Eretz Yisrael are aware of this and observe the custom between 5:40 and 6:40 on Friday evening.[12] Here in the United States, however, this adjustment is hardly known.

---

10. The time charts of that period were actually a bit more complicated. This is because there was one additional dispute regarding the clock. Our time system begins with the first hour after midnight. Sunset, the first hour of the halachic day, may therefore fall at 5 p.m. or 6 p.m. (or later). The old Arabic clocks began with the first hour of the new day at sundown. Midnight fell at approximately six o'clock and sunrise at approximately 12 o'clock. Many Jews preferred this system, which had been in place in Israel under the Ottoman Empire.

An article in the *Kol Yisrael* newspaper, dated 1925, is reproduced in *HaZ'manim B'Halachah* (p 91). The author encourages Jews, as a matter of religious principle, to use the Arabic clock, since it most closely reflects our tradition, by beginning the calendar day at nightfall. The newspapers and calendars of the time therefore had *three* columns; one for Arabic Time, one for Standard Time, and one for European/Eretz Yisrael Time. For example, the calendar for March first has sunrise at 6:25 Standard Time, 12:25 Arabic Time, and 6:04 European/Eretz Yisrael Time.

Confused by today's *luach*? Be thankful that you were not born one hundred years earlier!

11. See *Igros Moshe* O.C. 1:24 and 2:20, as regards *chatzos hayom*.

12. Recently, this was the subject of an announcement in the Hebrew-language newspaper of Belz Chassidim in Eretz Yisrael.

We Are Announcing the Wrong *Molad*!

Rambam and *Tosafos* set a time of *b'harad* for the first *molad*. This is the basis for our calculation of the *molad*. When they spoke of 204 *chalakim* after the fifth hour, they did not mean 204 *chalakim* after the 21st century's fifth hour. There was no Standard Time and the top of the hour, as we know it, did not exist. It is likely that they were referring to an hour that began with sunset at the equinox in Yerushalayim, where the *molad* is calculated. Or, perhaps, the reference is to an hour based on sunset the night before. One thing is certain. When announcements take place in our shul, announcing that the *molad* is at (for example) 5:23 a.m., this is not correct, for it implies use of our top of the hour, Standard Time. The announcement really should refer to the top of the hour as it was calculated in Yerushalayim at the time of *Ma'aseh Bereishis*.

Does this really matter? One could correctly argue that the purpose of our announcement is to recall that the new month is based on the sighting of the new moon. This reminder is accomplished, even if the announcement is imprecise. This presents no problem, so long as it does not affect Halachah.

The problem lies in the laws of *Kiddush Levanah*. Let us review some of these rules.

The Time for *Kiddush Levanah*

Once a month we commemorate the new moon by reciting *Kiddush Levanah*. When is this blessing to be recited?

There are two customs regarding the earliest time for *Kiddush Levanah*. Some wait until seven days of the new month have passed. Most *Acharonim*, however, rule that the earliest time for *Kiddush Levanah* is 72 hours after the *molad*. *Mishnah Berurah* (426:20) explains that when the moon presents only a slim crescent of light, the benefit is minimal. The blessing, which is related to man's benefit from moonlight, must be said at least 72 hours after the *molad*, when the light is greater. It is then that the amount of light is adequate for *Kiddush Levanah*.

The latest time for *Kiddush Levanah* is also related to the *molad*. According to the *Rema* (426:3), *Kiddush Levanah* may be recited until half the lunar month has passed (as stated earlier, the lunar month is 29½ days, 793 *chalakim*, which is equal to 44 minutes and 1 *cheilek*). This calculation begins from the *molad*. Half the time from *molad* to *molad* would be 14 days, 18 hours, 22 minutes and ½ *chelek* after the *molad*.

Beis Yosef explains the reason for this *z'man*. *Kiddush Levanah* is related to the benefit man has from moonlight. It is appropriate to make this blessing only at a time that the moonlight is increasing (the first half of the lunar month), and not once the amount of light has begun to decrease (the second half of the lunar month).

To sum up, *Kiddush Levanah* must be said between the time that the moonlight is significant (72 hours after the *molad*) and the time that the amount of moonlight begins to decrease. These *z'manim* are related to the correct *molad*.

We have demonstrated that the *molad* that we announce in shul is not precise. This becomes a problem when one is calculating the appropriate time for *Kiddush Levanah*. The calculations that appear on our calendars are based on the announced incorrect *molad*.

As a matter of practice, this difference is minimal. In Yerushalayim, the published *z'man* is off by 21 minutes. In the New York area, the difference is only a few minutes, depending on one's location.[13] It is rare that *Kiddush Levanah* is actually recited at the last minute. Still, if the calendars are printing *z'manim*, they should be accurate.

There are, however, other issues that result in a greater difference between the actual *molad* and the *molad* that is announced in shul.

◈§ A Second Issue

The *molad* that is announced in shul is based on *b'harad*, which is the original *molad* in Yerushalayim. When adding 72 hours to the *molad* to calculate the earliest time for *Kiddush Levanah* (or adding the calculation for the end of the *z'man*), we must bear in mind that the posted time is for Yerushalayim, and

---

13. New York City is 109° east of Yerushalayim. Each degree represents four minutes (there are 360 degrees, which cover the 24-hour rotation of the sun; this means that the sun travels 15 degrees per hour, or 4 minutes per degree), meaning that N.Y.C. is 436 minutes, or 7 hours and 16 minutes from Yerushalayim. Therefore, while the top of the hour in Yerushalayim is 21 minutes off, in N.Y.C., it is 16 minutes closer, or approximately 5 minutes off.

that an adjustment must be made for local time, deducting 7 hours for New York or 10 hours for California.

In addition, the announced *molad* does not make adjustments for Daylight Savings Time. The *molad* is figured every month by adding 29½ days, 44 minutes and 1 *cheilek* to the previous *molad*. This is done every month, regardless of changes in our local time. Thus, even in Yerushalayim, an adjustment must be made (during the winter months) when calculating the time for *Kiddush Levanah*.

A Third Issue

It is widely assumed that the *molad* time that we announce in shul is the actual time of the astronomical *molad*. In fact, this is not so.

Rambam (*Hil. Kiddush HaChodesh* 6:1 and 3) refers to our *molad* calculation as "the average cycle." The moon does not travel in a perfect circle around the Earth. Its path is an elliptical one; the lunar month is therefore not precisely the same every month. The Gemara's calculation of 29½ days, 44 minutes, and 1 *cheilik* is therefore only the average lunar cycle. The actual lunar month will vary, stretching to as long as 29 days and 20 hours. Thus, the *molad* announced in shul reflects this average cycle and does not represent the actual moment of the *molad*!

Once again, this information does not change the way we announce the *molad*. However, as in the earlier cases, the question remains: Should this change the way we calculate the times for *Kiddush Levanah*? After all, we have seen that the times for *Kiddush Levanah* are based on the amount of moonlight that is visible on Earth. This should depend on the actual facts, not on the average *molad*.

This issue is actually raised in *Beis Yosef*, quoting an earlier *Teshuvah*. "If there was a solar eclipse[14] such that the precise mid-month moment is visible, we certainly should not make this blessing afterwards. On a regular month, however, we can rely on the average

---

14. A lunar eclipse takes place at the moment of conjunction, which is the *molad*. This has been explained above ("Astronomy for Beginners").

A solar eclipse takes place when the Earth passes between the moon and sun. This is exactly half of the moon's monthly orbit, or half of the 29½ days, 44 minutes, and 1 *cheilek* from *molad* to *molad*.

calculation, which has been passed to us by our Teachers. This is true, even in a month where there had been a lunar eclipse, demonstrating that the *molad* time was not precise."[15]

Three issues regarding the *molad* have been raised. From these words of *Beis Yosef*, we see that the custom of following the announced *molad*, at least as far as this (third) issue is concerned, is correct. *Kiddush Levanah* is a *mitzvah d'Rabbanan* and it appears that this amount of leeway was included when the mitzvah was established. It is less clear if this leniency can be used in regard to the first two issues that were raised.

◆§ Yom Kippur *Katan*

There is one more area in which awareness of the correct *molad* affects practical Halachah. There is a custom, followed by pious Jews, to fast on Erev Rosh Chodesh, the day before the beginning of the new month. This is known as Yom Kippur Katan. *Magen Avraham* (417:3) cites *kabbalists* who have the custom to fast only until the time of the *molad*, even if this means that one is fasting for only a portion of the day. This custom is followed in some Chassidic circles. Their fast ends at the *molad*.

For those who follow this custom, awareness of the correct time for the *molad* is an issue of Halachah every single month!

◆§ A Final Thought

Rambam (*Kiddush HaChodesh* 11:4) writes, "Do not let these concepts be insignificant in your eyes just because they are not needed nowadays [since we no longer declare the month based on testimony of witnesses], for these are great and deep concepts."

Before our exile, the Jews in the Land of Israel would establish the calendar based on the sighting of the new moon. There was no preset calendar. Instead, each month, Jews

---

15. *Darchei Moshe* questions this.

would watch the heavens, searching for the appearance of that slender crescent that would herald in the new month.

The precise lunar calculations were kept secret by the Sanhedrin, so that people would search the heavens and anticipate the sighting of the new moon.

Each month, Jews all over Israel would look heavenward, searching the skies for a visible moon. Often, the Jerusalem area would be cloudy, and Jews from distant cities would be the first to observe the new moon. They would travel, even on Shabbos, to testify before the Sanhedrin. Every Jew knew that, on any given month, he might be the one on whom the nation would rely.

Our connection to the lunar cycle is not only a matter of setting the calendar. The Jewish People see the recurring lunar cycle as a symbol of our own renewal. We "are destined to renew, like her, and to glorify the Creator ...."

In studying the complicated lunar cycle, we see amazing similarities to our exile. We, too, search the heavens, eagerly awaiting our renewal. The timing of the Redemption, too, is shrouded in secrecy, so that people would continue to eagerly anticipate the renewal. The precise timing of the Redemption escapes us. We, too, are encouraged to understand that the Redemption is in our hands. Let every Jew know that with his personal *mesiras nefesh* for Torah, he might be the one on whom the nation will rely, to merit *Mashiach*.

We eagerly await the sighting of that new light, the *molad*, the rebirth of *Klal Yisrael*.

Rules of Dikduk

✥ Introduction

A righteous man was privileged to be visited by Eliyahu HaNavi.

The Chassid asked, "Why are your footsteps so distant? Come and announce the Redemption!"

Eliyahu replied, "The delay is because people do not know how to pray properly, mispronouncing the letters and the vowels…"

(*Yisod V'Shoresh HaAvodah* 5:3)

*T*he Mishnah in *Avos* (2:1), teaches, "Be as scrupulous in performing a 'minor' mitzvah as in a 'major' one." The *Rambam*, in his explanation of this Mishnah, cites the study of the Hebrew language as a mitzvah that is perceived to be a minor mitzvah, and is the subject of this Mishnah's admonition.

Regular Gemara *shiurim*, whether in yeshivah or in shul, rarely provide the opportunity or setting for a *shiur* regarding the study of *dikduk*.

More than a decade ago, in 1995, the Navi provided an opening for this type of *shiur*. The *shiur*, entitled "*Dikduk*, Rules for Hebrew Grammar," evoked an interesting set of responses. On the one hand, an unusually great number of people thanked me profusely and undertook to improve their *dikduk*.

On the other hand, there were many who expressed their lack of interest in this topic, owing mostly to their feeling of hopelessness in ever pronouncing words properly. I realized that these people were simply overwhelmed by the abundance of new information regarding an unfamiliar topic.

Since then, I have tried to share rules of *dikduk* a little at a time, often as the first fifteen minutes of a *Navi Shiur*. It seems to me that this "spoonful at a time" approach has helped even the latter group.

At first, it seemed somewhat ironic to me that I would be teaching rules of *dikduk*, given my own lack of knowledge regarding the subject. Later, I realized that this was precisely why I could connect with the average person. My presentations on this topic tend to be basic and straight to the point. I make no attempt to cover every exception to the rules or to answer every question. The result is a lesson with which most people can be comfortable, although the *dikduk* expert will certainly fault me for my omissions. To him I respond at the outset: These lessons are not aimed at the expert.

Below I present basic *dikduk* rules, culled from numerous *Navi Shiurim*. It is my understanding that these are *yedios* that everyone should know.

It is my hope that this small contribution will enhance the prayers and *Krias Shema* in *Klal Yisrael*. Perhaps this will provide some measure of *kaparah* (forgiveness) for my own shortcomings in this area.

⇜ Rules of *Dikduk*

Minchah had just concluded in the *Beis HaMidrash* of *Yeshivah Torah Vodaas* and I had davened for the *amud*. As I made my way back to my seat, my *Rebbe*, HaRav Avrohom Pam, *ztl*, called me aside.

Rav Pam held a *siddur* in his hands and showed me, "There are three-letter words in *Shemoneh Esrei* that have two vowels, each of them a *segol*. This includes the words *melech, keren, chesed,* and *tzedek*. Each of these words has two syllables (*me-lech, ke-ren, che-sed, tze-deck*) and should be pronounced *m'leil,* with the accent on the first syllable.

"When you daven, you pronounce them with the accent on the end of the word, *me-LECH, ke-REN, che-SED, tze-DEK*. This is incorrect, and it sounds strange to the listeners. Perhaps you should accustom yourself to the proper pronunciation."

At first I was taken aback, and, with a somewhat sheepish expression of thanks, I continued to my seat, rather dejected. Had my prayer sounded strange to many of the listeners?

Upon reflection, though, I made my way back to my *Rebbe*.

"*Rebbe,* you corrected one error, exposing my weakness in areas of *dikduk*. Is it possible that I made other mistakes, as well?"

With a gentle smile, Rav Pam replied, "Well, as a matter of fact, there were other mistakes ...."

With this, an interest in the practical rules of *dikduk* was kindled in me.

Although Rav Pam was himself a master linguist who had a wealth of knowledge in the rules of *dikduk* and a near perfect style in the numerous languages he spoke, he encouraged a more measured approach.

"*Dikduk* is like mustard. *Me'utan yaffeh, ree-boyun kasheh,* a measured amount is wonderful, while full study is a distraction," was Rav Pam's advice, quoting the *Chavos Yair* (*Teshuvah* 124).[1]

This took place close to thirty years ago. Since then, I have attempted to follow my *Rebbe's* advice. While I am confident that I did not violate the dictum of *ree-boyun kasheh* (too much is a distraction), I fear that I am still far from my *Rebbe's* measure of *me'utan yaffeh* (a measured amount is wonderful).

---

1. Rav Yaakov Emden was asked if the study of *dikduk* is permitted in a bathroom, where Torah study is prohibited. He responded (*Sheilos Yaavetz* 1:10) that this is permitted, as it does not constitute Torah study per se, but that the likelihood that one would think of Torah verses during these studies makes this inadvisable. He adds that his father, the *Chacham Tzvi,* read science books in the bathroom, and that he certainly would have given precedence to *dikduk* studies if this were feasible.

To quote the *Chavos Yair*: "A small amount of study of *dikduk* is necessary for every intelligent human being. Isn't a person ashamed to have studied, taught, and achieved the ability to decide matters of law, and still not know the simplest rules of *dikduk* regarding everyday prayer!?"

And so, let us study some basic *yedios* from the world of *dikduk*.

✺ Common Mispronunciations

Rav Pam, *zt"l*, would point out two serious errors that are often heard during *chazaras hashatz*.

- **The word *ba'al*** is found in the second blessing of *Shemoneh Esrei*. Pronounced properly, the sentence reads, "*mi chamocha ba'al gevuros*," which translates, "who is like You, Master of mighty deeds ...."

Often, the word *ba'al* is erroneously pronounced *bal* (as if there were no letter *ayin* in the word). This changes the meaning of the phrase. *Bal* is related to the word *al*, meaning *no*. This is used in many common expressions, such *bal tashchis* (do not destroy; do not waste) and *bal tosef* (do not add). *Bal gevuros* thus translates as "the one incapable of mighty deeds." This is the reverse of our true intention!

This phrase also appears in *Bircas HaMazon*, in the section that is added on Shabbos. This ends by describing Hashem as "*ba'al gevuros u'va'al hanechomos* — the Master of salvations and the Master of consolations." Here, again, the mispronunciation created when the word is read *bal* results in a terrible misstatement, describing God as incapable of these attributes.

The individual who reads from the Torah in shul is called the *ba'al korei*. I have visited shuls where people referred to the person designated to read the Torah as a *bal korei*, hardly a compliment. It was only later, when I heard the individual actually read from the Torah, that I realized that their characterization was quite accurate!

- **The word *oheiv*** is found in the conclusion of the eleventh blessing of *Shemoneh Esrei*. Pronounced properly, the blessing ends, "*melech* *oheiv tzedokah u'mishpat,*" which translates, "the King who loves righteousness and judgment."

Often, the word *oheiv* is mispronounced *oyeiv* (as if there was a *yud*). *Oyeiv tzedakah u'mishpat* translates, "the enemy of righteousness and judgment."

This reading is a disgraceful description of God, and people certainly should not answer *amen* to this blessing.

↞§ The *Chataf*

Often, a letter has a double vowel sign, comprising a *shva* and a second vowel. This can take any one of three forms: the *chataf patach* (a *shva* and a *patach*), the *chataf kamatz* (a *shva* and a *kamatz*), and the *chataf segol* (a *shva* and a *segol*).

■ **What is a *chataf* vowel?** A *chataf* vowel typically appears under one of the following four letters; *aleph, hei, ches,* and *ayin.*[2]

Whenever these letters are supposed to be vowelized by a *shva na*, the sound is enhanced by the addition of the second vowel sign. These letters might naturally have a softer sound. The added vowel sign is an indication that the letter should be expressed as a *shva na*, but a little stronger than might usually be the case.[3][4]

Whenever any one of these four letters appears with a *shva* alone, it is a *shva nach*, which has a negligible pronunciation.

■ **Does a *chataf* appear under other letters?** Occasionally, a *chataf* sign appears under other letters. Some Chumashim have this more often than others. This occurs when a *shva na* sound might be unclear. The *chataf* was added to remind the reader to pronounce

---

2. These are known as the *osyos geronos*, the letters whose sound is formed in the throat (as opposed to letters whose sounds are formed by the lips, teeth, tongue, or palate).

3. **Regarding the pronunciation of a *chataf patach*,** see Pri Megadim (Aishel Avraham 5:1). This is usually pronounced as a short *patach* sound (see Machatzis HaShekel 5:1).

4. The *chataf patach* also appears under a *hei* at the beginning of a word when the *hei* is meant to introduce a question (Rashi to Bereishis 4:9, 41:38; to Yirmiyahu 2:31, 49:1). If the second letter of the word is either an *aleph, hei, ches,* or *ayin*, this does not apply, and the *hei* has a regular *patach*.

the syllable clearly. Grammarians, over the centuries, have disagreed over how often this should be used. Some were quicker to add this *chataf* sign as *tiferes hakriyah*, to make the reading of the words flow more beautifully. Others rejected this approach. As we will see in our discussion of Ben Asher and Ben Naftali, virtually every parashah in the Torah has a least one example of this disagreement. The practical difference between the two approaches is minimal, since all agree that a *shva na* must be clearly expressed.[5]

๑๖ Moshe Takes Out and Caleiv Takes In

*T*he first vowel of God's name, under the *aleph*, is a *chataf patach*. This leads us to a fundamental question, as we shall now see.

■ **There are seven letters that are used as prefixes in Hebrew.** They are *mem, shin, hei, vuv, caf, lamed,* and *beis*. These letters spell the names of two of our great Biblical leaders, *Moshe v'Caleiv*.

When these prefixes appear before the Name of Hashem, how is the *aleph* sound to be pronounced? The addition of the prefix makes the difference in pronunciation very acute.

In fact, there is a difference between the prefix letters.

When any one of the first three ("Moshe") letters appears before the Name of Hashem, the *aleph* is expressed clearly and fully. When any of the other four letters ("v'Caleiv") appears as a prefix, the *aleph* sound is suppressed and barely pronounced.

Redak offers an expression by which this rule is easily remembered; "*Moshe motzee v'Caleiv machniss* — Moshe takes out [i.e., took the Jews out of Eygpt], and Caleiv takes in [to Israel]." In this context, this refers to the fact that the letters *Moshe* cause the *aleph*

---

5. In its early years, our *Beis HaMidrash* was blessed with an expert *ba'al korei* who wanted to pronounce these words in accordance with the opinion that uses the *chataf*, as this had been the approach of his *dikduk* teacher. I insisted that he follow the more commonly accepted approach, without the *chataf*.

In 1995, when our *Beis HaMidrash* moved to its new building, the Rosenthal family donated all new Chumashim. To my surprise (and our *ba'al korei's* delight), these Chumashim, the *Shul Chumash* (published by Vagshall), are punctuated with the controversial *chataf patach*!

sound to "come out," i.e., to be expressed; while the *u'Caliev* letters cause the *aleph* sound to be "taken in," i.e., to be suppressed.

The *Moshe motzee u'Caleiv machniss* rule applies as well, when these letters are a prefix to another of Hashem's Names that begins with an *aleph*, the Name *Elokim*. (The letter *hei* does not appear as a prefix for the four-letter Name of Hashem, but it does appear as a prefix for the Name *Elokim*.[6])

PRONOUNCING THE NAMES OF GOD

The following table gives the pronunciations of the Name when it appears with a prefix. In all these cases, the accent is on the last syllable (noy). The phrase "מֹשֶׁה מוֹצִיא וְכָלֵב מַכְנִיס" is used as a mnemonic. The prefixes ש, מ, and ה do not absorb or assimilate the vowel from the first letter of God's name, while the prefixes ו, ב, ל, and כ do absorb the vowel that follows.

בַּי-ה-ו-ה — Ba-doônoy
הַי-ה-ו-ה — Ha-adoônoy
וַי-ה-ו-ה — Va-doônoy
כַּי-ה-ו-ה — Ka-doônoy
לַי-ה-ו-ה — La-doônoy
מִי-ה-ו-ה — May-adoônoy
שֶׁי-ה-ו-ה — She-adoônoy

❧ An Unusual Word

*I*n the beginning of *Parashas Haazinu* (32:6), we find the Name of Hashem with two prefix letters, the *hei* and *lamed*, "*Ha'L'Hashem*." In our *Sifrei Torah* (and *Chumashim*), the

---

6. The *hei* prefix does not occur before any proper name. There is a logical reason for this. The prefix *hei* is typically a *hei ha'yideeah*, a *hei* that distinguishes the noun which follows. For example, the word *bayis* means *house*. If one were to refer to *habayis*, this would refer to "THE house," that is, the specific house under discussion, to the exclusion of others. When referring to a person by name, the *hei* is not necessary, because the reference is already to a unique individual. It is not necessary to exclude others. This is certainly true in regard to Hashem.

The name *Elokim* is different in that this word form is also used to refer to pagan gods. Thus, the *hei* is appropriate to distinguish the word as a reference to Hashem. [There is one exception. In *Yirmiyahu* 8:19, the *hei* appears before Hashem's name. There, however, this is not a regular *hei ha'yideeah*. The *hei* there denotes a question.]

letter *hei* is written as a separate word, although it is clearly meant to be understood as the prefix for the word that follows. How is this to be read?

The hei has a *patach* under it and is read normally. However, the *hei – lamed* combination is read as a single word, with the *lamed* read as a *shva nach*. This is followed by a pause (as between any two words) and then the Name of Hashem. Here, the *aleph* is read as if the word had no prefix (*Minchas Shai*, based on *Redak*).

This is an unusual configuration, which appears nowhere else in Tanach.

⋆§ "Yaihoo"

The *Ran* to *Kesuvos*, *daf* 7b (*daf* 2b in the *Rif*) refers to a rule of *dikduk* regarding "the *Yaihoo* letters." This section of *Kesuvos* is often learned in yeshivah, and the *Ran* is therefore a subject of discussion. Most (— almost all —) of the *talmidim* never heard of the *Yaihoo* rule and don't know where to begin searching for it. This is unfortunate, because the *Yaihoo* rule stares up at us from the siddur, every time we daven. As we shall see, this is actually one of the simplest rules of *dikduk*.

It is interesting that the Chassidic giant, the *Bnei Yisosschar*, in his opening to *Igra D'Kallah* (also in his *Mayon Ganim* 13:6), encourages the study of "the necessary rules of *dikduk*; *dageish*, the *Yaihoo* letters, and [*shva*] *nach* and *na* ...."

To understand the *Yaihoo* rule, it is first important to review the rules for the *dageish*. After studying these rules, we will return to examine the *Ran's* application of the *Yaihoo* rule.

There are six letters that sometimes receive a *dageish*, the dot in the letter that denotes a change in pronunciation.[7] These letters are known as *Beged Kefes*, the letters *beis, gimmel, daled, kof, fey*, and *sof*. Whenever these letters appear at the beginning of a word, they receive a *dageish* symbol. This is known as a *dageish kal*.[8] Thus, for

---

7. We pronounce the letters *beis, cof, pey,* and *sof* differently, depending on whether the *dageish* appears. The same should be true of the letters *gimmel* and *daled*, except that this distinction has become lost during our long exile.

8. **Dageish Chazak and Dageish Kal:** The *dageish* described above is called a *dageish kal*.

A *dageish* that appears on letters other than *Beged Kefes* is known as a *dageish*

example, the Torah begins with the words *bereishis bara*. Both words begin with the letter *beis*, both with a *dageish*.

There are occasions when this rule does not hold true. In the second verse of the Torah, the word *sohu* appears; although it begins with a *sof*, it does not take a *dageish*. In the first *berachah* of *Shemoneh Esrei*, the word *v'neihem* begins with a *beis*, but without the *dageish*. Why is this so?

The *Yaihoo* rule explains this. The word *Yaihoo* is a reading of the four letters to which this rule applies, *yud, hei, vuv*, and *aleph*: *Yaihoo*.

Beged Kefes at the beginning of a word receives a *dageish*, except if the previous word ended with one of the *Yaihoo* letters and is read together with the *Beged Kefes* word. In these cases, the *Beged Kefes* word is read together with the previous word, as a single expression. The *Beged Kefes* letters thus are not seen as being at the beginning of a word. They therefore lose their *dageish*.

When there is a pause in the reading of the sentence (as demonstrated by the *trop* on the words), the *dageish* remains.[9] In the words of *Minchas Shai* (to *Shoftim* 7:15), "The *Yaihoo* rules are ignored so that it reads properly."

In the examples cited earlier, the second verse of the Torah reads, "*V'haaretz hayisah sohu* ...." The word *sohu* is read with the previous word, which ends with the letter *hei*. The *dageish* therefore disappears.

The same is true for the first *berachah* of *Shemoneh Esrei*, in which we say, "*livnei vineihem*." The *beis* at the beginning of *v'neihem* follows a *yud* and therefore loses its *dageish*.[10]

Once you've learned the *Yaihoo* rule, you will notice it throughout Tanach.[11]

---

chazak, which also appears as a dot in a letter. This will be explained fully, below.

9. For example, in the *Baruch She'amar* prayer, we read, "*Baruch hu, baruch omer v'oseh*." The second "*baruch*" begins with a *beis* (with a *dageish*), despite the fact that it follows the letter *aleph*. This is because the words are not read together.

10. An exception: Where the *Beged Kefes* word begins with two identical letters, the first always retains its *dageish*. For example, "*Mah l'yedidi b'vaisi*," or "*Asher eeto b'Vavel*."

There is disagreement regarding the words "*kidishanu b'mitzvosov*," which appear in every blessing said before performing a mitzvah. The first letter in this second word is a *beis*. Nevertheless, because it follows a *vuv*, it should lose its *dageish*. Our custom follows Rav Zalman Henna (*Sharei Tefillah* 10) to retain the *dageish* (see there for an explanation; also in *Klalei Tamei HaMikrah*, p. 119).

11. See *Emes L'Yaakov* to *Parashas Bo* (10:24, 11:1). This would not be understandable to someone unfamiliar with *Yaihoo*.

◈ Back to the *Ran*

The *Ran* in *Kesuvos* discusses the *berachah* that we recite under the *chuppah* at a wedding ceremony. This *berachah*, recited before the actual *kiddushin*, ends with the words, "*Mikadeish amo Yisrael al yidei chuppah v'kedushin.*" This is typically translated, "(God) sanctifies his people Israel by way of *chuppah* and *kiddushin*."

Ran questions the language of this blessing. *Kiddushin* always precede *chuppah*. Why, then, do we recite "by way of *chuppah* and *kiddushin*"? The order should be reversed, "through *kiddushin* and *chuppah*."

Ran quotes the *Sefer Halttur*, who responds to this question by changing the letter *vuv* to a *beis,* as follows: "The correct version [of this blessing] is '*Mikadeish amo Yisrael al yidei chuppah b'keddushin.*'" This is translated, "(God) sanctifies his People Israel by way of *chuppah* through the *kiddushin* (that precede it)."

By changing the letter at the beginning of the word *v'kiddushin* to a *beis*, *b'kiddushin*, the meaning is changed and the question is resolved. We are indeed referring to a *chuppah* which follows *kiddushin*, and does not precede it.

Still, we always hear the word read *v'kiddushin* and not *b'kiddushin*, as the *Sefer Halttur* seems to recommend. Why is this so?

It is here that the *Yaihoo* rule comes to the rescue. "Those who read properly, read the *beis* softly [without a *dageish*] because it follows the letter *hei* [at the end of the previous word]. Because the letters *Yaihoo* soften the *Beged Kefes* letters, the scribes erred and [when hearing the *v* sound, wrote a *vuv* [rather than a *veis*]."

I explained this to the audience at a *Navi Shiur*. Immediately at the end of the *shiur*, I was attacked by a group of Sefardim armed with their *siddurim*. "But look, Rabbi, it *is* spelled with a *veis*!"

Indeed, the Sefardic *siddurim* have the word *v'kiddushin* spelled with a *veis* rather than a *vuv*!

◈ Mi Kamocha

The verse that begins with the words *mi chamocha* appears in the Torah at the Song at the Sea, and is repeated numerous times as part of our prayers.

INTRODUCTION TO THE RULES OF DIKDUK / 321

Each time, the verse begins with the words *mi chamocha*. The first letter of the second word does not have a *dageish*. This is in line with our *Yaihoo* rule, since the last letter of the preceding word is a *yud*.

However, when these same two words appear again in the second half of this verse, it is written as *mi kamocha*. Here the *dageish* is retained! Why would the *Yaihoo* rule apply to these words in one case and not in the other?

Rabbeinu Bachya and *Beis Yosef* (O.C. 51:9) are bothered by this question and suggest an unusual explanation. The Biblical figure Michah, whose story is recorded near the end of the Book of *Shoftim*, was the only Jew to take an idol with him during the Exodus from Egypt. Later, in the Land of Israel, he introduced idol worship to the area of Dan, in Northern Israel. We remember Michah as a disgrace to our People.

In the verse under discussion, Hashem's Name appears and is followed by the words *mi kamocha*. Had these words been vowelized in accordance with the *Yaihoo* rule, the words would read *mi chamocha*, and would begin with the syllables of the name *Michah*. In an effort to distance the name of this evildoer from the Name of Hashem, we retain the *dageish* and say *mi kamocha*.

However, there is an apparent difficulty with this answer. In the *Nishmas* prayer, we *do* express *mi chamocha* next to the Name of Hashem. There, we read, "*kol atzmosai tomarna Hashem, mi chamocha*"! Why don't we make the same change here, by changing the *chof* to a *kof*?

Beis Yosef asks this question, and answers that we are only concerned with mentioning Michah at the song related to *Krias Yam Suf*, because it was here that Michah showed the greatest audacity, carrying an idol through the sea even as Hashem showed the Jewish People such love by performing this wondrous miracle.

Minchas Shai (to this verse) quotes *Beis Yosef* and then offers an additional explanation. The first "*chamocha*" has a soft *chaf*, while the second "*kamocha*" has a hard *kof*. This demonstrates the fervor with which the *shirah* was said, beginning softly, but escalating to a more powerfully expressed praise of Hashem, "*mi kamocha*," who is like You!

◆§ Dageish Kal and Dageish Chazak

Once we have mastered the rules of *Beged Kefes* and the *Yaihoo* rule, we can turn our attention to a more complicated aspect of the *dageish*; the *dageish chazak*.

The *dageish* described above is called a *dageish kal*. This appears exclusively in the *Beged Kefes* letters.

A *dageish chazak* also appears as a dot in a letter, but is not limited to these six letters. The *dageish chazak* generally comes to denote a missing letter.

There are numerous circumstances in which a *dageish chazak* would replace a letter. This can occur when a letter is used as a prefix in place of a word.

One common example is the word *mibayis*, "from the house." To say, "from the house" in Hebrew, one could use two words, *min* (from) *habayis* (the house). It is easier to use the one-word form, *mibayis*, using a prefix in place of the extra word. In this case, the word *min* has become a one-letter prefix, maintaining the letter *mem* and omitting the letter *nun*. The missing *nun* is denoted by the *dageish* in the letter *beis*. This is a *dageish chazak*.

Similarly, we find the word *she'beirach*, "who blessed." To say, "who blessed" in Hebrew, one could use two words, *asher* (who) *beirach* (blessed). It is easier to use the one-word form, *she'beirach*, using a prefix in place of the extra word. The missing letters of the word *asher* are denoted by the *dageish* in the letter *beis*. This is a *dageish chazak*.

Another case is where a *shoresh* letter is dropped because of the conjugation of a verb. For example, the word *vayegash* (and he stepped forward) comes from the root *nagash*, spelled with the letter *nun* at the beginning. When the *nun* is dropped, this is noted by the addition of a *dageish chazak* to the letter *gimmel*.

A third situation involves root words that contain two identical letters. In the word "*sovav*," the letter *veis* appears twice.

There are word forms in which one of these letters fall away to make the word easier to pronounce. When this occurs, a *dageish chazak* is inserted to note the change. Thus, in the word "*sabosi*," the letter *beis* has a *dageish chazak*.

The *dageish chazak* denotes a stronger pronunciation of the letter. The letters *aleph, hei, ches, ayin,* and *reish* do not receive a *dage-*

ish chazak.[12] In the instance that one would normally be required to denote a missing letter, the vowel under the letter is changed, instead, to a *tenuah gedolah* (*Dikduk Sifoseinu,* Lesson 21).

✒ Closing Thoughts

A friend once questioned my interest in the practical rules of *dikduk*.

"In cases where the meaning of a word is changed by a mispronunciation, I can understand the importance of correcting the pronunciation. After all, in these cases, proper pronunciation is *m'akeiv*," he said.

"However, in most cases, the incorrect pronunciation does not change the meaning of the word. The mispronunciation isn't *m'akeiv*. Is it really important?" he asked.

I didn't answer.

Subsequently, I spoke to him, mispronouncing his name.

At first he smiled. Later, he mentioned that my behavior was annoying and asked me to stop.

I asked, "Is Hashem's name any less important than yours? You mispronounce the name of Hashem, Whom you are commanded to honor. I am only mispronouncing the name of a friend ...."

The Gemara teaches, "One who says that the entire Torah is from Heaven with the exception of one *dikduk* [lit., one small point], is included in [the verse[13]], 'For he despised the word of Hashem.'"

Beis Yosef (O.C. 142:1), quoting *Rabbeinu Manoach*, maintains that this is a reference to the rules of *dikduk*. As examples, he mentions the proper pronunciation of *shva na* and *shva nach,* as well as the proper use of the *dageish*.

We live in a generation that has a weakness in this area. Are we to accept that we are "included in [the verse], 'For he despised the word of Hashem'"? Heaven forbid!

---

12. There are exceptions to this rule.
13. *Bamidbar* 15:31.

Thus, the myth of the lack of importance of (at least) a minimal amount of knowledge of *dikduk* must be dispelled.

This is an area where a small amount of time and effort go a long way. Let's do it!

Rules for M'leil and M'lra

*D*ikduk errors are, unfortunately, commonplace. During the *Galus*, as Jews have adapted to the language of their host country, the nuances of the country's language have influenced our pronunciation of *Lashon Kodesh*. It is no wonder that Americans incorrectly pronounce most words *m'leil*. This is because most English words (and most Yiddish words) are pronounced with the accent on the first syllable. Try pronouncing *baseball* or *president* (or *shtreimel* or *cholent*) with the accent at the end of the word. The pronunciation sounds like that of a foreigner![1]

A man came to Rav Moshe Feinstein, *zt"l*, complaining vehemently about the mispronunciations that are common in yeshivah circles and about the lack of awareness of the most basic rules of

---

1. The *Beis Yosef* (end of 142), quoting *Orchos Chaim*, records a Sefardic custom to recite *v'hu rachum* after the reading of the Torah. He explains that this is intended as a prayer of forgiveness for our mispronunciations. (If the Sefardim need forgiveness, how much more so do we Ashkenazim, as our pronunciation is so much more corrupted!)

dikduk. The man carried on for a while. When his tirade finally came to an end, Rav Moshe responded softly, "You are right. And, by the way, allow me to correct you. The word should be pronounced *dik-DUK*, with the accent on the final syllable, and not *DIK-duk*, as you pronounce it. *M'lra*, not *m'leil*."

~§ "*Sheker* Is *Emes*; *Emes* Is *Sheker*"

Rav Pam had told me that three-letter words that are vowelized with two *segols* have their accent on their first syllable. It is interesting to note that people generally pronounce the word "*sheker*" (falsehood) correctly, with the accent on the beginning of the word. The word "*emes*" (truth) is also commonly pronounced *m'leil*, with the accent on the first letter. This is not correct. This is because the word *emes* is not vowelized by the double *segol*. The vowel under the letter *aleph* is a *chataf-segol*, a *segol* which is accompanied by a *shva* sign. This vowel *never* gets the accent. Thus, *emes* is correctly pronounced "*e-MES*," with the accent on the second syllable.

Rav Pam would take note of the strange situation, saying, "*Sheker* is *emes*; *emes* is *sheker*!" (i.e., the way people pronounce *sheker* is correct, while the way people pronounce *emes* is not).[2]

Three-letter words that are vowelized by two *kamatzim* are correctly pronounced *m'lra*, with the accent on the end of the word. This is also a word form that is commonly mispronounced. Thus, a groom is incorrectly called a *CHO-sson* (rather than the correct *cho-SSON*). Words such as *basar* (meat) and *chacham* (wise man) also have a double *kamatz* and are pronounced *m'lra*.

What is the rule of thumb? What decides when a word is *m'leil* and when it is *m'lra*?

---

2. A similar play on the word appears in *Aliyos HaGra* (note 75), "One who does not distinguish between *m'leil* and *m'lra*, hasn't said a word of *emes*, ever!" This is a reference to the "true" pronunciation of *emes*.

◆§ M'leil — M'lra[3]

To answer this question, Rav Pam loaned me a short *sefer* on *dikduk* rules. This is a softcover pamphlet titled *Dikduk Sifoseinu*, which was printed in Palestine in '36. I photocopied the *sefer*, and it is available to anyone who desires to make a copy for himself. I found the following rule regarding *m'leil* and *m'lra* particularly fascinating.[4] To share it with you it is necessary to first introduce two concepts.

■ **The first concept: The ten vowels (*tenuos*)** are divided into two groups, with five vowels designated as *tenuos gedolos*, major vowels, and the other five as *tenuos ketanos*, minor vowels. (The *shva* falls into its own category, as an unpronounced vowel.)

The method usually used to memorize the two sets of vowels is the pair of Hebrew words, *pituchei chosum* (these words appear numerous times in the Torah, including *Shemos* 28:11,21 and 36 and 39:6, 14, 30)[5]. The meaning (and context) of these words is academic to our discussion. It is the five vowels appearing in these two words that are to be memorized, because these five are the five *tenuos gedolos*, major vowels. Thus, they are: the *cheerik gadol* (*cheerik* followed by the letter *yud*), *shooruk* (which appears in the *vov* form), *tzeirei; cholum,* and *kamatz*.

The remaining vowels (including the *segol*) are *tenuos ketanos*. (The five minor vowels are *patach, segol, koobutz, cheerik katan* [i.e., without the *yud*], and *kamatz katan*.[6])

---

3. A word is *m'lra* if the accent is on the last syllable; it is *m'leil* if it is on the next-to-last syllable. The accent must be on one of the last two syllables. The common misconception that *m'leil* refers to a word with an accent on the beginning of the word is inaccurate. (Except, of course, in two-syllable words, in which the next-to-last syllable *is* the beginning of the word.)

4. As with most *dikduk* rules, this is not an absolute rule. There are other criteria that can contribute to the *m'leil – m'lra* designation. (See, for example, note 7.) Still, this rule is the starting point; it serves well to explain the cases under discussion.

5. Don't look this up! Strangely enough, these words appear in the Torah *without* the *cheerik maleh* (that is, there is no letter *yud* following the *cheerik*). Still, this *siman* works, based on the commonly assumed spelling of these words.

6. **What is a *kamatz katan*?** The *kamatz katan* is a *kamatz* that comes in place of a *cholum*. For example, the word *chok* has a *cholum* over the letter *ches*. When the word appears in connection with another word, the *cholum* becomes a *kamatz*, as in *chok olam*. Similarly, the word *chodesh* (month), with a *cholum* over the *ches*, becomes *b'chodsho*, with a *kamatz* under the *ches*. This is a *kamatz katan*.

■ **The second concept:** Two types of syllables (*havaros*) form all Hebrew words. All syllables have only one vowel. Most syllables also have only one letter. This is known as a *havarah pishutah*, a simple syllable.

Often, a syllable has two letters. This is known as a *havarah murkevet*, a syllable with a "passenger" letter. The first letter has the vowel, while the second letter has no vowel. Its sound "rides" on the letter that precedes it. This gives the syllable two letters.

Let us take, as an example, the word *melech*. This word has two syllables. The first syllable, the *me* sound, has only one Hebrew letter. This is known as a *havarah pishutah*. The second syllable, the *lech* sound, has two letters. This is a *havareh murkevet*, a syllable with a "passenger."

Once we understand that all syllables are divided between these two categories, we can move on to a follow-up rule for syllables.

A *tenuah gedolah* is a vowel with a longer sound. It is clearly heard, even without an additional letter attached to it. The grammatically ideal form would therefore have a *tenuah gedolah* appear as a *havarah pishutah*.

A *tenuah ketanah* is a vowel with a shorter sound. It is not heard as clearly without an additional letter attached to it. The grammatically ideal form would therefore have a *tenuah ketanah* appear as a *havarah murkevet*.

Not all words have these ideal grammatical forms. Often, a *tenuah gedolah* is a *havarah murkevet*, and a *tenuah ketanah* is a *havarah peshutah*. This syllable form is called a *havarah zarah*, a foreign syllable form.

We have now come to an understanding of these two concepts, the rules for vowels (*tenuah gedolah* – *ketanah*) and the rules for syllables (*havarah peshutah* – *murkevet* – *zarah*). We are now ready to understand the rule for *m'leil* – *m'lra*.

This *kamatz katan* is pronounced with a *uh* sound (*u* as in *cup*). The regular *kamatz* is pronounced as *awe*.

❧ Back to *Melech, Keren, Chesed,* and *Tzedek*

*T*he rule for determining accent is that we take a look at the last two syllables. If either one is a *havarah zarah*, it receives the accent. If both are *havaros zaros*, or if both are not, the accent remains on the final syllable.

To put it simply: A word is *m'lra* unless the final syllable is a *havarah peshutah*, and the next-to-last syllable is a *havarah zarah*.[7]

We now understand why the words with two *segols* must be *m'leil*, while the words with two *kamatzim* must be *m'lra*.

The *segol* is a *tenuah ketanah*. The first syllable (which has only one letter) is therefore the *havarah zarah*, and the accent appears there. *Melech, keren, chesed,* and *tzedek* are therefore *m'leil*.

The *kamatz* is a *tenuah gedolah*. The first syllable (which has only one letter) is a regular syllable. It is therefore the second syllable that receives the accent.

❧ *Eiss* or *Ess*?

*W*e have learned that a *havarah zarah* takes the accent of the word.[8] Single-syllable words, which have *only* a *havarah zarah* syllable, must therefore always take an

---

7. This rule is useful for understanding the examples noted here. There are, however, other rules that can change this. This includes the following.

■ **Rules for a suffix:** An easy rule to remember is that words with the most common forms of suffix are *m'leil*. This includes words that end with any of the following suffix forms; -*tee, -too, -nee, -nu, -nah, -hoo, -hu*.

However, a suffix that ends with a *mem* or *nun* (-*tem, -ten, -hem, -hen, -chem, -chen* suffixes) is always *m'lra*. This is so for a very practical reason. The *mem* and *nun* sounds are so similar that the accent is needed to stress the sound to the listener.

(Another example: When the word that follows begins with the letter *aleph, ayin,* or *hei,* and the words are read together, the first word is *m'lra* [*Emes L'Yaakov* to *Toldos* 26:10 or 22].)

8. This is only if the *havarah zarah* appears as one of the last two syllables of the word. The accent is never on any syllable other than the final syllable of the word (*m'leil*) or the next-to-last syllable (*m'lra*).

accent mark. This includes such common words as *eiss* (the), *kol* (all), and *bain* (son). Sometimes these words are connected to the word that follows and do not take an accent mark. In these cases the *havarah zarah* would have no *trop* (accent mark). This would contradict our rule; the vowel is therefore changed to a *tenuah ketanah*, so that the syllable is no longer *zarah*. Thus, the word *eiss* is changed to *ess* (with a *segol*); the word *kol* appears with a *kamatz katan*; the word *bein* becomes *ben*.

These changes are purely grammatical and have no bearing on the meaning of the word. (*Darshonim* who ascribe differences in meaning between them are therefore in error.)

☙ Other *M'leils*

The Name of God: The *Noda B'Yehudah* (1:2; also cited by *Mishnah Berurah* 5:2) was asked regarding the proper pronunciation of *Hashem*'s Name. The Name has three syllables: 1. the *chataf-patach-aleph*; 2. the *cholum-daled*; 3. the *kamatz-nun* with the letter *yud* following (a *havareh murkeves*).

Is the word pronounced *m'leil*, with the accent on the *cholum-daled*, or *m'lra*, with the accent on the *kamatz-nun* accompanied by the *yud*?

By applying the *havarah zarah* rule, we can conclude that the accent is on the final syllable. This is because the final syllable has a *tenuah gedolah* and has two letters, a *havarah murkevet*. This is a *havarah zarah*, which always commands the accent.

Indeed, this is the *Noda B'Yehudah*'s reply. The expression of his answer is of particular interest: "Regarding the wisdom of *dikduk*, I have no standing. But such a simple question can even be answered by a schoolchild …."

The *Noda B'Yehudah*'s subsequent explanation belies his humble claim,"I have no standing."

For those who find it difficult to remember the *Noda B'Yehudah*'s ruling (did he say *m'leil* or *m'lra*?), I quote the end of his ruling, "Anyone who pronounces [the Name of Hashem] *m'leil*, is himself *m'lra* …."[9]

---

9. This is a play on the word *m'lra*. The root, *ra*, also means bad or evil. Thus, one who pronounces the Name *m'leil* is himself bad.

■ **Kaddish:** After the passing of my father, z"l, I began reciting the Mourner's Kaddish in shul. I received an anonymous letter[10] pointing out the fact that all the words of Kaddish should be pronounced *m'lra* — only one word is pronounced *m'leil* — the word *l'eila*[11] (the one word in Kaddish that has the same word root as the word *m'leil*)!

The Kaddish is commonly mispronounced. In particular, the words in the line beginning "*Y'hei shlomo rabbah* ..." are erroneously pronounced *m'leil*.

We seek to do mitzvos with a proper level of *hiddur mitzvah*. A mitzvah performed in memory of a loved one certainly deserves to be done in its most beautiful fashion. The *hiddur mitzvah* for reciting Kaddish is the proper pronunciation.

■ **The Patach Genuvah** is a *patach* on the letter *hei*, *ches*, or *ayin* when it is the final letter of the word. This *patach* has an unusual pronunciation. It is read as if the *patach* were under an *aleph* that precedes the final letter.[12] This word is **never** *m'lra*, as a *patach genuvah* never takes an accent. Listen carefully to *chazaras hashatz* and you will hear that people generally pronounce them incorrectly.

Examples of this are the words (in *Shemoneh Esrei*) *soleiach* (forgiving), *matzmiach* (causes to flourish), and *shomea* (He who listens).These words all appear at prominent places in the *chazaras hashatz* and are often mispronounced. As Rav Pam would have said, this sounds strange to those listening, both here and up in Heaven.

---

10. Why anonymous? Apparently, this was because the author of the letter was afraid that I'd be offended by it. The letter was originally signed, but the signature portion had been ripped off before the letter was mailed. In fact, I'm grateful for the letter. If the letter's author is reading these lines, kindly accept my thanks.

11. Actually, there is one more word in the Kaddish that is *m'leil*. This is the word *aleinu*, at the end of *Kaddish Shaleim*. We have already seen (in footnote 7) that any word with the *nu* suffix is *m'leil*.

12. People are familiar with this in the case of a *ches* at the end of the word. When an *aleph* or *ayin* is the final letter of a word, this rule does not change our pronunciation (since our *ayin* sounds like an *aleph*). However, this is important (and not well known) in cases where the *patach hei* appears at the end of the word. It should be read as a *patach aleph* followed by a short *hei* sound.

[The first time a *patach genuvah* appears is in *Bereishis* 1:6; *Minchas Shai* there records a dispute regarding these rules. We have described the accepted opinion.]

❧ The Most Important *M'leil* of All

Although proper grammar is always important, it is rare that a *m'leil* – *m'lra* distinction would actually change the meaning of a word. Still, as we shall see, there are numerous words that have one meaning when the accent is *m'leil*, and a second meaning when the accent is *m'lra*. Many of these words appear in *Krias Shema*, the most important part of our morning prayers. It is particularly shocking that many of these words are mispronounced in ways that *do* change the meaning of the word.

Let us see a simple example.

The word *ahavta* translates as "you loved," in the past tense. Similarly, the word *amarta* translates as "you said," in the past tense. These are simple elementary-school translations.

It would follow that when the prefix letter *vuv* is placed before these words, the translation would remain the same, except that the "and" prefix is added.

Thus, *v'ahavta* translates "and you loved"; *v'amarta* translates "and you said," both in past tense. This is generally correct.

However, in the first paragraph of *Krias Shema*, this is not so. This paragraph opens with the command, "*V'ahavta es Hashem Elokecha* — and you shall love Hashem, your God." Here, *v'ahavta* is correctly translated in the imperative (command) future tense. Why is this so? Isn't *v'ahavta* a word whose meaning is "and you loved," in the past tense?

The answer to this is that the *vuv* prefix comes in two forms. When the letter *vuv* appears as a simple prefix, it is called a *vuv hachibur*, and does nothing more than to add the prefix "and" to the word.

Sometimes, however, the *vuv* prefix does more. In these cases, it changes the tense of a verb from past to future. This is called a *vuv hamehapeches*, a *vuv* that changes the tense. When the *vuv* is a simple *vuv hachibur*, it does not affect the pronunciation of the word. However, a sign of a *vuv hamehapeches* is that the pronunciation of the word does change. While the word *v'ahavta* is normally *m'leil,* the *vuv hamehapeches* causes it to change to *m'lra*. The same is true for other words in *Shema* that have the same word structure, such as *v'achalta*, *v'asafta*, *v'amarta*, and *v'dibarta*.[13]

---

13. The word *v'savata*, however, remains *m'leil*, despite the fact that the *vuv* is a *vuv hamehapeches*. This is because the vowels change when this word form appears at the end of a verse (or at an *esnachta*). This changes the *m'leil* – *m'lra* designation as well.

In all these cases, the correct *m'lra* reading is in the imperative (command) future tense. If any of these words is pronounced *m'leil*, the meaning changes to the past tense. There are additional words in *Shema* in which a *vuv hamehapeches* appears. This includes the word *v'nasatee*, which appears twice in the second section of *Shema*.[14]

Sadly, these words are mispronounced by the majority of Ashkenazic Jews.[15] It is generally the *Gedolei Yisrael* and the *baalei dikduk* who get this right. A *yirai Shamayim* should certainly look to be included in this group. It only takes a short while to grow accustomed to using the correct pronunciation.

One More Word

Kunteres HaTomas HaMilim[16] points out one additional word in *Krias Shema*, where the *m'lra* designation changes the meaning of the word. This is the word *v'charah*, which appears in the second paragraph. This word is *m'lra*.

---

14. In an effort to keep this discussion simple at the *Navi Shiur*, I mentioned only the five words with the *v'ahavta* form. I received a letter from a *baal dikduk*, pointing out that the *vuv hamehapeches* appears twenty two times in *Shema*. He included the many similar words in the plural form, such as *u'kishartem* and *u'kisavtem*. It is true that these words are indeed *m'lra*. However, the difference in meaning applies only to the words mentioned above (the *ani* and *atem* forms of the verb). Words ending with the *-tem* suffix are *always m'lra* (*Kunteres HaTomas HaMilim*).

15. In general, a mispronunciation that changes the meaning of a word causes a person to fail to accomplish the mitzvah of *Krias Shema*. Could it be that so many Jews are not *yotzei* this mitzvah?

Rav Yaakov Kamenetsky, *ztl*, in an attempt at *limud zechus*, suggested that these Jews are not pronouncing these words *m'leil* because they intend the past tense. Rather, they are expressing the word as if it appears at the end of a Torah verse. There, the rules mentioned here do not apply, and the word remains *m'leil* (see footnote 13)!

16. **Kunteres HaTomas HaMilim** is an excellent short *sefer* on *dikduk* rules, by Rav Avrohom Yitzchok Hoffman of Yerushalayim. I discovered this *sefer*, which is currently out of print, in Yeshivas Ohr Same'ach, shelf 309. I visited Rabbi Hoffman at his home in Yerushalayim and inquired about purchasing the *sefer*. He declined to sell me any of his few remaining copies, insisting that there were better *dikduk seforim* available. (I returned this *sefer* to its place in Ohr Same'ach, making it available to any of you who may be visiting Yerushalayim and wish to make use of it.)

In *Sefer Iyov* (30:30) this word appears in the past tense, "My bone was dried[17] (*charah*) by the heat." This word is *m'leil*.

Redak (*Sefer HaShoroshim*) explains that the *charah* in *Shema* is itself the root word (*ches-reish-hei*) and is always *m'lra*. This word, as it appears in *Iyov*, comes from a different root word (*ches-vou-reish*[18]) and is *m'leil* in the past tense.

Thus, the change in the *m'leil* – *m'lra* designation changes the meaning of the word to past tense.

---

17. This follows Rashi. Others translate it as "burned." This seems to be an attempt to relate the word to the *charah* of *Shema* (and elsewhere), which refers to a burning anger. While it may be true that there is a mystical connection between the two words, they must come from two different root words. The root *ches-reish-hei* (or any root word with a *hei* as the third letter) would not appear *m'leil*. (For example, the common words *assah* (he did) or *ratzah* (he wanted), are always *m'lra*.)

18. *Rabbeinu Yonah*, cited by *Redak*. Any word with a *vuv* as the middle letter of the root word can take the *charah* form, but is *m'leil* in the past tense. For example, the word *kum* (*kaf-vuv-mem*), becomes *kamah*; the word *shuv* (*shin-vuv-veis*), becomes *shavah*. Both are *m'leil*.

Redak himself suggests that the correct root may be *ches-reish-reish*. Either way, this is not the same root word as the *charah* in *Shema*.

[It seems puzzling that *Minchas Shai* to *Iyov* indicates that this is the only place where the word *charah* appears *m'leil*. This word also appears in *Yechezkiel* 24:11 as *m'leil*. There, *Minchas Shai* indicates that *this* is the only place that this word appears *m'leil*!

Upon reflection, I realized that the word *charah* appears *m'leil* only once. In *Yechezkiel*, the word has a *vuv* prefix (*v'charah*). *Minchas Shai* is saying that the word with the *vuv* prefix appears *m'leil* only once.]

Dikduk for Aramaic Words

*I*n addition to the ten Hebrew vowels, Hebrew uses the *shva* to denote a simple consonant sound. The *shva* itself can be pronounced in two forms. One is called the *shva nach* (the "resting *shva*"); the other is the *shva na* (the "moving *shva*").

For a **shva nach**, the consonant sound rests on the previous letter of the syllable (similar to the *t* sound in *rent*).

For a **shva na**, the consonant sound starts a new syllable and is more pronounced (similar to the *t* sound in *till*).

In Hebrew, there are five rules for designating a *shva* as a *shva na*. These are usually remembered as rules *aleph* through *hei*, as follows.

■ 1/א. A *shva* at the first letter of a word is always a *shva na*. There is no other way to pronounce this *shva*, since there is no preceding letter on which it could rest. This is remembered as Rule *Aleph*, for the first letter of the Hebrew alphabet.

- **2/ב**. If two consecutive *shva* vowels appear in one word, the second must be a *shva na*.[1] This is remembered as Rule *Beis*, the second letter, since it applies to the second *shva*.

- **3/ג**. The status of a *shva* is based on the vowel of the letter that precedes it. If the vowel is a *tenuah gedolah*, one of the five major vowels, the *shva* that follows is a *shva na*. If it is a *tenuah ketanah*, the *shva* that follows is a *shva nach*.[2] This is remembered as Rule *Gimmel*, for *gedolah* (which begins with a *gimmel*).

- **4/ד**. A *shva* under a letter that has a *dageish* is a *shva na*. This is remembered as Rule *Daled*, for *dagushah* (which begins with a *daled*).

- **5/ה**. A *shva* on the first of two identical letters is a *shva na*. The most common is the word *halilu* (or *halilu'kah*), the command to praise, which has a *shva* under the first of two *lamed* letters. This is remembered as Rule *Hei* for *halilu* (which begins with a *hei*).

~§ Aramaic Words

The Aramaic language is closely related to Hebrew. The *Rosh* refers to Aramaic as a "corrupted Hebrew." Sections of Nach (including large sections of *Daniel* and *Ezra*) appear in Aramaic. Aramaic words use the same vowels as Hebrew. The extent of this similarity raises several *dikduk* issues. The designation of the

---

1. The first of two consecutive *shva* vowels is always *nach*, resting on the previous letter.

- **A difficulty: What happens if two *shva* vowels appear as the first two vowels of a word?** The first *shva* must be pronounced *na*, in accordance with Rule *Aleph*. It is not even possible to pronounce it as a *shva nach*, given that there is no previous letter on which the *shva* could "rest."

It is because of this difficulty that a word never begins with two *shva* vowels. The letter *vuv* appears as a prefix meaning "and," which typically appears with a *shva* under the *vuv*. You will notice that whenever the *vuv* prefix appears before a word that begins with a *shva*, the vowel on the *vuv* is changed, sometimes to a *cheerik*, sometimes to a *shoorik*.

2. Exceptions to this rule are discussed in "Rav Zalman Henna and the *Tenuah Kallah* Controversy."

shva is one such issue. Are the rules for designating a *shva nach* and *shva na* the same as for Aramaic as they are for Hebrew?

This question is most significant when it applies to a *shva* that follows a *tenuah gedolah* (major vowel). In Hebrew, this would indicate a *shva na* (Rule *Gimmel*). Numerous words in Kaddish (which is in Aramaic) contain a *shva* that follows a *tenuah gedolah*.[3] How are these words to be pronounced?

Most people, Sefard or Ashkenaz, pronounce these as a *shva nach*. A source for this can be found in *Minchas Shai* to *Sefer Daniel* (beginning of Chapter 6), who presents the customary pronunciation as a *shva nach*. It appears from his words that the rules of *dikduk* do not apply to Aramaic.

Rav Zalman Henna follows the rules of *dikduk* in his *Siddur*, designating this *shva* as a *shva na*. Here, he is not alone in his opinion.

The *Siddur* of Rav Shabsi Sofer and the *Siddur Ishei Yisrael* follow this opinion. They designate the letter *tof* in the Aramaic words "*shichintei*" and "*givurtei*" as a *sof* (without a *dageish*). This indicates that the *shva* that precedes it is a *shva na*. This is also the opinion of the *Gra*, as recorded in *Ma'aseh Rav* #52.

Although Jews from *Taiman* follow this custom, it remains one of the issues in which Rav Zalman Henna's opinion has not been accepted by the multitudes of Jews.

৺১ *Yisgadeil V'yiskadeish*

Another Kaddish issue involves the first two words of Kaddish. Are they pronounced *yisgadal v'yiskadash* (with a *patach* at the end of each word), or *yisgadeil v'yiskadeish* (with a *tzeirei* at the end of each word)?

The earliest siddurim used the *patach* (*yisgadal v'yiskadash*). Rav Shabsi Sofer, in his *Siddur*, cited both possibilities. He based this confusion on two verses in *Sefer Daniel* (11:36, 37), where the two forms appear in apparent contradiction.

Rav Zalman Henna published his first two books in 1708 (when he was 21 years old). These were *Binyan Shlomo*, a work on *dikduk*, and *Shaarei Tefillah*, a siddur. In *Binyan Shlomo* (*Beis HaBinyanim* 7; p. 79-80), he endorses the *tzeiri* pronunciation (*yisgadeil*

---

3. Such as under the *lamed* of "*l'olmaya*" and "*b'alma*," or under the *reish* of "*u'poorkanei*," or under the *sof* of "*tzilus'hone*" and "*u'vaus'hone*."

v'yiskadeish). In *Shaarei Tefillah*, however, he retains the *patach* pronunciation.

Sixteen years later, Rav Zalman Henna published *Siddur Beis Tefillah*, in which he switched to the *tzeirei* form. However, he did so for all similar Aramaic words, not only for those at the beginning of Kaddish. (This includes *V'al kulam* in *Shemoneh Esrei*, which reads "*V'al kulam yisbareich v'yisromeim* ....")

Mishnah Berurah 56:2 (based on *Pri Migadim*, there) endorses the *tzeirei* reading for the first two words of Kaddish, but not elsewhere.[4] This is the predominant custom in Eretz Yisrael and the yeshivah world. Much of *chutz l'aretz*, and the Chassidic world in particular, use the *patach* pronunciation.

---

4. This is based on the understanding that these two words are Hebrew, not Aramaic (from *Yechezkel* 38:23).

Ben Asher and Ben Naftali

The "Aleppo Codex," known to Syrian Jews as "*Keter Aram Soba*," is a text of the twenty-four books of Tanach that had been safeguarded in the Syrian Community of the city of Aleppo, for many centuries. Significant portions of the Codex were destroyed during the Arab riots in 1948, when the Syrians marked the establishment of the State of Israel by setting fire to the Aleppo synagogue. Virtually the entire Torah portion (until *Devarim* 28) was destroyed. Most of Nach, however, remained intact. The portions that remained were recently smuggled out of Syria and are presently in Jerusalem.

According to Syrian tradition, this Codex is the text of Ben Asher, which the *Rambam* had endorsed as the most accurate version of the *mesorah*. If this is correct, the codex should be studied and used for our books of Tanach.[1]

---

1. For example, the Gemara instructs that *Shiras Devorah* be written in the poetic format known as "*ariach al gabei levena*." Our text of the Nach has the words set differently. *Shiras Dovid* (*Shmuel Beis* 26) also appears differently in our text as compared to the *Keter Aram Soba*. This will be discussed below.

In 1989, Rabbi Mordechai Breuer, working under the auspices of Mosad HaRav Kook in Eretz Yisrael, published a complete Tanach, using as his sources *Keter Aram Soba* as well as other ancient texts. In 1996, Rabbi Breuer published the *Horev* Tanach based on the *Keter Aram Soba*. Many saw this as a definitive Tanach text and argued that our Tanach scrolls should now be written in accordance with this text, even if this would entail changing the current practice.

This suggestion was not without controversy. Numerous *poskim* pointed out that we have no definitive proof that this is indeed the text of Ben Asher. The foremost *poskim* in Eretz Yisrael rejected attempts to change our *mesorah* based on this text, because its authenticity could not be verified. Some *poskim* who had previously expressed excitement over the resurfacing of *Keter Aram Soba* nevertheless refused to accept its use to change our *mesorah*.[2]

Rav Y. S. Eliyashev, *Shlita*, wrote (*Kovetz Teshuvos* 1:113), "Who can offer testimony that this is indeed the famous book found in Egypt, which was corrected by Ben Asher, on which the Rambam relied?"[3]

Rav Shlomo Zalman Auerbach, *zt"l*, argued that our *mesorah* could not be changed based on a new discovery. "Just as we ignore the arguments of Professor Felix, an observant Jew who argues that the world has an incorrect translation for '*shiboles shu'al*'[which is traditionally translated as *oats*], and we ignore this and continue to make a *mezonos* on it; and he also sought to disprove our translation of '*tamcha*' as horseradish, arguing that it did not exist in the time of *Chazal* and therefore should not be used for *marror*, and nevertheless we do not accept this argument and we follow our tradition; certainly then this, which [contradicts rulings that] are clear in the *Shulchan Aruch* ...."

---

2. Rav Shmuel HaLevi Wosner of Bnei Brak, who had written a letter of endorsement in 1988 regarding *Keter Aram Soba*, retracted the letter in 1995, asking that it no longer be used.

3. Rav Nosson Gestetner, in his *L'Horos Nosson* (10:73), cites an earlier source (*Teshuvos Ra'anach*), who discusses a dispute between the *Rambam's mesorah* and that of the Aleppo Codex. Since Rambam writes that he consistently follows Ben Asher, this would seem to indicate that the Aleppo Codex is not the work of Ben Asher, or that it was not his final version.

Rav Dovid Yitzchaki, of Kollel Chazon Ish (in Bnei Brak), wrote to Rav Gestetner in a letter that has been published in the *Ohr Yisrael Journal* (#9, p. 169, f. 30). In the letter, Rav Yitzchaki maintains that Rav Gestetner had been presented with inaccurate information, on which his *teshuvah* is based. He offers *mareh mikomos* in support of his defense, showing that there are no contradictions between the Aleppo Codex and known opinions of Ben Asher.

Rav Shlomo Zalman Auerbach also points out that the *Chazon Ish* was categorically opposed to the use of newly discovered manuscripts in formulating Halachah. In one letter (1:32) he writes forcefully, "The manuscripts that are uncovered serve almost no purpose in coming to the truth. Rather, they are used to bend the rules and twist the truth. It would be better to hide them ...."

By Jerusalem tradition, nothing worthwhile ever takes place unless placards denouncing it are plastered around the city. Sure enough, placards denouncing use of *Keter Aram Soba* appeared. Pamphlets were issued, containing letters from *gedolim* to this effect. Controversy followed controversy. There were accusations that some of these letters were forged, while others quoted only portions of letters, distorting their intent.

Then the unexpected happened. The pendulum swung back. Voices were heard defending the use of *Keter Aram Soba* and maintaining its authenticity as the text of Ben Asher. A letter was circulated, signed by Syrian rabbonim, attesting to their tradition that this was indeed the Ben Asher text. A letter signed by Rav Yaakov Posen, *Shlita*, on behalf of the Beis Din of Rav Nissan Karelitz, defended use of the *Keter* and accepted the likelihood that it was the work of Ben Asher.

In Elul of 1999, Rav Chaim Kanievsky, *Shlita*, wrote regarding the placards, "This is false, a lie! The *sefer* has a proper *mesorah*, and one who wishes to rely on it may do so. Evil people have spread rumors regarding it."[4]

It was pointed out that *Gedolei Yisrael* (quoted earlier) had expressed disapproval of changing an accepted practice based on *Keter Aram Soba*.[5] This applies to only a handful of areas in Tanach, where our practice follows an accepted tradition. In fact, we have no real *mesorah* regarding most of Tanach. In these areas, *Keter Aram Soba* is as authentic a source as one could find.

The disagreement continues. An excellent defense of *Keter Aram Soba* appeared in the *Ohr Torah Journal*, Volume 9. The subsequent

---

4. This letter is reproduced on the first page of the Introduction to the new printing of *Luach Eresh*. The other letters mentioned here appear there on p. 611 and p. 14. See also the *Ohr Yisrael Journal*, Numbers 9-11.

5. The letter of Rav Y. S. Eliyashev, quoted earlier, reads, "To change an accepted *minhag*, which has been accepted for many generations, based on the recently discovered manuscript, which is attributed to Ben Asher .... Who can offer testimony that this is indeed the famous book found in Egypt, which was corrected by Ben Asher, on which the *Rambam* relied?"

This letter refers to the issue of spacing of *Shiras Dovid*, as discussed below.

issue presented a counter-argument, along with a rebuttal. A third issue included letters on the topic. These essays give a concise and clear picture of the issues of dispute.

A short work, entitled *Ashureinu*, was published to defend the *Keter*. This was followed by a rebuttal in the form of a short *sefer* entitled *Mesoraseinu*. These excellent works also give a clear picture of the two sides to the dispute.

This debate centers primarily on the authorship of *Keter Aram Soba*. If authentic, the great respect worthy of the Ben Asher text is clear from the opinions of all involved.

❧ Who Was Ben Asher?

Most people never heard of Ben Asher. Who was he and in what way did he distinguish himself?

Aharon Ben Asher was a tenth-century expert in the text of the books of Tanach. Yaakov Ben Naftali was a respected contemporary of Ben Asher, whose text was often in disagreement with that of Ben Asher.

Little is known about the personal lives of Ben Asher and Ben Naftali.[6] They are presumed to have lived in Tiverya, and to have come from families with a few generations of expertise in the Masoretic texts. The *Machberes Ben Asher* is mentioned by *Redak* in *Shoftim* 6:19. Manuscripts throughout the centuries have contained pages delineating differences between the two texts.[7]

Rambam (*Hilchos Sefer Torah* 8:4), in his discussion regarding the proper text for Tanach, writes, "Because I have observed great errors in the books that I have seen regarding this, and because there are many disputes ... I have seen it appropriate to record, here, the different section breaks of the Torah, the closed breaks, and the open breaks, as well as the form for [writing of] the Songs, so that all *seforim* can be corrected. The text that we rely upon in these issues is the famous book found in Eygpt that contains all twenty-four Books, which had been in Jerusalem to be used to correct their *seforim*. All

---

6. There is even uncertainty regarding the first name of Ben Naftali. *Minchas Shai* records it as presented above.

7. *Encyclopedia Judaica* Volume 4 (under "Ben Asher" and again under "Bible") contains four reproductions of ancient Torah manuscripts that list differences between Ben Asher and Ben Naftali.

rely on this, because it had been corrected by Ben Asher, who spent many years correcting and revising it. I relied on him for the Sefer Torah that I wrote."

The first time that *Minchas Shai* mentions Ben Asher (*Bereishis* 1:3), he explains, "These men were two *roshei yeshivah* in the area of *mesorah*; one was named Yaakov ben Naftali and the second was Aharon ben Asher. The *Shalsheles HaKabbalah* writes that after the time of Rav Saadya Goan, there were two great men who often argued regarding words of the Torah and their *trop* ... we rely on the reading of Ben Asher, as the *Rambam* relied on him. This is the custom in the western countries. In the east, they rely on Ben Naftali."

The degree to which these two great men dominated their field is such that, if an opinion is specifically attributed to one of them, the assumption is that the other argues! See, for example, *Minchas Shai* (*Melachim Aleph* 13:4), "In one *sefer*, I saw written, 'according to Ben Naftali, this has a *dageish*.' From this we can understand that according to Ben Asher, it is soft [without a *dageish*]."

In Bnei Brak, a *Tehillim* was being written on parchment, for the Lederman shul. There was one word that was written one way in the *Tehillim* of the *Gra*, and another way in the text of Ben Asher. Rav Chaim Kanievsky, *Shlita*, was asked what to do. He responded that Ben Asher's version should be followed. He explained, "First, we cannot be certain that the *sofer* checked with the *Gra* regarding each word that he wrote. Second, even if he did, it may be that if the *Gra* had known that Ben Asher wrote it differently, he would have followed his opinion."

◆§ The Historical Background[8]

The story of Ben Asher and those who followed in his footsteps is the story of the preservation of the text of the Tanach. Already, during the time of the evil Jewish kings Achaz and Menashe attempts were made to corrupt the text of the Torah. The Gemara teaches that during the first decade of the reign of Yoshiyahu, no uncorrupted text could be found in all of Israel. The discovery of a Sefer Torah that had been secreted in the *Beis HaMikdash* during this period is recorded in Navi.

---

8. This is based (in part) on *History of the Jewish People: From Yavneh to Pumpadisa*, Chapter 40 (ArtScroll, 1986).

The Gemara (*Megillah* 3a) teaches that the proper use of the five "enderletters" had similarly been forgotten for even a longer period. *Rishonim* explain that this was a result of the earlier disruptions during the reign of these kings. (The characters that we use for the alphabet are known as *Ksav Ashuris*. During the period of Achaz and Menashe, Jews used *Ksav Ivris*, not *Ksav Ashuris*, for their everyday language. Use of our alphabet, containing the enderletters, was reserved for *kisvei kodesh*.)

Later, during the era of the Second *Beis HaMikdash*, the *Anshei Knesses HaGedolah* exerted great effort to restore the integrity of the text.

After the destruction of the *Beis HaMikdash*, the center of Jewish scholarship shifted to Bavel, where it remained for centuries. There, Talmud Bavli came into being, to preserve our *Torah She'baal Peh*, our Oral Tradition.

The leader of Babylonian Jewry was known as the *Reish Galusa*. Around the year 4280 (520 CE), Mar Zutra, the *Reish Galusa*, was executed, and his wife fled with their infant son to escape the vengeful anger of their enemies. She returned to the Land of Israel, settling in Tiverya. This infant grew up, and, as Mar Zutra II, he became *Reish Pirka* (a new title for *rosh yeshivah*). Soon, the tradition of Torah scholarship returned to the Holy Land.

Talmud Bavli remained the dominant basis for Jewish law, and during this period it became universally accepted. Nevertheless, there were areas in which the yeshivos and scholars of Tiverya distinguished themselves, namely, in the study of Tanach, Hebrew grammar, and the *Ta'amei HaMikra* (or *trop*), the melody by which the Torah is read.

The subsequent exiles and the Dark Ages (the period known to us as the *Savoraim*), when almost no Jewish works were published, certainly exacerbated this problem. The lifelong efforts of Ben Asher, Ben Naftali, and Rabbeinu Meir HaLevi saved the day by establishing the proper text for all time.

By the time of Ben Asher, the superiority of Tiverya in this field was undisputed. An example of this can be found in the words of *Ibn Ezra* (*Shemos* 25:31), "I have seen scrolls that had been examined by the sages of Tiverya, and fifteen of their eldest scholars took an oath that they had looked at every word, every point, and every [detail of spelling] three times [and the unusual spelling of this word is correct]. And I did not find this in the scrolls of Spain, France, or overseas."

The contribution of Babylonian Jewry during the millennia that followed the Churban is well known. The major contribution of Eretz Yisrael, in the preservation of the books of Tanach and an understanding of their grammar, is not.

Let us explore some of the issues related to the legacy of Ben Asher and his *bar-plugta,* Ben Naftali.

~§ The Problems

As we begin a discussion regarding different versions of the text of Tanach, it is important to point out that there is one standard text for the words of the Torah. It is well over three thousand years since the Torah was given at Sinai, and the text has been passed faithfully from generation to generation. Our Torah is identical to that which Moshe brought from Sinai. There is not a single word that appears in one text and not in others.

The difference between texts that we are discussing is in regard to various issues that pertain to the scribe as he transcribes the text, or to the pronunciation of the words and to the proper manner of reading certain words. Specifically, the issues cover three areas: spacing, full vowels, and pronunciation.

■ **A. Spacing:** There are breaks (i.e., areas, usually nine letters long, that are left blank on the parchment), that appear between sections of the Torah. Where is the scribe to leave space and in what manner should this be done?

There are also parts of Tanach, called *Shiros,* or Songs, that are written in a poetic format, with additional spacing. The style of the writing of these Songs is also sometimes in dispute.

■ **B. Full Vowels:** Some vowels can be written in a short or long version. These are the *cheerik* (which can appear with or without a *yud* following it), and the *cholem* and *milupim* (both of which can appear with or without a letter *vuv*). The difference between the two versions never changes the meaning of the word. They affect only the correct spelling of the words involved. Here, too, there is an occasional dispute over which version of the vowel to use.

■**C. Pronunciation**: There are sometimes disputes over the vowels and accents of specific words in the Torah. There are disagreements over the spelling of certain words in Nach. In addition, there are disagreements over the *trop* or cantillation of some words. All these affect the correct pronunciation of the word.

We will return to discuss the halachic issues in each of these three areas. First, let us meet the individuals who brought these issues to discussion.

Ben Asher or Ben Naftali?

Where these two luminaries disagree, whose opinion is followed?

Earlier we quoted *Minchas Shai* (*Bereishis* 1:3) who writes, "We rely on the reading of Ben Asher, as the *Rambam* relied on him. This is the custom in the western countries. In the east, they rely on Ben Naftali."

Chiddushei HaRan (*Sanhedrin* 4a), quoting *Rashba*, also writes that the eastern and western communities differed as regards Ben Asher and Ben Naftali.

Maharam Mintz (*Teshuvah* 8) writes that although we follow Ben Asher, one may rely on Ben Naftali as well. *Sha'ar Ephraim* (Chapter 6, *Pischei Sharim* 21) quotes *Maharam Mintz* but disagrees with him, maintaining that Ben Asher is followed.

The great *midakdeik* (grammarian) Rav Zalman Henna, in his *Siddur Shaarei Tefillah* (323), writes that Halachah follows the opinion of Ben Asher "in all cases."

As we shall see, there are individual cases in which Ben Naftali's opinion is followed. However, I am not aware of any source that categorically prefers the opinion of Ben Naftali (see following page).

Rabbeinu Meir HaLevi, the *Remah*

No Ben Asher text has survived the thousand years that have passed since they were written by Ben Asher. There are *seforim* (including the *Rambam*) that quote portions of his text, but we have not had a full copy of the Ben Asher text for a very long time.

It was through the great efforts of another *Rishon* that the teachings of Ben Asher and Ben Naftali were preserved. Rabbeinu Meir HaLevi Abulafia lived in Spain in the early thirteenth century. He

This list of Ben Asher/BenNaftali differences is part of the Lisbon Torah manuscript in the British Museum. These lists were part of Torah manuscripts for generations.
(Ilustration credit: M. Lustig)

is known by the acronym *Remah*, by which other *Rishonim* refer to him. *Remah* is most widely known for his *Yad Remah*, a halachic commentary on *Bava Basra* and *Sanhedrin*. He also wrote *Mesores Siyag LaTorah*, a *sefer* that contains alphabetically arranged Masoretic notes on the Torah. There, Rabbeinu Meir also records the correct spelling of many words in Tanach that might otherwise be called into question. This is used as a source for all Ashkenazic *seforim* (despite the fact that Rabbeinu Meir was a Sefardi). There are a few places where Rabbeinu Meir brings two possible spellings. For these, the Ashkenazic tradition relies on the *Sefer Ohr Torah*.

Minchas Shai, in his commentary to Torah, follows *Ohr Torah*. *Minchas Shai* added a commentary to the other books of Tanach. Rav Shlomo Ganzfried, too, bases his *Kesses HaSefer* (a widely used work on *safrus*) on the text of *Remah* and *Ohr Torah*. The *Remah* differs from the *mesorah* in six places. *Kesses HaSefer* follows the opinion of *Remah*. The widely available "Qoren" text (this is the large-size Tanach used by many shuls for the reading of the Haftorah) also follows *Remah* and *Ohr Torah*.

We have therefore been fortunate that this long line of experts has preserved a unified tradition for the writing of our Sifrei Torah.

৵ৡ Minchas Shai

Among *Acharonim*, *Minchas Shai* is generally recognized as the preeminent source for our *mesorah*. *Chasam Sofer* (Y.D. 270) writes that "all my teachers relied upon him." *Aruch HaShulchan* (275:15) writes, "We follow the *Sefer Minchas Shai* … all the scribes follow him, as his entire *sefer* is focused on this and he was meticulous in his work."

The author of *Minchas Shai* was Rav Yedidya Shlomo ben Avraham, born in Mantua in the late sixteenth century. He served as Rav in Mantua from approximately 1600 until his passing in 1626. He placed great effort into establishing the proper text of all twenty-four books of Tanach. He traveled extensively to secure authentic manuscripts, including that of Rabbeinu Meir.

He wrote two volumes, the first on the five books of the Chumash and the five Megillos, and the second on Tanach. He named his *seforim Goder Peretz* (*To Fill the Breach*). These *seforim* were first published one hundred years later, when the publisher renamed them *Minchas Shai*, in honor of the author (*Shai* represents the initials of Yedidya Shlomo).

Minchas Shai has appeared in the standard *Mikra'os Gedolos* Tanach, but not in the Chumashim. Recently, *Minchas Shai* has been republished by the late Rav Yehudah Aryeh Guttman, *zt"l*, and has begun to appear in some new editions of *Mikra'os Gedolos*

Chumashim, as well as in many editions of *Tikkun L'Korim*.

As mentioned earlier, there was a great deal of controversy regarding the publication of the text of *Keter Aram Soba*. A collection of Rabbinic statements was published, entitled *Berur Mesoras Nusach HaTanach*. There, numerous *poskim* maintain that *Minchas Shai* be followed as a final authority in these areas.

Now that we are familiar with Ben Asher, Ben Naftali, *Remah*, *Kesses HaSefer*, and *Minchas Shai*, let us review some areas in which these *seforim* are used *l'Halachah* today.

◆§ One Letter in the Entire Torah

A Sefer Torah contains over 304,000 letters. There is a significant dispute regarding one of these letters, the last letter of the word *dakah* (*Devarim* 23:2). This is one of the six places where *Remah* (who spells *dakah* with a *hei*) disagrees with the *mesorah* (where it is spelled with an *aleph*). Rav Ovadia Yosef (*Yichaveh Daas* 8:25:1) suggests that "perhaps this relates back to the dispute between Ben Asher and Ben Naftali."

Minchas Shai quotes *Redak*, who spelled this word with the letter *aleph* at the end. However, *Minchas Shai* himself disagrees and rules that *dakah* should be spelled with the letter *hei*, calling *Remah* "the man of authority." Rav Moshe Shternbuch (in *Mitzvas HaYom*) relates that the *Gra* instructed that a Sefer Torah in which *dakah* was spelled with an *aleph* should be corrected. Virtually all later *poskim* follow this ruling of *Minchas Shai*.[9]

The dispute may depend on the translation of this word, which is used here to refer to a specific physical injury. Some understand it to come from a root word related to *pounding* (the similar word, *m'duchah*, refers to a grinding tool). This is spelled with a *hei*. Others understand that it is related to a root word meaning *insignificant* (as

---

9. The list includes *Chidah* in *Shiurei Berachah* Y.D. 275:3 and *L'Dovid Emes* 11:16, *Teshuvah M'Ahavah* 1:71, *Beis Ephraim* 64, *Zera Emes* Y.D. 3:141, *Meil Tzedakah* 29, and *Kaf HaChaim* 143:34.

Ben Asher's opinion regarding this word is not known. The portion of *Keter Aram Soba* that contained this word was destroyed during the 1948 riots in Aleppo.

As we shall see below, the custom of Chabad rejects this ruling and spells *dakah* with an *aleph*, citing other sources.

in *Tehillim* 90:3), which is spelled with an *aleph*.[10]

It is interesting to note that although our Sifrei Torah spell *dakah* with a *hei*, when this word appears in the Gemara and *Shulchan Aruch* (and in most Rabbanic sources), it is spelled with an *aleph*. I have no idea why this is so.

~§ The Taimani Sefer Torah

Jews from Taiman have traditions that sometimes differ from ours. As regards the Sefer Torah text, there are nine differences between their text and ours. In three of these cases, Rabbeinu Meir had presented both versions. The remaining six differences are the six places where Rabbeinu Meir differed from the *mesorah* text.

May someone who is not a Taimani recite the *berachos* over a Taimani Sefer Torah?

A number of Sefardic *poskim* discuss this issue. *Kaf HaChaim* (143:34) cites his own *Be'air Mayim Chayim*, which does not allow a non-Taimani to read from this Sefer Torah. His main objection is in regard to the Taimani spelling of the word *dakah* with a *aleph*. *Divrei Chachamim* (#47) disagrees. He points out that the Taimani tradition attributes its text to Ben Asher and therefore rules that it may be used.

Rav Ovadiah Yosef, in *Yichaveh Daas* (6:56), also addresses the issue. He shows that there are sources for the Taimani text and rules (somewhat reluctantly) that to avoid dispute, one who is called to an *aliyah* in a Taimani Sefer Torah should recite the *berachos*, as usual.[11]

~§ The Chabad Sefer Torah

The Ashkenazic custom, like that of all non-Taimani *Sefardim*, is to spell *dakah* with a *hei*. There is one exception to this. The Chassidim of Chabad/Lubavitch spell *dakah* with an

---

10. I have heard this explanation attributed to *Shelas Dovid*.

11. There is an additional difference between the Taimani Sfrei Torah and all others. This is in the verse (Bereishis 9:29), "*va'yehi kol yimai Noach.*" The word *va'yehi* is written *va'yehiyu*, with an extra *vuv*. The two versions are found in *Minchas Shai*. This, too, is an issue of major concern to the aforementioned *poskim*.

aleph. Rav Shlomo Yosef Zevin, *zt"l*, (a world-renowned scholar with roots in Chabad) wrote a lengthy article on this topic, which is printed in *Otzar HaPoskim* to *Even HaEzer* (to *Siman* 5; page 165). There, he defends this practice and maintains that it has early sources. He cites a claim that a Sefer Torah of the Ba'al Shem Tov spells *dakah* this way. The source of Chabad's custom is the *Sefer She'aris Yehudah*, written by the brother of the *Ba'al HaTanya*, who rules that *dakah* be spelled with an *aleph*.

The Chassidim of Chabad are fiercely loyal to their tradition, even where this may differ from the custom of the rest of *Klal Yisrael*. Their Sifrei Torah are written in *Ksiv Ari*, which is common for many branches of Chassidus. If a Jew who is not a member of Chabad were to hire a Chabad *sofer* to write a Sefer Torah for him, the *sofer* would follow Chabad tradition unless specifically instructed otherwise. Many people know that it is necessary to specify the type of *ksav*. An individual must specify if he wants *Ksiv Beis Yosef* (which is the custom of most of *Klal Yisrael*) or *Ksav Ari* (the custom of the *kabbalists*).

However, most people are not aware of the difference in the spelling of *dakah*. Here, too, it is necessary to provide the *sofer* with specific instructions.

May someone who is not Lubavitch recite the *berachos* over a Lubavitch Sefer Torah? The question that Sefardic *poskim* had discussed in regard to a Taimani Sefer Torah is discussed by Ashkenazic *poskim* in regard to a Chabad Sefer Torah.

The consensus of *poskim* is that it is preferable not to use this Sefer Torah, but that a *berachah* may be made in a case when no other Sefer Torah is available.[12]

If one is unsure if a Sefer Torah was written by a Chabad *sofer*, what should he do? Winding the Torah to the end of *Devarim* (to check the word *dakah*), and then winding it back to the reading of the day, may be time-consuming. Is there another way to recognize if a Sefer Torah was written according to *Minhag Chabad*?

There is another distinctive characteristic of Chabad *sofrim*. The letter *hei*, as written in a Sefer Torah, has an upside-down *yud* as its left leg. Chabad *sofrim* also write the *hei* this way, most of the time. There is one exception. Look at the left leg of the *hei* at the end of

---

12. *Meil Tzeddakah* 29, *Beis Ephraim* Y.D. 64, *Minchas Chinuch* 613. *Be'air Moshe* (8:58) instructs that the *Sefer* be returned to the *aron* in favor of another Sefer Torah. If this is not possible (there is no other Sefer Torah or one is in a Chabad shul), he rules that a *berachah* may be made.

the Name of Hashem. In most Sifrei Torah, this *hei* is identical to the others in the Torah. In *Sifrei Chabad*, this *hei* is different. The left leg appears as a straight line or as a straight *yud*, not as an upside-down *yud*. If a Sefer Torah is written this way, it is likely that the word *dakah* was also written according to the custom of Chabad.

⇜ A. Spacing

*R*ambam (*Hilchos Sefer Torah* 8:4) lists the proper space to be left between sections of a Sefer Torah, based on Ben Asher. It would seem that there could be no dispute in this area, since the *Rambam* is clearly quoting the text of Ben Asher, which he himself had seen. Indeed, *Rama M'Pano* (106) writes, "Who can choose to disagree with [*Rambam's*] words, which are based on an old tradition?"

There is however, one place in the Torah where the issue of proper spacing remains in dispute. This is in *Parashas Tzav* (7:22), where *Rambam* does not instruct that there be any spacing at all. Some Sifrei Torah, however, do have a space. (Today, Taimani Sifrei Torah still contain this space.)

Rambam (7:11) rules that failure to follow the correct spacing of a Sefer Torah would invalidate the Sefer Torah. May these Sifrei Torah be used?

Shach wrote a responsum on this topic; it is published in the *Shulchan Aruch*, *Yoreh Deah*, after *Shach* 275:6. *Shach* concedes that it would be better to follow the Rambam, and adds, "If I had the power, I would abolish [this custom]."

Shach also agrees that improper spacing would invalidate a Sefer Torah. Nevertheless, he rules that if a Sefer Torah is written according to the custom of a community, even if it differs from the text of Ben Asher as quoted in the *Rambam*, the Sefer Torah may be used.

SPACING THE *SHIROS*

The Gemara (*Megillah* 16b) instructs that *Shiras Devorah* be written in the poetic format known as "*ariach al gabei levenah*." Our text of the Nach has the words written normally, with no distinctive *shirah* form. Many versions of the *Tikkun L'Korim* printed before the 1990s (including the popular *Mishor Tikkun*), have *Shiras Devorah* written as normal text. This is because the *Tikkun* is used to prepare for the reading from a Navi scroll, and scrolls were written this way.

We have been relying on our tradition for this, even though it does not follow the Gemara. This is similar to the situations described below (see "Full Vowels," below) regarding situations when our tradition contradicts the Gemara's text.

In *Keter Aram Soba*, *Shiras Devorah* appears as described in the Gemara. Does this indicate that our custom should indeed follow the Gemara and that our current practice is in error?

Those who argue that *Keter Aram Soba* is Ben Asher's text have suggested that we write our Nach scrolls in accordance with the Gemara and the *Keter*. Here *Minchas Shai*, too, writes that the *Shirah* should be written in a distinctive manner. He urges that it be written in sixty-five lines, in accordance with *Mesechas Sofrim* and in contradiction to the custom (in his time) of writing *Shiras Devorah* in sixty lines. Clearly, though, the custom in his time was to use the *shirah* form to space *Shiras Devorah*.[13]

Today, many *sofrim* (and a wide range of *Tikkun sofrim*) follow Ben Asher, as recorded in *Keter Aram Soba*.[14]

Shiras Dovid (*Shmuel Beis* 26) also appears differently in our text, compared to the *Keter Aram Soba*. Our Nach scrolls present *Shiras Dovid* written in the poetic format known as "*ariach al gabei levenah*." The *Keter* has it written in a different format, which is known as "*ariach al gabei ariach*." Both forms are mentioned in *Minchas Shai*.

It was in regard to this issue that Rav Y. S. Eliyashev, *Shlita*, wrote his letter, quoted above, urging that the accepted custom not be changed because of the discovery of the *Keter*. In fact, *Minchas Shai* (who mentions both customs) prefers our custom of "*ariach al gabei levenah*."

---

13. Curiously, the *Keter Aram Soba*, which follows the *shirah* form as in *Minchas Shai*, has only 58 lines.

14. It is interesting to note that the *Sinai Tikkun*, published before the '90s, has *Shiras Devorah* in the distinctive *Shirah* style. The *Sinai Tikkun* describes itself as based on a *Tikkun* from Amsterdam that had been published in 1866.

B. Full Vowels

We have seen that there are three vowels that can be written in a short or long version. These are the *cheerik*, which can appear with or without a *yud* following it, and the *cholem* and *milupim*, both of which can appear with or without a letter *vov*. These are known as "*chasseiros v'yeseiros*," vowels which have "missing or extra" letters. Although this does not affect the meaning of the word, the vowels in the Torah must be written precisely.

When reading the Torah, it sometimes occurs that a spelling mistake is discovered. When this happens, we return the Torah to its place in the ark and continue reading from another Sefer Torah. Does this apply to a mistake in the *chasseiros v'yeseiros*?

Over the generations, errors in these vowels have crept into our text. As a result, the *Rema* (O.C. 143) rules that we do not return a Sefer Torah to the ark. "Our Sifrei Torah are not so precise [regarding *chasseiros v'yeseiros*], that we could say that the others are more kosher [than the one being returned to the ark]."

Occasionally there are vowels that are mentioned in the Gemara as *chaseir* or *yoseir*. When a mistake in these cases is found, it would seem proper to return the Sefer Torah to the ark. Indeed, this is the opinion of many *poskim*.[15]

However, there are places where the standard text differs from the Gemara's text. We nevertheless continue to use our text (*Tosafos* to *Nidah,* 33a). How do we justify a practice that openly contradicts the Gemara?

Chidushei HaRan (*Sanhedrin* 4a) answers, "The *Rashba* wrote that these are part of the dispute between the east and west, between Ben Asher and Ben Naftali. Wherever we find this dispute, we follow the majority [of Sifrei Torah]."

These words are difficult to understand. How can the tradition of Ben Asher and Ben Naftali, who were *Rishonim*, override the text as it appears in the Gemara?

It seems that the *Ran* and *Rashba* considered the texts of Ben Asher and Ben Naftali to be sufficiently authentic, so that we can assume that their versions of the text existed as far back as the time of the Gemara. The Gemara is simply quoting one version. Since we assume

---

15. *Meieri* to *Kiddushin* 30, *Teshuvos Sharei Ephraim* #82, *Shev Yaakov* #56, *Chochmas Bezalel* to *Niddah* 33a. Cf. *Sidrei Taharah* to *Niddah* 33a and *Binyan Zion* 1:98.

that the text was already in dispute at that time, we are not bound to any one opinion and we therefore follow the prevalent custom.

In the current controversy, arguments have swirled around the correct spelling of a word in *Sefer Tehillim*. The word *succah* always appears in Tanach as a *chasier*, without a *vuv*. Rav Shlomo, the *dayan* of Vilna, in *Cheishek Shlomo* to *Meseches Succah* (2a), writes that there is one exception to this rule. In *Tehillim* 76:3, the word "*succo*" (his *succah*) is written with a *vuv*. Rav Shlomo writes that he checked the *Tehillim* scroll that had been written under the direction of the Gaon of Vilna, the *Gra*, and that *succo* appears with a *vuv*.

In the *Keter Aram Soba*, *succo* appears *chaseir*, without the *vuv*. Those who seek to discredit the *Keter* point this out as an indication that it is not reliable.

Others argue that it is unlikely that the *Gra* actually examined each word of the *Tehillim* scroll. The fact that it was written under his direction only indicates that issues that the scribe considered to be in dispute were placed before him. It is therefore likely that the *succo* spelling was not based on the *Gra*, and that this spelling is consistent with the rest of Tanach, without the *vuv*.

A *Tehillim* scroll recently written for the Lederman shul in Bnei Brak follows the *Gra's* version, as recorded in *Cheishek Shlomo*.

TODAY

The *Rema* ruled that we are not experts in *chaseir* or *yoseir*, and that we therefore do not return Sifrei Torah to the ark because of a *chaseir* or *yoseir* mistake.

Shaagas Aryeh takes this a step further. The 613th mitzvah in the Torah requires that every Jew write a Sefer Torah at least once in his lifetime. *Shaagas Aryeh* maintains that the mitzvah is to write a Sefer Torah that is entirely correct. Today, when we are no longer experts in *chaseir* and *yoseir*, it is most likely that our Sifrei Torah contain at least one error. One is not obligated to write a Sefer Torah if he cannot be sure that it is written in perfect compliance with the original text.

Birkei Yosef (in *Shiurei Berachah* 270:2) disagrees sharply. He maintains that today, thanks to the great efforts of *Rishonim* and the *Ohr Torah*, we once again have expertise in *chaseir* and *yoseir*.[16]

---

16. There appears to be another, more serious difficulty with the opinion of the *Shaagas Aryeh*.

There are disputes in many areas of Biblical Law. We can never be absolutely sure

Avnei Nezer (Y.D. 356:5) contends that things have changed. "Today, we are experts in *chaseir* and *yoseir*, despite the fact that they were not experts in the time of the Gemara. Through his hard work, *Remah* has clarified everything ...."

However one rules as regards the halachic aspect of this dispute, the historic significance of these comments is awesome. The diligence and hard work of these Torah giants have resulted in a text that may be the most accurate in well over a thousand years, going back past the time of the Gemara!

We see, once again, how the work of these giants has affected our Sifrei Torah in such a positive way!

C. Pronunciation

There are numerous areas in which *Minchas Shai* records a difference of opinion between Ben Asher and Ben Naftali regarding the proper pronunciation of words.

Minchas Shai to *Shoftim* (7:15) and *Melachim Beis* (16:5) records a dispute in regard to the *Yaihoo* rule, which is discussed in our section on *dikduk*. The disagreement involves the proper placing of a *dageish*, as explained there. *Minchas Shai* explains that Ben Naftali's position was based on a desire to make the words read more easily. This appears to be an instance where the opinion of Ben Naftali is accepted.

YISACHAR

Another well known dispute involves the pronunciation of the name of one of the *Shevatim*, Yisachar. *Redak* (*Yirmiya* 37:13) reports that the second *sin* is silent, in accordance with the opinion of Ben Asher. Rav Zalman Henna (in *Sharei Tefillah* 323), too, records this as the opinion of Ben Asher, "and the Halachah always follows Ben Asher." *Noda B'Yehudah* (E.H. 107) reports that this was the

---

that any halachic decision is identical to the ruling that Moshe Rabbeinu taught from Sinai. Still, the Torah allows for differences of opinion and has a system for *psak Halachah*. We follow the opinion of the majority of *poskim* and are 100% sure that we are performing the mitzvah properly. This rule should apply to the mitzvah of writing a Sefer Torah as well. The objections of the *Shaagas Aryeh* are therefore puzzling.

custom in Poland, where only one *sin* was pronounced. This is the custom in most Ashkenazic and Sefardic communities.

In some Chassidic circles, though, the second *sin* is pronounced (with a *shva nach*). This custom follows the opinion of Ben Naftali, as recorded in *Sharei Tefillah*. *Noda B'Yehudah* writes that after he moved to Prague, he saw that some people pronounce *Yisaschar* with both letters.

Redak, Ibn Ezra (*Shemos* 1:3), *Rashi* to *Divrei HaYamim* (15:24), *Minchas Shai* (*Bereishis* 4:18), Rav Zalman Henna, and Rav Yaakov Kamenetsky (*Emes L'Yaakov* to *Shemos* 1:3) understand that the issue regarding the pronunciation is a *dikduk* issue. The issue is not related to *Yisachar* alone. They cite other Biblical names (and words) that contain two consecutive identical letters and are subject to the same rule.

There are other traditions related to the reading of *Yisachar*, which are based on *drush*; see for example *Chasam Sofer* to *Parashas Vayeitzei* and *Shaar Rachamim* to *Sharei Ephraim* 6:14. These opinions sometimes pronounce the *sin*, and sometimes do not.

Rav Yaakov Kamenetsky (*Emes L'Yaakov, Bereishis* 30:18) questions these explanations, because we find another individual named Yisachar (also spelled with two *sin* letters, with only one *sin* pronounced) in *Divrei HaYamim Aleph* 26:5. It is difficult to imagine that the *drush* reasons attributed to the naming of Yaakov Aveinu's son would apply to this individual as well.[17]

This is more than a question of pronunciation. What is the correct spelling of the name Yisachar in a *get* or *kesubah*? *Noda B'Yehudah* (E.H. 2:107) rules that it be spelled with one *sin*.[18] Those who pronounce both letters would certainly spell it with the letter *sin*, twice.

•

---

17. It may well be that the recorded pronunciation (for *Divrei HaYamim*) that Rav Yaakov brings is based on Ben Asher. Those who pronounce both letters would maintain that Ben Naftali would hold of this pronunciation in *Divrei HaYamim* as well. This would allow for those reasons, *al pi drush*, to apply only to Yisachar the son of Yaakov.

18. This was the practice of my *Rebbe*, Rav Avrohom Pam, *zt"l*.

≈§ *Tiferes Hakriah* [19]

There are numerous places in the Torah in which Chumashim vary in regard to the placing of a *chataf* vowel. This is a vowel that appears in place of a *shva na*, to give the letter a stronger pronunciation. This can take any one of three forms: the *chataf patach* (a *shva* and a *patach*), the *chataf kamatz* (a *shva* and a *kamatz*), and the *chataf segol* (a *shva* and a *segol*). These usually appear under one of the following four letters; *aleph*, *hei*, *ches*, and *ayin*. These letters have a soft sound, and the *chataf* is useful in clarifying the pronunciation.

Occasionally, a *chataf* sign appears under other letters. Some Chumashim have this more often than others. This occurs when a *shva na* sound might be unclear. The *chataf* was added to remind the reader to pronounce the syllable clearly. There are variant traditions regarding the use of this *chataf*. This relates to a basic issue debated by Ben Asher and Ben Naftali: how quick should we be to modify the pronunciation of words for *tiferes hakriah*, to make the reading of the words flow more beautifully.

Virtually every *parashah* in the Torah has a least one example of this addition of a *chataf* sign.

Examples of this use of the *chataf*, from the first five *parshiyos* of the Torah:

- *Parashas Bereishis* (1:18): *U'lhavdeel* (and to separate): In the ArtScroll Chumash, this appears with a *shva* under the *lamed*. In the Shul Chumash, it appears with a *chataf patach*.

- *Parashas Noach* (9:14): *B'Anani* (when I place a cloud): In the ArtScroll Chumash, this appears with a *shva* under the *nun*. In the Shul Chumash, it appears with a *chataf patach*.

- *Parashas Lech Lecha* (12:3): *M'vorachecha* (those who bless you): In the ArtScroll Chumash, this appears with a *shva* under the *reish*. In the Shul Chumash, it appears with a *chataf patach*.

- *Parashas Vayeira* (18:21): *Ayrdah* (I will go down): In the ArtScroll Chumash, this appears with a *shva* under the *reish*. In the Shul Chumash, it appears with a *chataf patach*.

---

19. This section is based on the teaching of Rav Yisrael Belsky, *Shlita* (although the individual examples are mine).

■ *Parashas Chayei Sarah* (24:60): *Va'yivorachu* (and they blessed): In the *ArtScroll Chumash*, this appears with a *shva* under the *reish*. In the *Shul Chumash*, it appears with a *chataf patach*.

As you can see, this difference is common, appearing in every *parashah* of the Torah. Today, most Chumashim do not follow the practice of adding the *chataf*. Some do (the *Shul Chumash*, printed by Wagshall, is one popular example). This sometimes leads to confusion during the reading of the Torah.[20]

⇨ Reading Megillas Esther

On Purim, we read Megillas Esther. You may have noticed that during the Megillah reading, some words are read twice, each time with a different pronunciation. Why is this done? The answer lies in our discussion.

There are five places in Megillas Esther where the text of *Kesses HaSefer* is different than that which appears in the *mesorah*. Two of these differences affect the way the words are read.

The differences in reading occur at the following words: *l'harog* (8:11), which appears in *Kesses Hasefer* as *v'laharog*; and *b'fneyhem*, (9:2), which appears in *Kesses Hasefer* as *l'fneyhem*.

Ashkenazim generally write Megillos in line with *Kesses HaSefer*, but read these words twice, once each way. The importance of the second reading cannot be understated, as there are strong indications that this is indeed the correct text.

Sefardim and Taimanim follow the text of the *mesorah*. *Minchas Shai*, too, differs with *Kesses HaSefer* in regard to these words.

Some shuls also read the word *sorer* (1:22) twice, also pronouncing it *shorer*. This custom has no source and is not the practice of *Gedolei Yisrael*.[21]

---

20. The *Keter Aram Soba* (attributed to Ben Asher) does use the *chataf* in these cases.

21. One rav suggested, tongue in cheek, that the custom may have originated with a henpecked husband who was reading the Megillah in shul with his domineering wife in attendance. The verse, with the correct *sorer*, reads, "every man should rule in his own home." The meek *ba'al koreh*, fearing that his wife might hear him reading these words and respond angrily to them, quickly changed the reading to *shorer*. The verse now translates, "every man should sing in his own home."

The other three differences relate to the spelling, but not the pronunciation, of words. They are:

- 1. *V'hilbeesho* (6:9), spelled with (or without) a *yud* following the *beis*;

- 2. *U'mishloach* (9:19), spelled with (or without) a *vuv* after the *lamed*; and

- 3. *L'kayeim* (9:31), with the letter *yud* once (or twice) after the *kuf*.

Fortunately, misspellings in a Megillah do not invalidate it for use, so that these differences are not *m'akeiv*.

~§ Rav Pam's *Minchas Shai*

There were a few areas in the Torah where Rav Pam, *zt"l*, would discuss the opinions of the *Minchas Shai*. One of these was in the final verse of *Parashas Toldos* (28:9), where Esav marries a woman by the name of Machlas. There, *Minchas Shai* presents two ways to read this name.

One version, which *Minchas Shai* accepts as the primary opinion, places a *kamatz* under the first letter, the *mem*, followed by a *chataf patach*. A second opinion places a *patach* under the *mem*, followed by a *shva* under the *ches*.

Rav Pam would explain that the proper name of Esav's wife was Bosmas, as *Rashi* explains in *Bereishis* 36:3. There are two explanations of the Torah's nickname, Machlas. *Rashi* (ibid.) explains that the root of this name is related to the word *michilah*, forgiveness, and that this teaches that when a person is married, Hashem forgives his past sins, allowing him to start married life with a clean slate. Others explain that this is related to the root word *machlah*, disease, because Machlas was not a righteous woman, and her marriage to Esav caused pain and anguish to Yitzchak.

If we accept the first explanation, the *mem* would have a *kamatz*; the version that places a *patach* is following the second explanation, as the word *machlah* begins with a *patach*. (This explanation appears in *Chiddushei Maharal Diskin* to *Parashas Toldos*.)

Rav Pam would instruct the *ba'al korei* in yeshivah to read the word twice, to satisfy both opinions.

≈§ One Last Thought

Rav Yaakov Kaminetsky, *zt"l*, would say that there were areas of Jewish Tradition that were neglected in recent centuries for historical reasons. He would give, as an example, the study of Tanach and of *dikduk*, which had become the focus of the *maskilim*, the non-religious "intelligensia" of the nineteenth and early twentieth centuries. Traditional Jews, in reaction, shied away from these studies.

The *maskilim* are no more, having gone the way of all Jewish sects who reject the religious teachings of the Torah. We can safely return to a proper study of these neglected areas of our tradition.

The Mystery of the Missing Years

*E*very seven years the *Shemittah* arrives, heralded by much fanfare. The Keren HaSheviis is out in full force, raising funds to help the Israeli farmers. The laws of *Shemittah* are being reviewed.

This leads one to wonder. The *Galus* has been long. After all these years, do we still have it right? Is it really the *Shemittah* year? Of course it is! Still, it would be interesting to make the calculation, to prove that it is the *Shemittah* year. We may even find a surprise or two along the way.

৵ The Calculation

*C*alculating the *Shemittah* year seems simple enough. We simply need to calculate the precise date of the last *Shemittah* year that can be verified and add to it a recurring seven-year cycle.

The Gemara (*Taanis* 29a) teaches that the Second *Beis HaMikdash* was destroyed on a post-*Shemittah* year. This is the last *Shemittah* year that can be verified from the Gemara. But the Gemara does not tell us which year that *Shemittah* took place. How do we figure out the year that this last *Shemittah* took place?

To ascertain an accurate date, we should start at the very beginning — from the beginning of time — and calculate the years forward until that *Shemittah* year. Fortunately, the Torah provides us with information we need to be able to do so.

During *Ma'aseh Bereishis*, the first man and woman were created. Twenty generations later, Avraham Avinu was born. The Torah provides a precise accounting of these twenty generations. The chronology of the first ten generations (culminating in the birth of Noach) appears at the end of *Parashas Bereishis*. A similar listing of the next ten generations (culminating in Avraham's birth) appears at the end of *Parashas Noach*. By adding these figures, we learn that Avraham Avinu was born in the Hebrew year 1948.

This calculation is verified by *Rashi* (*Avodah Zarah* 9a), who identifies 1948 as the year of Avraham's birth.

Rashi continues the chronology: Yitzchak was born when Avraham was 100 years old. This sets his birth at 2048. *Rashi* then demonstrates that the Jews left Egypt 400 years after Yitzchak's birth. This places the year of the Exodus at 2448.

The next piece of the puzzle is provided by a verse in *Melachim Aleph* (6:1), which tells us that the first *Beis HaMikdash* was completed in the month of Iyar, 480 years after the Jews left Egypt. This brings us to the year 2928.

The first *Beis HaMikdash* was destroyed on Tisha B'Av, 410 years after it was built (*Rashi, Bava Basra* 3b). This brings us to 3338. This *Churban* was followed by a 70-year exile, which culminated in the building of the Second *Beis HaMikdash* (*Divrei HaYamim Beis* 36:21) in the year 3408. The *Churban Bayis Sheini* took place 420 years later (*Aruchin* 12b). This works out to the year 3828. Since the *Churban* took place during a post-*Shemittah* year, we may conclude that the year 3827 was that most recent verified *Shemittah* year.

We have now determined that 3827 was a *Shemittah* year, and simple arithmetic should allow us to calculate all subsequent *Shemittos*. The first post-*Churban Shemittah* took place seven years later, in 3834; the next occurred seven years later, in 3841, and so on. If we follow this formula, and add 277 cycles of *Shemittah* (or 1939 years), we will come to the year 5766 as the most recent *Shemittah* year!

This information would certainly be distressing to the thousands of farmers who observed *Shemittah* in the year 5768. Are they two years late?

A Partial Resolution, but Problems Remain

We are left with a two-year discrepancy between our calculations and the year which was observed as *Shemittah*. There is no one answer for the entire discrepancy. Let us try to deal with this one year at a time.

Rashi and *Tosafos* (*Avodah Zarah* 9a) disagree on the precise year of the second *Churban*. The Gemara teaches that the Second *Beis HaMikdash* "stood for 420 years." *Rashi* understands this to mean that the second *Beis HaMikdash* was destroyed 420 years after it was built. *Tosafos* argues that the *Beis HaMikdash* stood for 420 full years and was destroyed on Tishah B'Av of the 421st year. Our calculation followed *Rashi*, placing the year of the *Churban* exactly 420 years after the year the *Beis HaMikdash* was built, at 3828. *Tosafos* adds a year and maintains that the *Beis HaMikdash* was destroyed in 3829.

The *Tur* (*Choshen Mishpat* 67) writes, "[Regarding] the calculation of the Sabbatical year, there is a difference of opinion, according to Ri (i.e., *Tosafos*) it was in the year [50]88, according to *Rashi*, in the year [50]87."

The *Tur*'s calculations mirror those presented above. They result in the determination that *Shemittah* took place most recently in 5767 (according to *Ri*) or 5766 (according to *Rashi*).

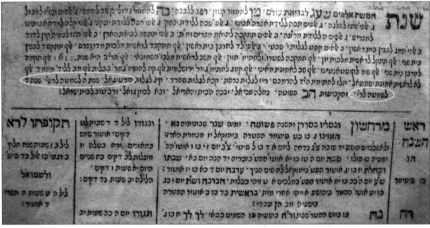

This 1612 calendar (from the recent Sotheby's Judaica Auction), lists the year as "the 5th year from Shemittah according to Rashi, the 4th year according to the Ri." This would mean that 1614–15 was a Shemittah year according to Rashi, 1615–16 according to Ri. Calculating forward, this means that 2006–07 was a Shemitta year according to Rashi; 2007–08 according to Ri.

THE MYSTERY OF THE MISSING YEARS / 365

Our practice follows *Tosafos*, establishing the year 3828 as a *Shemittah* year. This would mean that the most recent *Shemittah* was 5767. This is a bit closer, but still not consistent with our practice. We are still a year off!

Here, at least, we find that this problem is noted by Rav Moshe Isserlis. In his notes to the *Tur* (*Darkei Moshe* 3) he writes, "If so, the whole calculation [being used today] is in error, for if so, *Shemittah* should have taken place in the year 5263 and 5270...."

If we accept that our calculations are correct, we are faced with two possible resolutions of our puzzle. Either we must conclude that the calculations of the *Rishonim* listed above are off by a year, or, if they are accurate, we must conclude that this was not actually 5768. Neither resolution seems appealing.

৩৪ Solving the Mystery

The mystery can be answered only through a review of the origin of our calendar.

During the 16th century, Jews began to return to Eretz Yisrael and farm the land. The *Shemittah* calculation had somehow fallen into disuse and a disagreement erupted as to the proper year to be observed. Four different opinions were offered as to the precise year of *Shemittah*!

To resolve the problem, an inquiry was dispatched to Rav Levi Ben Chaviv (who was known by the acronym *Maharalbach*) requesting a definitive ruling. His response, printed in *Teshuvos Maharalbach* #143, deals with many facets of the *Shemittah* calculation. In part, he observes that different communities in Europe had conflicting designations of the year on their calendars. "This year, which is 5066 according to our understanding, is 5065 according to the Eastern communities."

He explains the basis for each opinion as follows:

Adam was created on Rosh Hashanah, the first day of *Tishrei*. The calculations offered above count time as beginning with Adam. This is the calculation accepted by virtually all *Rishonim* (including *Rashi*, *Tosafos*, and the *Tur* mentioned above); this is called *Cheshbon Adam*, the calculation [that begins from] Adam.

One can argue, however, that this is not accurate. Since the creation of man took place on the sixth day of Creation, the first five days of Creation actually fell during *Elul* of the previous year!

The Talmud (*Rosh Hashanah* 2b) teaches that "[even] one day of a year is reckoned as a year." These five days would thus be counted as the first year of Creation. Thus, one could argue that Adam was created at the beginning of Year Two. This adds one year to all our calculations. For example, the calculation of twenty generations leading to Avraham's birth (which adds up to 1948) would bring us to the year 1949. All the other calculations would also be advanced by a year.

This would lead us to conclude that the *Churban Bayis Sheini* took place in the year 3830. This places *Shemittah* at 5768! This is known as "*Cheshbon Tohu* — calculations [that begin from] emptiness," i.e., from the days prior to Adam's creation.

Drishah (to C.M. 67) quotes this letter in resolving the question of Rav Moshe Isserlis regarding our calculation. The *Tur* and *Beis Yosef* based their *Shemittah* projections on *Cheshbon Adam*. Like most other *Rishonim*, they would consider this year to be 5767. We, who count the years according to the custom of the "cities of the west," count from *Cheshbon Tohu,* and consider this to be 5768. Either way, we are precisely 1938 years from the *Churban Bayis Sheini* (according to the accepted opinion of *Tosafos,* cited above).

⋄§ Resolving the Problem

All our calendars place this year as 5768. The calendars also agree that this is a *Shemittah* year. This means that we are now 1938 years after the *Churban* (or 1938 years after the last pre-*Churbam Shemittah*). Our calendars, therefore, assume that the *Churban* took place in the year 3830 (5768 minus 1938 = 3830). We are following the custom of the communities of Western Europe (quoted by *Maharalbach*), who calculated the calendar based on *Cheshbon Tohu*. As we have seen, this calculation places the *Churban Bayis Sheini* at 3830.

In short: This year (whichever it is) is indeed the *Shemittah* year. However, it is not clear that this is truly 5768!

Most *Rishonim* seem to concur with the calculation of *Cheshbon Adam*. According to them, this is actually 5767.[1]

---

1. The common reference to the year of Avraham's birth as 1948 is based on *Cheshbon Adam*. Thus, a teacher who uses this (accepted) date and at the same time refers to this year as 5768 is being inconsistent!

~§ 5767 or 5768?

*D*oes it really matter if this year is 5767 or 5768? If we would agree that we are presently 1938 years after the *Churban*, does the labeling of the year have any halachic significance?

Maharalbach (in the response cited above) suggests that there is no halachic difference how a year is labeled. It is for this reason that he tolerates the different practices of his day, as the eastern communities counted from *Cheshbon Adam*, while the western communities counted according to *Cheshbon Tohu*. It would be interesting to know how the difference in the calendars was ever worked out. If European communities had different customs in the early 16th century,[2] what happened after that time that caused all Jews to agree to count by *Cheshbon Tohu*?

In a letter printed in *Avkas Rochel* (and quoted by *Birkei Yosef* in Y.D. 330:137), Rav Yosef Karo alludes to the confusion surrounding the precise timing of *Shemittah*. He mentions a specific agreement of "all of the scholars, some forty or fifty years ago" to set halachic policy by defining a precise *Shemittah* calculation, and urges that that policy be honored. One may theorize that such an assembly would also have set policy regarding the proper calendar designation of the year.

~§ Dating a *Kesubah*

*W*hen a couple is married, the husband gives his wife a *kesubah,* a contract, which must be dated accurately. Although a post-dated *kesubah* is valid, it takes effect only from the date inscribed on the *kesubah*. The day, month, and year must therefore be filled in properly.

The standard form of the *kesubah* contains the following language: "On the ___ day of the ___ month in the year ___ according to the count that we calculate here in the city of ___, etc." This language is puzzling. It would seem simple enough to fill in a date. Why add the explanation, "according to the count that we calculate here ...."? It is almost as if we are acknowledging that our calculations may be incorrect!

---

2. *Baal Hamaor* (*Avoda Zara* 9a) alludes to differing customs as early as the Geonic Period.

And indeed they may be. As we have seen, many *Rishonim* would not agree that this is the year 5768. We therefore play it safe in our *kesubos* and state clearly that the contract is meant to take effect in 5768 "according to the count that we calculate here." This would make the *kesubah* valid according to all opinions, since the date, as described, is unquestionably accurate.

The Gemara has an expression, *Teiku*, which is an acronym for "*Tishbi* [i.e., Eliyahu HaNavi] will answer unresolved problems." This will occur when Eliyahu will proclaim the advent of *Mashiach*. Among the questions to be answered then will be the exact count of that year.

Prayer Problems

It was the summer of '95 and I had undergone surgery on my leg. I knew that the next morning I would wake up in a hospital bed, unable to get out to join a minyan. I resolved to do the next best thing; and I set my alarm clock to wake up in time to daven *k'vasikin*, at sunrise.

There I was, early the following morning, exhausted from the experience of the previous day, davening flat on my back. I'm ashamed to admit it, but I must have drifted off in middle of reciting *Shemoneh Esrei*. I awoke a few moments later. I found myself unsure of what to do. What point in *Shemoneh Esrei* had I reached? How do I continue?

There was only one thing to do. I picked up the phone and called my Rebbe, Rav Avrohom Pam, *zt"l* (who woke up early to learn, every day).

"Rebbe, I'm in middle of *Shemoneh Esrei* and I need your advice ...."

*C*hayei Adam (24:21) discusses my *shailah*: the case of an individual who is in middle of *Shemoneh Esrei* but cannot determine at which *berachah* he is holding. He may be sure that he said the first *berachos* and sure that he hasn't said the final *berachos*, but is unsure at which point in the middle he lost his place. What should he do? At which point should he resume his prayers?

The *Chayei Adam* applies the well-known principle of *safek berochos l'hakel* — in case of doubt, a *berachah* is not recited. He therefore reasons that the individual who is in doubt should not recite any *berachah* that he may already have said. *Chayei Adam* therefore rules that he may continue only from a *berachah* that he is certain he has not recited. If he is in doubt regarding any *berachah*, he may not recite it, because he would be risking a *berachah l'vatalah*, a wasted *berachah*.

The Steipler Gaon, in his *Kehilas Yaakov* (*Berachos* #17), challenges this ruling. Indeed, our primary concern should be to avoid the risk of a *berachah l'vatalah*. However, there is a factor that the *Chayei Adam* has failed to take into account, as follows.

If a person misses any one of the *berachos* of *Shemoneh Esrei*, he has not satisfied his prayer obligations (*berachos m'akvos zu es zu*) and must repeat the entire *Shemoneh Esrei*. It would therefore seem to be most important to ensure that every single *berachah* is said, thus avoiding the possibility that there is a missing *berachah*, which would render all the remaining eighteen *berachos* as *berachos l'vatalah*. It would therefore follow that the person should recite every *berachah* that he *may* have missed. Although this risks an individual *berachah l'vatalah,* it avoids the greater risk of invalidating the entire prayer!

And now, we return to my situation in the hospital bed. I was familiar with the disagreement between the *Chayei Adam* and the Steipler. Still, I had not thought that I would need to decide which opinion to follow. I certainly hadn't ever imagined that this would happen to me!

What should I do? Do I follow the ruling of the *Chayei Adam*, who certainly surpasses the Steipler Gaon in his authority as a *posek*? Or should I take into account the seemingly correct argument of the Steipler Gaon, and recite the *berachos* that are in doubt?

Rav Pam, zt"l, responded (as best I can recall), "If one follows the opinion of the *Chayei Adam*, he is certainly okay."

This is the advice that I followed. Later, when I returned home, I resolved to attempt to find an answer to the question of the Steipler.

◆§ A Second "Steipler's Question"

*I*n another section of *Kehilas Yaakov* (*Berachos* #27; this issue also appears in *Beur Halachah* 101), the Steipler deals with another issue regarding *Shemoneh Esrei*.

A primary aspect of *Shemoneh Esrei* is the person's obligation to concentrate on the words he is saying. *Rambam* (based on *Berachos* 34b) rules that there is a minimum absolute requirement of concentration; if a person failed to concentrate on the words of the first *berachah*, the entire *Shemoneh Esrei* must be repeated.

The *Tur* (O.C. 101) rules that, as a practical matter, this should not be followed. This is not because the *Tur* disagrees with the fundamental ruling of the *Rambam*. Rather, it is because of our weakness in concentrating on our prayers. The *Tur* reasons that, in all likelihood, the second *Shemoneh Esrei* will also be said without proper concentration at the first *berachah*. Since the second *Shemoneh Esrei* is not likely to be any better than the first, there is no point in repeating the prayer. All subsequent *poskim* follow this ruling.

The Steipler accepts the ruling of the *Tur*. However, he points out that this presents a difficulty. It may happen that a person is in middle of *Shemoneh Esrei* and realizes that he has failed to concentrate during the first *berachah*. He would not repeat his prayer. Still, how can he complete the improper *Shemoneh Esrei* in which he is standing? This *Shemoneh Esrei* is a wasted one, as he has failed the minimum requirement of concentration. Aren't the remaining *berachos* thus wasted ones? Shouldn't he just sit down and hope for a better *Shemoneh Esrei* the next time around?

The Steipler struggles with this question and leaves it without resolution.

To deal with these issues, let us step back and seek a more complete understanding of the mitzvah to pray.

◆§ Why Pray?

*F*or most people, prayer is an opportunity to ask *HaKadosh Baruch Hu* for the things we need. We call this *bakashas tzrochim*, asking for the things we need.

There is another dimension to prayer.[1] When a person prays to

---

1. This concept is found in numerous earlier sources, including *Sefer HaIkrim* (4:16), *Akeidah* (#58), and *Maharal* (*Nesiv Avodah* 3). This is also discussed in many

Hashem, he recognizes that *HaKadosh Baruch Hu* is the source of all blessing. This recognition is fundamental to our faith in God as an active Ruler of the universe. The more we pray, the more we incorporate this belief into our psyche. We call this "*avodah*, service of God." This is a second aspect to our prayers, viewed by some as the most important purpose of our daily *Shemoneh Esrei*.

As we study prayer, we will find many clues to these two aspects of prayer.

The Gemara teaches that the three daily prayers are modeled after the prayers of our three *Avos*; "*Tefillah avos tiknum*."

We are also told that the three prayers are modeled after the three daily parts of our service in the *Beis HaMikdash*; "*Neged timidim tiknum*." Although the Gemara appears to bring these as two competing views, the *Rambam* accepts them both.

In fact, each of these models of prayer represents one of the two dimensions of prayer. *Avos tiknum* refers to the requests of our *Avos*; the *bakoshas tzrochim* part of prayer. The prayers of our *Avos*, as presented in the Torah, were requests in times of need. *Neged timidim tiknum* is clearly a reference to the *avodah* aspect.

The *Rambam* (*Sefer HaMitzvos*, #5) brings the Biblical verse (*Devarim* 11:13) that serves as a source for our prayer obligation, as "*l'avdo b'chol levavchem* — to serve Him with all your heart." Which service is based in the heart of man? This is prayer.

The *Rambam* (in his notes to *Sefer HaMitzvos*) offers a different source, from *Bamidbar* 10:9. "*V'Chi savo'ui milchamah b'artzichem ... u'sikatem bachatzotzros* — and when you go to wage war in your land against an enemy who oppresses you, you shall blow your trumpets [as a call to prayer]."

Here again, we have two verses that mirror the two aspects of prayer. "To serve Him with all your heart" is a clear reference to the *avodah* aspect. "When you go to wage war ..." clearly refers to *bakoshas tzrochim*.

Chassidic *seforim*, including *Degel Machneh Efraim* (*Parshas Eikev*), *Ben Poras Yosef* (on *Tefillah*), and *Maor V'Shemesh* (*Parshas Ki Savo*). *Igros Moshe* (O.C. 2), in a ruling regarding prayer in the public schools, presents the non-Jew's obligation to pray as part of his mitzvah of *emunah* (faith in Hashem).

❧ Why Pray for Everything?

*T*here are basic differences between these two reasons for prayer. If *bakoshas tzrochim* were the sole purpose of prayer, it would hardly make sense to *require* that a person ask for everything. A person should be permitted to choose those *berachos* that contain the requests he wishes to pray for on any given day.

Yet, the middle *berachos* of *Shemoneh Esrei* contain requests for virtually all of a person's needs. The *poskim* rule that if a person misses any one of these *berachos*, he has not satisfied his prayer obligations (*berachos m'akvos zu es zu*). Why should this invalidate the entire prayer?

If prayer were solely a request to Hashem, *bakoshas tzrochim*, it is difficult to see why we are required to ask for everything. However, the second aspect, the *avodah* part, uses prayer to reinforce our faith, requiring us to recognize Hashem's control over those things we ask for. Thus, we can understand that the requirement should cover every aspect of our lives. This explains why we pray for everything; to strengthen the *avodah* in all aspects of our lives.

In fact, in *Divrei Yoel* (*Bereishis*, p. 67), the Satmar Rebbe teaches that during the time that the *Beis HaMikdash* stood, a person was *not* required to mention all the *berachos* of *Shemoneh Esrei*. At that time, the *avodah* was in the *Beis HaMikdash*. This left only the *bakoshas tzrochim* aspect of prayer, which does not require that every *berachah* be mentioned.

This enables us to understand the Gemara's statement that the order of the middle *berachos* (which had originally been formulated by the *Anshei Knesses Hagedolah*, centuries earlier) was forgotten and had to be reformulated after the *Churban*. It seems difficult to understand how the *Shemoneh Esrei* prayer could be forgotten. Jews pray every day. How could the formula for prayer be forgotten by an entire nation?!

The Satmar Rebbe explains that the order *was* forgotten because it was not used during the time that the *Beis HaMikdash* stood.

~§ A Deeper Look

*T*his insight enables us to answer the Steipler's difficulty with the ruling of the *Chayei Adam*.

If a person finds that his mind has strayed during his prayers, to the point that he does not recall which *berachah* he has recited, how should he continue?

Chayei Adam had ruled that he may continue only from a *berachah* that he is certain that he has not recited. If he is in doubt regarding any *berachah*, he may not recite it, because he would be risking a *berachah l'vatolah*, a wasted *berachah*.

The Steipler Gaon's difficulty is based on the rule that if a person misses any one of the *berachos*, he has not satisfied his prayer obligations (*berachos m'akvos zu es zu*). He reasons that missing a single *berachah* would invalidate all the remaining eighteen *berachos*.

Given our understanding of the dual parts of prayer, the ruling of the *Chayei Adam* can be explained. It is true that if one *berachah* is missing, the individual has not satisfied his prayer requirement. As explained, this is a failure in the *avodah* aspect of prayer. Still, this does not render the rest of his *Shemoneh Esrei* wasted *berachos*. The prayer, even when missing a *berachah*, satisfies the *bakoshas tzrochim* aspect (similar to prayers during the *Beis HaMikdash* era), and are not *berachos l'vatalah*.

This would answer the second issue of the Steipler, which we presented earlier. It is true that there is a minimum amount of concentration that is an absolute requirement in *Shemoneh Esrei*. What is the source for this obligation? There are numerous other Biblical mitzvos which require declarations. These include *Bircas HaMazon*, *Vidui Ma'asros*, the prayer associated with *Bikurim*, and (according to many *Rishonim*) *Birchas HaTorah*. We do not find in a single one of these cases that a failure to concentrate invalidates the mitzvah. Why is prayer different?

Prayer is different, because of the Torah's obligation "*l'avdo bchol levavchem* — to serve Him with all your heart;" the source for the *avodah* aspect of prayer. Indeed, in the service of the *Beis HaMikdash*, we do find that the *Kohen's* failure to properly concentrate invalidates an offering.

We may therefore conclude that lack of concentration invalidates the *avodah* aspect of prayer. The *Rambam* therefore requires that the *Shemoneh Esrei* be repeated, since this aspect of prayer is missing. Still, the prayer that was said without concentration is *not* a wasted prayer! The obligation of prayer as *bakoshas tzrochim* has been fulfilled.

This explains why a person who is in midst of *Shemoneh Esrei* may continue, even if he realizes that he has failed to concentrate when saying his first *berachah*.

⋐§ This Also Explains ...

There is an additional source for this insight from the surprising ruling of the *Mishnah Berurah* (593:2), that a person who has no siddur may recite the *Shemoneh Esrei* from memory, as best he can, even if he knows he will not remember every *berachah*. This is permitted, despite the fact that he remains obligated to daven if a siddur would subsequently become available. Clearly, the *Mishnah Berurah* does not view an incomplete *Shemoneh Esrei* as a series of *berachos l'vatalah*!

There is another difficulty that is resolved based on this explanation.

The Gemara (*Berachos* 26a) teaches that if one has accidentally missed one of the daily prayers, he may compensate by adding a second *Shemoneh Esrei* to the subsequent prayer. This is true for the three daily prayers, Shacharis, Minchah, and Arvis.

Tosafos explains that one cannot compensate for a missed Mussaf prayer. This is because Mussaf is a prayer which is recited in place of the *korban mussaf* that was offered in the *Beis HaMikdash*. In regard to offerings, we have a rule that "*aver zemano, botla korbano* — if the time has passed, the opportunity is missed." Thus, one cannot compensate for a missed Mussaf prayer.

Tzlach (and others) questions this ruling. We have seen that all prayers are in place of offerings in the *Beis HaMikdash*, "*Neged timidim tiknum*." If so, the principle of "*aver zemano, botla korbano*" should apply to all prayers. Why are the three daily prayers any different than the Mussaf prayer?

Our understanding of the prayer obligation answers this question. The Mussaf prayer has only one purpose; the *avodah* aspect of prayer. Once this has been missed, no prayer obligation remains.

The other prayers are different. It is true that there can be no compensation for the *avodah* aspect of every prayer. Still, there is the added dimension to the three daily prayers, the *bakoshas tzro-*

chim part. For this, we have the rules of compensation for a missed *Shemoneh Esrei*.

⇜ Your Prayers

*G*iven this understanding of prayer, the language of *Shemoneh Esrei* takes on new meaning. In fact, if you pay attention as you pray, you will find the dual aspect of prayer in the language of many of the *berachos* of *Shemoneh Esrei*!

For example, in our prayers for healing, we start with *bakoshas tzrochim* ("Heal us ..."). Then we add, "For You are Hashem, the King, the faithful Healer ...," a statement of faith in God, the *avodah* aspect. This form of *berachah* holds true for almost every one of the middle *berachos* of *Shemoneh Esrei*.

As you follow the language of your prayer, you will find that this newfound insight gives you focus. Look for it as you daven and the prayers will take on greater meaning. You will find that the more you understand davening, the easier it will be to have *kavannah* when you pray.

Prayers may be the service of your heart, but it cannot succeed without the input of the mind. The more we understand the fundamentals of prayer, the more we apply ourselves to understanding prayer, and the more we will succeed in prayer.

Educating Children: Two Dinim

Raising a child is a challenge. It always was and always will be. We call this "chinuch," the parents' obligation to raise their child as the next link in the family chain that can be traced back to *Har Sinai*.

In a typical home, which parent is more involved in chinuch? Who spends more time training the child to make *berachos*, perform mitzvos, and behave in the manner befitting a *ben* or *bas Yisrael*? In most homes, it is the mother who is the main child-rearer, the trainer of her children.

Yet the mother's total involvement in her child is hardly reflected in Halachah. In fact, the Gemara (*Nazir* 29a) teaches, "A man is obligated to train his son in [the observance of] mitzvos, [but] a women is not obligated to train her son." This is a view taken by most *poskim*.[1]

---

[1] *Tosafos Yeshanim Yuma* 82a; *Terumas HaDeshen* 94; *Magen Avraham* 343:1; *Birkei Yoseif*, ibid.; *S.A. Harav*, ibid.; *Kaf HaChaim*, ibid.; *Matei Efraim* 616:6. See, however, *Orech Mishor, Nazir* 29a; *Aruch HaShulchan* 343:1, who take exception to this approach.

How strange! Can it be that the mother, whose talents and energies are described by *Chazal* as the mainstay of a home and who truly contributes more than anyone else to the child's physical and spiritual growth, does not bear the primary responsibility for chinuch? Can it be that she is not obligated *at all* in the chinuch of her child?

Actually the mitzvah of chinuch itself is puzzling. It is undeniably a keystone in perpetuating Jewish life and values over the generations, yet the Talmud tells us that it is only a *mitzvah d'Rabbanan* (*Chagigah* 4a). None of the *Rishonim* count chinuch as one of the 613 *mitzvos d'Oraysa*.

The teaching of Torah to one's children — in contrast to mitzvah observance — would seem to be a clear *mitzvah D'Oraysa*: "And you shall teach them to your children" (*Devarim* 11:19; see also *Ramban*, ibid.). The *Rishonim*[2] do not even count this as a mitzvah per se; instead, they view this as part of the more general mitzvah of Talmud Torah.

The unique ability of our people to persevere and grow throughout generations of exile certainly stems from our obsessive dedication to the chinuch of our children. How strange that at the Giving of the Torah at Sinai, Hashem did not specifically command us to ensure the continuity of generations!

⋯§ Defining Chinuch

*I*n attempting to attain a deeper understanding of this mitzvah, we come across two distinct explanations of chinuch. While we generally define chinuch as training, the Torah uses chinuch as a term of *has'chalah* — beginning.[3] These two definitions parallel two distinct explanations of the mitzvah of chinuch, as found in *Chazal*.

■ **Chinuch as a *has'chalah*:** Some[4] see chinuch as an early beginning of mitzvah fulfillment. Although a Jew is required to perform mitzvos beginning at age twelve (for girls) or thirteen (for boys),

---

2. *Sefer HaChinuch* 419; *Rambam, Asei* 11; *Yereim* 254; *Rav Sadya Gaon* 14. See also Rabbi Yerucham Perlow's commentary to *Rav Sadya Gaon*, Vol. 1, p. 234.

3. *Bereishis* 14:14; *Devarim* 20-25; *Rashi* in both places.

4. *Magen Avraham* 658:8; *Igros Moshe* Y.D. 137.

chinuch calls for these mitzvos to be performed at a younger age. According to this view, parental responsibility extends only to the mechanical performance of the deed.

- **Chinuch as training:** Others[5] see chinuch as the parents' obligation to make mitzvos and Torah values a part of their child's life, so that he will be accustomed, from an early age, to perform Hashem's mitzvos regularly and eagerly. Although this view certainly acknowledges mechanical mitzvah observance as basic, the emphasis is placed on attitudes and feelings. Accordingly, a parent who cannot afford to buy his son a kosher *esrog* might be fulfilling this aspect of his chinuch obligation by buying his son a flawed *esrog*[6] (providing, of course, that his son is unaware of the imperfection). Although this does not fulfill the technical requirement of the mitzvah, the father is still training his son in being accustomed to perform mitzvos, which is his basic obligation.

In short, we can refer to these two aspects of chinuch as the mitzvah observance, or *has'chalah* facet — and the Torah value, or training facet.

Involving a child in the mechanics of mitzvah observance, the *has'chalah* aspect, is not necessarily a Biblical obligation. This waits until maturity. It is the teaching of Torah-values, the training aspect, that would seem to be of utmost importance. In fact, a child is technically incapable of *kavannah* (moral intent) in the performance of individual mitzvos (and, indeed, children are not obligated to have *kavannah* in performing mitzvos[7]). Still, the general education in Torah-values is essential to his development as a Jew.

We may therefore suggest that it is only the technical part of chinuch, the *has'chalah* part, which is only a *mitzvah d'Rabbanan*. The all-important training aspect of chinuch may indeed be a *mitzvah d'Oraysa*. To establish this, we would still need to explain why chinuch (in any form) is not counted as one of the 613 mitzvos.

---

5. *Rashi, Succah* 2b; Rav Meno'ach, Commentary to *Rambam, Shvisas Asor* 2:10.

6. This is a *machlokes Rishonim*; see *Mishnah Berurah* 658:28; *Beur Halachah* 657.

7. *Turei Even* to *Chagigah* 6b.

৵§ Pouring a Foundation for Torah

*H*ashem created man with many *middos*, natural instincts. Among them are the *middos ra'os*, such as anger, haughtiness, and lust, which we are taught to stringently avoid. Yet, nowhere in the Torah are we specifically commanded to distance ourselves from these *middos ra'os*.

Rabbi Chaim Vital (quoted by Rav Elchonon Wasserman in *Kovetz Mamarim*, p. 34) explained this puzzling omission: "Proper *middos* provide the foundation for Torah. Without them, a Torah life would be unimaginable. Their acquisition, therefore, requires no specific commandment."

This observation can easily be applied to the Torah-value aspect of chinuch as well. At Sinai, Hashem did indeed give *Klal Yisrael* the responsibility to pass down the Torah for all generations. But precisely because this is so self-evident, it was not specifically commanded.

We find that Avraham Avinu influenced vast multitudes to accept monotheism, converting these people into truly righteous men. Whatever happened to these people and their descendants? Why do we find no reference to their descendants anywhere in the *mesorah*?

I once heard Rabbi Moshe Feinstein, *zt"l*, explain that, notwithstanding their personal righteousness, these men had failed to grasp the significance of chinuch. As a result, not one of their descendants perpetuated their convictions after the passing of Avraham and Sarah. Chinuch, then, is the most basic lifeline of *mesorah*, surely a Torah foundation of the type explained by Rav Chaim Vital.

This is the training aspect of chinuch.

Rabbeinu Manoach (Commentary to the *Rambam*, *Shivisas Asor* 2:10) explains that "*tri chinuchei yesh* — there are two parts to chinuch." The obligation to raise a child in the Torah way is certainly the paramount aspect of chinuch. However, there is a second aspect. The Sages of later generations added the second phase to the chinuch obligation; namely, the technical inclusion of minors in mitzvah observance, obligating the parent to make sure that the child actually performs the mitzvah, and that he does so properly. But the basic chinuch precept existed earlier.

This is the *has'chalah* aspect of chinuch.

To sum up: To satisfy the original, Biblical obligation, it would be enough to purchase a *posul esrog* for a child, if he thinks that it is a proper *esrog*. Using the *esrog* will certainly train the child to perform the mitzvah. The Rabbanan added a second phase to the chinuch obligation, requiring that the mitzvah be performed properly, with a kosher *esrog*.

⇜ The Heart

While a mother's role in chinuch is not specifically defined in the Gemara, it is alluded to (*Niddah* 31): "Three partners form a human being — Hashem, father, and mother. The father contributes the white, from which are formed the bones, sinews, nails, brain, and white of the eye. The mother contributes the red, from which are formed the skin, flesh, hair, and pupil of the eye. Hashem gives the soul, etc."

In *kabbalistic* teachings, we find that white is symbolic of purity of thought (*Maharal, Gevuros Hashem*, Ch. 28). Red and the faculty of vision are symbolic of proper action (*Alshich* and *Abarbanel* on *Shmuel Aleph* 16:12).

Reb Tzaddok HaKohen (*Dover Tzeddek* 22:1) explains this Gemara in a spiritual sense. He describes the father's contribution toward the development of his child as the *he'lem*, filling the child's mind with the proper knowledge, ideas, and plans. The knowledge itself is a "hidden" part of chinuch. Ideas exist in the depth of a person's mind. Proper actions, however, do not necessarily result from this knowledge.

The mother's contribution includes the formation of the heart — the center of a person's drives, emotions, and desires, which motivate him to act. Her task, referred to by Reb Tzaddok as the *nigleh*, is to inspire the child to transform the *he'lem* into physical action. Or, in the words of *Maharal* (*Derashos Maharal*, p. 28), "The task of a righteous woman is to prepare her offspring to accept and then apply Torah ethics and thought."

We find that a woman is likened to a garden (*Pirkei d'Rav Eliezer*, Ch. 21). A seed is planted into the earth of a garden, where it is nurtured and fed until it blossoms into a majestic tree. So, too, man contributes the seed from which a child is formed; but it is the woman whom Hashem has blessed with the anatomy capable of nurturing that seed and forming it into a human being.

✥ A Spiritual Garden

This analogy is true in the spiritual sense as well. As Rav Tzaddok explained, the father's *he'lem* role is to plant seeds of chinuch by giving his child the basic knowledge necessary for mitzvah fulfillment. To accomplish this, it would be sufficient to acquaint a child with the mechanical observance of mitzvos. The mechanical mitzvah observance of childhood, however, will not automatically guarantee that a child will continue to perform mitzvos as an adult. This is only a beginning aspect of chinuch.

The mother's role in forming a child, spiritually as well as physically, is far more complex. Hers is the training aspect that will influence the child to want to do mitzvos, to appreciate mitzvos and Torah values. Her task is to imbue him with the feelings that will inspire him to act upon his father's teachings. She is to provide him with the moral basis in which Torah and mitzvos will take root and flourish. She is primarily responsible for the training aspect of chinuch.

Later, a second aspect of chinuch was added, the *has'chalah* part. This is the obligation to make sure that the child performs mitzvos properly. When *Chazal* say that women are exempted from the mitzvah of chinuch, they are referring to this aspect of chinuch, the mechanical part. The Torah-value aspect of chinuch, however, falls under her jurisdiction. This is the chinuch role whose paramount importance can be presumed to be such an obvious Torah foundation that it is not specifically commanded.

Just as Hashem endowed woman with the anatomy necessary for the forming of a child, so too did He provide her with specific talents and abilities necessary for *chinuch habanim*. When *Chazal* (*Berachos* 48b) describe women as "*dabraniyos*"— more talkative — the intention is not to belittle them. The same applies for their observations that women are shyer,[8] more merciful,[9] emotional,[10] and less physically active[11] than men. Although these factors may seem to handicap her, in truth they are invaluable tools necessary for her life role.

---

8. *Kesubos* 67a; *Yevamos* 42a.
9. *Megillah* 14b.
10. *Lekach Tov* on *Esther*.
11. *Yerushalmi, Pesachim* 1:4.

➤ A Man's Faults; a Woman's Strengths

*A*s *Ramban (Bereishis 3:16)* points out, a woman's tendency towards shyness is a positive attribute, not a fault. Her lack of aggressiveness and physical restlessness make her less likely to thrust herself into the competitive business world for personal fulfillment. Perhaps these very tendencies enable many a mother to ignore pressing tasks and deadlines to spend unhurried, unscheduled time with her children when they need it.

"*Kol kevodah bas melech pnimah* — the princess's glory is within" refers to a woman's unique ability to find her main satisfaction within the four walls of her home. Her child, who has a keen awareness of his mother's feelings, absorbs this happiness. Because she is more emotional and expresses her feelings more openly and readily, her attitudes have a profound impact upon the development of her child.

Have you ever stopped to observe a mother putter around the house with a toddler at her heels? Listen and you will hear her non-stop commentary on the workings of a household and the mysteries of the grown-up world. Almost out of habit, she will describe each item she removes from the grocery bag, explaining its use as she puts it in its place. Now imagine a father unpacking the same bag of groceries. He will have the job done in half the time, but his child will be ignored during those few minutes. Our *nashim dabraniyos* have a natural quality that they use, almost subconsciously, to educate our children.

Indeed, the three basic qualities in which our nation prides itself — "*rachmanim, beishanim, v'gomlei chassadim*, being merciful, modest and charitable" — are all attributes in which a mother excels. Her chinuch activities cultivate these values in the hearts of our children.

➤ Don't Miss the Message

*T*oday's society is seeking to obliterate the social implications of male-female differences. "Liberation" demands that women seek to overcome what they perceive as feminine handicaps. As much as we may recognize this attitude as inimical to a Torah perspective, the values of the society around us invariably invade our own. The common perception of a housewife-mother as a maid-babysitter is diametrically opposed to *Chazal's* understanding of her role. A mother who stays home with her children should view herself as a full-time *mechaneches* — an educator of the young, not a simple babysitter.

A mother's failure to grasp the significance of her role can have a detrimental effect on her children. Aware of this, a mother who elects to go to work should make certain that her replacement, too, is a capable *mechaneches*. Parents who would shudder at the thought of sending their children to public schools nevertheless allow people with hard secular values — even non-Jews — to tend their school-age children for many hours a week. Were this mother to truly appreciate her child's needs and the ways in which she is constantly contributing to his development, she would select a babysitter with much more care. This is not to say that a babysitter must be well educated — only that she have basic, simple, Torah-oriented values. And while it may not always be possible to obtain an observant babysitter, a chinuch-conscious mother should put every effort towards attaining this ideal.

Big Bird or "Imma"?

Because many women fail to see themselves as educators of their children, they often entrust this assignment to Sesame Street-type programs. Big Bird and Captain Kangaroo might indeed have training abilities in certain areas that are superior to those of many mothers, but those areas do not constitute chinuch. Children raised on the lap of their TVs often learn to count at an early age and become conversant in many relatively worldly matters. But experience has shown that these children are often lacking in many *middos*, notably *beishanus* (sense of shame) and *yiras Shamayim* (fear of Heaven). While one may argue that educational programs can be beneficial as a supplement to chinuch, it is extremely difficult to limit such programs to a supplementary role. Children will absorb more from funny characters, bedecked in colorful costumes than from low-key, one-to-one experiences in their homes. Unpacking a bag of groceries can hardly seem exciting to a youngster accustomed to seeing Cookie Monsters and cartoon characters performing impossible feats. Professional educators perceive television as an impediment to *chinuch habanim*. If mothers saw themselves as educators, perhaps they too would feel that way. Again, the child is hurt by his mother's failure to appreciate her own importance.

HaKadosh Baruch Hu has blessed every child with a thirst for knowledge and a strong desire to imitate the grown-ups around him. These are his tools for building a proper foundation for his life. A parent-*mechanech* must supervise the use of these tools. This constant vigilance often causes inconveniences, but the rewards are great. As David HaMelech said, "Those who sow with tears shall reap with joy." Is there another harvest in life that is more important?

My Favorite Synonyms

Synonyms are words with the same meaning. The English language abounds with synonyms, as do all of the world's languages.

Lashon HaKodesh is different. This Divinely inspired language has no true synonyms. Although some words may initially appear to have identical meanings, there is always a significant difference between them (*Malbim*, Introduction to *Sefer Yeshayahu* and to *HaKarmel*).

There are many sets of words that need to be explained. Below I represent a few of them — my favorite synonyms.

⇜ *Al* / *Lo* — אל / לא

Al and *lo* both mean "no." What is the difference between these two words?

In regard to the *Korban Pesach*, we are commanded, (*Shemos* 12:9), "Do not (*al*) eat from it, when it is raw" and "Do not (*lo*) leave it [uneaten] until the morning."

The earlier commandment uses *al*, while the second uses *lo*. Are we to infer any difference between these two commandments, based on the language difference?

Another example is found in *Kedoshim* (19:4). "Do not (*al*) turn to the idols; and molten gods you shall not (*lo*) make for yourselves."

It is difficult to see any difference between the use of *al* and *lo*. These appear to be true synonyms!

Meshech Chochmah (*Shemos* 12:9) uses a story in Tanach to point out that there is indeed a difference between the words.

In *Melachim Aleph* (Ch. 3), we find the well-known incident of the two mothers, each of whom claims the living child as her own. Shlomo HaMelech "rules" that the baby be cut in half and divided between the two women.

Verse 3:26 records the protestation of the true mother. "And she said, 'I beg you my Master, give her the living child, and do not kill him!'" This verse uses the words "*al timisuhu*," "do not kill him."

The verse that follows, 3:27, records the response of Shlomo HaMelech. "The King responded. He said, "Give her the living child and do not kill him, for she is the mother." This verse uses the words "*lo timisuhu*," "do not kill him."

The difference is in the power of the "no" command. Wherever it is an absolute command, coming from a position of authority, the stronger word, *lo*, is used. Where it is a request, a plea that action not be done, the weaker word, *al*, is used.

Thus the mother who is begging for the child's life uses the word *al*. The king, who is commanding that the child's life be spared, uses the stronger word, *lo*.

This also explains the use of the word "please" (*na*), in the phrase, "please do not." The term used with "please" is *always* the word *al*, never the word *lo*.[1] This is understandable, given that the *na* request indicates some aspect of weakness on the part of the person making the request. The weaker form, *al*, is therefore appropriate.

We know that the punishment for violating the negative commandments of the Torah is *malkos*, lashes. The Gemara takes for granted that this applies to those commandments which appear using the word *lo*. The Gemara (*Eiruvin*, end of first *perek*), expresses uncertainty regarding those commandments that appear with the command *al*. The Gemara concludes that the *malkos* punishment applies in both cases. However, the initial uncertainty begs explanation.

---

1. As in "*Al na tehi k'mais*" (*Bamidbar* 12:12), "*Al na sa'vor mai'al avdecha*" (*Bereishis* 18:3), "*Al na yichar*" (*Bereishis* 18:31), and "*Al tasteer panecha mimeni*" (*Tehillim* 102:3).

If the words were synonymous, this would be difficult to explain. However, given our understanding that they are not synonymous, the difference becomes clear. The word *al* denotes a softer expression of request, which is why the Gemara speculates that the punishment is not as severe as when commandments are expressed as *lo*.

A question remains. There are some commandments that appear with the word *al*. Given that these are absolute God-given commandments, the choice of the softer *al* is puzzling.

Let us examine the two examples with which we began.

In regard to the *Korban Pesach*, we are commanded, "Do not (*al*) eat from it when it is raw" and "Do not (*lo*) leave it [uneaten] until the morning" (*Shemos* 12:9).

This commandment was given in Egypt, regarding the night of *Makkas Bechoros*. The first commandment, regarding the eating of the Korban Pesach, refers to the first half of the night, before the firstborn Egyptians died. At that point, the Jewish People had still not been redeemed from the bondage in Egypt. They obeyed the laws of the Torah as an expression of faith. At this point, the Jewish People had not yet been separated from their Egyptian hosts and the commandments were still only requests, using the word *al*.

After the firstborn Egyptians had died and the Jews were released from their bondage, they became God's people. Now they had a strict obligation to obey God's command. The second half of the verse is a commandment regarding the second half of the night and therefore appears using the more powerful term, *lo*.

The second example cited is found in *Kedoshim* 19:4. We are commanded, "Do not (*al*) turn to the idols; and molten gods you shall not (*lo*) make for yourselves."

Meshech Chochmah explains that absolute commandments are only possible in cases that the commandment pertains to an action. Where the commandment pertains to thought, the commandment is less absolute (in that man cannot absolutely control his thoughts) and the word *al* appears.

We also find this later, in *Parashas Kedoshim* (19:31), "Do not (*al*) turn to the sorcery of the *Ovos* and *Yidonim*." This, too, is a thought-based commandment, and *al* is therefore appropriate.

Similar explanations are in order wherever the *al* word appears without apparent justification.[2]

---

2. "Do not (*al*) drink wine or intoxicating beverages" (*Vayikra* 10:9). Here the drinking itself is not a prohibition. It is the act that follows while one is intoxicated that is prohibited. Thus, the prohibition on drinking cannot be expressed in absolute terms.

~§ Simlah / Salmah —
שִׂמְלָה / שַׂלְמָה

*S*imlah and *salmah* certainly appear to be synonymous. The words are almost identical, except for the position of two letters.

Ben Yehoyada (to *Shabbos* 113b) explains the difference between the words. *Simlah* denotes significant or expensive items of clothing, while *salmah* refers to simple or inexpensive items.

When the Jewish People left Egypt, they first "borrowed" items from the Egyptians. These are described as, "gold utensils, silver utensils and *s'malos*." All are items of significant value.

On the other hand, in presenting the obligations of a *shomer*, a guardian, to protect another person's items, reference is made to "*salmah*" (*Shemos* 22:8). This is to demonstrate that the obligation to safeguard items placed in a person's care extends to inexpensive items, as well.

In *Megillas Rus* (3:3), we find that Rus was instructed to wear "*samlosecha*" for her encounter with Boaz. The Gemara (*Shabbos* 113b) explains that this refers to her Shabbos clothing, which she wore for this occasion. Where did the Gemara see that reference here is to Shabbos clothing?

Ben Yehoyada points out that it is the choice of the word *simla*, which indicates that this refers to the finest clothing that Rus owned, her Shabbos clothing.

Pardes Yosef (*Vayeitzei* 28:4) makes the same observation, citing the Targum for *salmah*, which is *kesuso* (*Shemos* 22:25), indicating an ordinary item of clothing. In the very next verse, the Targum for *simlah* is *tosvei* (*Shemos* 22:26), indicating a significant item of clothing.

Pardes Yosef to *Mishpatim* offers additional examples of this distinction.[3]

---

3. *Tosafos Berachah* (to *Bereishis* 28:4) also refers to *simlah* as a significant item of clothing. However, he contrasts this with *beged*, which refers to a simple item.

[*Beged* often refers to clothing that is worn to project an image. Thus, the word is related to *ba gad*, an expression of rebelliousness, as garments are sometimes worn in a manner that conveys an image of rebelliousness. *K'sus* refers to clothing that is worn as a covering, without paying particular attention to the image it conveys. Thus, the word is related to *kisui*, covering.]

◆§ Kesev / Keves — כבש / כשב

The Hebrew word for sheep is *keves* (*kof-veis-sin*). Occasionally, this appears in the Torah with the letters inverted, as *kesev* (*kof-sin-veis*). In all cases, this refers to a sheep. It would therefore appear that they are synonyms.

Are these two different words, with different meanings?

Meshech Chochmah (*Parshas Vayikra* 5:6) explains that both words refer to sheep, but in two different stages of life.

A sheep usually cannot become pregnant during its first year. A sheep, at this stage, in its first year of life, is called a *keves*.

This name is similar to the word *kevesh*, suppressed, as in *Michah* 7:19, "*yichvosh avonoseinu* — suppress our sins." The word *keves* denotes that the reproductive powers of the sheep are suppressed, dormant, during this first year.

The general term for sheep, when referring to sheep of any age, is *kesev*.

When the Torah refers to the *chatos* offerings, which must be brought using sheep within their first year, the Torah labels them as *kivasim bnei shanah,* sheep in their first year. The *keves* form is used.

Olah and *shelamim* offerings, on the other hand, have no such restriction. These offerings may be from sheep, older than one year. In twelve of the thirteen places that the word *kesev* is used, reference is to one of these offerings, which are not restricted to first-year sheep.

The thirteenth place is during the episode involving Yaakov and the sheep of *Lavan* (in *Parshas Vayeitzei*), where the discussion involves pregnant sheep, and the form *kesev* is used exclusively.[4]

This is more than a simple word lesson. The fact that first-year sheep are used for *chatos* offerings is related to the *keves* identity of this animal, which has a name that relates to *Michah's* "*yichvosh avonoseinu.*" This is the function of the *chatos*: to bring forgiveness for specific sins.

---

4. There is one exception to this rule, as explained by *Meshech Chochmah.*

◈§ Metzitzah / Mitzah — מציצה / מיצה

An interesting set of synonyms relates to the controversy regarding *metzitzah*, the suctioning of blood from the *milah* wound.

The word *mitz* is well known in Modern Hebrew as the word for juice. Thus, *mitz tapuzim* is orange juice; *mitz tapuchim* is apple juice. The root of the word is related to the Hebrew word for squeezing, as in "*v'nimtzah domo al keer hamizbayach* — and [the *Kohen*] shall squeeze the blood onto the wall of the Altar."

If this word is related to the word *metzitzah*, the removal of the blood from the *milah* wound, it would indicate that squeezing is adequate for removal of the blood and that suction is not required. Are these two different words?

Binyan Zion (1:23-24) writes, "The root *mem-tzadik* is found in three forms ... recently, *dikduk* experts have understood them to be synonymous. However, after careful examination, I have come to the conclusion that there is a significant difference between them. This is all part of the beauty of our Holy Tongue [that each nuance of spelling is significant]. The root *mitz* refers to something removed by pressing or squeezing, as in *mitz chalav* (*Mishlei* 30)... the root *matzatz* refers to removal by suction, (as in *Yashayahu* 66:11)...the root *matzah* refers to both ...."

This interpretation leads *Binyan Zion* to conclude that the *metzitzah* procedure must be performed by suction. The *Chasam Sofer* had permitted this to be done by pressing on the wound to remove the blood. He based this ruling on the use of the root word in various verses referring to removal by squeezing. *Binyan Zion* disagrees. He contends that whenever this word is spelled using the letter *tzaddik* twice, it refers exclusively to removal by suction.

"If he [the *Chasam Sofer*] were still alive, I would sit on the ground before him and ask him to show me a single place in *Mikra*, *Mishnah,* or Gemara, where *metzitzah* is used for anything other than suction."

~§ Geshem / Mattar — מטר / גשם

Geshem and *mattar* are both translated as "rain." What is the difference between these words? Are they synonyms?

The difference between the two terms is particularly striking when we examine the language used in the *Shemone Esrei* prayer.

During the winter months, we add a reference to rain in two sections of the prayer. In the second *berachah*, we praise God as the Giver of rain, saying, "*Mashiv haruach u'morid hageshem* — He makes the wind blow and brings down the rain." We use the word *geshem*.

Later, in the ninth *berachah*, we ask God to give us rain, saying, "*V'sein tal u'mattar* — Give dew and rain." Here we use the word *mattar*. Why do we change from one expression to the other?

Rav Shlomo, the *dayan* of Vilna (in his notes to the beginning of *Masechas Ta'anis*) explains that the words are not synonymous. Both refer to rain, but in different ways. *Mattar* refers to blessed rains, which cause the crops to grow and bring sustenance to the world. The term *geshem* is a general term that includes all forms of rain.

Thus, in the ninth *berachah*, in which we ask that the crops be blessed with rain, we use the term *mattar*, blessed rain.

In the second *berachah*, we describe *gevuros Hashem*, God's exhibition of might in our world. There, we refer to all rains. The stormy turbulent rains of destruction, of typhoons and hurricanes, are certainly included as a most visible aspect of God's might in our world. The word *geshem* is therefore most appropriate.

On Shemini Atzeres, we begin the winter season with the Prayer for Rain. Here, we begin to say, "*Mashiv haruach u'mored hageshem*."

This prayer ends with the request, "For You are Hashem, our God, Who makes the wind blow and brings down the *geshem*, for blessing and not for curse, for life and not for death, for plenty and not for scarcity."

Rav Shlomo gives us a new appreciation of this prayer. Having used the term *geshem* in describing Hashem's might, we follow with a prayer that the only form of *geshem* we ever hope to experience is the rain that is "for life and not for death ...."

This also explains why the reference to *mattar* is phrased "... *v'sein tal u'mattar* — and give dew and rain." "Give" denotes giving something desirable. The second *berachah* is phrased "*morid hageshem* — brings down the rain," without the expression of giving.

We may add that this also explains why the request for *mattar* in the ninth *berachah* includes reference to *tal* (*v'sein tal u'mattar*), while the second *berachah* does not mention dew as well as rain.

In the request for *mattar* we mention dew, because it also serves to help the crops grow. In reference to *geshem*, however, *tal* has no place, as it is hardly an exhibition of Godly might. We therefore refer exclusively to rain.[5]

◈ Ess / Eis — אֶת / אֵת

The most common word in the Torah, spelled *aleph-sof*, appears with two types of vowelization. Most often a *segol* is used, and the word is read *ess*. Occasionally, the *tzeirei* vowelization appears, so that the word is read *eis*.

These are *not* two different words. The difference in vowelization is based on a rule of *dikduk*.

All single-syllable words receive accent marks, as evidenced by the *trop* on the word. When the word is linked to the word that follows, the primary accent mark of the two-word set is always on the second word. In this case, the vowel on the single syllable word changes and becomes a *tenuah ketanah*, a minor vowel.[6]

For the same reason, this is also true of other single-syllable words that appear two ways. This includes words such as *kol* and *chok* (both words appear two ways, either with a *kamatz katan* or with a *cholom*: קָל–כָּל; חֹק–חָק, or *ben* and *bein* בֵּן–בֶּן.)

These changes are purely grammatical and have no bearing on the meaning of the word. *Darshonim* who ascribe differences in meaning between them are therefore in error.

---

5. There appears to be an exception to this rule. In the curses of the *Tochachah*, we read, "Hashem will make the *mattar* of your land [bring up] dust and dirt" (*Devarim* 28:24). *Mattar*, here, is *not* a blessed rain. Why is the word *mattar* used?

Rav Shlomo explains that, on the contrary, this is precisely the meaning of this verse. If the Jewish People fail to fulfill Hashem's commandments, the *mattar*, blessed rain, will turn into a rain that brings undesirable dust and dirt onto the earth.

6. The reason for this is explained in our section on *dikduk*.

~§ Af / Gam — אף / גם

There are two Hebrew words for "also." The Torah sometimes uses the word *af* and sometimes uses the word *gam*. What is the difference between these two synonyms?

Pardes Yosef (*Vayikra* 26:16), based on the *Malbim*, explains this beautifully. The word *gam* is used when we are discussing two equal things. For example, "And *Tzeelah* also (*gam*) gave birth ..." (*Bereishis* 4:22) or "And also (*gam*), on that night, they gave their father wine to drink" (*Bereishis* 19:35).

The word *af* is used when the second item is more significant (or more surprising) than the first. (This is similar to the common use of the English word *even*.) For example, (*Vayikra* 26:42) "And I will remember My covenant with Yaakov and also (*af*) My covenant with Yitzchak, and also (*af*) My covenant with Avraham, I will remember." Malbim explains that the covenant with Yaakov, regarding his descendants, was obviously intended to apply to the Jewish People. Yaakov had no non-Jewish descendants. Yitzchak, however, had Esav's non-Jewish progeny, so that the application of Yitzchak's covenant is a greater kindness. Avraham had many more descendants (Yishmael's offspring, as well as the children of Kiturah), and the application of his covenant to the Jewish People is an even greater kindness.

This is also true of the use of the words *af* and *gam* in the Gemara. "Even (*af*) Daniel was only answered in the merit of Avraham" (*Berachos* 7b), or "Even (*af*) Hashem does not render judgment alone" (*Sanhedrin* 18a).

This explanation hints at a fantastic insight into human nature. The word *af* is also used in Tanach to denote anger. This would appear to have no connection to the "also" meaning of the word.

In truth, though, it has a profound connection. Anger and disappointment are related to a human being's expectations in life. If a person expects that there will be difficulties in a particular project, those disappointments neither anger nor frustrate him. On the contrary, he is prepared to roll up his sleeves and overcome the difficulties.

Anger is the result of unrealistic expectations. Difficulties become more significant (or more surprising) than they truly are. A person with unrealistic expectations is easily disappointed and quick to anger. To him, each additional difficulty is an *af*, a surprise. Life has a way of throwing surprises at a person; to this person, each is an *af*, a difficult burden, which leads to anger.

A wise man, however, says, "*Gam zu l'tovah*," "This, too, is for the best." To him the difficulty is a *gam*, an additional challenge in life, to be dealt with patiently and with a smile.

◆§ Melech / Mosheil — מלך / מושל

The difference between these two synonyms, as explained by the Vilna Gaon, is well known in the yeshivah world. *Melech* and *mosheil* both denote a king or ruler. The Gaon (in *Mishlei* 27) explains that a *melech* is someone who rules willing subjects. A *mosheil* is someone who rules with force, because the subjects are unwilling to subject themselves to his rule. We therefore find that Hashem is described as a *melech* over the Jewish People, but a *mosheil* over others ("*Ki la'Hashem ha'miluchah u'mosheil bagoyim*"). The description of the Messianic Era, however, describes Hashem as *melech* over all ("*V'hayah Hashem l'melech al kol ha'aretz*").[7]

We may offer an insight based on this. The Gemara (*Beitza* 32b) describes situations in which a person's life can become unbearable, "not really a life." These examples include an individual who is overcome with pain, God forbid. The Gemara's expression for this describes his pain as a *mosheil* over him ("*Mi she'yesurin moshlin b'gufo*").

By applying the insight of the Gaon, we may understand that a person's attitude to his pain or difficulty will control his appreciation of life. If a person can appreciate that the pain is purposeful, Hashem's *yisurin shel ahavah*, he will be able to accept his lot. This is a lofty level, indeed. To him, the pain is not a *mosheil*; his life is well worth living, for he senses purpose in all that transpires.

The Gemara is referring to the typical, simpler individual who has not risen to the occasion, who fails to see purpose in his suffering. He is angered by his pain and cannot appreciate his purpose. He is the unwilling subject of his suffering, one whose life is described as "not really a life."

The Gemara mentions another unbearable situation, one who has a wife who rules over him, and uses the term *mosheil* to describe the wife ("*Mi she'ishto mosheles alav*"). Here, the insight would point to the fact that the husband under discussion is unable to accom-

---

7. See also *Pachad Yitzchak* to *Succos* #128 in explanation of this *Gra*.

modate his wife's life needs and still maintain a normal husband-wife relationship. He seeks to guide his family by force, and his wife pushes back, compelling him to follow her lead. She rules over him, against his will, as a *mosheles*, dragging him to follow her lifestyle. The wise husband learns to retain the relationship, even as he makes his wife happy by agreeing to her needs, all the while patiently guiding the family to follow a Torah lifestyle.

"After all," he reasons, "if I'm going to do it anyway, I may as well smile about it!"

✑ Hod / Hadar — הוד / הדר

Hod and *hadar* are usually translated as "glory and majesty." These two words often appear together and seem to have the same meaning. Are they true synonyms?

Malbim (*Vayikra* 19:25 and *Tehillim* 104:1) explains that *hadar* is used to describe external beauty and majesty. The Torah therefore refers to the *esrog* using the term *hadar*, for it is a fruit with external beauty. *Hod* refers to internal majesty, a beauty that is a defining characteristic of that which is being described. Therefore, when Moshe was commanded to share his greatness with his disciple, Yehoshua, the term *hod* is used, "*v'nassata mai'hodcha alav*" (*Bamidbar* 28:20).

This explains why the twin attributes *hod* and *hadar* are not mentioned in regard to people. They appear often, however, always in reference to Hashem (*Tehillim* 21:6, 96:6, 104:1, 111:3 and 145:5 and *Iyov* 40:10).

This explanation clarifies a part of the siddur. The poem, *Ha'aderes v'ha'emunah l'Chai Olamim*, is part of the Shabbos davening (for *nusach* Sefard) and part of the *machzor* (for everyone). In *Ohr Gedalyahu* (*Moadim*, p. 141), the depth of this poem is explained. Each line of the poem mentions two attributes of Hashem. In human beings, each attribute is not fully compatible with the second attribute with which it is paired. We praise Hashem by declaring that, in Him, both attributes coexist fully and in harmony.

Regarding some lines of this poem, this can be easily explained. For example, the fourth line pairs "wisdom and speech." Generally, we understand that silence is a greater indicator of wisdom than speech. *Siyag l'chachmah shtikah*, the gate of wisdom is silence.

These attributes are therefore not fully compatible. "Kingship and dominion" (the thirteenth line), too, are not compatible. The Hebrew words used are related to *melech* and *mosheil*, which, as explained above, refer to rulership by the will of the people (*melech*) and against their will (*mosheil*), respectively. "Beauty and eternity" (the fourteenth line) generally do not go together. As things age, they tend to lose their beauty. "Might and modesty" (the sixteenth line), too, do not usually go together. "Desire and righteousness" (the eighteenth line) are certainly incompatible in humans.

The incompatibility of *hod* and *hadar*, glory and majesty, seem to present a difficulty. The *Malbim's* explanation resolves this. Humans who focus on external beauty will always sacrifice *p'nimius*, internal majesty. A person who focuses on achieving internal majesty will neglect external beauty. These attributes are not fully compatible.

In Aramaic, the word *hadar* has an additional meaning, "to turn back; to change direction,"[8] as in the Talmudic expression (*Bava Basra* 130b) "*hadarna bi* — I shall change my mind." Elsewhere, (*Sanhedrin* 107b) we find that Rav Yehoshua ben Perachya implores Yeshu, "*Hadar bach* — Repent!"

Aramaic words are generally related to their Hebrew counterparts. We would be stymied in an attempt to discern the relationship between *majesty* (the Hebrew *hadar*) and *turning back* (the Aramaic *hadar*).

Malbim makes it simple. The transience of physical beauty is a basic teaching of Jewish ethics. We are all familiar with Shlomo HaMelech's teaching, "Grace is false and beauty is vain," (*Mishlei* 31:30). Thus, the relationship between an expression used to describe external beauty and an expression describing the concept of turning back or changing direction is a profound one.

∾§ *Vayomer / Vayedaber* —
ויאמר / וידבר

This is perhaps the most common set of apparent synonyms in the Torah. The root word *amar* is normally translated *said*, while *deebeir* is translated *spoke*. The difference between "he said" and "he spoke" would appear to be minimal (at most).

---

8. This is probably based on *Daniel* 4:24.

A well-known explanation of these words is that *amar* denotes gentle speech, while *deebeir* denotes harsh speech.[9] As we shall see, numerous commentators point out that this is not really accurate.

Rashi, in numerous places,[10] explains that *deebeir* denotes harshness. The commentators on *Rashi*,[11] however, point out that this is not always so. *Netziv*, in the Introduction to his commentary on the Chumash (*Kidmas Emek* #9), writes, "There are many places where it is impossible to use this explanation, such as '*Speak to the Jewish People and say to them*' [*Vayikra* 1:2, *Bamidbar* 30:18, and others], where both words appear in the same command! Most commandments appear with the introductory verse, "*Hashem spoke to Moshe, saying ....*" Again, both words appear together.

There is no source in the Talmud for defining *amar* as a soft style of speech. We do, however, find a source for defining *deebeir* as a harsh expression: *Makkos* 11b. Still, the *Maharsha* and *Aruch LaNer* (to the Gemara) point out instances where this rule does not apply.

The *Sefer HaKsav V'Hakabalah* (*Shemos* 6:2) writes, "The intention [of this Gemara] is not that *deebeir* always denotes a harsh language, because there are countless places which show the reverse of this rule."[12]"

We are therefore left to find a definitive difference between these two words, one that would encompass (not contradict) the words of the Gemara and of *Rashi*.

Different explanations have been offered. The one that seems closest to *pshat* appears in the *Sefer Redifei Maya*. The term *deebeir* is used for intense speech between people who have a relationship and are discussing something of significance. *Amar* is used for less

---

9. This is usually mentioned in connection with the following verse, which appears before the Torah was given at Sinai. Moshe was instructed, "And so shall you say to the house of Jacob [referring to the women] and tell to the *Bnei Yisrael* [referring to the men]" (*Shemos* 19:3).

Rashi, based on *Mechilta*, comments, "To the house of Jacob, these are the women, say to them, with gentle language."

Many understand this to be based on the word *amar*, connoting soft speech. In fact, there is no indication in the *Mechilta* that this is based on the word *amar*.

10. *Shemos* 6:2 and 32:7 (*lishon koshi*, a term of harshness), *Vayikra* 10:19 (here, Rashi uses '*lishon az*', a term of force), *Bamidbar* 12:1, *Devarim* 2:17.

11. See, for example *Gur Aryeh* and *Sifsei Chachamim* to *Shemos* (ibid.).

12. "And he spoke to the young woman's heart" (*Bereishis* 34:3) could hardly imply harshness (*HaKsav V'Hakaballah*). Similarly, "And he spoke to the *bnei Cheis*" (*Bereishis* 23:3) refers to a soft request (*Aruch LaNer*).

intense talk, one which is not necessarily related to a relationship or to obligations between the people involved.

This is understood from a careful reading of *Targum Onkelos*. When *amar* is used, Targum translates, "And Hashem said to Moshe." However, when *deebeir* is used, Targum translates, "And Hashem spoke *with* Moshe." The word *with* indicates a more intense type of discussion. Thus, it is true that harsh words are offered with the *deebeir* form, for they are intense and affect the relationship between the people involved.

This would explain why the commandment regarding *tzitzis* begins with *Vayomer*. Most Biblical obligations are mandatory, and *Vayidaber* is appropriate. *Tzitzis* is known as a *mitzvah kiyumis*, one which need not ever be fulfilled, because the Torah requires only that *tzitzis* be inserted into a four-cornered garment. If one never wore such a garment, one would never be subject to the commandment. The *Vayomer* expression fits well (*Darash Moshe II, Parashas Shelach*).

The fifth book of the Torah is called *Devarim*, from the root *deebeir*. Moshe's entire talk to the Jewish People is referred to by this word, *aileh hadevarim*. This is more than a convenient title. At this point, the bond between Moshe and the Jewish People was strong. They had traveled together for forty years and had suffered through numerous challenges. Here, words of *deebur* were appropriate.

◆§ *Naar / Yeled* — נער / ילד

I hope you've enjoyed (and gained from) my favorite synonyms. I'll end with my most difficult discovery regarding synonyms.

Common understanding is that the word *yeled* is used to refer to a small child, while *naar* refers to an older child. See, for example, *Meshech Chochmah* to *Bereishis* 42:22.

In an astonishing comment, Rav Yaakov Kaminetsky (*Emes L'Yaakov, Bereishis* 34:4), maintains that these two words are true synonyms: "There is no difference between *naar* and *yeled*."

This is based on *Targum*, who does not differentiate between the two words in his translation. Rav Yaakov supports this based on *Malachim Beis* (4:26-35), where the two words are used interchangeably for the same child.

Rav Yaakov's comment contradicts the premise of this entire *shiur* — that the Hebrew language contains no true synonyms!

The issue appears to be an issue of dispute between Rashi and the *Ramban*, in regard to the verse, "… and behold, the child (*naar*) was crying" (*Shemos* 2:6). *Rashi* and *Ibn Ezra* indicate that *naar* implies an older child. *Ramban* disagrees, "for a child, from the day he is born, is called *naar*."

Still, *Ramban* leaves open the possibility that there are other differences in meaning between the two words. Rav Yaakov's statement that two words can truly be synonymous is surprising. I wonder if there are other sources for this.

SECTION III
Imponderables

Imponderables

*W*hat are "Imponderables"? *Navi Shiur* regulars would not ask the question. For the rest of our readers, I'll explain.

It was '01, during the final illness of my father, *olov hashalom*. I was in yeshivah during the day and I spent the nights with my father. I was wondering when I would have the time to prepare the week's *Navi Shiur*.

Someone had left a book entitled *Imponderables* near my father's sickbed. The book deals with everyday questions of general interest. These are questions which people enjoy wondering about; hence, "Imponderables."

I imagined what a book like that would contain if it were written by a religious Jew. I realized that a question regarding the Navi portion in that week's *shiur* would qualify. I thought about other questions (perhaps discussing some of them with my father) and soon, I had a *shiur*.

The response to the shiur was overwhelming. I have since offered a new Imponderables shiur each year. I receive more correspondence regarding the Imponderables than I receive regarding any other *shiur*.

It is impossible to predict which question will generate the greatest interest. The question regarding the *vuv* of *V'leYerushalayim Ircha* (see below) generated fifteen different answers. I regret that I did not save the correspondence. Some of the answers below come from these letters. I apologize for failing to attribute the answers to their authors. Although I remember the answers, I've forgotten their individual origins. Please forgive me.

Here, I present a selection of my favorite Imponderables. I hope you enjoy "*tumuling*" over these questions as much as I did!

◆§ Why Do Two *Yuds* Refer to God's Name?

We see it all the time. Our *seforim* constantly use two *yuds* as a reference to God. Where does this come from? Is it really God's Name? Is it prohibited to erase this name?

There is no early source for the two-*yud* notation. This appears to be a printer's method of writing God's Name, to avoid writing the Name that could not later be erased. *Mikdash Mi'at* (an early *sefer* on *safrus*) says of this notation, "*eino kilum* — it has no significance." *Mahari Asad* (*Teshuvos Y.D.* 304) and Rav Tzaddok (in a letter printed in the back of *Takanas HaShavim*, on p. 85) call this a "*siman b'alma* — just a symbol."

Rav Tzaddok offers a source for the two *yuds*. Printers used the first *yud* of one of God's Names (the *Shem Havaya*) and the last *yud* of another (the *Shem Adnus*) to create this sign.

Rema (*Y.D.* 276) brings a *three-yud* manner of writing God's name. This appears as two *yuds*, side by side, with a third *yud* above them. *Seforno* (*Parashas Bo* 12:22) refers to this as a *kabbalistic* sign of God's Name. *Rema* rules that this Name may be erased only if there is a need.

Rema's ruling would certainly apply to the two-*yud* name, which has less of a source! *Sefer HaChassidim* (935) and *Mahari Asad* (Y.D. 304) rule that the two-*yud* name may be erased for any need.

Kosher Giraffe Meat

We've never seen giraffe meat offered in our butcher stores. The giraffe has split hooves and chews its cud. These are the signs of a kosher animal. It has recently been discovered that giraffe milk curdles into cheese. This is also an indication that the giraffe is a kosher animal. Why haven't we ever enjoyed giraffe meat?

"Many people" say that this is because it is difficult to *shecht* (slaughter) a giraffe. Where on the long neck should the *shechitah* take place?

"Other people" explain that this reason is ridiculous. *Shechitah* may take place anywhere on the neck, subject to limitations delineated in *Shulchan Aruch*. The *easiest* animal to *shecht* is the giraffe (if you could get a giraffe to allow you to come close to it with a knife). We would be permitted to eat giraffe meat, if we could take hold of it.

These people explain that we don't eat giraffe meat for the same reasons that non-Jews don't: because it is expensive and doesn't taste very good.

What's the story? Are the "many people" right, or are the "other people" correct?

As with most controversies, neither side is entirely right. The idea that it would be difficult to find the proper spot for *shechitah* is indeed absurd. The giraffe is kosher and there is no halachic difficulty in the *shechitah*.

But wait. Don't rush to invest in this promising new fad. There *is* a problem.

The *Rema* (Y.D. 82:3) limits the consumption of poultry to those birds for which there is a *mesorah*, a tradition that it is kosher. *Chochmas Adam* 36:1 and *Chazon Ish* Y.D. 11:4-5 extend this limitation to wild animals as well, restricting consumption to the deer, for which there is a clear *mesorah*. This would seem to be a limiting factor, preventing the marketing of giraffe meat for Ashkenazic Jews.

How disappointing.

(There may still be a glimmer of hope. Rav Saadya Gaon, *Redak*, and *Targum Shivim* define the Biblical *zemer* as the giraffe. An argument can be made that this positive identification should suffice as the *mesorah* requirement. If giraffe meat were to come into vogue, we would need a final ruling on this issue.)

◆§ Why Are There Two Days of Rosh Chodesh?

The first day of every Jewish month is called Rosh Chodesh. On this day we recite Hallel and add a Mussaf prayer.

Half the Jewish months are 29 days long; the other half have 30 days. When there is a 30th day to a month, we call this 30th day Rosh Chodesh as well. Thus, every other month has two days of Rosh Chodesh. We are all accustomed to this aspect of our calendar, although this practice is not mentioned in *Shas*. Why do we have two days for Rosh Chodesh? Why should the last day of a month be called Rosh Chodesh?

Many assume that this is for the same reason that we observe two days of Yom Tov in *chutz l'Aretz*; because of *sifeika d'yoma*.[1] In fact, *Tzlach* (*Mes Berachos* 26b, *s.v. Rashi*) quotes *Binyan Ariel* who offers this explanation.

This explanation is very difficult, for two main reasons.

First, *sifeika d'yoma* would require that every month have two days of Rosh Chodesh, just as every Yom Tov has two days. After a 29-day month, Rosh Chodesh would be the first and second of the new month[2] (*Birkei Yosef* O.C. 427).

Second, in *Shmuel Aleph*, Chapter 20 (in a section known as *Machar Chodesh*), we find that King Shaul kept two days of Rosh Chodesh. Surely, Shaul, who kept close contact with the Sanhedrin, had no *sifeika d'yoma*!

Furthermore, we read that Shaul was aware *in advance* that there would be two days of Rosh Chodesh. He had no *safek*; he was not

---

1. During Biblical times, Rosh Chodesh was determined by witnesses who testified before the Sanhedrin that they had seen the new moon. This could not be known in advance. (Even when the astronomical facts were known, it could not be known if weather conditions would allow for a sighting of the new moon.) It was therefore impossible to create calendars in advance of a month. Only after the Sanhedrin's determination could that month's calendar be set. People who lived near the Sanhedrin were quickly informed of the Sanhedrin's decision. Those who lived far away remained unaware for a longer period, and kept two calendars, one for each of the possible Rosh Chodesh days. This resulted in two days of Yom Tov.

2. We do this on Rosh Hashanah, which has two days of Yom Tov. Rosh Hashanah follows a 29-day month. The Yom Tov is therefore observed on the first and second of the new month. This should be true of every Rosh Chodesh, according to *Binyan Ariel*.

unsure on the first day. In Biblical times, *sefeika d'yoma* situations could not be known in advance, since they depended on the appearance of witnesses in the Sanhedrin, something that could not be predicted.

Why did Shaul observe two days of Rosh Chodesh?

Rav Pam would explain that our two-day Rosh Chodesh is based on the *Rambam* (*Hilchos Kiddush HaChodesh* 8:4). *Rambam* maintains that Rosh Chodesh always occurs on the day of the *molad* (lunar conjunction), whether it is the first day of the calendar month or not. After all, this is the true Rosh Chodesh — the beginning of the new lunar month. In addition, the first day of the new calendar month is Rosh Chodesh. Thus, we observe Rosh Chodesh both on the first of the lunar astronomical month and on the first of the lunar calendar month. After a 30-day month, these days were typically the same. After a 29-day month, they occur on two different days. Thus, the two-day Rosh Chodesh!

(There is a source in *Magen Giborim* 108 for Rav Pam's explanation of the *Rambam*. Although the *molad* does not always occur on the 30th day of the month, Rosh Chodesh was established based on the usual *molad* [Rav Chaim Kanievsky, *Shekel HaKodesh* in *Beur HaHalachah* to this Rambam].)

≈§ The Missing Chicken Leg

A woman came to me with a bruised chicken leg. After examining it, I explained that it was *treif* and had to be thrown out.

"What about the other chicken legs in the package?" she asked.

I explained that the entire chicken is *treif*. However, she had not purchased a whole chicken. The other chicken legs in her package were fine. "The *treif* piece is a right leg of a chicken. The other chicken thighs in your package are also right legs. A chicken has only one right leg, so the other pieces must have come from other chickens, which we may assume are kosher."

Simple enough. Then, I began to reflect. Where *is* the *treif* left chicken leg? It is somewhere out in the marketplace. It cannot be distinguished from other left chicken legs. Should they all be prohibited because of the one missing *treif* chicken leg? Perhaps it is permitted because the *treif* piece cannot be distinguished from the other chicken legs. It is *botul b'rov*. Or is it?

There is an important exception to the rule of *botul b'rov*. This exception is known as *chatichah ha'roui l'hischabed*. This refers to a *treif* portion of food which is significant enough to be served at a meal. This portion of food does not become permitted when it becomes mixed with other food. In fact, it causes all other food in its mixture to be prohibited as well. This includes all portions that may become confused with the prohibited piece.

Following this logic, it would seem that all left chicken legs that originated from the same *shechitah* source as the *treif* piece should be prohibited! This may include tens of thousands of chicken legs!

Of course, this is not limited to left chicken legs; all other parts of the *treif* chicken are also out there, somewhere.

Can it be? Every time a chicken portion is found to be *treif* should we be announcing a recall on the other chicken parts that were processed on the same day?

Someone — please help me with this one![3]

◆§ Which Woman's Name Appears Most Often In Navi?

It is fascinating that the woman whose name appears most often is Navi is barely known and that her name has not been carried on among the Jewish People. Who is this woman?

Tzeruyah was the sister of Dovid HaMelech. She had three illustrious sons; the most famous of them was Yoav, Dovid's general. The Navi constantly refers to him as *Yoav ben Tzeruyah*, thereby repeating his mother's name dozens of

---

3. *Yoreh Deah* 110:5 rules that the rule of *kol d'porish mai'rubah porish* applies to this type of situation. This means that the other portions of chicken are permitted, provided that they were removed from the butcher store before the *treif* chicken leg was discovered. This is enough to permit the use of chicken parts that were purchased prior to the discovery of the damaged leg, but not those portions of chicken still in the store or *beis hashechitah*.

For those studying *Yoreh Deah*, see also 110:7 with *Shach* and *Taz*.

times. No other woman's name appears as often in Naviim. (In Kesuvim, only the name Esther appears more often.)

Our imponderable: Why was Yoav referred to by his mother's name? Most people assume that *Tzeruyah* is a man's name. This is because the Navi refers to everyone else as "*ben* his father." Why are the children of Tzeruyah different in that they are referred to as "*ben* their mother"?

Chidah (*Ayin Zocher* 200:7) suggests that Yoav and his brothers are referred to as *ben Tzeruyah* because their mother was a member of the royal family. The verse refers to them by the name of their most noteworthy parent.

Another possible explanation can be based on *Ezra* 2:61. There, we find that a person used the name of his maternal grandfather, because this was important for *yichus* purposes. When the mother's side of the family creates a halachic issue for the descendants, it is important that the lineage not be forgotten in subsequent generations. Using the maternal name ensures that the maternal lineage would not be forgotten.

This reason can be applied to the family of Tzeruyah as well.

We know that the status of Dovid's family was called into question during his lifetime. Dovid's father, Yishai, was a descendant of Rus, a Moabite woman who had converted to Judaism. The *yichus* status of the descendants of a Moabite convert had been the subject of a long dispute. Many held that a Moabite convert lacks proper *yichus* and is prohibited from marrying Jews (except other converts). It may be that the descendants of Rus continued to refer to themselves by that branch of their lineage, so that their *yichus* issues would not be forgotten. Only later, after the Prophet Shmuel settled the issue by anointing David as king (for which proper *yichus* is a requirement) did it become clear that the *yichus* of the descendants of Rus should not be questioned.

∽§ Caleiv Is Missing!

Yocheved and Miriam risked their lives on behalf of Jewish newborns in *Mitzrayim*. Heaven rewarded them for this. "And it was because the midwives feared God that He made them houses" (*Shemos* 1:21). *Rashi* explains that this refers to the Houses of Kohanim and Leviim, which descended from Yocheved, and to the royal House of David, which descended from Miriam. The Gemara (*Sotah* 11b) explains that the House of David was born from the marriage of Caleiv and Miriam.

This is a well known Chazal; even the youngest students learn this when they are introduced to *Parashas Shemos*.

Yet this seems to be impossible. At the end of *Megillas Rus*, the name of every one of David's ancestors is listed, from Yehudah through Dovid. Caleiv is missing! His name does not appear on the list! It therefore appears that Dovid did not descend from the marriage of Caleiv and Miriam!

One may argue that we often find figures in Tanach who had more than one name. Perhaps Caleiv, too, had more than one name, and one of the ancestors listed in *Megillas Rus* is actually Caleiv.

This would answer our Imponderable. However, this cannot be. In *Divrei HaYamim* (2:18), we learn that Caleiv was the son of Chetzrone (who was also known as *Yefune*; see *Sotah* 11b) and that he had a brother named Rom. Chetzrone and Rom do appear in *Megillas Rus* as ancestors of Dovid. It is therefore clear that the lineage of the House of Dovid does not descend from Caleiv!

This is a perplexing problem (mentioned in *Maharsha* to *Sotah* 11b) which would appear to defy an easy solution.

When I was preparing *shiurim* on Megillas Rus, a dear friend loaned me a rare copy of the commentary of Rav Vidal HaTzofasi (a 17th-century Moroccan *gadol*) to *Rus*. He addresses this question and suggests a possible answer. It may be that Caleiv and Rom were brothers, and that one of them married Miriam but died without children. In accordance with the laws of *yibum*, the surviving brother married Miriam. Their offspring, the ancestor of Dovid HaMelech, was the biological descendant of one brother; but, in accordance with the Torah's *yibum* laws, is referred to as the descendant of the deceased brother. Thus, both are true. Dovid descended from Caleiv and from Rom!

An ingenious solution to a difficult problem.

How Did the Dispute Between *Rashi* and *Rabbeinu Tam* Regarding Tefillin Begin?

Rashi and his grandson *Rabbeinu Tam* have different opinions regarding the order in which the parchment Torah sections are placed into the tefillin boxes. Each maintains that only his tefillin are kosher. How did this dispute begin?

When Moshe Rabbeinu came down from *Har Sinai*, he taught the Jewish People to wear tefillin every day and instructed them on how to insert the parchment sections into the tefillin. From that moment on, hundreds of thousands of Jews wore tefillin every day. At what point could a dispute have begun regarding the proper form of tefillin? At any point it should have been possible to examine the tefillin that were in use to determine the proper placing of the parchment inserts.[4]

Aishel Avraham (of Butchash) 493 suggests that the dispute began in a generation when few Jews were actually wearing tefillin. Confusion developed and it was difficult to find tefillin on which to establish the law. This is hardly a satisfying answer. It is certainly difficult to imagine that so few Jews wore tefillin, anywhere in the world, that this caused confusion among scholars.

There are two distinct schools of thought regarding the evolution of the *machlokes Rashi* and *Rabbeinu Tam*. Predictably, Chassidic circles, where the wearing of *Rabbeinu Tam* tefillin is more prevalent, have a more accepting approach. Yeshivah circles, where the opinion of the *Gra* is followed and *Rabbeinu Tam* tefillin are rarely seen, have a less accepting approach.

- **Approach A: There were always two pairs of tefillin:** Some maintain that there were always two ways of placing the parchment into the tefillin. The *Divrei Chaim* (quoted by his descendant, the

---

4. The Klausenberger Rebbe *zt"l*, in his approbation to *Sefer Divrei Yisrael*, adds another question. *Rambam* (*Hilchos Mamrim* 1:3) teaches that there are no disputes in areas that are related to tradition (as opposed to areas related to erudition and logic, in which there are many areas of dispute). This teaching should include this dispute, which relates to tradition; how then did this dispute develop?

Klausenberger Rebbe, in his *haskamah* to *Sefer Divrei Yisrael*) maintains that during the forty years that Moshe led the Jewish People to Eretz Yisrael, the tefillin of *Rabbeinu Tam* already existed.

This is the approach of many *kabbalists*, who attach great mystical significance to *Rabbeinu Tam* tefillin (see *Teshuvos V'Hanhagos* 4:15). *Ben Yohada* (*Mes. Menachos* 43b) suggests that Dovid HaMelech wore both *Rashi* and *Rabbeinu Tam* tefillin!

According to this view, there was always a primary pair of tefillin, for all to wear, and a second pair, which was worn as a sign of great piety. The dispute between *Rashi* and *Rabbeinu Tam* revolved around the two pairs of tefillin: which is the primary tefillin and which is secondary?

There is a difficulty with this approach. If both pairs of tefillin already existed, why doesn't the Gemara mention them? Why doesn't the *Rif* or *Rambam* (or any other Rishon) refer to the second pair, which we know as *Rabbeinu Tam* tefillin?

Rabbeinu Tam tefillin are generally reserved for people with great *yiras Shamayim*, who live their lives in a humble and holy manner. These tefillin were never intended for everyone. It may be for this reason that their existence was not publicized in the Gemara.

■ **Approach B: *Rabbeinu Tam* changed the accepted custom:** The second approach involves an understanding of the authority of a Torah giant to change an accepted custom based on his understanding. (This discussion regards changing custom; no *Rishon* could ever change a ruling that is found clearly in the Gemara.)

Michtav M'Eliyahu (4:56), in discussing this, maintains that *Rabbeinu Tam* did change the accepted practice. "Certainly there had been an accepted practice, but because there was no precise *mesorah* ... this remains a custom. Torah Law requires that the ruling be examined according to the rules of establishing [Halachah] ... and because this resulted in a conclusion that contradicted the custom, the custom was pushed away by the halachic conclusion."

This was the approach of the *Gra* and his disciples who discouraged the wearing of *Rabbeinu Tam* tefillin, treating the issue as any other *machlokes Rishonim* in which a definitive ruling already exists.

~§ Would *Rabbeinu Tam* Use Our *Rabbeinu Tam* Tefillin?

Rashi and *Rabbeinu Tam* disagreed regarding the order in which the parchment Torah sections are placed into the tefillin boxes. Those who wear both pairs of tefillin feel that they are satisfying both opinions.

However, *Noda B'Yehudah* (2:4) writes that our *Rabbeinu Tam* tefillin are *posul* according to the opinion of *Rabbeinu Tam*.

Why is this so, and why would anyone wear *Rabbeinu Tam* tefillin that are *posul* according to both *Rashi* and *Rabbeinu Tam*?

Noda B'Yehudah explains that aside from the dispute regarding the order of the tefillin sections, there was a second disagreement between *Rashi* and *Rabbeinu Tam*.

There is a well-known dispute regarding the placing of a *mezuzah* on a doorpost. *Rashi* maintains that the *mezuzah* should be placed vertically, while *Rabbeinu Tam* rules that the *mezuzah* must be mounted onto the doorpost in a horizontal position. Halachah follows *Rashi's* opinion, although the Ashkenazic custom is to place the *mezuzah* at an angle, out of deference to the opinion of *Rabbeinu Tam*.

Rashi and *Rabbeinu Tam* also disagree on how a Sefer Torah should be placed in the *Aron Kodesh*. We follow *Rashi's* opinion that the Sefer Torah must stand in the *Aron*. *Rabbeinu Tam* maintained that the Sefer Torah should be stored in a lying position.

This dispute has a third application as well. *Rashi* states that the parchment is placed vertically into the tefillin boxes. *Rabbeinu Tam* disagrees. He would place the parchment into the boxes horizontally. Here too, our custom follows *Rashi* and the parchment is placed into the tefillin in an upright position.

The problem lies in the fact that while our *Rabbeinu Tam* tefillin have their parchment inserted in the order which follows *Rabbeinu Tam*, they are placed vertically, in accordance with *Rashi's* opinion! This seems inconsistent; why is this done?

Noda B'Yehudah answers this question by explaining that the two disputes are very different. In the dispute regarding the order in which the parchment is placed, *Rabbeinu Tam* was not alone in his opinion. Those who wear *Rabbeinu Tam* tefillin do so because there were other *Rishonim* who concurred with *Rabbeinu Tam.*

In the second dispute, however, *Rabbeinu Tam* stood alone in his opinion that the parchment should be placed horizontally. Here, the opinion is not strong enough to be taken into account as a matter of practice. Those who wear *Rabbeinu Tam* tefillin therefore satisfy his opinion in one dispute (the order of the parchment) but not in the other (the position of the parchment).[5]

Thus, our *Rabbeinu Tam* tefillin are *posul* according to the opinion of *Rabbeinu Tam.*

~§ A Clean-Shaven Shimshon?

Biblical drawings that depict Shimshon as a long-haired but clean-shaven warrior are always amusing to us. These drawings were not created by God-fearing people. Still, they appeared on the introduction page to earlier printings of *Sefer Shoftim*. One wonders how people could make such a foolish mistake. Don't we all know that Shimshon was *the* Nazir of Tanach? And, of course, a Nazir is forbidden to use a razor — or scissors — on his hair. How could he have been clean-shaven?

I have no doubt that Shimshon, as all great *tzaddikim*, had a full beard. Yet these drawings help me remember a *Teshuvas HaRashba* (1:407). The *Rashba* explains that the prohibition of a Nazir is limited to the hairs of his head. This is the clear reading of the verse in the Torah (Bamidbar 6:5), "All the days of his Nazir vow a blade may not pass over *his head*, until the Godly Nazir days are completed, he shall be holy, growing the hairs *of his head* long."

A Nazir is the same as everyone else in regard to the restrictions on shaving the beard, which is prohibited only if done with a razor (or razor-like) implement! I doubt the artists were familiar with this *Rashba*. Still, their drawing serves as a reminder of this little known Halachah.

---

5. This is also the opinion of *Magen Geborim* 34:2. See also *M'asef Lechol HaMachanos* 34:4.

∽§ Kosher Succah Decorations?

Can succah decorations be "kosher" or "*posul*"? Are there rules for these decorations?

The *Mishnah Berurah* does express a rule for succah decorations. The rule is not our imponderable; the fact that most of our succah decorations violate this rule *is* something to ponder!

The concept of succah decorations appears in *Shulchan Aruch*, Chapter 638. The *Mishnah Berurah* (24) writes the following:

"It is not permitted to engrave [the verse] *baSuccos teishvu* on a gourd or the like, to hang it in the succah, because the [verse] will come to be neglected. In addition, one may not write verses from the Torah, unless it is part of a complete book, as we find in *Yoreh Deah* 283. Although we do write verses, this is for teaching purposes only, not for any other reason."

Today, we do not hang gourds in our succos. Still, the decorations that we do use should not contain verses. Verses of the Torah have a *kedushah* and should be used for teaching purposes only; they do not belong on decorations.

I once sent a child to a local store to purchase succah decorations, with the instruction that none should contain a Torah verse. The response? There was not a single poster without a verse on it. How strange!

This is apparently not a new problem. The *Chidushei HaRan* (*Shabbos* 5b) makes the point that signs that are posted in shuls should not contain Torah verses.

∽§ Why Do We Refer to the Splitting of The Sea as *Kriyas Yam Suf* — the Ripping of the Sea?

Everyone has heard of *Kriyas Yam Suf*. This is a most perplexing expression. The Torah (*Shemos* 14:21) refers to the splitting of the Yam Suf as "*VaYibaku hamayim* — and the water split." In *Tehillim* 136:13, we find the expression "*l'gozer yam suf l'gizarim* — He, Who divided the Yam Suf into parts." In all of Tanach, we never find this seemingly inappropriate word, *kriyah*, ripping, in reference to the miracle at Yam Suf! Yet the Gemara does use this expression, as in *Sotah* 2a, "Pairing [man and woman] is as difficult as *kriyas Yam Suf.*" This has become the common Hebrew term for the splitting of the Sea. *Kriyah*, ripping, usually refers to something solid, usually cloth or paper. Why is this expression used for the splitting of a body of water?

I have a good friend in Great Neck who was bothered by this expression, and has put great effort into finding an answer. He found this question in the Haggadah of the *Shem MiShmuel*. I find the answer offered there difficult to comprehend.

Likutei Yehudah, quoting his grandfather, the *Chidushei HaRim*, offers an answer. The Hebrew expression *kriyah* is used to refer to the ripping or separation of things that were originally separate, but were joined together. Cloth is made of many threads that were brought together. When these joined threads are ripped, we use the term *kriyah*.

We are taught that Hashem planned the splitting of the Yam Suf, from the moment of Creation. At the beginning of time, when the seas were first formed, "*tnai hisneh HaKodosh Boruch Hu im ma'aseh bereishis* — God already set in motion the great plan," which would bring the Jewish People to the Sea at a precise moment. In a sense, the Sea was preset to split.

As the Jews stood at the banks of Yam Suf, they had no way of knowing this. To them, the fear of the pursuing Egyptian army was very real. The Sea seemed to be an insurmountable barrier. To them, the Sea "split"; a single complete sea became two bodies of water. The words "*VaYibaku hamayim*" were most appropriate.

Torah She'Baal Peh teaches that this was preordained. From the beginning of time, these were actually two great bodies of water that touched, waiting for that great moment when they would reveal their preordained separation. The term *kriyah* is meant to teach this.

(This explanation has halachic ramifications. *Koraya*, ripping, is one of the thirty-nine prohibited melachos on Shabbos. The *Chidushei HaRim* was apparently following the opinion of the S.A. HaRav (340:13), who maintains that this prohibition applies only to the ripping of things that were originally separate [such as cloth, or two papers that were glued together]. He feels that there is no prohibition on ripping a single item, such as a piece of leather. This opinion maintains that kriyah is defined as the ripping of two items that had been joined. This opinion is rejected by many *poskim* (*Pri Migadim* 340, A.A.18, *Beur Halachah* 340:13, *Chazon Ish* 51:13; see also *Nishmas Adam* 29:2). According to them, the Imponderable remains unresolved.)

What Is the Hebrew Word for Sunrise: *Neitz* or *Haneitz*?

Virtually all *z'manim* calendars have a column for sunrise, labeled "*haneitz*," and a column for sunset, which is labeled "*shekiyah*." The *hei* prefix means "the"; thus *haneitz* translates to "the sunrise." Why is the word for sunrise always written with a *hei* prefix, while the reference to sunset is not written with the *hei* prefix?

Neitz, as a reference for sunrise, does not appear in Tanach. We usually understand that the word *neitz* comes from the Hebrew word for sparks, *nitzotzos*, referring to the early-morning sunrays. If so, the *hei* is a prefix and not part of the root word.

Many *ba'alei dikduk* have suggested that the *hei* is part of the root word (*hei-nun-tzadik*), and that this word is related to the Hebrew word for blossoming, as in "*heineitzu harimmonim* — the pomegranates have blossomed" (*Shir HaShirim* 6:11, 7:13). If this is true, the common expression for a *vasikin minyan*, which is often referred to as a *neitz* minyan, is incorrect. It should be the *haneitz* minyan. Many *ba'alei dikduk* emphatically insist that this is correct; however, it seems to me that they are not correct. Many *poskim* do not consider the *hei* as part of the root word. The *Mishnah Berurah* (493:6) refers to sunrise using the two-letter *neitz*, without the *hei*.

This is found in countless other sources (including such diverse *seforim* as *Pischei Teshuvah* Y.D. 184:6, 399:3; *Chavos Yair* 83, 219; *Chasam Sofer* Y.D. 197, *Rav Paelim* 2:2; *Har Tzvi* O.C. 106, and Y.D. 264; *Igros Moshe* O.C. 4:6 and Y.D. 1:180).

It therefore is clear that most *poskim* treat the *hei* as a prefix to *neitz*. Our calendar's constant reference to *neitz* with the *hei* and *shekiyah* without the *hei* therefore remains something of a mystery.

◈§ How Do You Forget Something Purposely?

There are a number of Torah Commandments related to agriculture. Non-farmers rarely have the opportunity to perform these mitzvos. Rav Chaim Kanievsky, in his *Derech Emunah* (*Hilchos Matnas Aniyim, Beur haHalachah* to 1:14) reports that the *Gra* strove to perform these mitzvos. Each year, he would purchase a piece of land that was ready for harvest and perform the three mitzvos that relate to harvesting: *leket, shikchah,* and *peah*.

Our problem relates to the mitzvah of *shikchah*. This commandment is accomplished when a person forgets a bundle of produce in his field, under specific conditions. The farmer is obligated to leave the forgotten produce in the field, so that poor people can retrieve it. How did the *Gra* go about performing the mitzvah of *shikchah?* Can a person somehow cause himself to "forget" something?

This Imponderable puzzled me for a long time; it seemed irresolvable. Then, a suggestion was offered by a *mispallel* who employs many people in his furniture business.

He asked whether *shikchah* applies only to bundles that were forgotten by the farmer himself, or also to produce forgotten by his worker. I pointed out that even if it was a worker who forgot the bundle, the farmer has a mitzvah to leave it in the field.

"In that case," he assured me, "the *Gra* could have accomplished the mitzvah easily. I have a number of workers who are sure to forget things every time — guaranteed!"

Could it be that the *Gra* used this method of performing this mitzvah?

Something to ponder.

୫୫ Why Is *Zichrono L'vrachah* Used To Refer to Someone Who Is No Longer Alive?

If you see the words *zichrono l'vrachah* after someone's name, you would understand that he is no longer alive. Yet, there seems to be no reason for this; *zichrono l'vrachah* means "may he be remembered for a blessing." Living people, too, should be remembered for a blessing!

We find a similar expression in *Bircas HaMazon*, where we say, *Horchamon Hu yishlach lanu es Eliyahu HaNavi zachur latov*. There it refers to *Eliyahu HaNavi*, the one person who hasn't died! Why has this expression come to refer to a person who has passed away?

*I*n 1921, a rav in St. Louis, Rav Chaim Hirshenson, published his *Sefer Malki BaKodesh*. In it, he made reference to a question which had been posed by "the author of the *Torah Temimah, zichrono l'vrachah*." Subsequently, he received a letter from Rav Boruch Epstein, assuring him that he was very much alive. In a subsequent volume of *Malki BaKodesh*, Rav Hirshenson apologized and explained that two Yiddish language newspapers, the *Der Togblatt* and *Der Morgan Journal*, had reported Rav Boruch Epstein's passing. ("Don't feel bad; they once published an obituary for me, too.") Overjoyed at the news that Rav Epstein was alive, Rav Hirshenson expressed the blessing, *Boruch Michayeh HaChaim*!

Rav Hirshenson ended his piece with a defense of the use of this term for a living person, arguing that nothing in the expression refers to death.

The Gemara in *Kedushin* (31b) instructs a son in the use of a title to refer to his deceased father. During the first year, the son appends *hareini kaporas mishkavo* — may I atone for his death — after the name. Once the year has passed, he says *zichrono l'vrachah l'chayei haOlam Haba* — may he be remembered for a blessing [and] eternal life. Perhaps this is the source for the abbreviated title, *zichrono l'vrachah*.

Maharsha, however, disagrees. He states clearly that *zichrono l'vrachah* refers to living people! Still, the custom may stem from those who have learned this Gemara without the *Maharsha*!

✨ Why Do We Refer to a *Choleh* by Using His Mother's Name?

A person is identified by his father's name (e.g., *Yosef ben Shimon*) in a *kesubah, get,* and in all other legal documents, as well as when being called to the Torah. Why is the mother's name (e.g., *Yosef ben Rachel*) used to identify a sick person when a prayer is offered for his recovery?

A common explanation is that the mother's identity is more certain than the father's. The child comes directly from the mother's womb and her identity can be verified by witnesses. When a person is ill, we want to be sure that we are identifying him correctly.

Ben Yohada (*Mes. Berachos* 55b, *s.v. anna*) rejects this explanation as an insult to a person's father.

(It is told that the Brisker Rav, when still a youngster, was asked the following question: We know that in most cases, *kibbud av*, honoring a father, takes precedence over *kibbud aim*, honoring one's mother. Why is this so? The mother's identity is verified with more certainty than the father's. If so, shouldn't honoring her take precedence?

To this, the young Velvel replied, "It is hardly an honor for the mother to suggest that this is not truly his father!"

This is the point of *Ben Yohada*'s objection.)

Ben Yohada offers a different explanation. When praying for a person who is ill and mentioning the parent's name, we wish to do more than identify the patient. We mean to mention a name that will bring merit to the sick person, in Heaven. A woman's merits are generally greater than a man's, in that some of the most difficult *nisyonos* (such as *bitul Torah* and *shmiras ainayim*) do not apply to women. In addition, she is not obligated in the performance of many mitzvos. Thus, we assume that her merits are greater, and it is therefore the woman's name that is mentioned.

We find a similar idea in *Birkei Yosef* (O.C. 284). He reports a custom regarding two people who have *yahrtzeit* on the same day. As noted earlier, the custom was to give precedence to a person observing the *yahrtzeit* of a father over one observing the *yahrtzeit* of a mother. Why should the father have precedence?

Birkei Yosef explains that the assumption is that the soul of a man needs merit in heaven more than does the soul of a woman. His *nisyonos* in this world are far more difficult. Thus, on the *yahrtzeit*, we view him as being in greater need.

This is the meaning of the Gemara, (*Berachos* 17a), "The promise made to woman is greater than that which was made to man."

܀§ Moshe Rabbeinu's Missing Year

"Moshe was 80 years old and Aaron was 83 years old when they spoke to Paroh" (*Shemos* 7:7). This verse refers to Moshe at the time he first stood before Paroh. This incident was followed by the ten *makkos* (plagues). The Jewish People left Egypt during the following Nissan. It is safe to say that the ten *makkos* took at least six weeks (one Midrash indicates that they took ten months). This would mean that Moshe's 81st birthday, on the 7th of Adar, took place after he first stood before Paroh, five weeks before the Exodus from Egypt. On the 7th of Adar, forty years later, Moshe passed away. He should have been 121 years old. In fact, the verse tells us that he was 120 years old. Where did the missing year go?

Rav Yaakov Emden, in his notes to *Zevachim* 118b, makes an astonishing suggestion. Due to difficulty with another mathematical calculation, he suggests that the Jewish People were not actually in the *Midbar* for forty years. We do find elsewhere (regarding the laws of lashes) that the Torah rounds a number to forty when it is actually thirty-nine. Rav Yaakov Emden suggests that here too, the figure of forty years in the *Midbar* is not exact.

Although this would answer our question, Rav Yaakov Emden's suggestion cannot be correct. *Shemos* 16:35 tells us, "The Children of Israel ate the *mon* for forty years."

The Gemara (*Kiddushin* 38a) quotes this verse and asks, "Did they eat [*mon*] for forty years? But they ate [*mon*] for forty years, less thirty days? This teaches us that the cakes that they brought out of Egypt tasted like the *mon*."

Clearly, the Gemara understands that the forty-year figure is accurate!

If so, our original question remains unresolved.

Chasam Sofer (*Teshuvos* 6:29) offers another possible resolution. He suggests that Moshe was not actually 80 years old when he stood before Paroh. The verse quoted earlier actually means that Moshe was in his eightieth year when he stood before Paroh. His 80th birthday took place on the following 7th of Adar.

This answer requires that we accept that this verse differs from the other references to age in the Torah. Still, this appears to be the only possible resolution of a difficult imponderable.

(Others suggested that the Exodus took place in a leap year, which had two Adar months. This could allow us to place the first visit to Paroh on the 7th of Adar, Moshe's 80th birthday. The ten *makkos* could have taken place over the next nine weeks, culminating in the Exodus on the 14th of *Nissan*. However, this is inconsistent with *Rashi* (*Shemos* 7:25) who teaches that the first *makkoh* alone took a month. Many *meforshim* understand that the *makkos* were spaced a month apart. This means that the ten *makkos* took ten months.)

⇜ How Many Verses Are There in *Parashas Tzav*?

That's easy! Everyone knows that *Parashas Tzav* has ninety-six verses, equivalent to the numerical value of *Tzav*. Every Chumash says so at the end of the *parashah*, where the Chumashim present a *siman* (mnemonic) to remember the number of verses in the *parashah*. Here, we find, "*Tzav siman* — the word *Tzav* indicates the number of verses" — ninety-six.

Or is it? A bar mitzvah *bochur* in our shul was to read *Parashas Tzav* from the Torah. I commented to him that he had ninety-six verses to prepare. He corrected me, "Oh no! It's ninety-seven. I counted them!"

I was sure that he was making a mistake, so I counted the verses with him. He is right! *Tzav* does have ninety-seven verses. Why is the *siman* incorrect — or is it?

*I*t is difficult to know the source for the *simanim* and whether it is important to try to answer this problem. Still, let's make an attempt.

The Gemara (*Kiddushin* 30a) teaches that the middle verse of the Torah begins with the word *V'Hisgalach*. This verse appears in *Parashas Tazria* (13:33). Rav Moshe Feinstein (*Igros Moshe* O.C. 35) points out that in our Chumashim, the division of verses is different. The middle verse appears in *Parashas Tzav*, 160 verses earlier than indicated in the Gemara.

Rav Moshe concludes that the division of verses in our Chumashim contains some errors. The first half of the Chumash contains numerous instances where two verses should be combined into one. The second half of the Torah contains some long verses that are actually two separate verses.

We are unsure in which verses these errors are found. Since the division of verses does not change the meaning of any verse, the precise division is of little practical consequence.

Given the information that there are some verses that appear (in our Chumashim) as two but should really be one, we may answer our question. *Parashas Tzav* may indeed contain ninety-six verses. Our Chumashim present ninety-seven, because this includes one extra division of a long verse into two smaller ones.

❧ How Many Verses in *Parashas Pikudei*?

In our Chumashim, the number of verses in every *parashah* is presented with a *siman*, a mnemonic, at the end of the *parashah*. For some mysterious reason, *Parashas Pikudei*, and only *Parashas Pikudei*, has no *siman* at the end. Why is this so? It seems easy enough to count the ninety-two verses of the *parashah*. Why not present a *siman*?

To add to the mystery, many Chumashim are published with the following Hebrew words at the end of *Parashas Pikudei*; "*ein kol siman* — there is no *siman*." Until recently, all Chumashim had this legend at the end of *Parashas Pikudei*. Why?

Could it be that there is in fact a *siman* for the number of verses in this *parashah*? The *siman* is the words "*ein kol*," which have the numerical value of ninety-two. Thus, Chumashim always contained the words "*ein kol siman*" at the end of *Parashas Pikudei*, informing us that the *parashah* has ninety-two verses. Publishers (and many others) misunderstood this to mean that there is no *siman* to this *parashah*. They began to delete these words because they saw no reason to publish what seems obvious, that there is no *siman*.

In truth, though, this *siman* belongs there in its proper spot, at the end of *Parashas Pikudei*!

◆§ Should Megillos Be Read Before *Krias Hatorah*?

There are four times during the year that we read a megillah during *Shacharis*. Megillas Esther is the best-known. It is also the most important, as reading Megillas Esther is a Rabbinic obligation. *Berachos* are recited before we read Megillas Esther.

The other megillos are Shir Hashirim, which is read on Pesach; Rus, which is read on Shavuous; and Koheles, which is read on Succos. There is no Rabbinic obligation to read these megillos; these are read as a *Minhag Yisrael*, and most communities do not recite a *berachah* when they are read. Clearly, the level of obligation for these *megillos* is not the same as for Megillas Esther.

Our practice in reading these megillos is quite puzzling. Megillas Esther is read during Shacharis, after *Krias HaTorah*. The other three megillos are read before *Krias HaTorah*. Why is there a difference between them?

The question is even more puzzling given the fact that Megillas Esther is the more significant megillah — yet it is read at a later point in the davening!

*H*ere are some of the answers that were offered in response to this question.

There is a Talmudic dictum, *"Tadir v'sheino tadir, tadir kodem."* This rule applies to the order in which mitzvos are performed. When one is faced with two mitzvah obligations, the one which occurs more frequently, the *tadir*, is performed first. For example, when Yom Tov falls on Shabbos, *Bircas HaMazon* contains two added paragraphs, one in honor of Shabbos and one for Yom Tov. Which one is recited first? We recite the Shabbos paragraph first, since it occurs more often than Yom Tov. This is an example of *Tadir u'sheino tadir, tadir kodem.*

Here too, *Krias HaTorah* occurs more frequently than the megillah reading and therefore precedes the reading of Megillas Esther.

Why, then, doesn't this rule require us to read the Torah before the other megillos?

Shagas Aryeh 28 explains that the rule of "*Tadir v'sheino tadir, tadir kodem*" applies only to obligatory mitzvos. That is why the mitzvah of tallis precedes the mitzvah of tefillin, every day.

This would answer our question as well. The reading of the other megillos is not a true obligation; it is therefore not subject to the "Tadir" rule. They may therefore precede *Krias HaTorah*.

Another answer has been suggested based on the Gemara (*Shabbos* 116b) that reports of an earlier *takanah* banning the reading of *Kesuvim* on Shabbos. The Gemara indicates that this enactment was aimed primarily at Shabbos afternoon.

The megillos are all part of *Kesuvim*. The reading of megillos on Shabbos, therefore, takes place as early as possible, before the Torah reading. Megillas Esther is never read on Shabbos and can therefore be read where it belongs, after *Krias HaTorah*.

These answers do not satisfy most people. The first answer does not explain why the other megillos *should* be read before the Torah; it only explains that they *may* be read then. The second answer employs a rule that is not *l'Halachah*!

Allow me to suggest a simpler answer. Our experience is that the reading of Megillas Esther tends to bring out the joy and levity of the Purim day; people completing the Megillah are often in a frivolous state of mind. Perhaps it was this consideration that caused this megillah reading to be delayed until after the Torah reading. (Too many people become caught up with the Purim spirit and neglect the end of davening. I often wish that we would also complete *all of the prayers* before the reading of Megillas Esther!)

✑ 3,550 Missing Jews!

We all know that there were 600,000 Jews who were counted in the *Midbar*. Actually, the Torah records a total of 603,550. It would seem that the popular figure is simply rounded off from the 603,550. There are, however, places where an exact number is mentioned — as 600,000!

Shulchan Aruch, in *Hilchos Shabbos* (345:7), considers a city with 600,000 people to be a *rishus harabim d'Oraysa*, a public domain. This is based on the number of counted Jews in the *Midbar*. One would think that the *Shulchan Aruch* would be precise. Still, one could argue that this too, is a rounded number.

In the following case, the 600,000 number is clearly precisely meant: *Tosafos* (*Megillah* 16a) discuss the 10,000 silver talents that Haman offered to entice Achashveirosh to kill the Jewish People. *Tosafos* explain that this is precisely offset by the 600,000 half-shekels donated by *Bnei Yisrael* in the *Midbar*. (*Chasam Sofer*, in his notes to *Mes. Megillah*, explains this calculation.) This calculation is based on the figure of 600,000 Jews in the *Midbar*! Why are the other 3,550 not counted?

I haven't found anyone who discusses this, so let me try my own answer.

When the Jewish People traveled in the *Midbar*, they were surrounded by *Ananei HaKavod*, Clouds of Glory. The Torah reveals that there were Jews who traveled outside these clouds: "those who were straggling behind" (*Devarim* 25:18). These were "weaklings because of their sins, whom the clouds expelled" (*Rashi*, ibid.). Some understand that these were the *Eirev Rav*, insincere converts who accompanied the Jews out of Egypt.

How many Jews were "straggling behind"? We are not told. If we could somehow determine that 3,500 Jews were outside the camp, expelled by the Clouds, we could answer our question. We would understand that there were indeed exactly 600,000 Jews in the Jewish camp.

But — how can we know the precise figure of Jews who were outside the Jewish camp?

I can't prove it, but I have a pretty good hint.

In *Parashas Pekudei*, we find that the donations to the Mishkan were used in its construction. Everything that was donated (precious metals, stones, cloth, and wood) was used somewhere in the sanctified area, the *Machaneh Shechinah*. There was one exception. Curtains surrounded the perimeter of the sanctified area. These curtains hung on hooks. Each hook was mostly behind the curtain, outside of the *Machaneh Shechinah*. These hooks were the only part of the Mishkan that "straggled behind," standing mostly outside of the sanctified area.

Who donated the silver for these hooks? The Torah explains (*Shemos* 38:24-28) that every Jew donated a half-shekel silver coin. These coins were melted down. Most of this silver was used for the *adanim,* the base sockets of the Mishkan walls. A small amount was used for the hooks, "And from the one thousand seven hundred seventy-five [shekels], he made hooks for the pillars ...."

1,775 shekels were used for the hooks. These were donated by 3,550 Jews, each contributing a half-shekel. Who were these 3,550 Jews, whose donation "straggled behind" the other donated materials? It would seem logical that these would be the same people who themselves straggled behind the camp during the travels in the *Midbar.*

If this assumption is indeed correct, it would explain that there were 600,000 counted Jews within the Clouds of Glory. This is the Jewish camp from which the laws of Shabbos are derived, establishing the *reshus harabim d'Oraysa,* the public domain, at precisely 600,000 Jews!

This explains why the calculation regarding Haman's coins uses the figure of 600,000 donated coins. These donations brought forgiveness to the Jewish People. It is no wonder that the other 3,550 coins did not bring forgiveness; they were the coins of the *Eirev Rav!*

✺ Where Was Bavel?

Conventional thinking identifies Bavel (Babylonia) as a region of Mesopotamia, in what is today Southern Iraq. There is virtually unanimous agreement on this, both in Jewish and secular sources.

Yet this seems to be impossible. Iraq is east of Israel; Southern Iraq is due east. The verses in Navi consistently refer to Bavel as to the north of Eretz Yisrael. *Yirmiyah* 1:14 (we read this as a *haftorah* during the Three Weeks) states: "Tragedy will descend from the north." This refers to the attack of the Babylonian army.

In the Gemara, too, we read (*Gitten* 6a, *Bava Basra* 25b), "But Bavel is to the north of Israel." Syria, Lebanon, and Turkey are north of Israel. Iraq is not. Where is Bavel?

av Yakov Emden (in his notes to *Gitten* 6a) answers this Imponderable. His words are crucial to anyone learning the *Book of Yermiyah*. Iraq/Bavel is indeed east of Eretz Yisrael. This was clearly known to the *Tanaim*, as we find the Babylonian Sages constantly referring to the Sages of Eretz Yisrael as dwelling "*B'Maarava* — to the West."

To travel from Bavel to Eretz Yisrael, in a straight western path, would require crossing the Syrian and Arabian Deserts. Today, this is difficult and unpleasant. In Biblical times it was highly dangerous. Travel from Iraq/Bavel to Eretz Yisrael was always plotted in a circuitous route, traveling north, then west, and then back down (through present-day Syria) to arrive in Eretz Yisrael from the north. This was the route of the Babylonian army. Thus, the Prophet correctly warns, "Tragedy will descend from the North."

Rashi to *Berachos* (61b, *s.v. havu*) writes, "Bavel stands to the east of Eretz Yisrael." Some Gemaras have a notation changing the wording of *Rashi* from "east of Eretz Yisrael" to "north of Eretz Yisrael." This change is not necessary, as *Rashi* (as it appears) is correct; Bavel *is* to the east of Eretz Yisrael.

Tosafos (*Bechoros* 55b, *s.v., matra*) identifies Bavel as lying to the southeast of Eretz Yisrael.

✥ When *Rashi* Is Not *Rashi*

Rashi's commentary to the Gemara appears on the inside column of the printed Shas. There is no notation on the page identifying this as *Rashi's* commentary. It is understood by all that these are the words of our great teacher, *Rashi*.

Now, turn to *Rashi's* commentary to the *Rif*. Here, the printer has headed the inside column of the page with the identifying name, "*Rashi*."

Similarly, the *Ein Yaakov* (a *sefer* containing the Agaddic sections of *Shas*) identifies *Rashi* with his name above the inside column.

Is there a reason that *Rashi's* name appears only in these places?

attended Rav Eliya Chazan's shiur for four years. During the very first *shiur*, (we began *Kiddushin*), he presented a question, showing that *Rashi* to the *Rif* contradicts *Rashi* to the

Mishnah. He paused, and then laughed. "This cannot be considered a contradiction. *Rashi* to the *Rif* was not written by *Rashi.*"

The rule for identifying *Rashi's* commentary appears simple (but somewhat convoluted).

Wherever the commentary *was* written by *Rashi*, his name does not appear. In places where the commentary was written by others, in an attempt to mimic *Rashi's* style, the printers have inserted the (false) heading, *Rashi'*

Rashi's name appears as a heading in five places: the commentaries to *Rif, Ein Yaakov, Nedarim, Pirkei Avos,* and *Megillas Taanis.* In all of these places, the commentary is not that of *Rashi*! Why did printers do it this way? Who knows!?

Wait a minute! You may ask regarding *Nazir*, which in our Gemaras has no "*Rashi*" heading. Yet *Maharitz Chayos* at the beginning of *Nazir* writes that the commentary is not *Rashi's*. Did the printers miss one?

Sidei Chemed 9:141 argues that the commentary to *Nazir was* written by *Rashi*, citing a *Teshuvas HaRosh* and *Kesef Mishnah* who refer to it as truly *Rashi*. The printers must have followed this opinion.

SHABBOS IMPONDERABLES

✍ Waving at the Candles

Why do women wave at the Shabbos candles after lighting them? Some women rotate their arms in a circular motion; others wave as if saying good-bye. What is the meaning of this?

This is an Imponderable which has defied all attempts to answer it. Some women have said that they are waving good-bye to the previous week. Others are waving hello to the new week. None of these ideas have a source anywhere.

When lighting Shabbos candles, we first light the candles and then recite the blessing on the mitzvah. The *Rema* (263:5) points out that this is different from all other mitzvos, for which the blessing is recited prior to the mitzvah. For this reason, the *Rema* records that there is a custom for a woman to block the candles from her vision prior to making the *berachah*. This would explain why a woman would cover her eyes or position her hands to block the candles. This does not explain why a woman would wave her hands in a circular (or any other) motion.

V'tzorech iyun.

~§ Why Say Half a Verse Before Kiddush?

Kiddush on *leil Shabbos* begins with *Yom HaShishi* ("the sixth day"). These are the last two words of a verse in the Torah. The custom is to preface these two words with the earlier words of the verse, saying "*VaYehi erev vayehi boker, yom hashishi*" ("and there was evening and there was morning, the sixth day").

The Gemara (*Megillah* 22a) teaches that a person should not recite a portion of a verse, only a complete verse. This would seem to be the reason for this addition. *Yom hashishi* is a segment of a verse. We therefore recite the beginning of the verse as well.

This is all fine and well — unless you look up the verse! In *Bereishis* 1:31, we read, "And God saw everything that He had made, and, behold, it was very good, and there was evening and there was morning, the sixth day."

Even after adding to "*yom hashishi*," we are still reciting only a portion of the verse! What do we gain by adding a few words?

The mystery is compounded by the fact that at the daytime Kiddush, too, the custom is to precede the Kiddush by saying a verse that begins, "*al kein beirach* ..."; this too is half a verse!

*B*en Ish Chai (*Rav Pe'alim* 1:11 and *Torah L'Shimah* 374) and *Magen Geborim* (quoted by *Chasam Sofer* O.C. 10) maintain that one may recite half of a verse, provided that he read the portion before or after the *esnachta*. By adding the few words before *yom hashishi*, we are satisfying this requirement.

Chasam Sofer (O.C. 10) rejects this explanation. He points out that this answer is contradicted by the Gemara. The Gemara (*Megillah* 22a) that teaches that one should not read a portion of a verse is discussing the portion before the *esnachta*! The Gemara is clearly prohibiting the reading of a verse segment, even if the segment begins (or ends) at an *esnachta*.

Chasam Sofer offers a *kabbalistic* explanation for our custom. The earlier portion of this verse, "And God saw every thing that He had made, and, behold, it was very good," refers to the creation of Satan. Reference to this angel at the Shabbos meal is inappropriate. Hence, the first portion of the verse is omitted.

Some *poskim* do not accept either of these answers. They maintain that the prevalent custom is incorrect and that the entire verse should be recited (*Siddur Rav Yaakov Emden, Aruch HaShulchan* 271:25).

܀§ Chassidim Making an Early Shabbos?

The time that halachic night begins is the subject of a well known dispute. In yeshivah circles, the opinion of the Geonim and the *Gra* is followed. They maintain that night begins shortly after sunset. Chassidim follow the opinion of *Rabbeinu Tam*. He maintains that night begins when three stars become visible in the sky. This is well after sunset, anywhere from 30 minutes to 72 minutes after sunset, depending on the geographic location.

This is the reason that Chassidim daven Minchah after sunset; it is still day according to *Rabbeinu Tam*.

Halachah allows a person to begin the Shabbos from *plag haMinchah,* an hour and a quarter (*sha'os z'maniyos*) before nightfall. Indeed, during the spring and summer months, many people choose to make an "early Shabbos" by davening *Kabolas Shabbos* after the *plag haMinchah*. In New York, sunset can be as late as 8:30 p.m. Many minyanim begin Shabbos as early as 7:00 p.m., which is *plag*. A person can never begin his "early Shabbos" before *plag haMinchah*.

An enduring mystery: Those who follow *Rabbeinu Tam's* opinion maintain that nightfall (in June and July), is much later than 8:30. For them, 7 p.m. is well before *plag haMinchah*. Davening the Shabbos prayers before *plag* is a *brachah l'vatalah!*[6]

How then, can we justify the widespread practice of starting an "early Shabbos" on the part of those who follow *Rabbeinu Tam's* opinion?

At the time that I introduced this Imponderable, I could come up with no resolution. Afterwards, I was shown the *Sefer Yisrael V'Hazmanim*, a contemporary compendium of the laws relating to *z'manim*, written by a *talmid chacham* who is a Satmar Chassid. In this *sefer* (Vol. 1, Ch. 12), he explains that according to many *poskim*, the determination of *plag* is not related to *Rabbeinu Tam's z'man* for nightfall. Rather, *plag* is calculated from sunrise to sunset. (See *Magen Avraham* 233:3.) The time for *plag* is thus the same for all!

This opinion can be supported by the fact that even according to the *Gra*, the calculation of *plag* is not based on daytime. Day begins at *alos hashachar*, 72 minutes before sunrise. Still, the daytime as regards *plag* is determined based on sunrise. *Rabbeinu Tam* would have the same opinion regarding the end of daytime, as regards *plag*, which would be at sunset even according to his opinion.

This would explain the custom of making an early Shabbos on the part of those who follow the *z'man* of *Rabbeinu Tam*. It should be noted, however, that this approach is the subject of great controversy.[7]

---

6. See O.C. 263:4 and *Beur Halachah*.

7. *Minhag Yerushalayim* is to follow the *z'man* of the *Geonim*. It is also the *Minhag Yerushalayim* to light Shabbos candles 40 minutes before sunset. *Minchas Yitzchak* (9:20) points out that this can create a problem for those who follow the *Rabbeinu Tam z'man*, since candle-lighting must take place after *plag haMinchah*. This issue was also addressed by *Eretz Zvi* (60; in a letter to the Gerrer Rebbe).

They rule that the reason for the *plag* requirement for candle-lighting is so that it is clear to all that the candles are being lit in honor of Shabbos. In a community where everyone lights the Shabbos candles early, it is not necessary to keep to the *plag* of *Rabbeinu Tam*, since it is clear that candles are being lit in honor of Shabbos.

Minchas Yitzchak apparently does not accept the reason of the *Sefer Yisrael V'Hazmanim*. His explanation is unique to candle-lighting. This seems to indicate that he would not approve of davening early.

⇜ Using Chickens to Determine Nightfall

The precise time for nightfall is the subject of disagreement. The Geonim maintain that night begins soon after sunset. *Rabbeinu Tam* holds that night begins later, when stars are visible in the sky. This is a difference of as many as 72 minutes.

We should be able to settle this dispute once and for all. The Gemara (*Beitza* 7a) teaches that (under normal conditions) chickens do not lay eggs at night. This is considered a certainty; the Gemara relates that we can rely on this assumption to determine Halachah.

If so, we should conduct an experiment, recording the times that chickens lay eggs all over the world. We should then take these records and examine them. If chickens lay eggs after sunset, this would prove *Rabbeinu Tam's* opinion that it is still daytime. On the other hand, if all the chickens lay eggs only until sunset, this would indicate that the *z'man* of the Geonim is correct.

Why didn't the *Rishonim* use this innovative idea to determine the Halachah?[8]

This suggestion caught the imagination of many listeners, but (to my knowledge) no one has yet undertaken to attempt this experiment. Some have suggested that chickens that lay eggs according to *Rabbeinu Tam's z'man* may be destined for Chassidishe *shechitah*!

[It was pointed out that this idea appears in *Pri Yitzchak* (Rav Yitzchak Blazer) 2:18, as a means of determining *bein hashemashos*.]

---

8. A similar question is posed by the *Ramban* (in the beginning of *Eilu Treifos*): Why didn't the *Amoraim* experiment with animals in order to settle disputes regarding *treifos*?

This type of question also appears in *Hilchos Basar V'Cholov* (91). There, we find a dispute between Rav and Shmuel regarding the transfer of taste from a hot food to a cold food. (This is known as the dispute of *tatai gavar/illa'ei gavar.*) Why didn't the *Amoraim* use a taste test to settle this dispute? (See *Kreisi U'Pleisi*, *Pri Migadim* 91:7, and *Tzvi LaTzadik* to 91:4.)

Their answers do not apply to our Imponderable.

Why Do Women Come to Shul for Mussaf?

On Shabbos, many women arrive in shul in time to join in the Mussaf prayer. Women are commanded to daven Shacharis and (according to many *poskim*) Minchah. They are certainly not commanded to daven Mussaf. The *Mishnah Berurah* (106:4) quotes two opinions regarding Mussaf. *Tzlach* maintains that women are prohibited from davening Mussaf. This is because the Mussaf prayer is in place of the Mussaf sacrifice in the *Beis HaMikdash*. Women did not take part in the Mussaf sacrifice and therefore have no connection to the Mussaf prayer. *Mogen Geborim* disagrees. He maintains that women may daven Mussaf, although he concedes that there is no obligation for them to do so.

It is therefore strange that women daven Mussaf, particularly if they haven't davened Shacharis!

In fact, women who arrive at shul when the congregation is at Mussaf should daven the Shacharis *Shimoneh Esrei*!

⁌ Sleeping Late on Shabbos

How strange! All week long, Shacharis minyanim typically begin between 6 a.m. and 8 a.m. On Shabbos, few minyanim begin that time. Most minyanim begin at 8:30 or 9:00 a.m., or later. Does this make sense? Shabbos is the holiest day of the week. Shouldn't we daven even earlier than on an ordinary weekday?[9]

A few possible answers come to mind:

- (A) People are tired after a busy week. If they awoke early, they would need to sleep during the day. It is better to sleep later in the morning, so that the entire day can be spent immersed in the *kedushah* of the *beis hamidrash*.

---

9. The Gemara (*Megillah* 23a) teaches, "On Shabbos, we rush to come [to shul early]." *Rashi* indicates that the Shabbos davening should take place at *vasikin*. Cf. *Rema* (281:1), who writes, "On Shabbos we come to shul later than during the week."

- (B) We are obligated to complete the *parashah* each week, preferably with *Rashi* and *Targum*. It is preferable that this task be completed before the Shacharis Torah reading. We therefore daven later on Shabbos morning, thus giving people time to work feverishly to finish the parashah in time.

- (C) All week long, people are rushed in the morning. Few people actually daven the *korbonos*, the section before davening. On Shabbos morning, people are sufficiently relaxed to daven the *korbonos* slowly and patiently. This is why the shuls are crowded before davening, as people carefully recite the *korbonos*.

- (D) All of the above (*hale'vai!*)

SIDDUR IMPONDERABLES

Where Is the *Neshamah*?

Most siddurim contain an introductory prayer that is said before tefillin are worn in the morning. This prayer contains the words, "and [tefillin are worn] on the head, for the soul is in the brain ...."
    Is the soul really located in the brain?
    The Gemara (*Berachos* 10a) appears to contradict this. There we learn, "just as God fills the entire world, so too does the soul fill the entire body."
    Why do we refer to a soul "in the brain"?

The soul is spiritual and therefore occupies no space, in the normal sense of the word. Still, *Ramban* in his *Toras HaAdam* (*Shaar HaGemul*, p. 287 in the Mosad Rav Kook edition) rejects the opinion of Greek philosophers, who maintained that the soul has no connection to space at all. *Ramban* writes, "It resides in [man], perhaps bound by space, or perhaps not bound by space for it has no physical body and anything without a physical body cannot occupy space. Still, the soul resides in man and is connected to his body ... for this small creation, the bright spirit, connects [the body] to life."

Thus, *Ramban* understands that the soul is the life force of man. As such, it resides in the entire living body.

Nefesh HaChaim (1:14) quotes the *Zohar*, in which the soul is described as a part of the head. How are we to understand this?

There are two aspects to the soul. *Ramban* describes the soul as the life force of man. The soul is also described as the source of man's faculty of wisdom and understanding. *Orchas Tzaddikim* (*Shaar Yiras Shamayim*) writes, "*HaNeshamah hee hachachmah* — The soul is the wisdom."

This view sees the soul as the portal of wisdom and understanding. If so, we can understand that the soul can be said to reside in the brain.

Indeed, *Orchas Tzaddikim* adds (*s.v. u'kmo*), "[God] planted the soul, the spirit of life, knowledge, and understanding, in the membrane of the brain, in the head ...."

We also find this idea in an earlier source, the *Siddur HaRokeach*, authored by one of the *Rishonim*, a disciple of Rabbeinu Yehudah HaChassid. He explains that the tefillin *Shel Rosh* are worn on the part of the body that houses the soul.

To sum up: there are two aspects to the soul. The human being's life force is part of the soul. When the soul departs, man dies. This part of the soul fills the body. The second aspect, the repository of knowledge and understanding, is an aspect of the soul that resides in the brain. The introduction to the performance of the mitzvah of tefillin refers to this when it says, "and [tefillin are worn] on the head, for the soul is in the brain ...."

[*Nefesh HaChaim* (1:14 ff.), based on the *Zohar* and the *Gra*, describes the *kabbalistic* approach to this issue, which describes the soul as hovering above man, not within him.[10]]

---

10. In a footnote to "The Longest Berachah," we introduced a dispute between the *Gra* and the *Baal HaTanya* regarding the description of the location of God. The *Tanya* describes God as everywhere, while the *Gra* rejects this expression. Regarding the soul too, the *Gra* (quoted in *Nefesh HaChaim*, ibid.) maintains that the soul's connection to the body is minimal, that it cannt be said to be contained by the body. One who understands the dispute regarding God will see that the *Gra*'s opinion regarding the description of the location of the soul follows his opinion regarding the description of the location of God.

~§ *Shimoneh Esrei*: Why Does Only One *Berachah* Begin With the Letter *Vuv*?

A *vuv* at the beginning of a word connects it to the preceding word. In *Shimoneh Esrei*, each *berachah* stands independently and is not connected to the previous *berachah*. It is therefore understandable that the *berachos* do not begin with a *vuv*, which would connect them to each other.

The fourteenth *berachah*, *V'LeYerushalayim earcha*, does begin with a *vuv*. Why should the *berachah* regarding Yerushalayim be unique, in that it is the only one of the eighteen original *berachos* of *Shimoneh Esrei* to be connected to the previous *berachah* by the letter *vuv*?

*T*he fourteenth *berachah* is a prayer for the *Shechinah's* return to Yerushalayim. The preceding *berachah*, *Al HaTzaddikim*, is a prayer for the welfare of the righteous Jews. Why should these *berachos* be connected by a *vuv*?

This is a true Imponderable, in that we recite the *Shimoneh Esrei* three times a day without ever wondering about such an obvious question. When this question was posed at the *Navi Shiur*, I knew of no answer. (I was not even aware of any source which posed the question!)

(In fact, it was pointed out that Sefardic siddurim do not have this *vuv* at the beginning of the *berachah*.)

I did receive numerous suggested answers.

■ 1. One well-known *talmid chacham* suggested that the *vuv* was based on the Gemara (*Megillah* 17b) that records the Biblical sources used (by the *Anshei Knesses HaGedolah*) to establish the *berachos* of *Shimoneh Esrei*. There, these two *berachos*, *V'LeYerushalayim* and *Al HaTzadikkim*, have a connection. They stem from one source. This could be a reason to attach them.

After studying the Gemara, however, this answer appears problematic. The source for many of the other *berachos* would also seem to attach them to the preceding *berachah*. Why are only these two *berachos* attached by a *vuv*?

■ 2. Rav Shimon Schwab (*Iyunei Tefillah*) explains *b'derech remez*, (that this is intended to hint at a message). He suggests that the *vuv* is not intended as a connecting *vuv*. Rather, the *vuv* hints at the word "and," implying that there is a second dimension to this *berachah*. This is a hidden reference to *Yerushalayim Shel Ma'alah*, the spiritual city of Jerusalem, which hovers above the physical Jerusalem. This is the portal through which all prayers ascend heavenward. Jews the world over direct their prayers toward Jerusalem. It is therefore fitting that the prayer for Jerusalem should contain a reference to the unique sanctity of the city.

■ 3. A most satisfying answer came in a letter from a mesivta *bachur*. I will let his words (as best I remember them) speak for themselves:

"We pray for a return to Jerusalem. What type of Jerusalem are we praying for? Is it a Jerusalem with *chillul Shabbos* and movie theaters? Of course not.

"We therefore connect this prayer to our previous request. We say to Hashem, 'preserve the righteous among the Jewish People, AND, together with them, let us return to Jerusalem.'"

How beautiful!

This *berachah* was written 2,500 years ago, but the nuance is especially appropriate today!

(Actually, there is another *berachah* that begins with a *vuv*. The twelfth *berachah* (*V'Lamalshinim*) also begins with a *vuv*. However, it is understandable that this *berachah* would be different because it is not part of the original *Shimoneh Esrei*; it was added many generations later.)

◈§ Forgiveness for a Previous Life?

The Gemara (*Megillah* 28a) teaches that before going to sleep each night, it is proper for one to forgive all who may have sinned against him. The Gemara expresses this as a four-word statement, "*shari l'chol man d'tzaron* — I forgive all who have caused me pain."

We are taught to repeat this each night, 365 days a year, so as to include anyone who may have sinned against us on that day.

For some unknown reason, our siddurim have "improved" on the Gemara's language, and replaced the four-word expression with a 98-word expression of forgiveness and prayer.[11]

We ponder the language of this prayer, which reads, in part:

"I hereby forgive anyone who angered or antagonized me ... whether in this life or in a previous life [this refers to the concept of reincarnation — *gilgul*] ...."

It is fine to forgive those who sinned against you in a previous life. But it makes no sense to repeat this forgiveness every single night, 365 days a year! Once forgiveness has been extended for a previous incarnation, it should be adequate. After all, it is no longer possible for anyone to anger or antagonize your previous life. Why repeat the forgiveness over and over?

This Imponderable spurred much interest, and included responses from some who made the novel suggestion that a person can live in two lives simultaneously (a split personality?).

A more reasonable suggestion: In a previous life, Reuven may have lived as Yaakov. Today, Yaakov is no longer alive. Still, Yaakov's enemies may be speaking *lashon hara* about him, even today. A person should want to forgive even these sins. Thus, each and every day he forgives anyone who sinned against Yaakov, his previous self.

The difficulty with this lies with Rav Yaakov Kamenetsky's *chidush* (in *Emes L'Yaakov* to *Parashas VaYeishev*) that there is no prohibition of *lashon hara* against people who have already died!

Still, Rav Yaakov records a *takanah* prohibiting slandering the dead. Although slander is not nearly as common as *lashon hora*, it may be that the nightly forgiveness is aimed at this.

◆§ *Bircas Kohanim*: Three Mysteries

During *Bircas Kohanim* (the Kohanim's Blessing), we recite a prayer related to our dreams. In this prayer, we recognize that we do not understand the meaning of dreams, and ask that God interpret them favorably.

---

11. This prayer does not appear in *Rishonim*. It does appear in *Kaf HaChaim* 239:2, and is alluded to by the *Kitzur Shulchan Aruch* 71:3.

This is an ancient practice, recorded both in the Gemara and *Shulchan Aruch*.

How is this prayer said?

Two customs are recorded. Some have a custom to recite this prayer three times, once after each of the three blessings of the Kohen. This custom is recorded in *Chayei Adam* (32:31) and *Mishnah Berurah* (130:5). Others say it only once. This custom is attributed to the *Ari*. *Kaf HaChayim* 130:1, 4 brings both customs.

Which custom is recorded in our siddurim? Is it printed once or three times?

Virtually every siddur contains this prayer twice, once after each of the first two blessings of the Kohen. Why? How did this error begin and why is it continued?

A point to ponder.

■ **A second Imponderable:** Why do our siddurim continue to print verses after each of the words of *Bircas Kohanim*? *Poskim* all seem to agree that these verses should not be said. This is the ruling of the *Shulchan Aruch*, *Rema*, *Gra*, and all who follow them. Why do printers continue to print these verses?

■ **A third Imponderable:** When the Kohanim finish reciting each blessing, we answer "Amen," as required by *Shulchan Aruch* (128:13).

When there are no Kohanim, the words of *Bircas Kohanim* are recited by the *chazzan*. When he finishes reciting each blessing, we answer, "*kein yehi ratzone.*" This is also mentioned in *Shulchan Aruch* (127:2).

Why are there two different responses to the identical words?

~§ A Prayer for Tomorrow

The morning blessings conclude with a request. In part, we beseech God to "rescue me today and every day from *azei panim v'azus panim* ... shameless men and shameless behavior."

Given that we recite this blessing anew each morning, why is it necessary to add the request that we be rescued today "and every day"? Isn't it enough to repeat the *berachah* every day for that day?

*R*av Eizel Charif was on his way to shul one morning when he was accosted by a *nudnik*, a man who questioned him incessantly. The Rov was unable to shake the man off.

Finally, he turned to the man and said, "Thank you; you've answered a question that has bothered me for years."

The man was puzzled, "But I only asked questions. I didn't offer any answers."

Rav Eizel Charif replied, "Each morning I ask God to 'rescue me today and every day from *azei panim v'azus panim* ... shameless men and shameless behavior.' I wondered why I add 'and every day,' since I plan to make this request separately tomorrow. Now, I know. I realize that when I am traveling to shul, I also need God's protection from *azei panim*. But I have not yet recited the prayer for today. Thanks to you, I realize that it is also necessary to pray for the morning of the next today."

⋐ The Last Words of *Shemoneh Esrei*

The final words of *Shemoneh Esrei* are said after we take three steps back. We say, "He Who makes peace in His heavens, may He make peace upon us and upon all of Israel, and now respond, Amen."

These words are recited silently. No one hears them. To whom are we saying, "*v'imru Amen* — and now respond, Amen"?

*R*av Shimon Schwab explains that this expression refers to the angels that protect the Jewish People and help a person's prayers ascend to heaven. To them we say, "... and now respond, Amen."[12]

It would truly be wonderful for us to appreciate the significance of our prayers. Our intensity in prayer would be greatly enhanced if we would stand in prayer with the image of two angels accompanying us.

---

12. There is a source for this in *Magen Avraham* (66:7).

The *Migdal–Migdol* Mystery Revisited

One of the enduring siddur mysteries involves the final portion of *Bircas HaMazon*. There, we find the verse beginning, "*Magdil yeshuos malko.*" This is a verse from *Shiras Dovid*, Dovid HaMelech's song of praise. This song of praise appears twice in Tanach, once in *Shmuel Beis*, Chapter 22, and again as the eighteenth chapter of *Sefer Tehillim*. (In both places, this is verse 51.)

There are numerous minor differences between the two versions of the *Shiras Dovid*. One difference is in the aforementioned verse, which is punctuated as "*mikdol*" in *Shmuel Beis* and as "*magdil*" in *Tehillim*. In *Bircas HaMazon*, the siddur instructs us to read this verse with the *Tehillim* punctuation (*magdil*) during the week and with the *Shmuel Beis* punctuation (*migdol*) on Shabbos and Yom Tov. This is an unusual and unique occurrence in the siddur and begs explanation.

The best known explanation is that of the Rabbi Boruch Epstein (author of the *Torah Temimah*), in his *Mekor Boruch*. He suggests that this is actually the result of a printer's error. According to this explanation, the verse may actually be read either way, both during the week and on Shabbos. The printer had indicated this by printing the word as *magdil* and adding a notation reading, "In *Shmuel Beis: migdol*." The words "In *Shmuel Beis*" were abbreviated as "*beis shin beis*," a common abbreviation. Later, an ignorant typesetter spelled out the abbreviation, but misunderstood this as an abbreviation for "*B'Shabbos* — On Shabbos." Over time, this has become the norm in all our siddurim — erroneously!

As intriguing as this suggestion may be, it is simply incorrect. The book of *Shmuel* is actually one volume of Neviim. The division into two volumes, *Shmuel Aleph* and *Shmuel Beis*, came to the Jewish world as the work of Christian printers in the seventeenth century. Yet the custom of reading *migdol* on Shabbos is found in the *Avudraham*. He lived in the fourteenth century, well before the book of *Shmuel* was divided into two volumes! Thus, the *migdol–magdil* custom began at a time that *Shmuel Beis* did not yet exist!

What, then, is the reason for this custom?

Tzofnas Paneach suggests a different reason for our custom. The Gemara (*Shabbos* 116b) indicates that there was a *takanah* prohibiting the reading of the books of *Kesuvim* on Shabbos. *Tehillim* is one of the books of *Kesuvim*; *Shmuel Beis* is part of *Neviim*.

The verse in *Bircas HaMazon* may be read either way, as *magdil* or as *migdol*. On Shabbos, out of deference to this *takanah*, Jews would deliberately switch to the *Neviim* version of this verse, reading it as *migdol*.

Others (see *Avudraham*) suggest another explanation. Grammatically, the *migdol* pronunciation is considered a fuller expression, "*maleih*." Shabbos, as the holiest day of the week, was thus accorded the fuller reading of the word, *migdol*. The less-significant reading, *magdil*, was left for the weekdays.

ﬆ Why Does the *Chazzan* Face the *Aron* When Saying "*Gadlu*"?

On Shabbos, after the Sefer Torah is removed from the Ark, the *chazzan* leads the people in reciting three verses. The custom is that the *chazzan* faces the people when reciting the first two verses. The third verse is customarily said as the *chazzan* turns back to face the Ark. Why is this so?

This is even more puzzling when we consider the verses that are recited.

We would understand that when the *chazzan* addresses the congregation, he faces them. The first two verses are certainly not addressed to the people. First, the *chazzan* says "*Shema Yisrael* ...," something he said earlier without turning to face the people. He then declares "*Echod Elokeinu* ...," praising Hashem, which is also a type of prayer that is routinely said when facing *mizrach*.

Gadlu, on the other hand, *is* addressed to the people, as the *chazzan* says, "Declare the greatness of Hashem with me, and let us exalt His name together." Shouldn't this be said facing the people? Yet at this point, the *chazzan* turns back to the Ark.

This question is found in the *Siddur Va'Yaas Avraham*, which refers to this practice as an error. He adds a second reason to object to the custom of facing the Ark. The Sefer Torah is generally carried from the Ark to the *bimah* along its northern side. This is the right side of the *chazzan* as he faces the people, and fits with the custom (mentioned in *poskim*), to take a route that is to the person's right. If the person is facing the Ark, this would require him to turn to his *left*. This seems to indicate that the *poskim* understood that a *chazzan* does face the people.

Yam Shel Shlomo (appended to the end of *Bava Kamma*) lists fifty differences in custom between *bnei Eretz Yisrael* and *bnei Bavel*. Difference #36 reads, "*Bnei Bavel* turn their faces to the people and their backs to the Aron Kodesh. *Bnei Eretz Yisrael* turn their faces to the *Aron Kodesh*."

The wording is ambiguous. To what does this refer? At what point do *bnei Bavel* face the *Aron Kodesh* and *bnei Eretz Yisrael* face the Aron?

We are unaware of any point in the davening where these two customs are found. Could it be that *Yam Shel Shlomo* was referring to the saying of *Gadlu*?

(As to the contention that this custom is not mentioned in the *poskim*, it was pointed out that the *Aruch HaShulchan* (134:4) does bring this, although he offers no explanation.)

◈§ Why Do We Refer to a "Second And Third" Kiddush in Our *Zemiros* of Shabbos?

When we return from shul on the night of Shabbos, we sing *Shalom Aleichem*. Afterwards, many sing (or say) the *Ribbon Olamim*, which is a beautiful prayer found in most siddurim. In it, we describe our Shabbos preparations, and say: "... and I shall bear witness that You created everything in six days, and I will repeat a second and third time, over my [Kiddush] cup, in great joy."

The reference to a second Kiddush is understandable, since we recite Kiddush at the morning Shabbos meal. Reference to a "*third time*" is puzzling. The custom to make Kiddush at the third Shabbos meal is not a prevalent one. Why then do we pledge to offer a third testimony to creation "over my cup"?

Some siddurim seek to rectify this problem by changing the *nikudos* to read past tense at the first two references to Kiddush, with only the third reference in the future tense. The words would then read; "... *and I bore testimony that You created everything in six days, I repeated it again and I will repeat it a third time over my [Kiddush] cup, in great joy.*"

This would refer to the two times that we mentioned Creation in shul (once in the Maariv *Shemoneh Esrei* and once afterwards in *Mayein Sheva*). Only the third reference is over the Kiddush cup.

This appears in many siddurim, but it appears to be contrived. The two words, *v'ashaneh v'ashalesh*, follow each other. The *aleph* prefix, which appears in both words, usually denotes future tense. It seems forced to assign different grammatical forms to each word.

Others suggest that only the first reference is past tense, referring to the Maariv prayer. The two other references (*v'ashaneh v'ashalesh*) are future tense, referring to the two cups of Kiddush still to come, one before the evening *seudah* and one before the first day *seudah*.

A third suggestion is based on the *Rambam* (*Sefer HaMitzvos* 155), who views *havdalah*, the blessing at the end of Shabbos, as a form of Kiddush. The *Rambam* sees Kiddush and Havdalah as two parts of one mitzvah, "to sanctify the Shabbos when it arrives and when it leaves." We can therefore understand that the "*third time*" is a reference to Havdalah.

This explanation allows us to leave all three references in future tense. This also allows them all to refer to testimony "*over my cup.*" The reference *is* to three cups to come — the two Kiddush cups, followed by the cup of Havdalah.

CHASUNAH IMPONDERABLES

◆§ Why Do the Mothers Break the Plate?

Our custom is to have a *Tanaim* ceremony before the wedding. At the conclusion of the *Tanaim*, an earthenware plate is broken. The custom is that the mothers of the bride and groom break the plate. Why is this honor accorded to the women? Why not have the groom break the plate, just as he breaks the glass under the *chuppah*? Or perhaps the two fathers should break the plate. After all, it is they who have accepted the *Tanaim* obligations upon themselves. Why the women?

There are many *seforim* that discuss wedding customs. Interestingly, I have not seen a single *sefer* that explains this custom or offers a source for it!

I'll offer a suggestion of my own.

Traditionally, the *Tanaim* was a business document that outlined the financial obligations that each side accepted upon itself in regard to the support of the young couple. Today, in most circles the document is essentially meaningless and creates no new obligation. Still, we continue to write *Tanaim* in deference to the original custom.

The custom to involve the women may relate to the times that the document created a real financial obligation. When a person accepts a financial obligation through a contract, his real assets are pledged to secure the obligation. In the event that those assets were previously pledged to another obligation, the earlier obligation would take precedence. Every married man does have a prior financial obligation to which his assets are pledged. This is the *kesubah* document, which every man undertakes as an obligation to his wife when they marry. A child is married off many years later. The father's *kesubah* obligation precedes the new *Tanaim* obligation.

At the *Tanaim*, we wish to have the new obligations supersede the earlier *kesubah* obligation. This can only be done by the consent of the wives, who may waive their rights in favor of the *Tanaim*. By having the women take part in finalizing the *Tanaim* obligation, they become partners in the new obligation. Their rights are thereby subordinated to the *Tanaim*, giving it precedence.

How Do You Say "Son-in-Law" in Hebrew?

A homograph is a word that has two meanings. The Hebrew language does not contain any true homographs. When a Hebrew word appears to have two meanings, the meanings are actually related by a single theme.

The Torah uses the word *chasan* to mean both a groom and a son-in-law; *kallah* to mean a bride and a daughter-in-law.

We are all familiar with these words as referring to groom and bride. The status of groom and bride lasts for only seven days. For how long are the children-in-law considered *chasan* and *kallah*?

An in-law relationship is always a fragile one. Parents are accustomed to correcting their child's behavior; after all, they've raised him from childhood. This behavior cannot be carried over to a child-in-law, who needs to be accepted and is not accustomed to their criticism.

Parents sometimes say to me, "I love my son-in-law. I will treat him just like my own son!"

I correct them. "No, no! Don't treat him like a son. Your son is accustomed to your criticism; your son-in-law is not. Treat him like a son-in-law."

Rav Chaim Kanievsky finds this wonderful lesson in the words *chasan* and *kallah*. To parent-in-laws, their new child must forever be viewed with the appreciation, joy, and acceptance of the original *sheva berachos* week. Indeed, they should remain *chasan* and *kallah* forever.

◆§ Why Doesn't the *Kesubah* Contain the Family Names of the *Chasan* and *Kallah*?

Traditionally, the names of the *chasan* and *kallah* are written in the *kesubah* in the style described in the Gemara. The person is described as the child of the father, e.g., "Reuven ben Shimon," without mentioning a family name. (This is based on *Rema* in *Seder HaGet* 129:19.)

Rav Moshe Feinstein (*Igros Moshe* E.H. 1:178; also *Maharsham* 1:83) rules that today, when use of family names has become the standard means of identification, the family name should be used.

Our Imponderable involves Rav Moshe's own behavior. I have friends for whom Rav Moshe was *misader kiddushin*. Rav Moshe wrote their *kesubah* without use of family names! This contradicts Rav Moshe's own *teshuvah*. A real Imponderable!

After this was asked at the *Navi Shiur*, I was contacted by one of Rav Moshe's grandchildren. He explained that Rav Moshe did indeed maintain that the family name should be used. Still, Rav Moshe was afraid that the exclusive use of a family name in a *kesubah* may lead people to question the validity of *gitten*, which do not have a family name. He therefore continued to write *kesuvos* in the old manner.

◆§ Why Does the *Kallah's* Family Pay for the Wedding?

The predominant custom is for the *kallah's* side to bear the cost of the wedding. This was not always the practice. The Gemara (*Kesuvos* 3a and 10a) assumes that it is the *chasan* who pays for the wedding meal. We find in the *Shulchan Aruch* (E.H. 64:4), "If the *chasan* does not wish to make a wedding feast and the *kallah's* family wants one, we compel the *chasan* to make an appropriate feast …."

None of the commentators to the *Shulchan Aruch* indicate a different custom.

Thus, for at least 1,600 years (from *Shas* through *Shulchan Aruch*), it was the custom for the *chasan* to pay for the wedding meal. When did this change — and why?

This is truly a mysterious change in our practice. Someone presented an answer from the *Piskei Teshuvah*, quoting the *Sfas Emes* (footnote to 194).

The Gemara (*Berachos* 6b) teaches: "One who enjoys the *chasan's* meal but fails to rejoice with him violates the five *kolos* ...."

The *Sfas Emes* maintains that our practice has changed in order to protect those who enjoy the wedding feast but do not really help in the celebration. In order to avoid the strict reprimand of this Gemara, we have ceased to make a "*chasan's* meal" (mentioned in this Gemara). Instead, we have turned the wedding feast into a "*kallah's* meal," to which this Gemara does not apply.

This is a difficult explanation. The Gemara is referring to a wedding feast. It does not really matter who pays for it; the idea is simply that one who benefits from the wedding feast must also give to the couple by rejoicing with them.

↦ Why Is the *Kesubah* Signed by People Who Haven't Read It?

The next time that you attend a wedding, watch the procedure for the signing of the *kesubah* document. In the United States, this is usually done at the *chasan's* table, before going to the *badekin*. Witnesses watch a *kinyan*, smile for the camera, and then sign the *kesubah* — without reading it! Can these be valid witnesses if they don't know what they are signing?

Recently, I've seen some *misadrei kiddushin* who insist that the witnesses read the *kesubah*. Isn't that the right way to do it?

*I*ncredible as this may sound, the "new" practice of insisting that witnesses read the *kesubah* is incorrect!

Rema (E.H. 66:1) writes that one should not insist that witnesses read the *kesubah*. The long-standing custom (even in the 16th century) was that witnesses signed the *kesubah* without reading it. The *Rema* feared that if we would start to insist that witnesses do read the *kesubah*, people would assume that the previous *kesubos* are invalid. To avoid this error, the practice of not insisting that the *kesubah* be read is continued.

Why is the *kesubah* kosher if the witnesses haven't signed it?

The *Shulchan Aruch* (*Choshen Mishpat* 45:2) rules that witnesses should read a contract before signing it. However, if a witness trusts the individual who wrote the contract, the *Shulchan Aruch* allows him to sign as a witness without reading the document. At a wedding, the witnesses place their trust in the *misader kiddushin* who completes the *kesubah*. They sign the *kesubah* based on his say-so.

It should be noted that the *Rema* refers to the person in charge of the *kesubah*, advising him not to insist that the witnesses read the contract. The witnesses themselves are not restricted from reading the *kesubah*. Indeed, it seems from the *Rema* that this is preferable.

◈§ Why Do We Say "Mazel Tov" at a Wedding?

Ashkenazic Jews seem to use "Mazel Tov" as an expression of congratulations. The origin of this expression is unclear. It does not appear in the Gemara, *Rishonim*, or early *Acharonim*.

The meaning is equally unclear. *Mazel* is commonly defined as "luck"; *Mazel Tov* means "Good Luck." This has nothing to do with congratulations.

Why are we are telling the *chasan*, "Good luck!" as he prepares to head to the *chuppah*?

*T*he students of Rav Eliyahu Dessler, in a footnote in *Michtav M'Eliyahu* (4:p98), recall their Rebbi's explanation.

Mazel is not "luck." It is a reference to an individual's unique purpose in this world. We say that a person's *mazel* is to be poor or rich or to be healthy or ill. Some people take this as an expression of a person's luck. In reality, it is an expression of a person's purpose in this world, his *tafkid*. Wealth, poverty, and illness are examples of tools that a person uses to fulfill that *tafkid*.

When a person is married, his new partner must be an individual who can help him fulfill his life's role and respond properly to his life challenges.

Thus, at a wedding (or any other major event in a person's life), we offer the most significant blessing. We wish the new couple success in fulfilling their individual *tafkid*, their special purpose in life. Mazel Tov — may you do well in fulfilling your *mazel*.

[See also the Munkatcher Rebbe in *Divrei Torah* 1:7, who offers a *kabbalistic* explanation for this expression.]

✑ Why Don't We Make a *She'hechiyanu* at a Wedding?

Every Yom Tov, we thank Hashem for having brought us to the joyous festival by reciting the *berachah* of *she'hechiyanu*. We thank Hashem for giving us life so that we may experience the occasion. When we wear a new suit, or eat a new fruit, or perform a new mitzvah, we also thank Hashem "Who has kept us alive, sustained us, and brought us to this moment."

A wedding is the most joyous moment in a person's life (it certainly beats the new-fruit experience!). Why don't we recite the *she'hechiyanu* blessing on our wedding day?[13]

---

13. *Tamei HaMinhagim* p. 411, quotes *Halachos Kitanos*, as follows: "*Ri Buton* wrote that one who is married may recite a *she'hechiyanu*, but when they asked the advice of the *Ohr Shraga*, he replied that you should have inquired regarding the blessing *dayan haemes* [the blessing recited upon a relative's death]."

In its original source the statement was made in reference to one who was marrying a woman for her money. In context, the statement is sensible. The partial quote is perplexing.

I attended the *semichah shiur* of my *Rebbe*, Rav Avrohom Pam, *zt"l*, for two years. During that time, I cannot remember Rav Pam digressing from the halachic topics of *Yoreh Deah* — except once.

We were studying the laws of *shechitah*. The question came up: Does a *shochet* recite a *she'hechiyanu* the first time that he performs this mitzvah?

Here, Rav Pam digressed to ask why a *she'hechiyanu* is not recited at a wedding.

He paused, looked at his class of young married (and soon-to-be-married) men, and explained. "The *she'hechiyanu* would imply that the joy of marriage is already complete. It isn't. Marriage is what you make of it."

A brief, but powerful, message.

Chasam Sofer (O.C. 55) offers a different explanation. The language of the *she'hechiyanu* blesses God for bringing us to this moment. A wedding day is different. It is the responsibility of the individual to do whatever is necessary to marry. Man must exercise great *hishtadlus* to arrive at his wedding day. This message is so important that we would not wish to recite a blessing that implies that it is God's job to bring us to the *chuppah*.

◆§ *Bashert* or Not *Bashert*?

People ponder this issue often: Is a person's match guaranteed or not? *Bashert* or not *bashert*?

The Gemara discusses the issue. Incredibly, there are two versions of this Gemara, which differ in regard to one apostrophe. If we read the Gemara with the apostrophe, it is teaching us that a marriage is guaranteed to happen. The version without the apostrophe clearly teaches that a person can marry outside of his *bashert*.

*T*he best-known Gemara related to this topic teaches, "Forty days before a child is formed, a heavenly voice comes forth and declares, 'the daughter of *piloni* is for *piloni*.' "

Does this mean that the two will certainly marry? This Gemara is unclear.

There is a second, lesser-known Gemara that deals with the issue more directly. In *Mes. Moed Katan* 18b, in the popular version of the Gemara, as it appears in our Shas, we read:

> Rava overheard a man praying. He said, "Let me marry Plonis."
> Rava said to him, "Do not pray this way. If she is right for you, you won't lose her. If she is not, you will end up denying God [because you will not marry her and you will feel that prayer does not help — *Rashi*].'"

The final word of this section, referring to God, is spelled *lamid-hei*, with an apostrophe over the *hei*. This signals that the letter *hei* is an abbreviated reference to God.

This version of the Gemara maintains that a person is sure to marry his *bashert*.

The second version of the Gemara, which appears in *Ein Yaakov*,[14] differs in the slightest of ways. A single apostrophe is missing from Rava's words, so that the final word of this section is spelled *lamid-hei*, without an apostrophe. This word, *lah*, is Hebrew for "her." This changes the meaning of the Gemara dramatically. The Gemara now reads:

> Rava overheard a man praying. He said, "Let me marry Plonis."
> Rava said to him, 'Do not pray this way. If she is right for you, you won't lose her. If she is not, you will end up fighting with her [because you will marry her and not get along with her — *Rashi* in *Ein Yaakov*].'"

The final word of this section, "her" is spelled *lamid-hei*, without an apostrophe.

According to this version, a person can marry anyone — but the results are best when marrying a *bashert*.

This is an incredible difference resulting from the slightest of textual discrepancies (see following page).

I checked the old Vatican manuscripts of the Talmud Bavli (a copy of these manuscripts is available in our yeshivah library) to

---

14. *Rashi* (*s.v. shema yikadmenu*) to the *Rif* apparently had this version as well. *Rashi* there explains the Gemara in line with *Ein Yaakov's* version and not in line with *Rashi* to the Gemara. (*Rashi* to the *Rif* was not authored by *Rashi* himself.)

see which version it contained. I was surprised to see that Rava's response is completely missing from the manuscripts! The confusion remains. (It must be *bashert*.)[15]

Above, the Gemara in Moed Katan 18b as it appears in the Vilna Shas. This version of the Gemara teaches that a person's bashert is predetermined and cannot be changed by prayer.

Below, the Ein Yaakov presents two versions of one word of this Gemara, with the difference of an apostrophe between them. The new version (without the apostrophe) teaches that prayer can change a bashert, but that the results may not be desirable. Note that Rashi's commentary, as it appears in the Ein Yaakov, explains both versions.

---

15. There are numerous additional sources for the *bashert* discussion (including the *Chasam Sofer*, mentioned in the previous note regarding *she'hechiyanu*). The *sugya* in *Moed Katan* is the only Talmudic source.

INDICES

PARASHAH INDEX
Find a thought on the weekly Parashah...

Parashah Reference:	Page
BEREISHIS	
Bereishis 1:31	49, 83, 432
Bereishis 2:18	183
Bereishis 2:23	97 – 98
Bereishis 2:24	93
Bereishis 5:24	128
Noach	44
Chayei Sarah	39, 199
Toldos 28:9	361
Vayeitzei	118, 206
Vayeitzei 32:2	38
Vayishlach 33:14	38
Vayishlach 33:20	129
Vayishlach 36:3	361
Vayigash 45:14	233
Vayigash	152
Vayechi	230
SHEMOS	
Shemos 1:21	411
Va'eira 7:7	423
Bo 12:9	387-389
Beshalach	417-419
Beshalach 16:33	178
Yisro	250
Yisro 20:12	71, 73
Yisro 34:1	80
Mishpatim 22:8	390
Mishpatim 24:1	129
Pikudei	425, 428
VAYIKRA	
Tzav	424
Tzav 5:6	391
Tzav 7:22	353
Kedoshim 19:4	387-389
Emor 19:25	397

Parashah Reference:	Page
BAMIDBAR	
Nasso	49
Nasso 6:5	416
Nasso 6:26	148
Beha'aloscha 10:9	373
Masei	44
DEVARIM	
Va'eschanan 4:2	66
Va'eschanan 5:16	80
Eikev 8:10	164
Eikev 10:12	148
Eikev 10:16	191
Eikev 11:13	373
Re'eh 12:30	67
Re'eh 13:1	66
Re'eh 15:8	105
Ki Seitzei	175
Ki Seitzei 23:2	350
Ki Seitzei 25:18	428
Ki Savo 28:24	394 fn 5
Vayeilech 30:15	210
Haazinu 32:6	318-319

INDEX

Achav, 187
Adar Sheini, 278
Aleppo Codex see *Keter Aram Soba*
Alos Hashachar, 286-299
   first rays or lit sky?, 287 fn 3
   morning star?, 287
   two ways to calculate, 288
altars (*bamah*), 68
angel – God's Will, 216
   accept *ol malchus Shamayim*, 216-217
   described in prayer, 215-218
   with us during prayer, 443
anger –controlling, 192
   from unrealistic expectations, 395
   ways to control, 28
apology – don't demand, 147
appreciating Eretz Yisrael, 230
Ashrei – *poseiach es yadecha*, 159, 164
   why at Minchah?, 169
astronomy – 27 day lunar month, 301 fn 1
   conjunction, see molad
   mitzvah to study?, 272-273, 286
   determines midday, 293 fn 11
   Steady State Theory, 283-285
   the "morning star," 287
Ataliyahu, 93
Attributes of Hashem – First *midah*, 125 – 135
Avraham Aveinu – his *geirim*, 381
ayin hara, 75
baalei teshuvah – unique *nisyonos*, 45-46
bal tosif, 66
"Baruch Hashem" – saying, 154
bashert?, 454
Bavel – location, 429
bechirah, see free will
Beged Kefes, 319
   Mi Chamocha, 321
bein hashmashos, 293 fn 10, 435
Ben Asher/Ben Naftali – Who were they?, 343

Ben Naftali's view accepted, 357
   chataf, 359
   chaseiros v'yeseiros, 355
   origin of disputes, 344-345
   override a Gemara?, 355
   tiferes hakriyah, 359
   whom do we follow?, 347
   Yisachar, 357-358
Beruria, wife of Rav Meir, 255-256, 259 fn 1
biographies of *Gedolim* mislead, 48
Bircas HaMazon – On *kezayis* of bread, 165
   u'vituvo chayinu, 157
Bircas HaKohanim – three mysteries, 441-442
bitachon, 161
   achieved by exile, 28
   in yourself, 162
   purpose of prayer, 373 and fn1
   Shema, 218
   source of happiness, 131
bluff – a world of, 155
Caleiv, 411
calendar – calculating *Shemittah*, 363-369
   Cheshbon Tohu, 367
   dispute regarding correct year, 366
   two-day Rosh Chodesh, 408
   year of *Churban* disagreement, 365
Chabad – Sefer Torah is different, 351-352
Chanoch – was *Matat*, 128
charity – *dei machsoro*, all he's accustomed to, 105, 110
Chasam Sofer – *hesped* for Tzfas earthquake, 61
   love of Jerusalem, 55
   on Eretz Yisrael, 58, 60
   on marriage, 199-200
chaseiros v'yeseiros, 355-356
   greater experts today, 357
chataf, 316-317

chataf vowel – dispute regarding, 359-360
chatzos (noon), 293 fn 11
cheilek – as measure of time, 280 fn 9
cheshbon tohu, 367
   our custom is contradiction, 367 fn 1
chickens – lay eggs only by day, 435
child sacrifice, 66
chinuch – mother exempt?, 378-386
   d'Rabbanan obligation?, 379, 383
   two understandings, 379
   using *posul* esrog?, 380-381
   each parent's role, 382-383
Churban – dispute which year, 365
   zecher l'churban story, 84
Chushim ben Dan, 229-230
clichés – are probably true, 96
clocks – *see* Time
complaining, 53-54
dageish – *chazak* and *kal*, 319 fn 8, 323-324
dating – purpose of, 172
David, King – realized he'd succeed, 43
depression - and yeshivah *bachurim*, 258 fn 5
   better than Rothschild, 158
   expectations cause, 104-121
   fall and pick yourself up, 48
   focus on what you deserve, 51
   not a time to make decisions, 52
   not rooted in reality, 155
   Rav Hutner to disciple, 48
   understanding what's happening, 46-47
   use *bitachon* to fight, 131
   when you get a raise, 76
difficulties – attitude, 396-397
   opportunity for greatness, 222
dikduk – *see also* m'liel and m'lra
   see also havarah
   Bnei Yisaschar on, 319
   chataf, 316-317
   considered Torah Study?, 314 fn 1
   dageish chazak/kal, 319, 323-324

emes is *sheker*, 327
for Aramaic words, 336-339
frequency of *chataf* use, 359-360
God's Name, 331
havarah zarah, 329
hei haydeeah, 318 fn 6
importance, 312, 324
in Shema, 333
kameitz katan, 328 fn 6
m'liel and m'lra, 326-335
mistakes delay *Mashiach*, 312
Moshe v'Caleiv rule, 317-318
patach genuvah, 332
Rav Pam's advice, 313-314
rules for *Beged Kefes*, 265
rules for *shva na/nach*, 264
rules for *tenuah kallah*, 265
rules for *vuv* at beginning of word, 266 fn 5; 267
shva na/nach, 336-337
tenuah gedolah/ketanah, 328
two common errors, 315
Yaihoo, 319-320
disagreements – a good thing, 200, 203
disappointments, 82-83
Dr Asch's experiment, 207-209
dreams – and *Bircas Kohanim*, 441
eclipse, 309-310
   solar – and the *molad*, 282
Emden, Rav Yaakov *see* Rav Yaakov Emden
entropy, 210
Eretz Yisrael
   difficulties, 59
   during times of danger, 233-234
   highest spot in the world, 55
   talk respectfully about, 58
   what to see, 62
Esav – his death, 230
   his wives, 361
evil people – relating to, 93
exile – personal exile of great men, 26
faith – *see bitachon*
   purpose of prayer, 373 fn1
fast days – *z'man achilah* in morning, 292

Feinstein, Rav Moshe – *bamos* in Tanach, 68
   ein onshin min hadin, 144,162
   name in *kesubah*, 450
   number of verses in Torah, 425
   praying for someone else's *ruchniyus*, 256
   purpose of punishment, 144,162
   stop learning to say Tehillim?, 227
forgiveness – for previous *gilgul*, 440
free will – affected by prayer?, 256-262
   can someone hurt you?, 131 (fn)
   See also Nekudas HaBechirah
giraffe meat, 407
God – "Knowing Hashem," 137
   accepts bribes, 148
   gives man his desires?, 160, 164
   judges a person *m'dato*, 150
   m'lo kol ha'aretz kivodo, 219-220
   pronouncing His Name, 317-318
   punishes only to repair, 144, 162
   spelled with two *yuds*, 406
   takes revenge?, 139
good – requires sustenance, 210
happiness – *Orchos Tzaddikim*'s method, 28, 131, 154
Harugei Lod, 227
Hashem – see God
havarah – *havarah murkevet, pishutah, zarah*, 329
Henna, Rav Zalman see Rav Zalman Henna
humiliation – dealing with, 131
   Rav Chaim Kanievsky, 224
husbands – work for their wives, 100
in-laws – critical of children, 143
   and *kibud av*, 72
   criticizing child-in-law, 94
   favor their own child, 99
   interfering, 201
   on children, 93-94
Iyov – 228
Jerusalem – cares if you remember her, 61
   in *Mashiach's* time, 64
   jealous of other cities, 55
   never crowded?, 58
   places to visit, 62
   talk nicely about, 57-58
   visiting *lishmah*, 63-64
   Yom Yerushalayim, 56
Jews in desert – 600,000?, 427
judging favorably, 195-196
judgment – trading *aveiros* for *mitzvos*?, 189
Kaddish – *m'liel* and *m'lra*, 332
   shichintei, givurtei, 338
   yisgadeil v'yiskadeish, 338-339
kal v'chomer – *ein onshin min hadin*, 145
kameitz katan – what is a, 328 fn 6
kesubah – see wedding
Keter Aram Soba, 340-343
   dispute regarding *succo*, 356
   Shiras Devorah, 354
   Shiras Dovid, 354
   chataf, 360 fn
kibbud av v'eim, 71
   standing for them 72
Kiddush Levanah – in month with lunar eclipse, 310
   not after a solar eclipse, 309
   time for, 307-309
kosher – missing *treif* chicken leg, 209
Kriyas Yam Suf, 417-419
Kuzari – prayer for Eretz Yisrael, 231
leap year – year left Egypt, 424
   schedule of, 278
life – goes in streaks, 42
Luchos – two sets, 80
m'leil and m'lra – how to determine, 328-330
   God's name, 331
   Kaddish, 332
   most important, 333
   never three syllables from end, 328 fn 3
   patach genuvah, 332
   rules for a suffix, 330 fn 7
manna, 178
marriage – afraid of disagreements?, 200
   communication, 174

courtship must continue, 172
deserve her respect, 180
disappointments, 88-89
each is a product of his home, 97
expecting differences, 114
feeling of partnership, 175
her standard of living, 106, 113
not alike at all, 198-204
spending, 177
stop trying to change her, 115
things change after the *chupah*, 198
when newness wears off, 174
why not create man with wife, 172
wives criticize, 183, 201
to relatives, 97
Matat, 128
his mission, 135
mazel tov – meaning, 453
Megillos – read before/after Torah, 426
l'fneihem or *b'fneihem*, 360
llarog or *u'lharog*, 360
mesorah – changing accepted custom, 414
changing based on manuscripts, 341-342, 355-356
chaseiros v'yeseiros, 355-356; of Tanach based in Tiverya, 345
Remah, 347-348
spacing *Shiras Devorah* and *Shiras Dovid*, 353
middos – why not a mitzvah?, 381
milah – *metzitzah*, 392
Minchah – why *Ashrei*?, 169
Minchas Shai, 349-350
Rav Pam quoted (*machlas*), 361
mitzvos – for ulterior motives, 62
mizrach – determine by seeing moon, 273-274
molad – adjust for DST, 310
affects *Kiddush Levanah*, 307-309
affects Yom Kippur *Katan*, 310
at Creation, 303, 307
based on average *molad*, 309
calculating for 5768 years, 303-304

coincides with eclipse?, 282
errors in time announced in Shul, 302-309
how is it calculated?, 301
monthly calculation, 279-280
one time everywhere, 302
we use average *molad*, 282
moon – see also molad
direction that crescent faces, 273-274
monthly orbit, 300-301
monthly orbit is 27 days, 301 fn 1
path in sky, 274, 275, 277
seen by day?, 301 fn 2
Moshe Rabbeinu – age, 423
Moshe v'Caleiv, 317-318
Mashiach – death of *yetzer hara*, 187
who will live in Jerusalem? – 64
Motza'ei Shabbos – *Gehinnom* opens, 18
movies – trip to Israel, 63
names – *ben* mother or father, 411, 422
for *choleh*, 422
family name in *kesubah*, 450
nazir – cuts beard?, 416
Nechemiah, Ch. 3
building, 12-13
Nekudas HaBechirah, 257-258
night – begins when?, 291-292
three average stars or small stars?, 293 fn 9
way to figure when begins 435
Nitzotzos HaKedushah, 34
Orchos Tzaddikim – faith as key to happiness, 28, 131, 154
Rav Pam encouraged study of, 154
ordination – see smichah
Pachad Yitzchak – Letter 128 (*chizuk* to talmid), 47-48
Letter 96 (depression), 52
Pesach 18 (*v'halachta b'drachav*), 127
Rosh Hashanah 31 (judging others), 141
Rosh Hashanah 8:4 (good requires sustenance), 210

"lose a battle and win a war," 48
pain – caused by expectations, 106
Pam, Rav Avrohom – *alos hashachar* time, 298
and *dikduk*, 313-315
"Courtship must continue," 172
don't demand apologies, 147
"*Emes* is *scheker*," 327
goes to a *din Torah*, 90
"learn *Orchos Tzaddikim*," 154
love for Nach, 79-80
machlas, 361
marriage and money, 177
missed opportunities, 44
mistake during *Shemoneh Esrei*, 370
Nechemiah builds wall, 12-13
Noach after the Flood, 44
not all can be helped, 91
pushing a *shidduch*, 89-90
relating to Jerusalem, 58
respect Eretz Yisrael, 58
segulos, 70
sheli sheli, 196
shortcut to Gan Eden, 192
tenuah kallah, 266, 268
terrorists, 232
vatranus, 192, 196
why two day Rosh Chodesh, 409
parents – honoring see *kibbud av v'eim*, 71
patience – Rav Moshe's example, 74
prayer see also *Shema*
see also words
Ashrei, 159
Ashrei at Minchah, 169
based on Tanach, 242
bedtime *Shema*, 440
Bircas HaTorah v'harev na, 174
Bircas Krias Shema, 214-225
chupah v'kiddushin, 321
contradiction regarding prayer for *ruchniyus*, 261-262;
difference between *Kedushah* and *Yotzer Ohr*, 219 fn
different before *Churban*, 374
earliest time in morning, 286-299

ein od m'lvado, 167
expression of faith, 373 fn 1
for another person's *ruchniyus*, 256-258
for Eretz Yisrael (*re'ai b'anyeinu*) 234
for *Yiras Shamayim*, 251, 255-262
forgot where holding, 370-377
gadlu, 445;
Ho'Aderes V'haEmunah poem, 397
Kaddish pronunciation, 337-338
Kedushah on Shabbos, 220
kidshanu b'mitzvosov, 320 fn 10
last Minchah of year, 164
lishma, 259 fn 6
m'lo kol ha'aretz kivodo, 219-220
Mi Chamocha, 32
migdal/migdol, 444
Mizmor L'sodah, 112 fn
Monday's *Yom*, 56
Motza'ei Shabbos Maariv, 18
neshamah she'bmochi, 437
past or present tense, 245-246
Prayer for Eretz Yisrael (Kuzari), 231
She'asah li kol tzorchi, 245
She'targileinu b'sorasecha, 174
Shema, 215, 218
Shemoneh Esrei –
Bareich Aleinu, 164
baal gevuros, 315
morid hageshem, 393
oheiv Tzedakah, 315
re'ai na, 234
without *kavanah*, 372
without *kavanah* is wasted prayer?, 375
v'imru amen, 443
v'leYerushalayim ircha, 439
v'sabeinu m'tuvecha, 157
source for mitzvah, 373
stuck without a siddur, 376
Tefillas Zakah, 50 fn
two dimensions to, 373
V'eirastich lee l'olam, 178

why pray for everything?, 374
why pray?, 372
prophets – the greatest, 116
punishment – trade *aveiros* for *mitzvos*?, 189
    never for sake of punishment, 144, 162
Purim, 223, 231
    Haman's silver talents, 428
    read Megillah after Torah, 426
    which words read twice, 360
Rabbeinu Tam – *yemei ha'ahavah, yimei hasinah*, 60
Rambam – angels are God's will, 216
Rashi – on which *mesechta*?, 430
    to the *Rif/Ein Yaakov*, 430
Rav Avrohom Pam *see* Pam, Rav Avrohom
Rav Moshe Feinstein *see* Feinstein, Rav Moshe
Rav Tzaddok HaCohen – believe in yourself, 162
    controlling anger, 28
    failure brings success, 49
    father/mother roles in chinuch, 382
    God never punishes, 144
    King Chizkiyahu, 49
    personal *galus*, 28
    pick yourself up again, 47
    Sesame Street problem, 385-386
    two *yuds* for God's name, 406
    what are angels?, 216
Rav Yaakov Emden – *see also* Rav Zalman Henna
    dispute with Rav Zalman Henna, 241-253, 260
    meets Rav Zalman Henna, 247
    Siddur Rav Yaakov Emden, 241
    Luach Eresh, 248-249
    Bavel to the north?, 430
    dikduk in bathroom?, 314 fn 1
    Jews in desert 39 years, 423
Rav Zalman Henna *see also* Rav Yaakov Emden
    Binyan Shlomo, 238-240
    his apology, 240, 242 fn 5

    kidshanu b'mitzvosov, 320
    Siddur Beis Tefillah, 339
    tenuah kallah controversy, 263-271
    Yisgadiel v'yiskadeish, 338-339
Remah (Rabbeinu Meir HaLevi), 347-348
revenge – emulate Hashem?, 140
    emulating Hashem? A second approach, 144
    reason for prohibition, 131
    replace with kindness, 126
Rosh Chodesh – Why two days?, 408
sacrifices – on a private *bamah*, 68
Sefer Torah – *see* Torah Scroll
segulah – a Brisker, 167
    for *shidduch*, 73
    for wealth, 75-76
    Rav Pam, 70
    Steipler, 70
Sesame Street – is a problem, 385-386
Shabbos – a second and third Kiddush?, 446
    early Shabbos, 433
    Kiddush, 432
    Kiddush and Havdalah are one mitzvah, 447
    koraya, 418
    meal between 6 and 7 p.m., 306
    minhag Yerushalayim, 434 fn 7
    Motza'ei Shabbos Maariv, 18
    sleeping, 436
    waving at the candles, 431
    women and Mussaf, 436
Shema *see also* prayers
    see also words
    calculating the *z'man*, 289 fn 5
    mispronunciations that change meaning, 333-334 and fn 14
    shva na/nach rules, 267-269
shemittah – calculating year, 363
    Maharalbach decides, 366
shidduch – *segulah* for, 73
    couples are different, 97
    pushing, 89-90
shikchah, 420
Shimshon – clean-shaven?, 416

Shiras Devorah – style of writing, 353-354
Shiras Dovid, 444
siddur see also prayer
see also words
V'yehi Noam, 18
Siddur Siach HaSadeh, 238-242
Sidei Chemed – author's story, 133
silence – a *segulah*, 74
Iyov's, 228
when upset, 51
Simchas Beis HaShoeivah – why water?, 112
smichah – unbroken chain, 141
Sod Halbur, 282, fn 13;
soul – where located, 437
south – represents light, 276
succah – always spelled *choser*, 356
decorations, 417
Succos – *Z'man Simchoseinu*, 111
sun – see also astronomy
path in sky, 301
sunrise – *neitz* or *haneitz*, 419
syllable see *havarah*
Tadir v'she'eino tadir, 426-427
Tam Elyon, 250
Tammuz 17, 81
tefillah – see prayer
tefillin – how parchment inserted, 415
neshamah sh'bimochi, 437
our *Rabbeinu Tam* tefillin, 415
Rashi and *Rabbeinu Tam* – origin of dispute, 413
V'eirastich lee l'olam, 178
Tehillim – during learning *seder*?, 227
for *choleh*, 227
spelling dispute (*succo*), 356
teshuvah – means returning, 118
time – Arabic time, 306 fn
10 "o'clock," 305 fn 9
clocks over the generations, 305-306
origin of Greenwich Standard Time, 305
what determines beginning of an hour?, 305
when night begins, 291-292
Tomer Devorah – importance of book, 124
Rav Moshe Cordevaro, 26
personal *galus*, 26, 29
reacting to insults, 223-224
v'halachta b'drachav, 126
Torah – arguments bring peace, 229
reciting half a verse, 432-433
tam elyon controversy, 250
verses used as decoration, 417
Torah Scroll – Chabad, 351
mitzvah to write nowadays?, 356
spacing between *parshiyos*, 353
Taimani, 351
travelers – *ovrei derech* and *holchei derech*, 37
traveling – among non-Jews, 29-32
trop, 250
tzeddakah see charity
Tzeis HaKochavim, see night
tzitzis – commanded thru *vayomer*, 400
v'ahavta l'reacha kamocha, 127
v'halachta b'drachav – emulate vengeance? one approach, 139
a second approach, 144
judging people, 137
Maharal, 139-140
Pachad Yitzchak, 127
vacation – plans, 181
Israel or Europe?, 62, 230
vatranus, 188-197
wealth – dealing with *nisayon*, 76
segulah for, 75-76
wedding – *bashert*?, 454
chupah v'kiddushin, 321
kesubah, 450
kesubah signing, 451
"Mazel Tov," 452
shechiyanu, 454-456
tannaim, 448
who pays?, 450
women break plate, 448
Weissmandel, Rav Michoel Ber, 217
wife – pays for damages at home?, 99-100
see women
women – and vacations, 181-182

appreciating her, 172
break plate at wedding, 448
closer to Hashem, 183, 185
critical of husbands, 183, 21
feminine nature, 383
kvetch too much?, 176
more merits than men, 422
Mussaf, 436
respecting husbands, 180
spend too much?, 177
Tzeruyah, 410
words – commonly mispronounced –
   baal, 315
   ha'l'Hashem, 318
   oheiv, 315
   questions regarding spelling –
      dakah, 350-352
      malchuso, 265
      Yisachar, 358
   questions regarding *dikduk*
      bein or *ben*, 331
      Borei pri hagafen, 245
      charah, 334-335
      eiss or *ess?*, 330-331
      in *Shema*, 333
      kidshanu b'mitzvosov, 320 fn 10
      ner shel Shabbos, 245
      shehakol nehiyeh, 245
      shichintei, givurtei, 338
      shiur, 246
      Yisachar, 357-358
      Yisgadeil, 245
      Yisgadeil v'yiskadeish, 338-339
      zochreinu lachaim, 245
   questions regarding meaning –
      charah, 335 fn
      chai olamim, 243
      chinuch, 379-380
      dorom, tzafone, 276
      k'dai, 244
      kriyah, 418-419
      mazel tov, 452
      neitz, 419-420
      olamim, 243
      sha'ah, 243
      Shacharis, Aravis, 244
      shiboles shoal, 341

      tamcha, 341
      u'nitalasni rucha, 247
      v'chof es yitzreinu, 251, 260
      zichrono l'vrachah, 421
   Synonyms: *al/lo*, 387
      af/gam, 395
      ben/bein, 331
      es/eis, 394
      geshem/matter, 393
      hod/hadar, 397
      kesev/keves, 391
      melech/mosheil, 100-101, 396
      metzitzah/mitzah, 392
      naar/yeled, 400
      simlah/salmah, 390
      vayomer/vayidaber, 398
Yaihoo, 319-320
Yehoshafat, King, 93, 102
Yehoyakim, 137-139
   to *Olam Habah?*, 146
Yehu, 80
yeshivah – leaving, 205
yetzer hara – eulogy on, 187
Yirmiyahu – and *ovdei Baal*, 65-66
   compared to Moshe, 116
   complains/stops complaining, 104
   expectations and disappointments, 115-116
   prophecy on Yehoyakim, 137
   Rav Breuer's insight into, 105, 116
Yisachar – Pronunciation dispute, 357-358
   spelling in *get*, 358
Yom Kippur – giving of *Luchos*, 81, 85
   Tefillas Zakah, 50 (fn)
   what is *teshuvah*, 118
   Yom Kippur *Katan*, 310
Yom Yerushalayim, 56
Zeh lo chashuv, 193-194
Zichrono l'vrachah, 421

This volume is part of
THE ARTSCROLL SERIES®
an ongoing project of
translations, commentaries and expositions
on Scripture, Mishnah, Talmud, Halachah,
liturgy, history, the classic Rabbinic writings,
biographies and thought.

For a brochure of current publications
visit your local Hebrew bookseller
or contact the publisher:

Mesorah Publications, ltd

4401 Second Avenue
Brooklyn, New York 11232
(718) 921-9000
www.artscroll.com